The Camp Fire Girls

Expanding Frontiers:
Interdisciplinary
Approaches to
Studies of Women,
Gender, and Sexuality

SERIES EDITORS:

Karen J. Leong
Andrea Smith

The Camp Fire Girls

Gender, Race, and
American Girlhood,
1910–1980

Jennifer Helgren

UNIVERSITY OF NEBRASKA PRESS | LINCOLN

Portions of chapters 1 and 3 were previously published in "Gender and Generational Identity: Camp Fire Girls and Cultural Production in the Interwar Years," in *Essays on Women's Artistic and Cultural Contributions, 1919–1931*, ed. Paula Birnbaum and Anna Novakov (Lewiston NY: Edwin Mellen Press, 2009), 37–50.

Portions of chapter 2 were previously published as "Native American and White Camp Fire Girls Enact Modern Girlhood, 1910–39," *American Quarterly* 66, no. 2 (June 2014): 333–60. Copyright © 2014 by the American Studies Association.

The University of Nebraska Press is part of a land-grant institution with campuses and programs on the past, present, and future homelands of the Pawnee, Ponca, Otoe-Missouria, Omaha, Dakota, Lakota, Kaw, Cheyenne, and Arapaho Peoples, as well as those of the relocated Ho-Chunk, Sac and Fox, and Iowa Peoples.

Publication of this volume was assisted by the College of the Pacific, at University of the Pacific, Stockton, California.

Library of Congress Cataloging-in-Publication Data
Names: Helgren, Jennifer, 1972– author.
Title: The Camp Fire Girls: gender, race, and American girlhood, 1910–1980 / Jennifer Helgren.
Description: Lincoln: University of Nebraska Press, [2022] | Series: Expanding frontiers: interdisciplinary approaches to studies of women, gender, and sexuality | Includes bibliographical references and index.
Identifiers: LCCN 2022001509
ISBN 9780803286863 (hardback)
ISBN 9781496233080 (paperback)
ISBN 9781496233660 (epub)
ISBN 9781496233677 (pdf)
Subjects: LCSH: Camp Fire Girls. | Girls—Societies and clubs. | Girls—United States—Social conditions—20th century. | Girls—United States—Social life and customs—20th century. | BISAC: SOCIAL SCIENCE / Children's Studies | HISTORY / United States / 20th Century
Classification: LCC HS3353.C3 H45 2022 | DDC 369.47—dc23/eng/20220803
LC record available at https://lccn.loc.gov/2022001509

Set in Arno Pro.

To my mother, Julie Hillman

Contents

Illustrations

Acknowledgments

With gratitude, I acknowledge the numerous people and institutions that have made this book possible. Its real beginning was in 1977 when I joined a Blue Bird group at my elementary school. I stayed in Camp Fire for seven years, made lifelong friends, and found that Camp Nawakwa in Angeles Oaks, California, helped me see the world in new ways. During graduate school, where I studied U.S. women's history, I uncovered old Camp Fire workbooks that featured a blurb about Charlotte Gulick and began to wonder about the organization's history.

I am grateful to my dissertation advisor Janet Farrell Brodie, who believed in the project when girlhood studies was considered an emerging field at best. Her guidance ensured the project reflected American cultural shifts and not just one organization's whims. Her mentorship and friendship have meant much to me over the years. Hal S. Barron, too, pushed me to connect my work to broad historiographical questions. Mary Rothschild served as an outside reader on my dissertation committee and has continued to offer advice and share a passion for girls' organizations as women's history.

Although this book started out as a dissertation, it incorporates more than fifteen years of new feminist scholarship on girlhood. Many readers, colleagues, and friends have helped shape my thinking over the years. I appreciate the critical feedback of Sarah Fieldston, Amy E. Davis, Marcia Chatelain, Susan A. Miller, Susan Eckelmann Berghal, Marcia Hernandez, Greg Rohlf, Kristine Gunnell, Molly Quest Arboleda, Anne Hartfield, Kelly Fuller, Sara Patterson, and the two anonymous readers, all of whom read either the entirety or portions of the manuscript. My writing groups at the University of the Pacific, especially Marcia Hernandez and Traci Roberts-Camps, and Judith L. Bishop, my writing buddy since COVID set in, have helped me focus and reminded me of what matters. I am thankful for their friendship and encouragement. I presented my research on Camp Fire Girls at numerous research conferences, too many to list here, and benefited immensely from the comments that I received. Meetings of the Society for the History of Children and Youth and the Berkshire Women's History Conference have brought me into contact with many scholars whose work I admire, and our conversations at panels and beyond have resulted in deeper inquiry. The influence of conversation and panels with Kristine Alexander, Miriam Forman-Brunell, Mischa Honeck, Lisa Jacobson, Catherine Jones, Ben Jordan, Stephanie Olsen, Leslie Paris, Rebecca Jo Plant, and Clifford Putney can be found in these pages. The Southern California Women's History Reading group, too, enlarges my perspective on women's history, making me a better teacher and scholar.

I would not have been able to write this book without the support of Camp Fire's local and national leaders and staff. To a person, they have been curious to learn about the history of the organization that they have inherited. Over the last twenty years, Mary Kay Roberts, Debra Huwar, Stewart Smith, Jeff Randolph, Cathy Tisdale, Erin Reisner, LaShee Thomas, Ernie Tilford, Julia Fleenor Bejarano, Greg Zweber, and Ben Matthews have accommodated my visits, answered my questions, helped dig up archival materials, and Zoomed. Former director Hester Turner, who passed away in 2020 at the age of 103, also offered her recollections—of being a Camp Fire mom to girls with vision impairments and of heading the organization during the turbulent 1960s and 1970s. Camp Fire personnel at numerous local councils showed similar generosity, allowing me to sift through scrapbooks and memorabilia. I thank Sandra Rutherford at Camp Fire Inland Southern California, Upland; Becky Gardocki-Elmore and Steve Elmore at the former San Andreas Council, San Bernardino, California; Karen Koeder at San Diego Council; Jerry Findley of the former Roganunda Council, Yakima, Washington; Bobbie Henderson of Camp Fire Green Country, Tulsa, Oklahoma; and Phyllis Morris, Oklahoma City Council, for their time and attention.

Numerous alumna shared Camp Fire experiences with me in person, over the telephone, and via email. They provided the voices that make this book about girls and not just organizers. Although I cannot fully integrate each woman's story, each interview shaped and informed this history. Thank you to Celia Anderson, Ann Chenhall, Sally Dunn, Carol Ferrell, Pat Flammini, June Hyman, Barb Kubik, Marty Lakin, Ann Lena, Sonia Littrell, Lynne Newman, Gail Oblinger, Lisa Reeder, Mary Alice Sanguinetti, Marlinda Stearns, and Mary Lee Turner. Phyllis Raines also opened her collection of Camp Fire memorabilia to me.

It has been a pleasure to work with the team at the University of Nebraska Press. Wrapping up a book project amid a global pandemic has not been easy. Emily Casillas has been supportive and flexible and has always shared great ideas about organization, content, and framing. I also thank Amy Pattullo for her attention to detail in copyediting, as well as Alicia Christensen, Sara Springsteen, and Erika Rippeteau for their assistance at various stages of production.

Several fellowships and grants facilitated my research and writing. I received a Claremont Graduate University Dissertation Grant; a Rodney G. Dennis Fellowship in the Study of Manuscripts at the Houghton Library, Harvard University; and a Schlesinger Library Dissertation Support Grant at the Radcliffe Institute, Harvard University. Since I completed my dissertation, I extended my research with internal grant funding from the University of the Pacific. These institutions allowed access to their collections, as did the Haverford College Special Collections; the Holt-Atherton Special Collections, University of the Pacific; and the Center for Sacramento History.

My family members have also supported my research and writing. My husband, Erik Helgren, is a physicist and a well-rounded intellectual. He has provided excellent feedback on many chapters and conference papers. My children have exposed me to a new era of youth organizations, and they continue to demonstrate how children shape their worlds and are not merely shaped by historical circumstances. My father, Charles Hillman, also supported my education financially and emotionally.

Special thanks to my mother, Julie Hillman, who was my Camp Fire leader. When I was in grad school, before the advent of Newspapers.com, she accompanied me to hunt for Camp Fire news on microfilm reels. She still deploys her skills as a former high school English teacher and checks my work.

The Camp Fire Girls

Introduction

The Camp Fire Girls Confront a
Crisis in American Girlhood

Charlotte Gulick, who with her husband Luther Gulick founded the Camp Fire Girls, explained to a *New York Times* reporter in 1912 that American girls faced a crisis. The many "changing conditions of our National life" made urgent the need for a national organization for America's adolescent girls. Charlotte Gulick worried that "woman's natural activities" were "weakened at the foundation" as many economic, educational, and caregiving functions, which had been the province of the family for much of the nineteenth century, moved to public institutions. Girls were no longer learning to sew and cook because ready-to-wear clothing was inexpensive, and boarding houses and bakeries provided food. Girls, therefore, were not learning creative work or the discipline needed to complete it. Even baby care, Charlotte Gulick feared, was being taken away from girls. Although she believed that scientific infant study was a "fine thing" for the babies, she lamented that regimented baby care "robbed girlhood" of a "character-building delight." When girls learned home tasks like cooking, sewing, and baby tending at school, the domestic science emphasis there meant that girls did not learn to serve "for the delight and comfort of the other members of the family and to their own ample satisfaction."[1] Girls learned the mechanics of home tasks without connecting to what Luther Gulick—a physician and expert on physical education and playgrounds—called elsewhere the "race history of woman," a phrase that invoked for Americans in the 1910s both the human race and an ambiguous white American nationality.[2]

Girls, Charlotte Gulick argued, needed to be useful, but "mere utility" would not suffice. Charlotte insisted, "We must also supply poetry, adventure, emulation as a stimulant to achievement. Girls must have romance." To do so, the Camp Fire Girls introduced American Indian imagery to connect members to an imagined timeless feminine past of women tending the family and hearth fire. Picturesque imagery would help "to bring back to women" a "real interest in the everyday affairs that used to fascinate [her] sex." Noting that work outside the home "has now a certain status" because a girl "takes money home," Charlotte and Luther Gulick wove into Camp Fire recognition for everyday home tasks as incentives for girls to work in the home.[3]

The Camp Fire Girls: Gender, Race, and American Girlhood, 1910–1980 tells how America's first and, for its first two decades, most popular girls' organization filled a space between the school and the home. Through youth clubs, the Camp Fire Girls created a model of citizenship for girls that stressed usefulness and beauty. It used racial tropes and distinct gender expectations to articulate for girls a model of womanhood that mixed traditional and forward-looking roles. This model of girl citizenship remained flexible and productive until the social and cultural shifts of the 1960s forced organization leaders to reevaluate the program. New civil rights laws and federal antipoverty initiatives, as well as the emerging feminist movement, forced reflection. In the late 1960s and 1970s, Camp Fire grappled with the structural barriers and limiting, gendered imagination that had made the organization an emblem of early twentieth-century girlhood but had foreclosed a more inclusive membership.

Believing firmly that girls and boys had distinct natures, Camp Fire's founders reenvisioned traditional domesticity for an age of consumerism, industrial production, and expanding women's rights. The Camp Fire Girls was to be the corollary to the Boy Scouts of America, which many of the same organizers had founded just a few years earlier. Camp Fire trained girls for a twentieth-century womanhood that embraced new opportunities for education, careers, athletics, and civic reform while still emphasizing women's connection to family and home. Organization officials found this philosophy, or what Luther Gulick called "essential feminism," adaptable to various social and political demands until the 1970s when coeducation and multiculturalism laid bare its limits. Essential feminism resembled the "maternalism" that women's historians have identified as undergirding women's participation in turn-of-the-century reform and the development of the early welfare state. Women claimed that their contributions to the family and society were founded upon their roles as mothers and that motherhood itself was "both a familial and civic act."[4] The organization's watchword, "Wohelo," an acronym of work, health, and love designed to sound Indian, spoke to these values. Girls and their leaders carved out new roles in public life based on the belief that women brought moral values and a unique concern for women and children to policy discussions. Youth organization leaders framed girls both as future mothers and citizens with rights and responsibilities in the current moment. Luther Gulick's term "essential feminism" called to mind the biological essentialism that characterized many Camp Fire leaders' thinking and structured organization policy for over fifty years. From industrialization through the Great Depression, two world wars, and the midcentury civil rights and feminist movements, the Camp Fire Girls adapted the founders' essential feminism (though most rejected the term "feminism") to articulate a valued role for girl citizens while maintaining a core belief in gender differences.

The Camp Fire Girls probes Camp Fire leaders' efforts, in the founding years and beyond, to raise women's status, first, by elevating those qualities and duties traditionally associated with womanhood and, second, by embracing women's expanding roles. Institutional histories, as well as early scholarship on Camp Fire, celebrated it as a "feminist movement" that regarded women as the "natural leaders of social life."[5] However, most recent scholarship on Camp Fire describes a plan that was reactionary or "politically naïve."[6] The disagreement is not surprising since Camp Fire's founders, especially Luther Gulick, held contradictory views on women's roles. Indeed, the book showcases the difficulty for a mainstream girls' organization to bridge the competing demands regarding girls' roles in the twentieth century. Whereas most histories of girls' organizations address the founding years alone, *The Camp Fire Girls* traces the contradictory approach to women's rights through the twentieth century.[7] Camp Fire's national program provided ways for girls to create broader civic identities. That they ultimately built an organization that was also reactionary reveals the limits of Camp Fire's essential feminism throughout the twentieth century.

Race History and Inclusion

Racialized understandings of citizenship and belonging also shaped the Camp Fire Girls. On the one hand, the Camp Fire Girls' 1914 certificate of incorporation committed the organization to inclusive membership open to *all* girls. Camp Fire included girls with disabilities, Black girls, new immigrants, and American Indians. This "civic nationalism" was in line with an American political and cultural tradition that, as historian Gary Gerstle writes, expresses "the promise of economic opportunity and political freedom to all citizens, irrespective of their racial, religious, or cultural background."[8] Camp Fire's inclusion policy was quite bold given the deep racism and nationalism that maintained Jim Crow and produced eugenic and anti-immigrant laws in the early twentieth century. On the other hand, Camp Fire accommodated local racial patterns and traded in racialized discourses related to eugenics and settler colonialism. When Luther Gulick explained that Camp Fire Girls would use American Indian symbols to pass through the "race history of woman, as the boy in his games and athletics passes through the race history of man," he embedded racialist notions into the organization's rhetoric and policies.[9] The organization's limited outreach, willingness to accept segregation, and appropriation of stereotyped Indian and Gypsy imagery divided girls. The organization was complicit in the broad acceptance of segregation and its associated unequal provisions and lack of accessibility, and in spreading narratives that obscured racial violence and tension.

A discourse of universal child development involved the coerced erasure of cultural identities and the dissociation of immigrant and subcultural identities. The Camp Fire Girls' founders and leaders elevated assimilation above pluralism. Camp Fire's model citizen was Protestant, middle-class, and white; she idealized self-reliance, hygiene regimentation, hard work, and women's connection to the nation through service and nurture. In

Camp Fire, native-born girls undertook assimilation projects, mentoring foreign-born girls. These undertakings fostered unequal relationships among girls, privileging native-born girls and their middle-class white feminine standards. Camp Fire, as a national organization, set limits on which girls achieved full citizen recognition.

In addition, Camp Fire's publications pretended that there was a cultural universality to girlhood that did not exist. The concept of inherent biological childhood stages, which emerged from turn-of-the-century childhood studies and child psychology, enabled Americans to view girls across class, religion, national background, and often even across race and disability, as the same malleable clay to be shaped into ideal women. However, this universal language of youth obscured the variants in children's development that resulted from poverty and discrimination.[10] Marginal girlhoods, though nominally included, were not easily incorporated into Camp Fire's unstated norm of white, middle-class, Protestant womanhood. Ignoring these circumstances made social hierarchies easier to uphold. Camp Fire's leaders embraced inclusion, championed improving girls' status, and aimed to improve society through deliberate intervention. But its clubs were often out of reach to girls and mothers who did not have free time and spare money for recreational activities and volunteering. The very effort to raise women's status through biological essentialism placed any who were not "beautiful" and "useful" in the way that Camp Fire articulated outside the new girl citizenship model.

At the same time, joining allowed a diverse population of girls to participate in a national girls' culture. In some places the girls defined modern girlhood in ways that were unique to their social location. Camp Fire clubs, at times, provided marginalized girls with the space to explore (often in segregated environments) their relationship to the broader national girls' culture that took hold in the twentieth century. Black leaders adopted the Camp Fire Girl program to promote the patriotism, community pride, and civic training that was often denied to Black girls. American Indian girls, forced to join extracurricular activities at boarding schools, used Camp Fire's Indian themes to explore their own heritage and background. And girls with disabilities and those quarantined due to Hansen's disease found a place of belonging.

The white, middle-class girls—who predominated in the Camp Fire Girls—sometimes challenged but often contributed to a dominant discourse on gender, race, and nation. They regularly shared the political ideologies of adults in the organization, and their agency often took the form of complicity. However, these girls, along with those from more marginalized backgrounds, also used Camp Fire Girl rituals and spaces to define gender and nationhood in generational terms. A white girl who donned an Indian-like costume was as likely to connect to the popular portrayal of suffragists as "on the war path" as she was to be thinking about the "race history of woman." Depending on their class, race, nationality, and disability or ability, Camp Fire Girls understood what it meant to be a twentieth-century citizen in ways that substantially overlapped with, but also diverged from, adult Camp Fire leaders' ideas.

Youth organizations like Camp Fire should be regarded as "hybrid cultures" created and mediated by youth and adults alike.[11] Girls found in Camp Fire a space to develop their own identities, which were often consistent with, but sometimes countered, Camp Fire's vision of twentieth-century American girlhood. In their meetings, activities, and camps, girls developed unique subcultures that operated in relation to, but also separately from, the dominant American middle-class culture. Girls reacted to and adapted prescriptive cultural elements, developing distinct values and activities, associations, friendships, language, rituals, and symbols based on understandings they shared with their peers. These perspectives were sometimes consistent with adult expectations and sometimes diverged from them. Feminist scholarship provides a valuable tool for explaining how girls disrupted the hierarchical transmission of values that often took place in adult-run organizations such as the Camp Fire Girls.[12] While youth organizations socialized girls, peer culture offered a medium for negotiating adult expectations, and youth rarely share the same nostalgia-driven sense of moral panic about social change. Those changes are part of their daily lives. Girls sometimes brought about change as they figured out how they fit into adult-created structures, seeking autonomy even as they adopted those structures. As historian Susan A. Miller contends, we should not be surprised that youth adopt the ideologies and practices of adults that they are close to since they share common class and race interests, not to mention affectional bonds.[13]

Modern Adolescent Girls

In its founding years, Camp Fire's target members were girls ages twelve to twenty, a group that drew increasing attention from child experts, reformers, and marketers in the early years of the twentieth century. In 1923 the average age of Camp Fire Girls was fourteen and a half. Although Camp Fire added a Blue Bird program for nine- to eleven-year-old girls in 1913, its focus was the adjustment of adolescent girls to the demands of modern womanhood. Each local club had six to twenty members of "about the same degree of maturity" to produce "team spirit" and "intimate acquaintance among the girls."[14]

The Camp Fire Girls appeared just as a modern girls' culture materialized. By the early twentieth century, American children enjoyed a virtual explosion of institutions and artifacts that enabled a unique youth identity to develop. As early as the 1870s, middle-class girls had experiences that enabled them to shape identities separate from the home and family. Attending public school, taking long walks, shopping, and even reading and letter writing brought them into contact with one another. By the early 1900s, middle-class girls attended high school, read girls' series fiction, watched films featuring girls, went to summer camps, and joined girls' organizations. Middle-class young people had more leisure time to spend together. Urban girls—across classes—pursued amusement at the theater and in downtown spaces. Modern girls fashioned new concepts of female identity.[15]

By the late nineteenth century, childhood and adolescence were increasingly the focus of study and intervention. Although childhood, adolescence, and youth are biological phenomena, adult concerns and young people's behaviors create the meaning societies attribute to these age stages. The child study movement at this time infused the research on child development with scientific expertise. By the early twentieth century, one of the child study movement's central figures, G. Stanley Hall, had redefined the earlier concept of "youth" as adolescence by applying

Among the many youth-centered enterprises to emerge during the Progressive era, Camp Fire stood out in the careful, deliberative way that its organizers drew upon racial and gender stereotypes to define female citizenship. Camp Fire emphasized private domesticity in its ritual and symbolism whereas Girl Scouts touted a public service image. In addition, although most youth organizations made use of American Indian imagery in camping programs, the Camp Fire Girls went much further to weave Indian play throughout the program and to retain Indian symbolism as core to Camp Fire identity far longer than did Girl and Boy Scouts, which also emphasized pioneering. In the 1910s and 1920s, Camp Fire, with its more conservative gender norms and connections to Boy Scout leaders in the United States, held the advantage in competing for members with the Girl Scouts. However, that emphasis and the racial stereotyping and romantic ceremonies limited the Camp Fire program's flexibility and its appeal across American regions, classes, cultures, and time. Although the Camp Fire Girls was national, its popularity was strongest in the Northeast, Midwest, on the Pacific Coast, and in budding councils in Texas and Oklahoma. The Girl Scouts, which began in the South, built a larger national following by cashing in on pioneer, explorer, and even military imagery. The Girl Scouts, identified with self-reliant, empowered girlhood, had worldwide resonance by the 1930s.

Building a National Membership of Girls

Camp Fire enjoyed rapid expansion in its early years, reaching a prominence that made it a shaper of twentieth-century girls' cultures and womanhood. It quickly became established as a national organization with clubs in all the states and the territories of Hawaii and Alaska. It grew to sixty thousand youth members by 1913 and reached nearly five hundred thousand in 1970 at its peak.[22] The scouting movement was also transnational; due to the flexible youth organization framework, groups were adaptable to distinct national concerns and political systems. While scouting and guiding became a global force in the interwar period, the Camp Fire Girls also spread to overseas American territories and countries. By the 1920s these included groups in Argentina, Bolivia, Brazil, Canada, Chile, China, Costa Rica, Cuba, England, Holland, India, Japan, Korea, Mexico, Panama, Peru, the Philippines, Samoa, Scotland, Siam (Thailand), South Africa, Spain, Turkey, and the West Indies. England had the most Camp Fire Girls—about 2,500 girls—while most countries outside the United States had only a handful of clubs.[23]

Camp Fire's U.S. success in adding new members and retaining those who joined shows that American girls found that the Camp Fire Girls had much to offer them. Although adults played a part in the enrollment of their daughters in youth organizations, children's willingness to join and continue their participation reveals that their desires and choices overlapped with adults.[24] By 1933 Camp Fire estimated that it had served a million and a half members. Its strength in the earliest years was in the cities, but as America's suburbs grew with the advent of rail lines and the availability of automobiles, Camp Fire took hold there as well. Early on the fastest growth occurred in New York, Massachusetts, Pennsylvania, and Ohio but it shifted to the Mountain States and the Pacific Coast by the 1920s. By 1930 Camp Fire's local councils in Chicago, Denver, Greeley (Colorado), Los Angeles, Detroit, Portland, Spokane, Seattle, and Boston each had over a thousand members.[25] The Camp Fire Girls and the Girl Scouts each had over 150,000 members by the mid-1920s and together served about 5 percent of the girls in the United States, a number just under the 6 percent of U.S. boys served by Boy Scouts. Although Boy Scouts recruited better than the Camp Fire Girls, Camp Fire retained girls slightly better. Most girls stayed in Camp Fire for a little more than two years. Only about one-fourth moved up in rank each year, however.[26] Rank advancement required time in the organization—at least four months for the first and nearly two and a half years for the highest rank of Torch Bearer. Girls also had to recite the Camp Fire Law, earn specific honors, and for Torch Bearer, develop leadership skills and mastery of their chosen craft. Still, a considerable number of Camp Fire Girls went on to lead groups of their own, indicating that they found participation meaningful. By the mid-1930s, 37 percent of the current leaders had been girl members at one point.[27]

The Camp Fire Girls was the most prominent girls' organization until 1930, when membership in the Girl Scouts surpassed that of the Camp Fire Girls. Camp Fire continued to enroll between two hundred and five hundred thousand girl members from the 1930s through the 1960s, while

Girl Scout membership reached one and a half million in 1950 and four million in 1970. Camp Fire continued to offer an important alternative. Indeed, through most of the twentieth century, the organization loomed large in American iconography, symbolizing an idealized American girl-hood. The *Saturday Evening Post* regularly used the phrase "a camp fire girl" in the mid-twentieth century to evoke an exaggeratedly wholesome, albeit naïve, girlhood. And *Time* magazine borrowed the moniker, dripping with irony, to characterize Marilyn Monroe's birthday serenade of President John F. Kennedy as sung "in a sincere, Campfire Girl voice."[28]

Although mothers served from the outset, Camp Fire targeted young women just out of college as group leaders—guardians, in Camp Fire terminology. Through extensive summer camp and college courses, many at normal schools, young women learned the skills needed to lead clubs. In 1915 *Wohelo*, Camp Fire's magazine, reported that 2,199 college girls and graduates were "Guardians of the Fire" and that they were making "their college education of service to others."[29] Many young women in this first substantial cohort of college women finished their education with, as Jane Addams called it, "no recognized outlet for their active faculties" and were searching for a "social claim."[30] Although Camp Fire provided no income to these young women, it offered an opportunity to put their knowledge and training to use. Camp Fire valued relationships of near equals where leaders offered subtle guidance rather than strict authority. A Rhode Island council boasted that "it results in real comradeship between the individual girl and her Guardian" since the leader "is in the background as a friend and adviser, rather than in the foreground as a dictator." In addition, Camp Fire officials advised these early guardians to associate closely with regular members, wear the same uniforms, earn honors, and participate in the same activities.[31] Girls and guardians appeared alike, and guardians offered a model for the womanhood girls would soon inhabit.

A Note on Sources

This book is based on a wide range of historical sources, including Camp Fire's promotional literature, guidebooks, and official correspondence, as well as girl-created records. Girls' writings indicate that they internalized, in large measure, key aspects of the Camp Fire program, but that they also often understood their participation in different terms than did adults. In camp journals, diaries, letters, scrapbooks, creative writing, health charts, and photographs, Camp Fire Girls recorded routine events, commented on meetings, noted their goals, and evaluated their relationships with other club members and leaders. This book recognizes that adults often mediated girl-created sources, asking girls to produce certain forms of writing, artwork, and photographs. Like all cultural producers, girls had in mind specific audiences when they produced texts. These sources, produced by youth and adults together, nonetheless provide insight into girls' receptivity or resistance to adult ideas.

Memoirs and oral histories also document girls' pasts. They present a separate set of challenges. As women remember their pasts, sometimes they are nostalgic for the organization of their youth and eager to share fond memories of friendships and camp. These are often longtime members who share valuable insider information, but they may not represent the many American girls who came into briefer contact with the organization. Another concern is that oral history and memoirs contain memories filtered through time and represent an adult's construction of her identity. Nonetheless, they record how women perceive their childhood activities as constitutive of their youthful identities. Before the 1970s, local communities recorded the activities of youth groups in the women's pages of local newspapers. These organizational and girl- and woman-created sources collectively provide evidence of girls' attitudes and responses regarding how Camp Fire fit into their coming-of-age stories.

Although some youth organizations have deliberately controlled their archives to shape the narrative they wish to tell about their programs, Camp Fire's collections are dispersed and decentralized.[32] No single archive houses Camp Fire memorabilia, though the Camp Fire National Headquarters in Kansas City, Missouri, retains many historical records. And although Camp Fire's official sources promote a picture of inclusion and progress, the national headquarters, local councils, and private collections do not coordinate one story. For many years Camp Fire has lacked an archivist. Archival collections such as Harvard University's Arthur and Elizabeth Schlesinger Library and the Sacramento History Center, and local councils across the United States house documents. Although some councils have carefully organized records, others have stored them haphazardly. At one location girls' journals from the 1920s were stored under a sink in available cupboard space. At another council the records were kept in cardboard boxes in a storage shed. When the director collected them for me, he brushed off the mouse droppings before digging in to see what was inside. Camp Fire's council leaders make little systematic effort to control the historical narrative. They recognize that alumni stories matter and are frustrated that, with little space and few resources, more cannot be preserved. Personnel with whom I have worked at Camp Fire National Headquarters and at local councils have been universally eager to share their records and learn about their organization's history. As Camp Fire has shrunk in the twenty years since I began this work, councils have closed their doors, and records have been lost in that process. This loss of girls' documents is a constant challenge for children's historians as well as for Camp Fire alumni. Some alumni maintain collections that serve as museums. Both adults and girls tell their stories about Camp Fire in the twentieth century through these diverse sources.

The chapters that follow proceed chronologically and thematically, examining the two strands of the book's argument—that Camp Fire presented a model of female citizenship that centered girls' and women's connection to the home as it broadened girls' opportunities to participate in civic life and outdoor athletics, and that Camp Fire adopted a commitment to inclusion that was hemmed in by its acquiescence to local racial practices and a false universal vision of girlhood. *The Camp Fire Girls* does not tell a thorough history of the organization but highlights stories that illuminate the workings of gender, race, and age in the twentieth century. Each chapter strives to center girls' voices as they responded to and shaped a key organization in their own lives.

The first four chapters address Camp Fire in the years before World War II, a time when U.S. white women secured the vote and found broader acceptance in the public sphere of education, entertainment, consumerism, reform, and paid employment. These years also saw the entrenchment of Jim Crow conditions, the spread of white supremacist groups such as the Ku Klux Klan, immigrant exclusions, and the consolidation of America's western conquest and territorial expansion through coercion and assimilation. Chapter 1 explores the Camp Fire Girls' founding philosophy, tracing essential feminism's connections to eugenic feminism and binary gender roles. The Camp Fire Girls advanced a racialized form of girls' national citizenship and a Protestant middle-class mandate for usefulness. Girls themselves created a generational culture and identity as they mediated the prescriptive program provided for them by adults. The girls' shared membership, friendships, and activities guided their sense of belonging to a modern girls' culture that they contrasted with their mothers' and grandmothers' experiences.

Chapter 2 examines the Camp Fire Girls' appropriative dress and symbolism and its different meanings for white and American Indian girls. Camp Fire Girls enacted temporary American Indian identities and went on "Gypsy trips" as part of an effort to construct a mythic concept of universal girlhood. Through mimicry, white Camp Fire Girls explored racial and sexual identities that were carefully bounded within symbolic spaces such as camp. White, middle-class girls used Indian imagery to critique white, middle-class feminine decorum, but Indigenous girls found in Camp Fire's "Indian lore" an avenue to exercise cultural authority. In the 1930s, white girls began to reject Indian lore as passé, and the Gypsy woman took the place of the Indian maiden as a symbol of romance, fantasy, and outdoor adventure.

Chapter 3 addresses Camp Fire's stated commitment to provide an education and recreation program to all girls. The organization accorded limited opportunities for national belonging to working-class and immigrant girls and girls of color, many of whom sought out the self-esteem and social responsibility that Camp Fire promised. Against a backdrop of rising nativism and racism, Camp Fire officials embraced pluralism and celebrated the cultural gifts of immigrant youth. The Camp Fire Girls moved immigrant girls into the mainstream of American society, marking them as white and training them and their families to adopt the white, middle-class gender system. Black Camp Fire leaders along with a few white leaders made progressive racial arguments and articulated Black childhood as a space deserving of protection. Still, Camp Fire's practice of forming clubs among children within the same neighborhoods, schools, and churches resulted in segregated clubs that only rarely reached beyond the white middle class. The de facto segregation and privileging of white girlhood that resulted was more pronounced in the South. Chapter 4 extends the discussion of inclusion to girls with disabilities and illness in the United States and in the territory of the Philippines. Camp Fire offered a space of inclusion for those who could demonstrate their usefulness and cheer. In homes for the blind and deaf children and in Hansen's disease (or leprosy) centers in the Philippines, Camp Fire articulated a concept of civic belonging that included able-disabled girls—those who can fit in without radically altering ableist structures and assumptions.[33]

Chapter 5 examines the impact of World War II on girlhood and American concepts of inclusion and diversity. Imbued with a strengthened service ethic born of the war and a new dedication to antiprejudice work, Camp Fire encouraged democratic citizenship, fostering tolerance even as it uncritically taught Camp Fire's civic ethic to Japanese American girls detained in War Relocation Authority camps. Camp Fire also elevated spiritual commitments connected to combating fascism and communism. For the first time, it asked members to pledge to "worship God." World War II was a turning point for ideas about inclusion but not all were admitted equally. Chapters 6 and 7 examine the gender and racial constructions of girlhood and womanhood in the early Cold War. Camp Fire officials began to interrogate their founding models of girlhood but ultimately recommitted to them, postponing a reckoning with changing gender roles and racial and class barriers until the 1970s. At the same time, the Cold War and the expanding civil rights movement called for more meaningful antiprejudice work. Camp Fire's language and imagery embraced the moment, but local race policies continued to privilege white communities and produce segregated groups. Underresourced girls from marginalized communities stood little chance of participating fully in Camp Fire's postwar councils.

Chapters 8 and 9 describe how, in the 1960s and 1970s, the Camp Fire Girls, under new leadership, reevaluated the structure and function of the organization. Not only did Camp Fire Girls admit boys, as its adherence to strict gender roles became increasingly untenable, but the organization adopted policies that deepened outreach efficacy and strengthened multiculturalism. This resulted from three shifts. First, all mainstream youth organizations (despite the baby boom) faced membership challenges in the late 1960s and 1970s as many young people, influenced by the counterculture, viewed civic organizations with suspicion. Second, the Camp Fire Girls' claims to women's difference seemed increasingly outdated as second-wave feminists called for equal rights. And third, as identity politics gained momentum in the 1960s and 1970s, youth organizations changed their approach to marginalized groups. Camp Fire leaders strengthened outreach efforts, and in doing so, they found that the organization's structures, symbols, and sometimes its message thwarted diverse membership. In 1975 the organization launched the "New Day" program, which prioritized local autonomy to serve diverse community needs. An epilogue examines Camp Fire within the current landscape of American youth organizations and its most recent diversity, equity, and inclusion efforts.

Camp Fire's founders designed it to integrate nineteenth-century feminine values of service to the family with emerging "modern" ideals of civic-minded, educated, and sporty American girlhood. Organization officials adapted Luther Gulick's essential feminism to various twentieth-century political and social contexts to create a version of girl citizenship that began with service to the home and extended outward. At the same time, Camp Fire was committed to a civic nationalist vision of American inclusion, but a narrow model of womanhood that left existing social hierarchies and racialized assumptions unchecked also shaped its program. Despite this, the Camp Fire Girls provides a lens for the historian to explore how American girls responded to mainstream progressive character-building institutions. Many American girls adopted Camp Fire's vision as their own. Others adapted Camp Fire's girl citizen ideal in ways that made sense from their unique historical and social positions. In the process, girls shaped the organization and the category of girlhood itself. As a socializing institution positioned between the home and the school, Camp Fire provided girls the means to identify themselves as a distinct modern generation.

1

"Preparing for Sex Equality"

Gender Ideals and the Founding Years

In 1911 founder Luther Gulick described in national newspapers, as a headline put it, "How the 'Camp Fire Girls' Are Preparing for Sex Equality." Indeed, the organization sought to raise women's status but did so by emphasizing girls' and boys' distinct gendered natures. Responding to what they perceived as a crisis surrounding American girlhood, the Camp Fire Girls reflected the cultural contradictions of an era of dramatic change in women's roles. Even as Luther Gulick rejected as "alarmist" the view that the home was "decaying" due to women entering public life, he and the other reformers who established the Camp Fire Girls defined their task as training "the girls to be womanly just as the boy scout [*sic*] activities train the boys to be manly."[1] Its program, especially its law and elective honor activities in home craft, hand craft, health, camp craft, nature lore, business, and patriotism, was designed to adapt nineteenth-century traditions of feminine grace and aesthetic taste, nurture, and domesticity to the increasingly active lives of girls and women in education, sports, social and civic reform, and meaningful work.

Innovative and experimental in their approach, Camp Fire's founders nonetheless shared what historian Alice Kessler-Harris calls the "gendered imagination."[2] Deep-seated beliefs about men's and women's roles in the workforce and the family found their way into the organization's policies and practices. "Essential feminism" was the term Luther Gulick used to capture the belief, shared by those women's rights advocates who sought to improve women's status and condition based on the perceived differences between men and women, that girls' civic responsibilities entwined with familial roles. Women's nature, Luther Gulick believed, derived from a biological race history that was distinct from that of men. "The set of ideals" associated with women, he noted, were "primarily social in their character." Motherhood and the home, however, had lost respect in the industrial age. He echoed maternal feminists as he explained that women and girls needed a "new-fashioned and community-wide power and responsibility." Through "community motherhood," they would "[apply] affection and understanding to the desires and hopes of all, especially in their social relationships" and usher in "a spiritual life never before even thought of."[3] What women and girls—indeed what the nation—needed was proper recognition of supposed eternal feminine values as well as a way to harness those characteristics for the good of modern industrial America. The Gulicks articulated a "new relation of women to the world" that directed girls to gaze outward toward service.[4] This thinking was intertwined with the period's popular eugenic and recapitulation theories. Like eugenic discourse, Camp Fire prioritized and positioned girls' reproductive and familial contributions as responsibilities to the nation and race. As Charlotte Gulick saw it, the work of the Camp Fire Girls was of vast "racial importance."[5]

The Camp Fire Girls: An Organization Distinguished from the Boy Scouts

The first Camp Fire club formed when girls and their families called for civic roles on par with those for boys. In 1910 William Chauncy Langdon, promoter of civic programs and writer for the Russell Sage Foundation, began to organize a historical pageant for Thetford, Vermont's, town anniversary the following summer. He called on Ernest Thompson Seton to form a Boy Scout troop there to appear in the final scene about the "promise of better citizenship." Just as the British Boy Scout founder Robert Baden-Powell had been surprised by thousands of girls who appeared at a Boy Scout rally in London in 1909, girls who showed up for rehearsals expecting parts caught Langdon off guard. Not having planned any part for girls in the pageant but believing that girls needed an equivalent organization, he called on his colleague at the Russell Sage Foundation, Luther Gulick, to help organize the girls. Gulick hesitated at first because he worried that an organization modeled on the Boy Scouts would promote masculine characteristics among girls, but he soon proceeded to advise Langdon as he developed the first Camp Fire Girl group for the pageant.[6]

The girls in Thetford were not unique in calling for a place in the expanding scouting movement. James West, head of the Boy Scouts of America, reported a constant inquiry from the public regarding girls' groups. Although work with girls made up only 5 percent of the youth work in the United States, girls' organizations and camps began to emerge across the nation.[7] By 1911 Clara Lisetor-Lane had formed a group called the Girl Scouts in Iowa, and Reverend David Ferry had organized Girl Guides in Washington State. The YWCA started the Health and Honor League for young women, Lina Beard was gathering materials to form an organization called the Girl Scouts, and in 1912, Juliette Low brought the Girl Guide program, renamed the Girl Scouts of the United States of America in 1913, to the United States from Great Britain.[8]

Amid these stirrings, the organizers of the Camp Fire Girls, many of whom had served as consultants to the Thetford pageant, as well as those who had begun to develop girls' camps and vocational programs, met to design a gender-based organization comparable to the Boy Scouts. In March 1911 they came together at the Horace Mann School of Teachers College in New York City to establish a national youth organization for American girls. Luther Gulick, Boy Scout organizer and head of the Child Hygiene Department at the Russell Sage Foundation, chaired the organizational meeting. A collection of accomplished progressive reformers also contributed time and ideas.[9] Many of them, like Luther Gulick, came from the playground movement and others, like Charlotte Gulick, had roots in camping, mothers' clubs, and the YWCA. The women were fairly well educated. Charlotte received her education at Washburn Preparatory College in Topeka, Kansas, Drury College in Oberlin, Ohio, and Wellesley, although she never graduated from Wellesley. Others, like Mary S. Woolman, professor at Columbia University, were involved in home economics and girls' vocational training. Numerous Boy Scout officials also lent their support and advice. Although a growing Girl Scout membership would eclipse that of the Camp Fire Girls in the 1930s, the early support of Boy Scout officials was crucial to Camp Fire's marketing and deepened its reputation for distinct gender-role training. The Girl Scouts, by contrast, irked American Boy Scout leaders by using the name "Scout" and copying much of the Boy Scout outdoor program. In the Camp Fire Girls, founders attempted to write a girls' program from scratch.[10]

What emerged was a gendered ideology that promoted separate citizenship norms for boys and girls. Luther Gulick, who had told Langdon that a program for girls modeled on the Boy Scouts without adaptation was "all wrong," articulated his idea that a girls' program should foster a traditional womanhood emphasizing beauty and usefulness. He defined women's usefulness in maternal terms: "The bearing and rearing of children has always been the first duty of most women, and that must always continue to be. This involves service, constant service, self-forgetfulness and always service." Luther Gulick insisted that there existed a "sharp dividing line between manhood and womanhood." He argued that this grew out of "a difference in the instinct feelings" as women evolved serving home and family while men served tribe and nation. Hence, to ignore gender distinctions in the formation of a girls' organization seemed to Luther Gulick to go against history and biology. These ideas would find their way into the organization's symbols. Gulick recommended that they adopt Langdon's title of "Camp Fire Girls," emphasizing that the name symbolized the "domestic fire" of the hearth and home and "not the wild fire."[11] The title accentuated women's duty to provide sustenance, beauty, and service within the home even as it suggested an outdoor spirit.

The Committee on Organization, chaired by Woolman and made up of influential women youth workers, worked with an all-male advisory committee over the next year.[12] Both of these groups worked to ensure that the Camp Fire Girls adhered to strict gender lines. At the second organizational meeting, Seton agreed with Luther Gulick that girls' work "should be undertaken to develop womanhood" and argued that "beauty should be brought in at every point." Lee Hanmer, Boy Scout organizer and member of the men's advisory committee, also insisted that since "men are the fighters" and "women are the home-makers," the new organization "should be founded upon feminine instincts and tendencies; not patterned after those of boys." The women organizers offered support for gender distinctions in youth programming as well. Clara Lisetor-Lane, who for a time affiliated with the Camp Fire Girls, noted that although she had organized her Girl Scout program to follow the Boy Scout movement, she carefully "discouraged among the girls anything like rowdyism" and altered activities "to suit the girls."[13] A Camp Fire press release in newspapers across America quoted Charlotte Joy Farnsworth of the organization committee stressing girls' connection to the home: "The nucleus of the home is the fire and its guardian. Activities to arouse what is most womanly in the girl are to center around the camp fire and the hearth fire and appeal to the girl's instinct to please, as the boy's impulse to compete is made the basis of his activities."[14]

Not all organizers, however, were of one mind concerning the gendered content of the new program. In May 1911 a bulletin subcommittee made up of well-known suffragist Grace Seton; dance educator Mary Beegle; and physical education pioneer Maria Dowd, prepared a program guide that the women of the organizing committee, including Woolman and Farnsworth, rejected as unsuitable for girls. Woolman and Farnsworth took the bulletin to members of the male advisory committee at the Boy Scout office, whose members declared it "neither significant nor attractive" for girls. First Chief Boy Scout Executive, James E. West, complained that many of the activities "were not only unsuited to girls, but would not be interesting to them." Presuming that the men could define feminine activities better than the women could, Langdon agreed, without irony, that the program outlined by the all-female committee was "entirely too masculine." Dr. John Alexander, another Boy Scout official, was the most emphatic. He argued that even the titles of "camper" and "leader," used to denote girls and their leaders, were inappropriate. He argued, "Girls . . . develop in an entirely different way [than boys]. . . . They grow up purely through imitation of their elders. Moreover, they do not have the group instinct. They do not work well together except in twos, and they depend almost entirely for their ideals and their activities upon the personality of the person guiding them." He assailed the bulletin as a "'slavish imitation' of the Boy Scout manual." Pressured by growing competition, however, all agreed that there could not be much delay in sending out a bulletin and so they resolved to write a new draft quickly.[15]

In addition to consulting on the bulletin concerns, West recommended combining rivals into one girls' organization, something he had successfully done with competing boys' groups. At West's urging, Lisetor-Lane and Ferry came to New York to discuss the possibility of amalgamating. For a short time in 1911, Lisetor-Lane's Iowa Girl Scouts and Ferry's Girl Guides merged with the Camp Fire Girls as the Girl Pioneers of America. This group went public that summer with the Bulletin Committee's revised program, which retained the term "camper" and went to 280 addresses. But by the fall, the Girl Pioneers had unraveled, and the different groups went separate ways. A 1911 report blamed the collapse on the unwillingness of any of the three organizations to cooperate.[16]

As far as Juliette Low's Girl Scouts of the USA were concerned, a merger was never a real possibility. Although Low had the friendship and esteem of British scout leaders, officials at Boy Scouts of America gave their support and advice to the Camp Fire Girls and actively pressured Low, once she adopted it in 1913, to stop using the Scout name. West sought to ensure that girls did not infringe upon the masculine image he was cultivating for the Boys Scouts. West wished that the Girl Scouts would just become Camp Fire Girls, and in 1924, the Chief Boy Scout of America had his attorneys file an unsuccessful patent lawsuit for the name's use.[17] Low was keen to bring other groups into the Girl Scout orbit, but she resisted any merger that subordinated her organization to the Camp Fire Girls. Low complained that the Camp Fire Girls did not really serve "every girl," citing the requirement to sleep with wide-open windows as "impracticable" for city girls and noting that burning campfires in the summer was "not well adapted to the Southern climate."[18] Luther Gulick, likewise, saw no advantage in altering the Camp Fire Girl program to combine with what was at that time a much smaller organization.

In September 1911 the original Committee on Organization reconvened, and members committed themselves once again to creating a unique girls' program. This time Luther and Charlotte Gulick took a clearer lead. The new Committee on Organization included Charlotte Gulick, Woolman, and YWCA national health secretary Dr. Anna Brown, and they asked Luther Gulick to chair it. Some members from both the original men's and women's committees joined. Charlotte Gulick drafted a new manual based on the Gulicks' experiments with camping activities at their private camp at Lake Sebago in Maine and on the home economics techniques that Woolman pioneered with her graduate students at Teachers College and the Manhattan Trade School for Girls. *The Book of the Camp Fire Girls,* the guidebook printed in 1912, remained true to the original plan to provide activities distinct from the Boy Scout honor program with its emphasis on merit badges and mastery. Camp Fire Girls would earn colored wooden honor beads to sew in symbolic patterns onto Indian-style gowns. The beads rewarded the completion of modest tasks in the seven elective honors. The core "crafts" were home and hand craft. The activities listed in these two sections of the handbook led girls through various domestic lessons and cultivated an eye for design and aesthetics. Health introduced best practices in fitness, sports, and games, emphasizing form rather than competition. Camp craft introduced the benefits and knowledge of outdoor life. Nature lore mixed scientific and poetic appreciation of nature. Business stoked girls' interest in earning and saving money. And patriotism encouraged historical awareness and service.[19] Luther Gulick drew up a statement of objectives as well as the Camp Fire Law.

Key leaders in educational and social reform lent their reputations and program advice to a council of advisers. They included Boy Scout organizers Daniel Carter Beard and Ernest Thompson Seton, reformers Jane Addams and Gaylord S. White, and philanthropist Grace H. Dodge, along with what *American Monthly Magazine* referred to as "two score other scarcely less prominent in philanthropic and sociological work."[20] The Camp Fire Girls received funding from prominent benefactors in 1912. The largest donation was $18,000 for three years from Margaret Olivia Slocum Sage, the wife of Russell Sage. In March, the committee embarked on two actions that marked its birth as a permanent national organization. First, it initiated a nationwide publicity campaign through publications like *Ladies Home Journal,* the *Outlook,* and the *Journal of Education.* Second, the Camp Fire Girls incorporated in Washington DC. By 1913, with a growing membership of sixty thousand girls, the Camp Fire Girls was an established part of the American organizational landscape.[21]

The Whole Child and the Law of Camp Fire

The Camp Fire Girls reflected the progressive education ethos of its organizers, including the mission to educate the "whole child."[22] Penned by

Luther Gulick, the Camp Fire Law, which girls recited when they joined the organization and at every meeting thereafter, expressed this commitment to girls' emotional, physical, and social well-being. Its seven lines—"Seek beauty, Give service, Pursue knowledge, Be trustworthy, Hold on to health, Glorify work, Be happy"—expressed Camp Fire's commitment to service along with permission for children to seek beauty and happiness.

"Seek beauty," the first line in the Camp Fire Law, was a girl's responsibility to counter the alienation that the urban, industrial era threatened. Although beauty included "beauty of person, clothing, character, and conduct," more important, it was "a certain attitude toward life, an appreciation of the beauty and romance and wonder of it."[23] Luther Gulick stated that this was a specific task for girls and that "making life beautiful and worth while is just as necessary as is the wonderful business world that man has built."[24]

Service meant usefulness, which in the historic white Protestant tradition gave spiritual meaning to worldly activity. A critical component in Camp Fire's concept of female citizenship, service invoked the nineteenth century's feminine duty to the family along with the expanding possibilities for social usefulness at the turn of the century. Luther Gulick urged, in an address that was printed and made available to girls, that they enact a "new patriotism" in the modern civic world, influencing politics and public culture by bringing the "activities born and raised in the home . . . out into the community." This included "love and service and spiritual relations." Women's talents might create a higher state of civilization. The responsibility of girl citizens was "to serve their country and their times by consecrating to it the most precious quality of womanhood; to bring about more sympathy and love in the world."[25]

The exhortation to "pursue knowledge" linked service to education. Girls prepared "to take part effectively and intelligently in the great readjustment that is going on in the world today." It meant studying domestic science and nature, and it also meant learning to work with other girls and women toward social reform. "Be trustworthy" was another condition of service. It countered a prevalent belief that girls and women lacked constancy and asserted that they could learn to "be loyal to other women" and to their "own ideals." The law next called on girls to "hold on to health," a key to

1. The Camp Fire Law appears, framed with Camp Fire symbols, in *The Book of the Camp Fire Girls*. The founders believed such drawings invoked authentic American Indian connections to nature. The top figure is the symbol of the Camp Fire with the crossed logs. The others represent Camp Fire themes. The symbol in the top corner means far seeing. Midway down, the doorway indicates opening the way for someone. The "V" indicates voyage, and the upside-down triangle in the bottom corner is resilience. *Book of the Camp Fire Girls*, 1914. Image courtesy of History Nebraska, The Camp Fire Collection. Reprinted with permission of Camp Fire.

all the other precepts. Not an end in itself, health was akin to civic fitness and enabled girls to "bring so much more zest and vigor to the business of living and . . . enter so much more efficiently into the work of the world." It included exercise and games as well as "essential facts in self knowledge of women." "Glorify work" called on girls to find meaning and satisfaction in daily necessary chores. The last line called on girls to "be happy." Happiness derived, the law posited, from the fulfillment of the other six points, and Luther Gulick believed it was a learned habit. "Be happy" both mirrored and surpassed the Boy Scouts' and the Girl Scouts' edicts to be "cheerful." Gulick explained that the law called girls to hide pain lest they spread suffering to others, but also held that individual happiness was a natural right that belonged to girls as much as it did to any citizen. The law thus legitimized their pursuit of fulfillment. In short, the law provided the pathway to female citizenship and for girls to be better "mothers, workers, voters and comrades."[26]

In addition to the law, the child-centered practices of progressive education emerged in Camp Fire's efforts to capture girls' imaginations and channel their energies toward productive and democratic ends. Luther Gulick directed youth workers to connect girls' ideals to their supposed natural habits and desires. He cautioned guardians against didacticism by asking, "Have you endeavored to use Camp Fire Girls to get girls to do what you think they ought to do, thus making it a sort of missionary affair?" and warned that "the organization will always fail where it is used for this obvious purpose." Here Camp Fire's founders followed educational philosopher John Dewey, who promoted the socialization of children by directing their usual activities and enjoyments toward cooperation and the "social consciousness of the race." In Camp Fire, this child-centered practice meant that leaders "help girls do the things they like to do best."[27] Progressive educators believed that play and interaction with the environment fostered learning better than rote memorization and passive instruction because they engaged the "instinctive traits" and channeled them toward lifelong wholesome ideals and habits.[28] Camp Fire's leaders thought that churches and public schools failed to do this. Public schools taught material knowledge without the social feeling necessary to bind societies together. As a result, Luther Gulick explained, children "know more about the use of tools and the physics and chemistry of cooking . . . than did our grandmothers," but they lacked the "social feelings and customs of the family." Children needed social responsibility; Luther Gulick found children who only studied and played to be "pretty worthless." He also found factory work exploitative, but he hoped to "discover again something in the community that children can do." The Camp Fire Girls would educate for social and emotional connections, thereby supplementing the school and church to anchor girls' service to the family and the community in the new industrial context.[29]

The Camp Fire Girls did so by offering the protective setting that the home had long offered middle-class children as well as exposure to public life. Camp Fire clubs brought girls into the public sphere by meeting in churches, schools, and community centers, and special activities like field trips, community pageants, and camps allowed girls to meet a still wider cohort. Although these acquaintances rarely went beyond their social circle, Camp Fire planners hoped to develop the social relations that progressive educators believed underpinned democracy.[30]

The Camp Fire Girls provided the intimate associations of close youth-adult relationships in the tradition of domestic apprenticeship and the close peer bonds of the female community. Camp Fire's selection of the term "craft" for its elective honors evoked the skill, autonomy, and dignity of artisan labor. In this, it reflected the influence of the arts and crafts movement of the late nineteenth and early twentieth centuries, which sought to improve design aesthetics and acknowledge the process by which labor skills were acquired.[31] It extended those preindustrial work traditions to women and girls. Camp Fire instruction followed what Charlotte Gulick called "the apprenticeship method." Mothers and college-educated women trained in domestic science might teach Camp Fire Girl apprentices to participate in domestic work. Charlotte Gulick envisioned a communal rather than a strictly private system, and one where compensation quantified women's work. She praised the efforts in "a western town" where "domestic science is being taught in the homes of the pupils. Mary's mother takes the girls for bread making, Mina's mother for marketing, Clara's mother for household accounts, and the mothers are paid for this work."[32] Charlotte's apprenticeship plan addressed common fears that the American girl was increasingly estranged from her mother and her labor, and therefore becoming "vulgar, unfeminine, and unladylike," in short, "a real problem for her mother."[33] Camp Fire promised to shore up intergenerational bonds and to ensure that the aesthetics and nurturing touches associated with domestic sentimentality would not be lost to the nineteenth century. Teaching not mere tasks, Camp Fire hoped to enable women to demonstrate the dignity and beauty of their work and instill pride in girls for women's work generally.

A Recapitulation Pathway for Girls

In addition to child-centered education, the Camp Fire Girls drew upon the era's eugenic and recapitulation theories to formulate a unique developmental experience for girls. The symbolism Camp Fire founders selected to grab hold of the girl's imagination relied on the theories of educator and psychologist G. Stanley Hall. Luther Gulick and Hall regularly shared a stage at education conferences and formed an intellectual friendship. Luther and Charlotte Gulick attended his lectures at Clark University, and Hall stayed with them in Springfield where, according to Charlotte, "Luther sits at his feet and asks questions."[34] In 1904 Hall's *Adolescence* transformed what the nineteenth century had known as youth—a critical period for character formation—into adolescence, the modern biological, developmental stage characterized by "storm and stress," with its need for protective attention and specialized education. His pioneering work in adolescent psychology connected white fears about Anglo-Saxon Protestant race suicide and child development theory.[35]

Hall was concerned that a "declining birth-rate" "among the cultured classes" would soon undermine national strength, and he sought a remedy for it. He was convinced, remarking on the trend for educated women to postpone marriage, that "if women do not marry before twenty-seven or -eight, the nation would in time die out." They simply would not have enough children "to keep up the population." Hall said "the duty of parenthood" was as necessary to the nation as paying taxes or military defense. Like Luther Gulick, his solution was "to make young men more manly and young women more womanly" through education and training. Hall's criticism of women's education was far more severe than anything the Camp Fire founders would make, but they came to the same conclusion about maternal training. Hall argued that girls became discontented when they observed, through coeducation, the prerogatives of boys and men and so he advocated education that would fit girls for motherhood. Although he believed that women were intellectually capable, he wrote that higher education left them too depleted physically and emotionally for this primary maternal role. Education for motherhood, Hall insisted, included domestic training and developing the "power of maternity in soul as well as in body." For this, he and the Gulicks turned to the "primitive races."[36]

Hall's racially metaphorical recapitulation theory, which argued that every stage of child development corresponded to a specific phase of human evolution, offered scientific justification for appropriating American Indian imagery for youth organizations. Prepubescent boys were most like "little savages," as Seton had called them in his book about Indian play, while adolescent boys underwent a transition from the "savage" stage to the "civilized stage" of adulthood. Turn-of-the-century Americans used "civilization" in a variety of ways. Although feminists and Black activists have used the term to demand civilized treatment such as safety from lynching and other political and social rights, white race science theorists posited a biological evolutionary stage that only whites had reached. One of its markers was gender differentiation. The dominant version of civilization "denoted a precise stage in human racial evolution—the one following the more primitive stages of 'savagery' and 'barbarism.'"[37] Hall, who overwhelmingly focused on boys in his research, argued that the boy needed to experience and embody the ostensibly natural, wild, warrior-like, savage stage to be inoculated against the "overcivilization" that many Americans believed threatened masculine vitality in the industrial age. The racialized primitive body was at once naturally healthy and deficient. Properly nurtured in clubs replete with rituals and symbols, boys would maintain the physical vitality of the "savage" as they gained the intellectual and cultural maturity of Western civilization. Hall anticipated the emergence of a race of supermen able to meet the challenges of modernity.

The Camp Fire Girls created ways for girls to maintain the gender differentiation that race theorists thought was a marker of civilization. Luther

Gulick wrote that in Camp Fire activities girls would pass through "the race history of woman, as the boy in his games and athletics passes through the race history of man."[38] Hall suggested that for girls, the magnanimity and idealism of adolescence were especially pronounced and that, in fact, girls stayed in this adolescent mindset, making them altruistic caretakers for life. In Hall's framing, "woman," like "savages," "never outgrows adolescence as man does, but lingers in, magnifies and glorifies this culminating stage of life." For Hall, summer camps developed girls' maternal sensibility as they studied the poetic rather than scientific aspects of nature and the "myth, custom, belief, [and] domestic practices of savages."[39] As the next chapter explains in more detail, Hall's race theories were the basis for Camp Fire's Indian imagery.

Still, the Camp Fire Girls diverged from Hall's scheme on several points. For Hall, proper education allowed for ample rest during what he considered to be sensitive adolescent years balanced by moderate outdoor recreation and nature appreciation. Whereas Hall believed that adolescent girls should not exert themselves during menstruation lest they damage their reproductive capacities, the Gulicks rejected female convalescence during adolescence.[40] Luther Gulick argued, "Girls who are established solidly in their monthly function during the years from twelve to twenty are not depressed or incapacitated by their periods during the balance of their lives." He concluded, "Women who are as well as possible during the teens have just as dependable working ability throughout the month as men do."[41] Although the Camp Fire Girls rejected sporting competition, the core activities in camping and health supported lifelong vigor, and Camp Fire materials celebrated feats of skill and strength and girls who undertook hundred-mile treks. One suspects that having had four active daughters, one who died as a teenager, may have helped shape the Gulicks' view.

Luther Gulick maintained that the ages of twelve to twenty were crucial for establishing the lifelong health and regularity that were necessary for girls' current and future usefulness. "It is brave to be happy though an invalid, but real big living demands health, power, [and] reserve," he declared. The list of activities for Camp Fire Girls betrayed no suggestion that girls were frail. Gulick wanted each girl to "walk a hundred miles each month," bicycle forty miles in five days, play team games for fifteen hours in a month, set up and live in a camp, and build fires.[42] In Camp Fire, girls learned to blaze trails, follow rivers to towns or seek out telegraph lines when lost, construct a shelter in the woods, and sleep outdoors. In 1915 the Madrona Camp Fire Girls of Oregon hiked 240 miles in two weeks from Grants Pass, Oregon, to Crescent City, California, working through numerous obstacles as they moved their horses and carts from one place to another and set up new camps at each site. The Camp Fire Girls integrated much that fit the masculine "strenuous life," as Theodore Roosevelt had called the "hard and dangerous endeavor" that he associated with national greatness.[43]

Luther Gulick nonetheless emphasized feminine fitness and rejected the idea that girls' athletics should mirror boys' contests. He regarded the "biological history of the sexes as sufficiently divergent to make it improbable that athletics, which, in their origin, involve movements and instinct feelings of the combative and hunting type," would appeal to girls. He argued that they "should be adapted to the feminine physiological, psychological, social or aesthetic needs." He believed that throwing, running, and jumping evolved in men from early ancestors' work as hunters. The women who survived, however, "were the best mothers, [the] most true to their homes, [and] the best workers." The Camp Fire Girls emphasized health, grace, and form rather than competition. Folk dance was the most emblematic of the female physical education pantheon, and Camp Fire embraced it enthusiastically. Readily learned, folk dance was the "most primitive of the arts." It characterized human rituals from weddings to funerals and, therefore, built the social connections deemed critical for girls. According to Luther Gulick, girls loved to dance because the rhythmic movements resonated with instinctive emotions and understandings of "what is beautiful and noble."[44]

"What a Girl Needs to Know about Herself": Sex Education

The founders not only supported girls' physical fitness, but they also were quite forward thinking about sex education and sexual expression. They attempted to teach girls about their growing bodies. At a time when American girls were, due to improved health and diet, reaching earlier menarche—a shift that for conservatives signaled disorder and possibly the promiscuity associated with supposedly inferior races—Camp Fire's leaders aligned the organization with progress and science. Camp Fire's founders believed that learning about menstruation promoted healthy motherhood as it increased girls' knowledge and represented a supportive approach to future motherhood. To earn Camp Fire's second rank, that of Fire Maker, girls were required "to know what a girl of her age needs to know about herself." A long list of hygiene concerns, including "the best use of hot and cold baths," "cleanliness of the hair," and sound exercise and sleep practices followed. The inclusion of menstruation, however, suggests a broader conversation about sex education. The experts that Camp Fire founders admired advocated adolescent knowledge about sexuality. British sexologist Havelock Ellis, whom Charlotte Gulick quoted on the cover of *Wohelo*, believed teaching sex education to girls fostered "responsibility in the guardianship of her own body and soul." Ellis pressed for a more technical discussion of sexual organs, their functions, and gestation. Hall, too, frankly recognized adolescent female sexual desire, which he thought was restrained by an innate female disposition toward "anatomical, physiological, and psychological modesty," and the need to combat superstitions surrounding menstruation.[45] For its part, the Camp Fire guidebook still used euphemisms for sex education, such as "hygiene" and "those intimate things which careful mothers tell their daughters about the personal life of women."[46] Leaders nonetheless taught facts about female biology to the girls in their groups. One woman who had been a Camp Fire Girl in the 1920s in Oregon recalled that she received lessons in female biology that she was not getting anywhere else. Although her leader's lessons did not extend beyond menstruation, they "eased minds." Her mother had been "tight lipped" about menstruation, citing only biblical explanations for its causes. To her, Camp Fire's teaching "what a girl needs to know about herself" eased the process of growing up. Other Camp Fire Girls agreed. One leader in training appreciated how "plain personal talks do more toward answering the unasked questions of young girls than anything else I know of." Such frankness helped her "a great deal to understand [girls'] half-asked questions."[47]

Several young women training to be Camp Fire leaders, however, disagreed about this part of the program. One thought sex education beyond Camp Fire's purview. As the instructor detailed an assignment for each woman to write a letter describing what she would tell her girls about puberty, one pupil recorded, "[The lecture] shocked or astonished some of the girls while the *youngest* one in the group shed a few tears—thinking it the mother's duty—But Mrs. McCormick [the instructor] had no pity on her and she had to take the medicine along with the rest of us.—*Ha*." The assignment prompted three more days of discussion among the young women, making the instructor glad she had included it.[48]

Charlotte Gulick rejected other forms of Victorian rigidity and encouraged girls to see their developing bodies as natural and therefore beautiful. She allowed the girls to prance around together in nightgowns tied high on one leg "for elegance." Rather than scold them, one camper remembered that she "told us how beautiful our bodies were and that there was nothing to be ashamed of." She also let them skinny dip in the lake. As these memories indicate, the Camp Fire Girls provided space for girls' self-acceptance to blossom.[49]

Charlotte Gulick was not necessarily representative of leaders' comfort with girls' emerging sexual expression, however. Other leaders' responses demonstrate discomfort. One Boston leader scribbled out camp rules on bits of paper. "[Don't] speak to any boy or young man without an introduction by a proper person" and "Don't wear an Annette bathing suit," she wrote, referring to the form-fitting, one-piece, skirtless suit popularized by swimmer and designer Annette Kellerman in the 1910s.[50] That the camp leader believed she needed to formalize such rules indicates that at least some girls were engaging in the disfavored activities. Indeed, when New Hampshire campers got caught at the swimming pool in the rain, one girl recorded, they "vamped an automobile & we all hoped [*sic*] in" to avoid the storm.[51] Her use of "vamp," a common expression for using one's feminine wiles to secure a favor, implied that the girls flaunted their femininity to hitch a ride back to camp. This act likely included speaking to boys and men without a "proper introduction."

The leader's notes also demonstrate her growing discomfort with girls' intimate same-sex relationships. In the nineteenth century, romantic, emotional, and even physical connections between young women were acceptable. In the early twentieth century, girls' intimacies remained commonplace at camp and in women's colleges and boarding schools. However, modern psychologists and educators increasingly advanced concerns that such same-sex relationships led to abnormal lesbian desire. The Boston leader forbade girls from getting "into bed with another girl."[52] Indeed, the proximity that was part of camp life, more than the ordinary weekly meetings, inspired girls' physical and emotional intimacy. Historian Leslie Paris has noted the prevalence of girls climbing into bed with one another to share secrets at summer camp.[53] One fifteen-year-old bragged in a letter home from the camp at Lake Sebago: "Mother, we all get in the lake in our bathing suits and scrub each others [sic] spines off—and you know that my spine is a popular washboard!"[54] Girls' letters home detailed new "adorable" best friends, mapped the sleeping arrangements to indicate relational intensities, and noted who invited whom to whisper late into the night.[55] Even when girls did not develop romantic friendships, they referred to one another as big and little sisters, and their friendships often lasted decades.[56]

Positive Eugenics in the Camp Fire Girls

Many girls welcomed the Camp Fire Girls' openness about puberty and developing bodies. Even as the Camp Fire Girls was open about puberty and developing bodies, the health program, of which the menstrual lessons were part, sought to disrupt race suicide. Menstrual health concerns meshed with other hygiene matters to support what historian Susan A. Miller describes as girls' "eugenic responsibilities."[57] By the 1910s, eugenics, the study of "more suitable races or strains of blood," as its founder Francis Galton defined it, was a fashionable scientific discipline. Popular science magazines ran articles regularly about the risks of racial "degeneracy," and over four hundred universities offered courses or programs devoted to it.[58] Eugenics was a topic of discussion in the extended Gulick family. Luther Gulick's mother expressed an interest in it in a letter to him and expected that it would shape how Americans approached marriage. Luther reportedly relied on so-called positive eugenics in his decision to end an engagement with a paramour because the two partners both had red hair, suffered headaches, and had "highly organized nervous systems."[59]

The Camp Fire Girl program was in step with "positive" eugenic thought in elevating motherhood and women's health to improve American racial stock. Although they served as a source of power for girls and women, maternal roles were turned toward the wider social aim of fostering a stronger nation and race. Camp Fire's organizers never called for the negative eugenics of "weeding and breeding out 'inferior' stock" that led to eugenic sterilization laws across the United States. These statutes targeted people with disabilities and mental illness and became models for Nazi sterilization laws. As chapter 4 discusses, the Camp Fire Girls accommodated girls with physical disabilities. Indeed, Camp Fire literature did not refer specifically to breeding. The program nonetheless responded to the decrease in marriage and fertility rates among the white middle classes over which prominent eugenicists fretted. The Camp Fire Girls aimed to shore up girls' health for the future of the nation. Here they were not far different from eminent progressives like Theodore Roosevelt, who cautioned Americans against "race suicide" and extolled physical activity, and feminist Charlotte Perkins Gilman, who placed motherhood and women's reproductive powers as the center of nation-building. Staying healthy for motherhood was good for the race and nation.[60]

Charlotte Gulick's pregnancy offers a model of the connection between physical activity, female strength, and maternal health. During her second pregnancy in 1890 and 1891, when most American women went into "confinement" during their last trimester, Charlotte rode her bike daily until one week before the baby arrived. She urged her in-laws to take up the sport as well and insisted that the muscle she built riding her bicycle accounted for her swift recovery following childbirth. She viewed bicycle riding as an investment in female strength and as a benefit to motherhood, and she connected it to her low-intervention labor. "Women who wear corsets and do not rest and exercise I suppose cannot be treated naturally but those of us who do I believe can have a more natural confinement," she wrote.[61] The low-intervention birth, in turn, allowed her to tend to her baby and home more quickly after delivery. Recreation served both individual health and eugenic purposes in that it promised better babies. The fortification of maternal health for national service found expression in Camp Fire's health program.

Luther Gulick's experiences, too, though they did not translate to maternal health claims, provided him with insight into the struggles adolescents faced as they tried to cultivate the "zest" for work that the modern era demanded. As an adolescent boy, Luther had struggled with health and purpose. The son of famous foreign Christian missionaries to China and Hawaii, he and his siblings, most of whom also established missionary careers, came of age with a mindset that emphasized uplifting and improving others by spreading Christianity and democracy.[62] However, headaches, backaches, possible depression, and what family members regarded as bouts of laziness prevented Luther from exhibiting this Protestant usefulness. When Luther was sixteen, he stayed for a brief time in Hanover, New Hampshire, with his brother Sidney Gulick, who chastised his brother's habits: "*Luther* . . . has been here a week without work, but today he has commenced sawing wood (this morning); and now after little more than an hour's work; he is back & on his back on the sofa. He can play in the gymnasium two hours a day & not feel particularly tired; but an hour's work exhausts him."[63] Luther Gulick's hours in the gymnasium were his source of inspiration for the playground movement and the Camp Fire Girls. Years later, Luther wrote in *The Efficient Life* that the best way to combat depression was to cultivate the habit of cheerfulness consciously and to balance work, exercise or play, and rest.[64] Hiking, physical activity, and rest did much for his well-being.

Physical training and habit formation provided the means to success for Luther. In 1885, at the age of twenty, he headed to the Sargent School for Physical Education in Cambridge, Massachusetts, a leading institute for training in physical education methods. Luther had learned of the Sargent School and about the field of physical education through Dr. Delphine Hanna, a female teacher of physical culture at Oberlin College, where he had studied. (She must have convinced him of women's athletic abilities.) While at Sargent, Luther discovered a profession that suited his temperament and skills far better than foreign missionary work did. Many schools needed physical education specialists as the field was rapidly expanding. He soon took a job at a YMCA as gymnasium superintendent, an appointment that combined Luther's religious and physical education interests. Still planning to follow his father's footsteps into missionary work, Luther soon enrolled in New York University Medical College to become a medical missionary. He earned his medical degree in 1889 but was drawn deeper into YMCA work in Springfield, Massachusetts. As he recognized the contribution that he could make there, he gave up the commitment to foreign missionary work and devoted his life to programs for play, recreation, health, and human usefulness.[65] His medical education lent his ideas scientific and professional credibility, giving traction to his organizational efforts. In educational and organizational work, he sought to motivate youth to solid habits by teaching them through the activities they already enjoyed, inspiring them through adventure, and offering them recognition for accomplishments.

Health and Habit Formation

The Camp Fire Girls taught a detailed health regimen that required extensive self-monitoring. The hygiene program included charts on which girls recorded daily over twenty diet, rest, hygiene, and exercise habits. Such record keeping reflected Luther Gulick's efforts to instill regular patterns of healthy living, and it was popular among youth organizations. The rural 4-H instructed its girls to keep health scorecards and subject themselves to examination by doctors and nurses, who would judge them for prizes according to a eugenic rubric at state fairs.[66] A Camp Fire Girl's record was more personal, though she would show it to her club leader, and it monitored habits rather than physical qualifications. On her chart, the Camp Fire Girl tracked whether she slept with wide-open windows, kept her clothes and hair neat, refrained from chewing gum, took one hour of exercise out of doors daily, and had a regular bowel movement.[67]

In the 1920s, keeping these charts with 90 percent success for at least two months out of the year was required for those girls who wished to earn the second rank of Fire Maker.[68] The 1924 annual report announced that 40 percent of Camp Fire members successfully kept such charts.[69] Surviving charts show that some girls carefully marked their habits, whereas others were inconsistent. One Massachusetts girl's chart showed diligence for the first five days. Then a few boxes were unchecked. After ten days, no further markings appeared on the chart, suggesting that she gave up that month.[70] Another girl's chart showed remarkable firmness in all categories; she marked nearly all spaces every day for a month, missing only a few glasses of water and occasionally forgetting to wash her hands before each meal. Even girls without the printed charts attempted to track the

CAMP FIRE GIRLS HEALTH CHART

Name _Marian Louise Hall_   Address _1615 Marietta Street_
Guardian's Name _Mrs Castle_   Month _April_   Year _1936_

PIN THIS CHART ON YOUR WALL AND CHECK UP YOUR RECORD EACH NIGHT

		Points	Total
1	MORNING HABITS: Drank one or more glasses of water slowly, on rising	1	26
2	Took five minutes' general exercise.	1	10
3	Took cool shower, plunge or sponge.	1	7
4	Cleaned teeth.	1	30
5	Ate wholesome breakfast, fruit, milk or cocoa, some form of bread; if underweight, eggs or bacon.	1	30
6	Had regular bowel movement.	1	30
7	DAY HABITS: Washed hands before eating.	1	30
8	Did not eat between meals, except milk and fresh fruit. Refreshments once a week at parties.	1	30
9	Ate three regular meals.	1	30
10	Drank at least two glasses of milk today (½). Did not drink tea or coffee today (½).	1	30
11	Ate my food slowly and chewed it thoroughly.	1	30
12	Ate at least one cooked and one raw vegetable in addition to potatoes.	1	28
13	Drank at least five glasses of water, including morning glass.	1	30
14	Walked briskly or exercised at least one hour out of doors.	1	30
15	Tried to stand and sit correctly all day.	1	30
16	Wore sensible shoes except for dress occasions.	1	30
17	RETIRING HABITS: Cleaned teeth before retiring.	1	30
18	Slept with open windows or out-of-doors.	1	30
19	Slept at least 9 hours (if over 16, 8 hours).	1	30
20	MONTHLY ACCOUNT: Walked 25 miles this month. / Walked 50 miles this month.	5 / 10	5
*21	Weight within 10 lbs. all month.	10	10
22	Washed hair at least every 2 weeks.	5	

Total number of points 536

REMARKS:

1. If 31, 30 or 28 days in month, the maximum totals are 614, 595 or 557 respectively; 90% for each of these will be 552, 535 or 501 respectively.
2. If 90% for the month is attained, the girl is entitled to wear the Health Symbol, adding a red dot to each section of fringe as the 90% average is won monthly.
3. If 90% of total is earned for 12 months in succession, a National Health Honor is awarded on receipt of the 12 Camp Fire Health Charts at Headquarters, 41 Union Square, New York City.
4. These must be correctly checked, added and accompanied by a letter of verification from Guardian.

*Height-weight tables on separate cards may be procured from the American Child Health Association, 370 Seventh Ave., New York City, for 1c each.

NOTE:—If working for a National Health Honor (12 consecutive months) a Camp Fire Girl must indicate a doctor's and dentist's examination in the 12 months and any necessary corrective work.

Date ....

2. Camp Fire's hygiene program included charts on which girls recorded daily over twenty diet, rest, hygiene, and exercise habits. The charts helped girls monitor their own health so that they might better serve the nation. Camp Fire Girls Health Chart, 1936. Author's collection. Reprinted with permission of Camp Fire.

same healthy routines. One girl who lived in a home for orphans probably did not purchase the twenty-five cent charts available through the Camp Fire Outfitting Company. Still, she followed her habits in her journal, registering when she "[ate] between meals," "put fingers in mouth," or "didn't take shower."[71]

It is impossible to know what girls thought of the charts. Some likely found them handy for monitoring progress toward self-improvement goals. For others, as a "body project" that channeled girls' energies and time into control of the body, the charts may have become a source of frustration.[72] Those who did not fill them out or stopped midway through the month subtly resisted Camp Fire's efforts to compel them to police themselves. Despite the tedious charts, health craft was, overall, quite popular, with its mix of sporting activities, health habits, and first aid. Health craft consistently ranked second in the number of honors girls earned, and in 1922 Camp Fire Girls earned over 350,000 health craft honors.[73]

Camp and Health

In addition to the hygiene regimen, camping fostered healthy girls and future women. The organization offered various avenues for camping. Girls attended the emerging girls' camps, such as those established by the Gulicks and fellow organizers Charles and Charlotte Joy Farnsworth in the early 1900s. The Gulicks' camp, Wohelo (later Sebago-Wohelo) on Lake Sebago, hosted seventeen New York City girls in tents in 1910, most for several weeks at a time. Girls swam and canoed in the lake. They donned bloomers with long black stockings and white tennis shoes, hiked, cooked out of doors, and performed rituals and skits at ceremonial camp fires. Employed personnel taught hand craft and camp craft skills such as knot tying. Girls who did not attend formal camps took trips near their towns and cities with their groups, staying at farmhouses, army forts, campgrounds, wooded areas, or seashores.[74]

Camp Fire organizers understood outdoor activity to be advantageous for a girl's constitution, an idea that reflected an American cultural belief about the restorative effects of nature. Youth leaders believed that outdoor activity away from urban centers restored and strengthened vitality, making a girl more useful to her community and nation.[75] According to Charlotte

Gulick, outdoor activity provided girls with "not only physical strength but a freedom and development which prepares her for the spiritual side of motherhood." The woman who loved the outdoors more easily "found romance in daily life, and enjoyment in all the wholesome activities and occupations of womanhood." She was thus "far better equipped to fulfill the functions of motherhood than the young girl brought up in an atmosphere of artificialities."[76]

Girls themselves cherished camping. In the early 1920s, between 70 and 80 percent of Camp Fire Girls went camping with their local clubs, with a little over 40 percent attending residential Camp Fire camps.[77] Girls showed their enjoyment of camping by taking photographs and keeping journals or scrapbooks of their trips. Often, Camp Fire Girls and their clubs maintained such memory books only when they went camping. Their care and attention to their camp memories reveal the significance of these novel experiences to them. They carefully decorated the pages of their scrapbooks with drawings and symbols, often writing the text in verse. Girls wrote odes to the scenery and camp landscape. Most often, they recalled friendships that developed at camp. Photos captured the joy of physical activity, companions, and adventure, all of which girls identified with camping.

Girls developed camp rituals that further showed that they valued camp. Experienced campers, for example, collectively referred to first-time campers as "tenderfeet" and poked fun at them for being "arrayed in all the splendor of full dress bathing suits, of silk or other city material."[78] Such teasing created a camp social hierarchy with more experienced campers at the top. It recognized those campers who mastered camp feats of strength and skill as well as the routine practices of camp life.

Camp offered girls opportunities to develop their physical strength, confidence, and athletic skills. Most campers got the chance to swim, most often in lakes, rivers, and creeks, since most early twentieth-century camps did not have swimming pools. Swimming was the activity in which girls earned the most honors while at camp. Other typical sports were baseball, volleyball, "group games," tennis, archery, and hiking.[79] Girls delighted in physical activities. Luther Gulick's niece, Ethel Gulick, wrote letters from Camp Sebago-Wohelo reflecting her pride in her own and other girls' ath-

3. Camp Fire Girls cooking a meal at a campsite near Ames, Iowa. Most girls indicated that camping was the most significant aspect of the program. They experienced adventure, activities like canoeing and boating, friendships, and appreciation for nature. They also practiced domestic skills like cooking out of doors. Their scrapbooks are filled with camping activities that were not possible in weekly meetings. Courtesy of Ames History Museum.

letic abilities. Ethel admired her fellow campers. Only one girl could not swim, despite the arrival of nearly forty new campers that summer. "Don't you think that does well?" she asked. She wrote with pride to her mother that she had "easily" passed the hundred-yard swim test, a mandatory test before being allowed to go in a canoe. Her relatives had not thought she was ready for it. Her excitement grew as she described a canoe trip and overnight campout. "We had a whooping good time," she exclaimed, and she later excused her neglect of letter writing due to the girls taking "a long tramp—12 or thirteen miles." Ethel's pride turned to annoyance, however, when girls did not enjoy physical activity as she did. Despite the fact that so many girls knew how to swim, most of them waded at the shallow beach rather than enter the deeper waters, she complained.[80]

Like many early twentieth-century girls, Ethel seemed to gain from the opportunity to participate in outdoor activities and sports a greater appreciation for the world of boys.[81] At age sixteen, she explained, "Yesterday our new Camp Fire of seven went on a picnic." Though she said they had "a fine time" finding flowers, she thought she would go with her brothers next time because "then we can build a dam across the river or something. When we go with the girls, they never want to go wading."[82] Ethel also voiced distaste in her letters for the secrets, gossip, and frivolity associated with girls. To her older brother, she wrote, "Girls are the funniest things in the world. They are *so* afraid of bugs and worms and they aren't at all afraid of telling on others. Thats [*sic*] what the matter is with a girl in the other tent. One girl said something she shouldn't and now the girl who didn't want it told is having fits." She quickly rebuked herself, however, for bothering her brother with the business of girls, apologizing, "I guess this isn't very interesting to you." Still, she filled him in on the other troubles she was having anyway.[83] For girls like Ethel, Camp Fire camp provided a space for adventure and new challenges even if the self-imposed limits of other girls disappointed her.

Elevating Women's Work through Ceremony and Recognition

After health, the Camp Fire Girls turned attention to usefulness. The Camp Fire Law instructed girls to "glorify work," which organizers defined primarily as tasks in service to the home and family. Camp Fire went beyond practical training in domestic skills to assert a philosophy of work that simultaneously veiled the drudgery of household labor and, organizers hoped, elevated women's status. The Gulicks believed that a loss in women's standing had accompanied the modern industrial era. Although women's opportunities outside the home were expanding, Luther Gulick wrote that "things which women have done during the entire history of the world, during our lifetime have lost their status." Charlotte agreed. "Motherhood," she wrote, "is extolled in poetry, but ridiculed in general."[84] She decried the incipient antimaternalism that would grow and eventually challenge the moral authority that undergirded organized women's reform efforts in the twentieth century.[85] Privately she lamented a crisis in girlhood: "It seems a great pity that school girls are given to making fun of the idea of even having a family, or of getting married."[86] The Camp Fire Girls glorified roles traditionally associated with womanhood, particularly motherhood and homemaking, to elevate women's position. Women's status would rise once their traditional roles received proper acknowledgment, its founders insisted.

Camp Fire Girls glorified domestic work through the elective honors, the tasks listed in the guidebook that girls did to earn beads. The home craft honors were "the most important factor in the Camp Fire organization," and thus home craft was the largest of the elective honor categories, accounting for a third of Camp Fire's total elective honors. Still, the founders did not want to relegate their daughters to lives of drudgery but to redefine daily chores as esteemed labor. This reconstruction of the meaning of work involved a two-pronged approach: quantifying work by delineating its specific components and romanticizing work by imbuing it with symbolic beauty and ritual. When the process was complete, homemaking and child-rearing, according to Luther's philosophy of essential feminism, would be "part of a definite social status."[87]

Camp Fire was in line with other programs designed to ennoble domestic work. It borrowed heavily from the home economics movement, through which women demanded professional recognition of the complexity and scientific basis of domestic labor. Embracing modern, scientific, efficient housekeeping, early twentieth-century home economists moved domestic science courses into colleges, high schools, settlement houses, and mothers' clubs. In line with progressive reformers' concern for social science and health reform, home economists sought to prevent disease by employing scientific hygiene principles in the home, teaching immigrants and rural women about nutrition and the chemistry of proper food handling, and helping women to save money by making wise consumer choices.[88] The emphasis on systematic efficiency and science ran through the home craft honors, many of which were developed in the Manhattan Trade School for Girls' home economics program. Luther Gulick noted that modern girls rarely cared to learn "how to care for babies," but if instructors called it "learning the causes of infant mortality," it sounded "like modern social service," and girls jumped at the chance to hear more.[89]

Camp Fire's founders also intended to show that women's work was quantifiable; it could be measured and remunerated. Camp Fire Girls did not actually earn wages for their domestic training, though some no doubt drew allowances for chores and some may have been employed part-time. Camp Fire Girls instead received small, colored wooden beads for specified tasks listed in the Camp Fire handbook. The Gulicks explained that in obtaining a concrete award for their labor, girls would recognize the importance of their work and take greater pride in it. Charlotte noted, "The Camp Fire program is the nearest approach we have to measuring the work in the home as the girl passes from one rank into another, and attains her beads."[90]

Still, quantification and efficiency were not the end goals for Camp Fire organizers, who rejected a laboratory approach to domestic work as too impersonal. Instead beads presented as part of a ceremony made the work a romantic adventure. Luther Gulick explained: "When a girl appears before her camp fire and reports that she has learned to make ten standard soups . . . that she can describe three kinds of baby cries and know the cause of each . . . and that she has received for each of these an award of honor . . . the spirit of romance has been suggested to her. . . . [A]s she stands before the camp fire and receives these tokens, the things which are everyday drudgery are thereby indicated as romantic and adventuresome."[91] Further romanticizing women's chores, Camp Fire's hand craft honors augmented housework by focusing on beautifying the home and balancing the systematic approach of domestic science. Camp Fire guidelines required girls to create articles that "show skill, ingenuity and taste," as well as originality in "designs, symbolizing some personal characteristics or something about this organization."[92] By giving awards for creativity and skill in housekeeping, Camp Fire hoped to inspire pride in girls' domestic skills and to maintain a personal touch—the infusion of beauty—in the industrial era.

How did girls respond to the simultaneous quantification and romanticization of female labor? If their engagement in the program is any indication of their approval, they absorbed the message that home and its sibling, hand craft, were important to female citizenship. The most honors awarded to members were in home craft. In 1922, for example, Camp Fire Girls received over 636,000 home craft honor beads. Combined with the other domestic category, hand craft, the third most popular category (240,000 beads awarded), nearly half the awards girls earned were in domestic pursuits.[93]

The high rates of domestic honors indicate that girls internalized Camp Fire's message about domesticity, but home craft was also convenient and it contained the most activity suggestions. (Together, home and hand craft made up 42 percent of the honor activities listed in the guidebook.) Girls could select familiar activities from this category and perform them without leaving home and with minimal adult help. As a practical matter, it was certainly easier, for example, to "make bread in two ways and two kinds of cake" than to "make a shelter and bed of material found in the woods," a typical camp craft activity.[94] Viola Collins of Springfield, Massachusetts, for example, commented, "Most of my honors have been won in Home Craft for I enjoy working at home therefore it is not hard for me to earn honors in this craft." Domesticity required neither participation with the group or a foray into the wilderness. A girl like Viola, eager to earn beads, could readily do so on any given afternoon.

Still, some girls framed their experience through Camp Fire ideals, expressing how earning beads had changed their attitude toward labor. Viola explained that Camp Fire ideals had enhanced her appreciation of housework. "Before I became a Camp Fire girl it was merely work; now it is more like play, it is like a game that does not grow tiresome for there are so many different things that can be done. When such honors are completed there is a satisfaction because you feel that something worth while has been accomplished."[95] Oral history and girls' letters record similar perceptions. Celia Anderson, who had been a Camp Fire Girl in the 1920s and later led a group as an adult, agreed that learning feminine skills like cooking and crafts fostered pride and a sense of accomplishment for girls. She remembered that when leaders conferred awards at council fires, "you had worked very hard, and this was your recognition."[96] Fifteen-year-old Clarissa Fairchild made sense of her camp chores through the Camp Fire ideal of glorifying work too. In her letter to her mother from Camp Sebago-Wohelo, she wrote, "I think that it really takes a whole lot of time and brains to see beauty in things, and that that is why work so rarely seems beautiful, because we are so used to it we don't *notice* any more. I hope there is such a thing as a habit of noticing, because if there is, I am forming it, because if anyone ever enjoyed cooking and washing more than I have this past week, I would like to see them."[97]

Not all Camp Fire Girls came to romanticize domestic tasks. One Columbus, Ohio, Camp Fire Girl in the mid-1920s recalled many years later that with her best friend, she had "shared in a new Campfire Girls program, but I was somewhat at a disadvantage, not bringing much confidence to handiwork."[98] Others recorded domestic labor without commenting on Camp Fire's philosophy. Frances Pass merely jotted in her 1920s diary that she "swated [sic] 40 flies for a Camp Fire bead" and "took account" of her Camp Fire records. She noted that "work was plentiful" on camp kitchen patrol but never indicated that she found particular beauty in it.[99]

Still, other Camp Fire Girls had a different view of women's perennial labor altogether. With her Sebago-Wohelo campmates, Ethel Gulick wrote a "playlette" that illustrated a generational concept of female labor. The short dramatic piece featured a mother and her friends talking about babies, quilts, and dishes. Then a "new fashioned lady" enters the scene and reads a "Declaration of Freedom." The girls' declaration compared their perceived opportunities favorably to the limitations that they associated with past generations of American women. Their grandmothers, they wrote, had "thru the tyranny of circumstance" their "noses . . . held to the grindstone of duty." Their "aspirations were throtteled by the hangmans noose of tradition [sic]," and their "joys were stamped out in the treadmill of drudgery." Describing themselves as "the flower of the United States, the fount of new life, the hope of future eons," the girls resolved to "blaze new trails for our sisters to follow" through the Camp Fire Girls. These Camp Fire Girls associated progress for women both with their generation and with Camp Fire. For these girls, being modern Camp Fire Girls meant leaving behind drudgery. They imagined that they were blazing new trails and moving into the "broat [sic] sea of the new opportunity," not merely recasting drudgery as meaningful work.[100]

Service in the Community

In addition to domesticity, girls' service was significant for her useful contributions to the community. Outlined in the patriotism (later citizenship) section of the handbook were specific projects for harnessing "the Spirit of the Home" to improve public life.[101] Camp Fire Girls earned honor beads for a broad set of progressive reform commitments, especially those supporting women's and children's welfare. They prepared, for example, plans "to improve the conditions under which girls work in your community." Camp Fire similarly rewarded girls who became "familiar with your national history as it affects woman's welfare," suggesting several readings on women reformers and women's rights activists, including Helen Keller, Lucy Larcom, Joan of Arc, Florence Nightingale, Jane Addams, Elizabeth Cady Stanton, Julia Ward Howe, and Mary Livermore. The guidebook urged girls to study women's labor conditions, organizations such as the Women's Trade Union League and the National Consumers' League, and women's property rights under state law, and advised girls to compare the United States to other countries.[102] Camp Fire founders deemed reform to be an integral part of the new relation of women to the world.[103] Indeed, Luther Gulick lamented that unlike their brothers, girls had little chance "for team work." The Camp Fire Girls intended to "give a girl the chance to go out and do some definite organizing work." Luther Gulick believed this would instill confidence, "a power of training which will make her invaluable anywhere."[104]

The Camp Fire organization, nonetheless, separated such reform from suffrage politics. Despite its promotion of participation in political life, the Camp Fire Girls took no official position on the suffrage debate. Its magazines failed to mention even the ratification of the nineteenth amendment. Camp Fire leadership separated civic activities, whether or not they developed girls' political consciousness, which it seems reading about Elizabeth Cady Stanton was likely to do, from suffrage activism. *The Book of the Camp Fire Girls* noted that "girls and Guardians are entirely free to identify themselves as they please" but also asked girls not to wear their ceremonial costumes if they marched in suffrage parades.[105] Nonetheless, Charlotte and Luther Gulick supported the suffrage cause. Charlotte Gulick considered joining suffrage groups around New York, writing, "I am trying to make up my mind whether I will join some of the societies or not. I believe it is coming, that it is the only logical outcome but I have no time for it now."[106] Records do not indicate that she ever joined any of them. Luther Gulick, too, believed that "woman is as sure to have the suffrage as the tide is to rise." He argued, however, that "the vote is no end in itself," but mattered so far as it brought women's unique service through nurture and love out of the home and into the community.[107]

Girls embraced the association between womanhood and civic participation. Luther Gulick's warning to girls not to wear Camp Fire costumes in suffrage parades hints that some girls did so, and newspaper reports indicated that Camp Fire groups marched in suffrage parades. But more commonly, girls embraced the less divisive aims of municipal housekeeping. In her literary voice, Hazel Murray, fourteen, of Littleton, Massachusetts, echoed the municipal housekeeping and essential feminism of the Camp Fire founders. She wrote short stories and sent them to Camp Fire headquarters to see if *Wohelo* might print them. In one story, a girl visits a dilapidated country town. In true Camp Fire fashion, the young woman suggests ways to beautify the town and improve its economy and reputation in the process. Not only do the townspeople need to plant flowers, but they need to erect a welcoming entrance to the town and organize a cleanup. "Why doesn't your women's club get busy?" she asks.[108]

Hazel was not alone. The 1922 annual report praised Camp Fire Girls' citizenship accomplishments, including the "100 per cent of the Camp Fire Girls who have given service of the first kind." They listed groups that had taken care of families' needs, provided summer camp for children, and visited "Old People's Homes" as the kind of civic work girls should be and were, in fact, doing. The report indicated special pride for several cities where the girls built community fire places, enormous stone or brick hearths constructed in parks and community centers to serve as the heart of community gatherings.[109] These public reform activities were rarely divisive and derived from traditional women's and girls' responsibilities. *Wohelo* explicitly impressed upon girls that they were part of a nationwide community and that this came with responsibility.

Service and World War I

World War I provided the Camp Fire Girls with an opportunity to showcase its model of healthy, useful girl citizenship. The term "service" itself was wrought with meaning during the conflict. It resonated with those Americans who supported wartime measures, registered for the draft, and volunteered for the Red Cross.[110] The war, Luther Gulick said, opened "as definite a place for the girls of the community in the national teamwork as there is for the women and men."[111] His maternalist essential feminism proved adaptable to wartime political demands. Although many pacifist women in the early twentieth century invoked the values of maternalism to defend their antiwar political positions and to claim that women were nurturers, not warriors, Camp Fire's leaders found maternalist claims to citizenship strengthened by war service. An alternative to passivism, historian Jean Bethke Elshtain writes, is the tradition of the noncombatant woman as the "beautiful soul," a repository of innocence, nonviolence, "succor and compassion" during wartime. Her "unselfish devotion" comforts other citizens via nurture and aid.[112] When Anna Howard Shaw addressed the girls of America from her post as president of the Woman's Committee of the Council of National Defense through the Camp Fire magazine, she made that connection. She explained that the call "into service for their country and for the freedom of the world" was not just for men and women, but for girls too. The call "asks you to put your watchword [Wohelo] to its test, to work, to build up your health, to cultivate a spirit of love which will teach you to sacrifice for your country as you have never sacrificed before."[113] Compassion and love would translate into actions to support the war effort.

With this in mind, Camp Fire officials drew up the "Minute Girl Program" for girls to contribute to the war effort. Gulick sent his plan to President Wilson, who gave his hearty approval and accepted the title of Camp Fire's honorary president. (This designation later went only to first ladies and female dignitaries.) To reach as broad a swath of American girlhood as possible, Camp Fire advertised the war program widely. Girls could participate without joining Camp Fire, performing ceremonials, or working on the organization's ranks. In doing so, Camp Fire recruited almost seven hundred more girls per month than it had before the war.[114] Camp Fire worked with other organizations, such as the National Red Cross, and the federal government to coordinate women's home front contributions. The organization helped the Department of Agriculture publicize food conservation guidelines; turned *Wohelo*, Camp Fire's monthly magazine, into a "service magazine" to educate American girls in food conservation; cooperated with the Woman's Committee of the Council of National Defense; and assisted the Children's Bureau in taking care of America's children.[115] Not surprisingly, girls earned a higher proportion of honor beads in patriotism than they had before the war—nearing the typically high totals in hand craft. Of the nearly 1.5 million beads earned in 1917, 221,000 recognized wartime public-spirited activities.[116]

Camp Fire Girls' war work included drumming up war support. One Camp Fire report claimed, "Healthy, happy, beautiful girls can call the attention of the community" to food-saving strategies and other civilian programs "better than any other class in the community." Indeed, American girlhood—invoking innocence, the nation's future, and youthful vitality—symbolized the fight to make the world safe for democracy. At banquets, plays, and parades, Camp Fire Girls, acting as "young hostesses," publicized government guidelines and the Red Cross menus that gave emergency mealtime suggestions.[117] The "Minute Girl" title itself, which meant "girls ready on the minute as were the Minute Men of 1812," evoked, whether intended or not, George Creel's "Four-Minute Men," the federal propaganda machine that used local volunteers to harness war support, though no other evidence connects the two.[118] Like Creel's speakers, Camp Fire Girls engaged in public entertainment designed to build, through the "dramatic cultivation of intense emotion," a consensus in support of the war.[119] One of the fundraising entertainments girls gave during the war, "The Slacker's Dream," condemned civilians as "slackers," the same label used to deride draft evaders. The main character is a Camp Fire Girl, and she dreams that the other girls in her unit are speaking badly about her. They accuse her of "eating all sorts of good things like chocolate cake and fudge, *all by herself!*" "How selfish!" "And unpatriotic!" they growl. In another scene, the Camp Fire Girl dreams of soldiers entering into battle. One does not have a sweater because his battalion has run out of provisions. His comrade attributes the lack of supplies to young women. "What a shame!" he complains. "There must be some slackers among the girls back home!"[120] This dialogue upbraided lazy girls who shirked their patriotic duty.

But Camp Fire Girls were rarely slackers. They supported their nation's war effort in a multitude of ways. Often, they coupled service with domestic responsibilities. For example, a Camp Fire group in Temple, Texas, established a day nursery at the local Red Cross headquarters to free older women to engage in war work. The girls entertained younger children with games and storytelling while gaining the valuable childcare experience Camp Fire championed. Almost fifty thousand Camp Fire Girls reported to national headquarters that they had helped take care of small children during the war.[121] In addition, they sewed bandages and raised funds for the Red Cross, worked on Liberty Loan drives and the Food Conservation program, performed in patriotic pageants, tended war gardens, and helped orphan children around the world.[122] Camp Fire's World War I efforts to send clothing to babies in Belgium and other war-struck countries launched an annual tradition as the organization would tie a major service project to its anniversary each year.[123]

War service firmly established the Camp Fire Girls in the American organizational landscape, but war work also marked the Gulicks' final contribution to the Camp Fire Girls. The Gulick family provided the kind of wartime service that they asked of American girls. Luther not only spread the Minute Girl program, but he also went to France as part of the War Work Council of the YMCA, where he surveyed "the moral and physical welfare of the American expeditionary forces." His second daughter, Frances Gulick, then in her twenties, also traveled to France as a YMCA welfare worker with the First Engineers in Europe. In August of 1918, in ill health and still committed to war work, Luther Gulick resigned his official position in the Camp Fire Girls. He died of a heart condition a week later at Camp Sebago-Wohelo. Lester F. Scott, a national board member who shared Luther's background in the playground and camp movements, was named president. Charlotte Gulick also left the Camp Fire Girls, turning her attention to organizing the National Association of Directors of Girls' Camps.[124]

The Camp Fire Girls' founders attempted to bridge the gap between traditional femininity and women's expanding roles. They hoped to offer girls a path to self-fulfilled womanhood without altering the nineteenth-century associations of care, nurture, and beauty with femininity. Such ideas found resonance in early twentieth-century social reform circles and educational reform movements. Camp Fire founders imagined a social structure that valued both women's and men's labor and acknowledged women's claims on physical activity, self-sufficiency, and political activism, but the Camp Fire Girls' founders also upheld women's primary identification with domesticity and motherhood. The Camp Fire Girls imported to motherhood and domesticity a national purpose, portraying women's work as scientific and quantifiable even as it romanticized domesticity and motherhood to encourage girls to take on these roles. Charlotte Gulick meant for girls to undertake work of "racial importance," the rehearsal of their future roles as mothers in the industrial bureaucratic context of the twentieth century. She saw this work as necessary for "the girls in all parts of the country, for girls who come from wealthy homes and for those who must work for their living." She declared, "It is for the city girls and the country girl; in short it is for all girls."[125] Nonetheless, as the next three chapters will show, the organization presented its program as universal and inclusive, but its policies solidified racial and class hierarchies. Camp Fire made race an everyday presence in the organization through racial mimicry. Segregation along the lines of race, ability, and religion within the organization also muddled the founders' inclusive pronouncements. When they did join, girls outside the white middle class made creative use of the Camp Fire program to fit into the national girls' culture they saw unfolding around them.

2

"Wohelo Maidens" and "Gypsy Trails"

Racial Mimicry and Camp Fire's
Picturesque Girl Citizen

Camp Fire officials used appropriative dress and symbolism to construct a mythic concept of universal girlhood. Camp Fire's ceremonial costume, council fires, and camping activities invoked American Indian and sometimes Gypsy imagery. At regional council fires and at weekly meetings, Camp Fire Girls adopted as their own what they thought of as American Indian names and symbols. For special occasions, such as when girls advanced in rank or earned honor beads, girls wore a brown, fringed dress decorated with symbolic designs and worn with a beaded headband depicting their personally chosen symbol. Wearing Indian-style gowns, the thinking went, girls from various backgrounds would appear comparatively alike, and sharing rituals and symbols created a collective Camp Fire identity. The guidebook insisted that when "girls from every station in life came together all clad alike," the costume was "just as becoming to the poor girls as to the rich girl." It created "a true democratic feeling between girls of all classes," and each Camp Fire Girl was "one in this great sisterhood."[1]

Dressed as Indian Maidens, or as Wohelo Maidens, as the organization literature regularly called them, Camp Fire Girls enacted what organization officials asserted were cross-cultural, timeless female roles. Like the boys who, according to G. Stanley Hall's recapitulation theory, lived through a so-called savage stage in their play, girls accessed a female race history through Indian play. Both American Indians and women in general—associated with reproductive capacities—have been historically viewed as "rooted more directly and deeply in nature," to borrow Sherry Ortner's phrase.[2] As historian Philip Deloria explains, early twentieth-century youth leaders like Charlotte and Luther Gulick and Ernest Thompson Seton were part of a group of Indian fanciers who placed "Indians outside the temporal (and societal) boundaries of modernity" where they stood for the "authenticity and natural purity" that might undergird a new modern identity. Camp Fire's American Indian symbolism "was about reaffirming female difference in terms of domesticity and service."[3] Although Camp Fire presented Indian play as universalizing, the practice magnified racial hierarchies and, as historian Abigail Van Slyck notes, "served to embed ideas about race into children's daily lives."[4] Seton and the Gulicks popularized the Indian imagery that took hold at camps across the United States in the 1920s and 1930s.

In addition to Indian mimicry, or mythologizing, Camp Fire Girls enacted other tropes in their performative play. The Gypsy image was similarly untethered to historical fact—certainly not based on the experiences of actual Roma immigrants. It, too, presented camping and wandering through fantasy and poetic portrayals. On occasion, Camp Fire Girls performed blackface, but it never won the organization's endorsement the way Indian and Gypsy play did. One suspects that it lacked the middle-class respectability that the other two signified. Only occasional images in scrapbooks and reports in newspapers feature Camp Fire Girls in blackface, and some of these sought to assert a degree of propriety. One Indiana group, for example, performed a version of *Cinderella* with blackface characters and "Negro dialect." They called this rendition "modern" because it followed the recent Broadway trend of featuring Black casts.[5] Although Broadway may have indicated style and taste for the Indiana group, at its core, minstrelsy was "a white obsession with black (male) bodies." Its "fleshly investments," disavowed "through ridicule and racist lampoon," were not mysterious nor picturesque and did not invoke a noble ideal.[6] In the gender and racial discourse of the early twentieth century, Indians and Gypsies (but not blackface) were deemed appropriate for white, middle-class girls.

Picturesque Indians and the Camp Fire Aesthetic

It may seem perplexing that only a few decades after the military campaigns against Native people had ended, white, middle-class youth leaders embraced Indianness for girls, who Camp Fire leaders viewed as society's most vulnerable and protected members. After all, nineteenth-century characterizations of Native women as promiscuous, dirty, and uncivilized were not so far in the past. Yet youth organization imagery reflected the next step in the ongoing colonial struggles that marked U.S. and American Indian relations: confinement to reservations, allotment, and coercive assimilation in boarding schools. Seemingly positive images worked to obscure violence still being committed on the population as conquest continued through new efforts to assimilate American Indian youth in boarding schools. Indeed, conquest and assimilation programs made Camp Fire's use of feminine Indian imagery for white girls viable by setting authentic Indianness safely in the past. Camp Fire's imagery reflected the prevalence in early twentieth-century popular culture of Native people as noble, picturesque relics of the past. As anthropologist S. Elizabeth Bird writes, "Once Indians were no longer a threat, they became colorful and quaint."[7] Seton and the Gulicks admired and emulated American Indians. They reinforced familiar "tropes, in which the Indian was," as one white camp architect explained, "an inheritor of old cultures and of wise, poetic and beautiful customs and beliefs, marvelously harmonious with his temperament and environment."[8] Luther Gulick used terms like "romance" and "picturesqueness" to describe American Indians. He maintained that Camp Fire's ritual and symbolism invoking Indians "would take hold of the girl's imagination and find its way into her soul." It would form "an attitude toward life" wherein "beauty itself would enter her mind and heart."[9] The tropes placed Native people outside modern industrial society, denied their contemporary identities and political concerns, and "urged white children to see themselves as the rightful inheritors to North America."[10] Common narratives about the successes of assimilation further obscured the systematic harms that allotment and boarding schools were inflicting on Native populations.

Assimilation policies had particular importance for the Camp Fire Girls because of its presence as an assimilation agent in American Indian boarding schools. In 1913 the Carlisle Indian School in Pennsylvania started a group. By the 1930s, clubs met at the Yakima Indian Mission in Washington and several government Indian schools, such as the Phoenix Indian

School in Arizona and the Fort Sill Indian School in Oklahoma.[11] The Phoenix Indian School required students to participate in at least one extracurricular activity such as Camp Fire, Boy Scouts, YWCA, Holy Cross, home economics clubs, literary societies, or athletics. Assimilation policies also had particular implications for Native girls. According to many assimilation advocates, girls as "mothers of the race" were critical targets of acculturation efforts. Boarding schools detached children from family, language, culture, and community and educated them for subservient roles in the capitalist economy. The tactics destroyed cultures by upending familiar gender systems and ties between generations. Boarding schools functioned in tandem with federal land allotment policy to undermine "collective land ownership" and "matriarchal forms of gender practices" by granting larger allotments and authority to male heads of household.[12] Against this backdrop, Camp Fire clubs appeared as an assimilative agent within some residential schools for Indigenous children.

Authenticity, Eclecticism, and Indian Consultants

Camp Fire adults praised the authenticity of the imagery they presented to girls. In reality, they sought an Indian aesthetic, what Seton called "the best things from the best Indians," rather than historical or cultural accuracy.[13] In this spirit, Camp Fire advocated making up Indian-sounding words, mixing and matching eclectic practices from distinct tribes, and taking up white depictions of Indians, especially Henry Wadsworth Longfellow's epic *The Song of Hiawatha*. Still, the Camp Fire Girls sought advice on American Indian cultures from Native authors, translators, and storytellers to lend an aura of genuineness to the program. These cultural brokers, or intermediaries, such as Charles Eastman, a Dakota Sioux doctor educated at Indian boarding schools and American colleges, and Ella Deloria, a Dakota linguist and author who worked with Franz Boas, offered their ideas to white Camp Fire leaders. By 1930 Camp Fire had an advisory committee on Indian lore that included Native leaders like Gertrude Bonnin (Zitkala Sa) and white Indian experts Mary Austin, John Collier, Edward Sapir, and Frances Densmore.[14] Local Camp Fire groups invited Native speakers to give presentations about their cultures, performing their Indianness in white institutions where they were, in Bird's words, "the object of the White, colonialist gaze." At the same time, the Native consultants could "document and legitimize their Indian backgrounds for readers and scholars," using white institutions for their own ends. Progressive American Indian organizations such as the Society of American Indians and the *Real American*, a Hoquiam, Washington, weekly that argued for U.S. citizen rights for American Indians, for example, cautiously promoted Camp Fire as a means to increase awareness about contemporary Indigenous people.[15]

Eastman's writings for Camp Fire Girls and Boy Scouts reappropriated, or adopted on his terms, the white romanticized Indian, casting the portrayal in contemporary and positive terms. Desirous of showing the presence of real modern American Indians participating fully in American society, Eastman showcased his "hybrid life." As Deloria explains, "When Eastman donned an Indian headdress, he was connecting himself to his Dakota roots. But he was also . . . imitating non-Indian imitations of Indians."[16] Eastman's reproductions of Dakota culture complemented Camp Fire, but Eastman also influenced the group's teaching as he instructed young people to connect to nature and improve their health, strength, and outdoor skills. He also echoed the gender distinctions central to the Camp Fire Girls, prohibiting girls from the masculine Sioux traditions of wearing head feathers and adopting the symbols of bears and wolves, recommending instead activities such as a "maidens' feast." Here girls took a vow of purity, prepared and served a meal, and gave a gift of service. Eastman's *Indian Scout Talks: A Guide for Boy Scouts and Camp Fire Girls* also challenged the notion that girls were frail and countered negative stereotypes of American Indian women. "Contrary to the popular opinion," he wrote, "our Indian girls and women are not mere drudges, but true feminine athletes." Young female readers who saw themselves as strong and independent would have been encouraged by activities laid before them that included vigorous physical activity and team competition in the form of field hockey and "canoe ball" (a type of water lacrosse).[17] Eastman provided reassurance that Camp Fire's gender-specific program was authentically Indian as he used his alliance with Camp Fire to recast perceptions of Native people.

Ella Deloria, likewise, gave lessons on Native cultures to Camp Fire groups, gaining "access to American cultural institutions in order to reshape popular conceptions of Indianness." She was ambivalent about Camp

Fire, chiding the "cut-and-dried, stereotype designs [which they] try to read into Indian material."[18] Nevertheless, she used the organization as an avenue of influence. Deloria reappropriated American Indian imagery by reintroducing elements of the Lakota Sun Dance ceremony, which the U.S. government outlawed in 1904. In "The Wohpe Festival," a pageant that Deloria wrote in 1928 for children's summer camps, the language resembled that used by Seton and the Gulicks. Deloria wrote that "the Indian way of presenting" a kinship with nature "is particularly picturesque and impressive."[19] Her use of "picturesque" to describe Native dances would have fit into the expected Indian aesthetic and increased the acceptability of Indigenous dances in youth programming. At the same time, she was introducing a banned ceremony into a new context. Through the subversive use of children's productions, Native leaders like Deloria found a way to reappropriate and enact their traditions. In this context, we should understand Native participation in the Camp Fire program.

Campfires and Council Fires

Camp Fire wove American Indian imagery, presented as both mythic and authentic, through campfire events. The campfire was not only the name of the organization, but also Seton and the Gulicks theorized that ritual at campfires connected youth to primitive emotions. The "protection, warmth, [and] place of meeting and comfort," Seton said, "are deep in our nature, ground in through the ages as we sat about the fire."[20] Youth organizations modeled ceremonial meetings on Indian tribal councils, calling them council fires and making them occasions of ceremony and ritual. Camp Fire Girls learned hand gestures that represented fire and came "from the sign language of the early American Indian." They began each ceremonial campfire with a ritualized lighting, preferably without matches.[21] Camp Fire Girls also collected Indian legends and told them around campfires. One group recorded them—especially those focusing on reverence toward nature—in a special scrapbook.[22]

Camp Fire leaders believed that individuals could reach a deeper level of spirituality by accessing what they assumed were primitive emotions. The first Camp Fire guidebook suggested that girls say an "Ode to Fire" at the monthly ceremonial meetings, where they would give thanks for the protection against animals, cold, and hunger.[23] Luther Gulick suggested that girls be allowed to sit alone by the campfire. "Let her make it an hour of consecration" to experience the "very devout feeling [that] comes over one" when one "watch[es] alone with the Great Spirit," he wrote.[24] Camp Fire had not abandoned Judeo-Christian religions but offered the "great mystery" as a nondenominational means of worshiping authentically.[25] A Camp Fire leader in Ottawa, Kansas, found the terminology and ritual meaningful. "I have learned a new phase of religion," she wrote, and "feel the presence of the Great Spirit when the cares of the world are left behind and we meet him in his natural sanctuary, the great out-of-doors."[26] The Cawemaco Camp Fire Girls of Western Maine similarly referred to their Sunday nondenominational service as "Worshipping the Great Spirit."[27]

The Camp Fire Girls' fire imagery centered on the home. When Camp Fire Girls cooked outdoors, they glorified daily tasks by connecting to timeless women's duties. Charlotte Gulick explained, "A girl goes ... to the woods ... and cooks her dinner in good, primitive style. It is just as essential for girls to cook over an open fire outdoors as it is for boys to play their team games; it is giving the girls in play the lessons they need to learn."[28] Moreover, just as the organization's name invoked the hearth, so too did Camp Fire's ranks: Wood Gatherer, Fire Maker, and Torch Bearer. The titles ceremoniously granted at council fires "emphasized service and the duties involved in tending the hearth."[29] The torchbearer was responsible for passing her torch undimmed on to future generations, further emphasizing the timeless roles that Camp Fire promoted. Just as Seton believed the campfire formed "a sacred bond" among men, Luther Gulick believed fires—even candlelight—invoked romance and beauty in "the common things of life" for girls.[30]

The hearth fire signified the community as an intimate gathering. Although Seton had maintained that council fires were governance structures, an idea that led to the construction of permanent rings at many camps, for the Camp Fire Girls council fires were also often smaller, intimate, egalitarian, and mobile. Signified by the circle of the people, fire rings might be formed in a clearing in the woods, on a beach, or even in a school gymnasium or community center.[31] They signaled the equality and belonging of those who met together.

4. Camp Fire Girls held ceremonial meetings in a ring. The meetings were intended to be intimate gatherings. The ritual of wearing their Indian-style headbands and gowns decorated with the honor beads they had earned made the ceremonials solemn and connected them to supposed cross-cultural women's traditions. *Book of the Camp Fire Girls*, 1914. Reprinted with permission of Camp Fire.

Girls Enact the Indian Maiden

Girls' responses to the American Indian imagery varied and were regularly at odds with Camp Fire's stated goal of creating a timeless, universal femininity. The meanings that girls made out of Camp Fire's race play are significant because, as young people, they were learning to articulate their place in the nation and to use and shape the discourse about race, ethnicity, and belonging. Moreover, because youth itself is a "transitional identity," it brings into sharp relief—as does racial mimicry—how all identities are under construction, historically contingent, situational, and intersecting.[32] Both American Indian and white girls donned Camp Fire's "Wohelo Maiden" attire and experimented with the organization's naming and symbols.

Girls had unequal access to authority and varying abilities to construct meaning discursively within patriarchal social structures. Age and gender limited their social and cultural power. Still, white Camp Fire Girls usually made a choice to join the organization; boarding school rules forced Native girls to select among assimilative programs.

At times the identities Camp Fire Girls tried on for size legitimized institutional power; white and Native girls' participation in the organization's gendered, racialized rituals naturalized both patriarchal and colonial systems. At the same time, girls resisted patriarchal and colonizing signification and, within Camp Fire clubs, carved out distinct self-portraits. Because of the complex interplay of gender, race, and age, Wohelo Maiden imagery could serve multiple—even competing—interests: a white Camp Fire Girl's challenge to gender roles using Indian imagery reinscribed racial hierarchies whereas a Native girl might use it to explore her roots or express a hybrid cultural identity. Signifying the nation through Indian play was complicated and contradictory. In one scene, Native Camp Fire Girls dressed like white girls dressing like Indians as they put on Camp Fire costumes in assimilationist institutions. In another, like the Native adults who were Camp Fire consultants, the Native girls honored their own heritage.

White girls, when they used the Indian Maiden voice in their naming, scrapbooks, and costumes, extended a colonial gaze. They explored what they believed Indians were like and how their own visions of femininity related to that image. But they did not do so just as adults prescribed. Many Americans perceived modernity and its secular, technological, and urban developments with anxious eyes. They designed rustic camps and American Indian imagery to access an authentic past.[33] Girls' writings indicate that they did not see the modern with the same anxieties that adults did. Children often have a different perception of their social and physical environment because they grow up in it; what appears to adults as destabilizing change can be, for children, an acceptable reality.[34] Some of what white Camp Fire Girls did met adult expectations, but some of their Indian interpretations represented competing generational values.

White Camp Fire Girls chose Indian-style names and symbols to exemplify gender-specific ideals. Their adult leaders provided models, adopting names of their own. Charlotte Gulick was Hiiteni for "Life, more abundant life"; Luther Gulick was Timanous for "Guiding Spirit"; and Seton was Black Wolf, which he said American Indian friends called him. Girls found lists of Indian words in Charlotte Gulick's *Name Book*, a dictionary of translations of words from various American Indian languages (primarily Dakota), and in Charles Eastman's *Indian Scout Talks*. They created their own supposedly Indian-sounding amalgamations. The Camp Fire watchword, "Wohelo," was one such combination, blending the first two letters of work, health, and love.

Many Camp Fire Girls enthusiastically adopted the feminine identities their leaders suggested. Whereas in boys' organizations, names were "in recognition of some exploit or personal gift," girls chose titles that stressed homemaking, beauty, and nature appreciation. Typical were "Songrow," who chose her name for the song of the sparrow; "Pan," who both "liked to cook" and wanted to commemorate the woodland spirit; and "Waw-o-ki-ye," who said her name meant "One who helps." Not all white girls found their authentic selves in Indian-style names, however. One girl, who chose "Little Crow" as her moniker, explained in her Camp Fire memory book, "The reason I chose this symbol was just caws."[35] For her, the naming was a source of humor.

Like Little Crow, many white girls were not entirely comfortable role-playing. One camper at Lake Sebago in Maine recounted how her club acted out Indian legends, but fell to "more giggling than acting."[36] Giggling made light of the ceremony's cultural significance and diminished their adult leaders' claims that such performances offered access to timeless gender identities. Similarly, when a Stockton, California, Camp Fire group characterized—in what Camp Fire literature called Hiawatha meter, no less—the Native dances they learned as "weird old songs of Indian lore," they distanced themselves from Camp Fire Indian imagery.[37] When other San Joaquin County Camp Fire Girls met actual California Indian women selling baskets near Yosemite, they contemptuously recorded that the women "only jabbered, / Smiled and then departed."[38] Seeing little that was useful for their modern identity formation, these Camp Fire Girls ignored the Indian theme, laughed uncomfortably at their leaders' attempts to teach femininity through cultural appropriation, and expressed negative stereotypes about Native people. Such behaviors regarded Indianness as foreign, strange, and degraded and placed American Indian identity outside the racial nation as they conceived it. These girls rejected Camp Fire officials' attempts to essentialize gender through Indian mimicry, but they still asserted white, non-Indigenous racial identity as superior.

Other white Camp Fire Girls found the Indian Maiden voice productive, but rather for challenging traditional ideas of feminine frailty than for affirming timeless domestic duties. Sebago-Wohelo campers adopted Eastman's strong and vigorous Indian Maiden. Their scrapbooks captured a spirit of athletic toughness, rejected feminine frivolity, and invoked masculine warrior imagery. Thus girls who quit a hike and "rode in white man's horseless wagons" were criticized as "lazy maidens" by their peers. One recorded a song about a Camp Fire Girl who "lost her frocks and frills" and replaced them with "bloody war paint" and tomahawks. The song celebrated her athleticism, saying, "She can hit the pace that kills, Because she is a Camp Fire Girl."[39] The lyrics mocked middle-class conventions and crossed gender lines by adopting an aggressive, warlike image of Indians. Scrapbooks used the Camp Fire aesthetic to praise favorite counselors' physical strength and grace, only thinly veiling a same-sex attraction, which psychologists and popular culture increasingly stigmatized. Describing the arrival of a popular female counselor, Stockton Camp Fire Girls were typical when, in Indian Maiden voice, they retold in rich, seductive prose that she "danced upon the scene of action / An Indian maiden, brown and lithesome."[40]

By wearing feathers in their headbands, Camp Fire Girls could also disrupt the costume's feminine symbolism. Despite Camp Fire's usual eclectic approach to Indian imagery, organization officials demanded greater accuracy in costume when its definition of gender was at stake. The 1914 Camp Fire manual warned girls that those who wore feathers in their headbands would have their photographs omitted from later editions. According to Eastman, the feather signified masculine warriors' accomplishments and was, therefore, inconsistent with the nurturing, domestic womanhood that Camp Fire envisioned. Luther Gulick wrote that although artists often depicted Indian women with a single feather, "The best authorities on Indian lore tell us that the feather, standing up-right from the head-band is never worn by the Indian woman. It is distinctively a man's decoration and is symbolic of certain definite attainments." For a woman to wear a feather was "a violation of Indian traditions."[41]

In spite of repeated reminders through the years, unpublished photographs in private albums, even one of a Gulick daughter in an early guidebook, show that girls wore feathers. Some girls likely found the masculine imagery appealing. For them, feathered Indians invoked courage, woodcraft mastery, and maybe even violence. Others likely were responding to the prevalence of feathered Indians (male and female) in popular American culture.[42] Images of Native women such as the statue of Pocahontas at Historic Jamestowne, erected in 1922, and Virginia Watson's illustrated narrative of her life, published in 1916, show a single feather standing up at the back of Pocahontas's headband. While it is unlikely that girls consciously rebelled in this manner, the ongoing presence of feathers suggests that girls incorporated masculine Indian stereotypes as well as the feminine imagery into their Indian Maiden concept. The Indian Maiden they enacted thus expressed their generational version of womanhood.

Girls also wrote in what Camp Fire called "Hiawatha meter," the trochaic tetrameter that Longfellow had used in his epic poem. In "count books," memory books that groups wrote collectively, the pretended Indian rhythm made camp experiences seem poetic, expressed the beauty and spiritual significance of nature, and infused their camp routines with mythic legend. The following passage from a 1914 memory book written at an Iowa Camp Fire leadership training course illustrates the typical structure and language of Camp Fire counts. It dramatized what was otherwise the rather ordinary first day of camp, complete with lectures by Luther and Charlotte Gulick. Young women, in their rather poorly constructed poem, sprinkled in what they likely considered Indian-sounding names and calendar months:

> Around the flame of Mongotasse [the Camp Fire name of Frances
> Gulick, who tended the fire]
> At the feet of the oracle great Timanous [Luther Gulick]
> On the 19th day of the beautiful Rose moon
> They started their stunts in the morning early
> Sing! Said the flame and they sang.
> Work! Said the flame and they worked.
> Dance! Said the flame and they danced.
> While gracefully dancing she [Charlotte Gulick] guiding them
> To the campanile she lead [sic] them
> To learn the secrets of nature
> Then the oracle bid them seek
> Seek the mystical meaning of Camp Fire

Express the wonderful truth that is in you
And live the glorious life of Wohelo.[43]

The use of the Indian-style names, "Rose moon" instead of the calendar month, the ascription of singing, working, dancing, and even a lecture at the "campanile" to the call of a fire spirit, and adjectives such as "mystical" and "glorious" to identify Camp Fire activities bespoke the organization's assumption that American Indians were particularly in tune with nature and able to see the beauty in ordinary events. By playing Indian and writing like Longfellow, girls approached the Camp Fire ideal.

Writing as Indian Maidens, girls also identified and critiqued characteristics of the white world. Describing a day at camp, "Kahona" wrote:

Next the day of white man's ice cream
Weekly dissipation for Wohelo
Sanctioned by our Hiiteni [Charlotte Gulick],
Ice Cream made in the white man's village,
Five mile walk for Indian Maidens.

Calling ice cream "dissipation" was humorous, but the girls also implied that the pleasures associated with civilization came with a moral cost. The idealized noble savage would pass from the scene as industrial modern life triumphed. These young women borrowed themes associated with Indians that marked luxury as corruption and Indian ways as purer. The Indian Maiden voice also became for Kahona a vehicle for analyzing white relationships to nature. In the following Sebago-Wohelo count book passage, girls critique mastery over nature. From their position as Indian Maidens, they observe the beauty of nature lost through "white man's uses." They identify Indians as living harmoniously with nature and whites with environmental devastation:

Larch and pine and beach [sic] and hemlock,
Fir and oak and red-wood cedar
Grown to breast the storm in winter
. . . Supply bending to the breezes,

Growing fit for white man's uses.
See them lie there in the water,
Heavy, stubborn, dead to feeling,
Stripped of all their robe of beauty,
Mastered by the loggers' pitchfork—
They who mighty storms could weather
Yet they lie there white man's master,
Beams to build the white man's shelter,
Withes to weave the white child's cradle.[44]

In this count, to be white means to master nature, a trope common in white literature and speeches extolling westward expansion; to be Indian is to coexist with nature. Here Camp Fire Girls and guardians used the count books as Camp Fire intended. They created a language that focused their attention on finding beauty in nature and balancing modern life with an appreciation of nature. But the Camp Fire Indian Maiden voice also allowed for a critique of the modernity that they were inheriting.

Similarly, white Camp Fire Girls used the Indian Maiden role to criticize feminine consumption and display. One passage in the Camp Sebago-Wohelo scrapbook noted how non–Camp Fire girls obsessed over their looks and fashion: "Thither came some pale-faced maidens / Decked with hair and various trimmings." True Camp Fire Girls and true Indian Maidens relinquished such frills. The record continued:

The great peace of wide Sabago [*sic*]
Has made every Indian Maiden
Every true Wohelo Maiden
Leave all vanity behind her
In her trunk and locked behind her.

Through her temporary identity, she critiqued her consumer-oriented white peers and adopted a seemingly more authentic and "true" natural beauty. Describing their group dressed once again in typical middle-class feminine fashion, she wrote:

Strange the maidens looked at dinner
In the white man's fads and fancies
Knew we not our Indian sisters
For they all wore white man's dresses.[45]

Camp Fire Indian Maidens described their own white culture as if from the outside.

Following the form of popular pageants, Camp Fire Girls also used the imagery to stage aggressive, treacherous, even libidinous characters. Young Camp Fire leaders at training courses who would have been in their early twenties, for example, created a sense of high drama that did not resemble the romantic, docile femininity that the usual ceremonials suggested. Rather, they acted out a flirtatious kidnapping of Black Wolf (Seton), and turned on its head the traditional captivity narrative in which male Indians captured white women. One of them wrote:

40 delilahs [sic] marched in procession to meet Black Wolf,—with base smiles lured him into their possession

With the greatest ease he was tied & bound, though offering resistance, intense & appalling to see; he was like a fly in a net.

The gentle maidens threw him over their shoulders, & gracefully ran lightly down the steps, & scornfully flung the once great chief into a rusty chariot, & with clashing of cymbals, blowing of trumpet & howling of hostile animals he was carried to his land.

With much chest swelling Black Wolf opened his council. . . .

Then came fierce & fiery contests, many fierce and fiery contests.

The exultant maidens bore away in triumph the scalp of Black Wolf.[46]

The same episode is recounted elsewhere in the same scrapbook without the fanfare as "the planned capture of Black Wolf." The Camp Fire trainees had brought him to the campfire where "contests in tilting, resuscitating the drowned or many other stunts" were performed. In the half ironic guise of Indian Maidens, they could play with notions of sexual allure, female aggression, and loud, raucous behavior. They even temporarily challenged the authority of the male camp official, all the while maintaining a feminine foundation, describing their actions as "gentle" and "graceful."

Although such Indian play was ubiquitous at camps and in youth organizations in the 1920s and 1930s, Camp Fire's use of Indian imagery occasionally prompted suspicion of the organization's spiritual effects on girls' lives. As Black Wolf's capture suggests, Camp Fire officials still needed to worry about stereotypes of Native women as sexually exotic and non-Christian. When girls sometimes wore their gowns to non–Camp Fire events like school banquets and pageants, Luther Gulick reminded them that the gowns were for ceremonial purposes and that casual public exposure might make it "appear that we are endeavoring to inculcate Indian or pagan customs or ideals."[47] In 1922 Girl Scout national board member Genevieve Brady spoke before the National League of Catholic Women in Omaha, Nebraska, and encouraged Catholic women to adopt Girl Scouting. Though she did so without the explicit approval of Girl Scout officials, she accused Camp Fire Girls of "a worship of nature rather than a reverence for God" and of "over-emphasiz[ing] the emotional appeal to the girl of nature." The executive committee of Camp Fire reported that this kind of publicity caused problems for Camp Fire in several locales. Though the board of directors had written to the Girl Scouts asking for a retraction and Camp Fire's president had met with Brady, the status of the concerns remained "inconclusive."[48] For some white women, race play threatened to undermine Christian womanhood, but Camp Fire, nonetheless, adhered to it.

When they enacted the Indian Maiden, white, middle-class Camp Fire Girls embraced much of both the critique and accommodation of modernity characteristic of their parents' generation. Still, their generational interpretation differed. White girls built their self-concept in part on Luther Gulick's racialized femininity, which prescribed a foray through Indianness to immunize them from the excesses of modernity. But the racialized femininity they developed was more than timeless domesticity. Through it, girls explored how they could be at home in nature, tough, independent, and sexually expressive.

For white, middle-class Camp Fire Girls, the Indian Maiden voice was temporary; girls could slip in and out of this role and thereby experiment without abandoning their modern, "civilized" feminine identities. Indeed, role play was most common at summer camp, a space participants understood to be special and unique. Cut off from wider society for a definite period of time, camp life offered the prospect of experimentation with identities.[49] Thus, girls might use nature-inspired words to mark time in their memory books, but they stuck to strict camp schedules and routines. They may have expressed reverence for nature, but they could hop in a car when hikes became too strenuous. Since the costume was symbolic and impermanent, challenges to feminine decorum through Indian dress never seriously threatened girls' service to family and nation. Indeed, white Camp Fire Girls used the Indian identity to expand their opportunities as white women. They continued to see Native people through a colonial lens that might pique curiosity but failed to challenge how romanticized Indian imagery obscured ongoing colonial struggles.

American Indian Camp Fire Girls

The symbol of the Camp Fire Indian Maiden functioned differently in distinct contexts. In 1932 Camp Fire Girls from the Phoenix Indian School donned ceremonial gowns—which they called Camp Fire Maiden costumes—to attend a regional Camp Fire meeting. They encountered hundreds of other mostly white, middle-class Camp Fire Girls from Arizona's cities and suburbs, similarly attired but calling themselves Indian Maidens. Native and white girls performed an idea of Indianness, but each articulated their own unique identities as modern girls. Both Indigenous and white girls laid claim to a national, peer-oriented youth culture that asserted independence and physical and intellectual toughness while rejecting adult condemnations of girls as trivial. American Indian girls also rejected the binary that rendered them either authentic or assimilated and adopted hybrid cultural practices, embracing universal girlhood while exploring tribal cultures. For Native girls, Camp Fire could be a space for reinterpretation and resistance. Whereas Camp Fire's use of Indian imagery privileged whiteness by placing Native people in the past and ignoring their contemporary voices, when Native girls adopted it, they exhibited an assimilated identity within a national girls' culture that they described as modern. At the same time, they used it to claim tribal traditions that undermined the boarding school project.

White Americans viewed Indian boarding schools as transformative; they turned primitive children into citizens. Assimilation promised that Native girls could be transformed into respectable U.S. female citizens, diminishing the taint of drudgery and sexual debauchery long associated with Indian women.[50] Boarding school girls would need training in race history as much as white girls did.

The Camp Fire Indian Maiden reflected white, middle-class notions of beauty, which Camp Fire leaders and boarding school advocates used the same language to describe. Charlotte Gulick's esteem for what she referred to as the simplicity, "beauty in form," and "beauty of color" of the Camp Fire costumes mirrored reformers' praise for Indigenous girls who had "fallen out with their old ways of doing things" and now "arranged becomingly" their hair and clothes with colors that "adorn" and "correspond."[51]

Boarding schools, which were the primary hosts of Native Camp Fire clubs, were spaces of "multiple, mixed, and diverse" experiences. According to American Indian studies scholar Amanda Cobb-Greetham, the women who had studied at Bloomfield Academy, a Chickasaw boarding school for girls in Oklahoma, were ambivalent about their experience. They described cultural loss even as they acknowledged that the school "showed them a different world and a different way to be in the world." K. Tsianina Lomawaima similarly finds that at the off-reservation Chilocco Indian School, despite the racist and oppressive efforts to assimilate girls and teach them subservient roles as domestic servants and wives, parents often chose to send their children as an uncomfortable but practical form of cultural negotiation. The women educated there found opportunities to forge solidarity through peer groups based on and sometimes crossing lines of tribe, skin color, language, religion, and gender.[52] In short, boarding school girls had opportunities to create situational and multidimensional identities.

In Camp Fire, Indigenous girls experimented with hybrid identities. A photograph of an "all-Indian" Camp Fire group at the Yakima Indian Christian Mission, a Disciples of Christ boarding school in White Swan, Washington, shows girls demonstrating their Indianness alongside their Camp Fire accomplishments. The girls wear both traditional Yakama dresses and Camp Fire headbands complete with proscribed feathers.

5. Camp Fire Girls at the Yakima Indian Christian Mission in Washington pose as an "All-Indian Camp Fire Girls' Group." Girls wear both traditional Yakama dresses and Camp Fire headbands complete with proscribed feathers. One girl wears a traditional ornamented basket hat typical of Yakama women. The girls demonstrate their American Indianness alongside their Camp Fire accomplishments. *World Call* 12 (April 1930): 19. Used with permission of the Center for Indigenous Ministry.

One girl wears a traditional Yakama ornamented basket hat.[53] The feathers are noteworthy since Camp Fire officials claimed that American Indian women did not wear head feathers and used the rule to maintain gender distinctions. These modern American Indian girls wore head feathers. Camp Fire officials' understanding of head feathers was predicated on a view that authentic Native cultures were static, unchanging, and relegated to the past. That the Yakama girls added head feathers to their Camp Fire headbands suggests that they reinterpreted Camp Fire's appropriation of Indian symbols to blend their traditions with popular culture. Although it is impossible to know what these girls thought about their dress, the photograph captures a hybrid moment that is simultaneously all-Indian and all–Camp Fire, retaining Yakama culture and accommodating assimilation.

Camp Fire Girls also appeared at federal boarding schools, such as Phoenix Indian School in Arizona. Here girls similarly constructed identities that rejected the rigid binary positioning of authentic and modern.

Pima, Navajo, Hopi, Tohono O'odham, and Apache students attended the Phoenix Indian School, and its Camp Fire clubs reflected this diversity. By the 1930s, many students were second-generation boarding school students and were conversant in institutional cultures. The school's curriculum emphasized, but was not limited to, vocational education (skilled trades for boys and home economics for girls).[54] Students were required to participate in at least one extracurricular activity such as Camp Fire. The librarian Nettie Willis, a white woman who had been a Camp Fire Girl before working at the school, brought Camp Fire there in 1929.[55] By 1935 the school had nearly sixty Camp Fire Girls between the eighth and twelfth grades. School instructors led most groups, but high school seniors led the youngest girls, and local Native college students led several clubs.[56]

Camp Fire Girls at Phoenix Indian School were among those who were most successful under the assimilative education model. They included valedictorians, writers for the school paper, and many who earned high marks in the school's merit system for attendance and behavior. Christian girls joined; one eighth grader wrote into the paper to urge her classmates to attend Christian religious instruction, no longer mandatory at Phoenix in 1932, to learn "the habit of doing right things."[57]

Camp Fire Girls at Phoenix Indian School described activities in the school's newspaper, the *Phoenix Redskin*, that were nearly identical to Camp Fire circles across the United States. They hiked, cooked outdoors, hosted teas, decorated a basement meeting room, and baked.[58] As Camp Fire Girls did nationwide, Phoenix's Camp Fire clubs emphasized friendship. One column celebrated the fun and friendship girls experienced on a campout, recording how girls sang, "giggled far, far into the night," and clung to one another in amused fear after hearing ghost stories.[59]

The national Camp Fire magazine, however, portrayed these members as outsiders to modern girlhood. One article introduced the Phoenix Indian School girls to the predominantly white membership, asking, "Isn't it interesting to think that Hopi or Pima or Osage girls enjoy working for Honors and winning Rank just as you do!" The article borrowed from a narrative of race improvement through assimilation, noting dismissively about the Phoenix girls' abilities that "some of the things you can do without much effort are a great achievement for them." Repeating the themes of boarding school practitioners, the article complimented Native girls who had learned to sew and dress in "pretty print or woolen dresses" and seemed surprised by "the nice way" the girls were "taking care of their hair and teeth and nails." By contrast, the magazine suggested that Indigenous girls came naturally to other aspects of the program. The "Camp Fire room" at Phoenix Indian School, for example, was "a thing of beauty . . . decorated with symbols and colors characteristic of the Indian."[60]

The Phoenix girls had written about their activities in the *Phoenix Redskin* in anticipation of the national article appearing in Camp Fire's monthly. Their description contrasted with Camp Fire's racist evolutionary progress narrative. They saw themselves as neither representatives of timeless gender roles, primitives in need of service, nor culture brokers. The girls described themselves as Camp Fire Girls who participated in the same girls' culture that Camp Fire represented across the nation. The girls explained that they had their pictures taken "in gowns and in regulation uniforms, exhibiting craft work . . . for which they have claimed Camp Fire honors." The article would highlight, they thought, "the work, accomplishments, and other activities of the Indian school Camp Fire girls."[61] Rather than emphasize "Indianness," or try to instruct a white audience about their traditions, as many Indigenous adults had done, they drew attention to "regulation" attire and how their accomplishments mirrored those of Camp Fire Girls everywhere. Their description of their work drew attention to their organizational accomplishments not as the assimilation successes of "Indians," but rather as those of any Camp Fire Girl. In some sense, they adopted the ideal of universal girlhood that organization leaders created. They must have been disappointed, then, by the caricature of their achievements that Camp Fire finally published.

A broader discourse about modern Indigenous girlhood was captured in the Phoenix Indian School magazine, where one home economics student announced that she was a modern girl.[62] To her, that meant a peer-oriented generation that was committed to education and independence, but also homemaking. She also invoked the transmission of women's roles between generations, which she claimed was an Indian practice. Her writing would have gratified Charlotte Gulick. "Modern Indian girls" wanted "home training" that mirrored that of a girl "a century ago" who knew from her mother that homemaking was the first duty of every woman, she wrote. Next, she described a peer-focused girls' culture. "When we are with our friends," she wrote, "we talk about our work, play, dress, eats, and friends." Most important to girls, she said, were education and independence. An American Indian girl desired "an opportunity to show that she can stand upon her own feet, and to show that she is no different from thousands of other girls who are making their own living." Lastly, she challenged the caricature of the modern girl as an overly flirtatious and frivolous flapper, a stereotype that white girls also contested. She saw herself as serious minded. "If 'modern' means straight-forward, clean, healthy, industrious, wanting friendship, mirth, and the love of our fellow man," she wrote, "we are 'it,'" borrowing a reference to flapper icon and Hollywood "It Girl" Clara Bow.[63] For this student, Phoenix Indian School girls were distinctly "modern Indian girls." They belonged to a national girls' culture interested in adventure and friendship—with a serious and independent side.

Even though Phoenix Indian School girls shared much with other Camp Fire Girls, they did not enact the Camp Fire Indian Maiden the same way that white members did. For example, when the newspaper reported that the girls chose their Indian names and worked on their symbols, Phoenix girls usually referred to them as their "Camp Fire symbols," whereas white Camp Fire groups commonly referred to these as their "Indian symbols."[64] Phoenix girls also translated the Camp Fire Law into Native languages and selected words from their languages rather than Indian-sounding names. When a new group formed at Phoenix Indian School in 1934, they chose *Na-a-si lid*, a Navajo word for rainbow, for the club's name.[65] While the word "rainbow" resembled the choices of many Camp Fire Girls to signify tranquil natural beauty, when Navajo girls chose words from their own language, they strengthened ties to their cultural roots.

At Phoenix Indian School, Camp Fire's emphasis on Indian imagery presented an opportunity for Native girls to learn about their own and other American Indian traditions. As Indigenous studies scholars K. Tsianina Lomawaima and Teresa McCarty point out, after several generations of boarding school experiences, many young people knew little of their cultures.[66] Thus Camp Fire meetings where girls taught their own dances, songs, holidays, and rituals to other Native girls were potentially spaces for resisting the dominant culture's marginalization and for facilitating pan-Indian alliances.[67] When Native college women led Camp Fire clubs, this kind of exploration of girls' cultural traditions was more common. One club's nature hike included sharing "Indian legends which are told by their people."[68] At the next meeting, the girls gave talks about the marriage traditions among their people.[69] In the 1930s, boarding school curricula increasingly included Native handicrafts, which taught girls to earn a living, and cultural lore. Native dances and clothing became useful publicity as tame "picturesque relics of the past."[70] (History lessons on treaties did not appear.) While records do not indicate what these girls thought of the inclusion of their traditional cultures in the curriculum, Lomawaima and McCarty submit that "young Native women must have found a refuge in these classes, a small space carved out of an oppressive institution where they could express, or at least feel, the precious presence of Indigenous identity, knowledge, language, and daily practices."[71] One imagines that some leaders created such a harbor in their Camp Fire clubs too.

When Native girls joined Camp Fire, they used Camp Fire's Indian imagery to fashion Native identities even as they assented to the assimilationist program of the Indian boarding school. Whereas adult cultural brokers sought opportunities to teach white Americans about Native ways, Native girls instructed white adults what it meant to be a modern girl and each other about their tribal heritages. Thus Camp Fire was a space where Native girls accessed a national girls' culture and created a generational identity. Still, individual clubs enabled Native girls to pursue their tribal histories and traditions. Youth organizations produced assimilation, but girls' choices also mediated adaptive pressures to generate hybrid identities.

Camp Fire continued to encourage Indian imagery in its camps and club program with little reflection into the 1970s. The naming and selection of symbols as well as the decoration of gowns continued as core elements that set Camp Fire apart from Girl Scouts and other organizations. Still, program literature gradually deemphasized the performative elements and replaced them, in the 1930s, with more ethnographic approaches. More white girls viewed museum exhibits about American Indians, and fewer wrote in Hiawatha meter. The Girl Scouts' popularity outpaced Camp

Fire's, as the patriotic connotations of "scouting" made Camp Fire's race play seem quaint and outmoded.[72] After World War II, even camps relegated Indian mimicry to the margins, though names and structures like council fire rings remained. Camp Fire would come to find, as chapter 8 discusses, that as inclusion and multiculturalism encouraged outreach to girls beyond the white middle class, few had interest in the appropriative imagery. The organization would begin to suggest alternatives to Indian-style gowns in the 1970s.

Gypsy Trails

Indian imagery was not the only way that Camp Fire girls played with identity. By the 1930s, as Camp Fire Girls were more likely to encounter American Indians through anthropological and historical lenses that placed Indians as artifacts in museums or characters in history books, the Gypsy became a substitute for the American Indian in the Camp Fire Girl aesthetic.[73] In 1930, for example, the Camp Fire magazine for leaders recommended that councils adopt a Gypsy-themed ceremony for their late-summer events. Girls replaced their Indian-like headbands with a "dashing gypsy scarf" and followed a "patteran" trail, which the girls prepared as they believed Gypsies did through coded messages to one another by scattering grass and leaves to direct one another to the fire circle. Additional suggested activities included a treasure hunt following clues placed in the woods and sharing about a favorite "bit of road" or a "woodsy path." The Gypsy theme now invoked romance and fantasy as girls were encouraged to "let imagination wander free," think up "cloud movies," and interpret bird songs.[74] The Gypsy woman took her place alongside the American Indian to symbolize mystery, romance, and outdoor adventure.

"Gypsy trails" was not a Camp Fire invention but built on popular images in American culture. Outdoor enthusiasts and camp manuals referred to trips out of camp and those with a wagon outfit as "gypsy camping." A considerable categorical cultural fluidity marked fashion in the decades of the 1920s and 1930s. As suntans became markers of wealth and travel for social elites, one could buy Helena Rubinstein's Gypsy Tan Foundation to darken one's skin.[75] Fashions in the 1920s also brought together bohemian and Gypsy themes as designers such as Paul Poiret looked east,

6. In the 1920s and 1930s, the Gypsy theme vied with the American Indian imagery for popularity. It invoked fantasy and freedom to wander. It was associated with camping. On the cover of *Everygirl's*, Gypsy Camp Fire Girls cook over an open fire in a Gypsy-like encampment. *Everygirl's*, May 1926. Reprinted with permission of Camp Fire.

incorporating orientalism through turbans, pantaloon skirts, lampshade tunics, and vivid colors. Greenwich Village artists and intellectuals came to be called bohemians—referring to the region of Europe associated with the Romany—for their association with free-spirited nonconformity.[76] Finally, anthropology, travel literature, and fiction established a "discourse on the gypsy as the embodiment" of "exoticism, primitivism, eroticism and nature."[77]

The Gypsy was associated with freedom despite the legal codes and structures that oppressed Roma people in the United States and Europe.[78] White Americans and Europeans associated Gypsies, as they did Indians, with wandering and the out-of-doors. The May 1926 *Everygirl's* called gypsying "another way of saying adventure" and likened it to the "open road of your vagabonding."[79] An "imaginary popular image of Gypsies" became an "avenue of escape" for individuals who sought to evade social strictures temporarily. Linguist Ian Hancock explains, "In the popular mind, Gypsies are the very epitome of freedom." Through hundreds of literary pieces and songs, audiences associated the Gypsies "with freedom: freedom from nine-to-five jobs, freedom from having to attend to personal hygiene, freedom from sexual restrictions, freedom from the burden of material possessions, freedom from responsibility, freedom from the law."[80] The flipside of freedom was license, and as with other forms of mimicry, the Gypsy figure was both desired and despised. The Gypsy woman, especially, has been depicted, from at least as far back as nineteenth-century English literature, as "oriental, dark, romantic, free and impetuous." She shares with other forms of primitivism an association with spiritual, intuitive, physical, sensual—and less rational—ways of being. Girls were not supposed to abandon hygiene, sexual mores, or responsibility to home and family. Although the Gypsy woman in literature and art is often sexualized, Camp Fire's use of the image cast the girl as modern and wholesome. Camp Fire's magazine for leaders said that girls needed "the right idea of the meaning of the word, 'gypsying,'" no doubt an attempt to distance girls from the sexual exoticism that gypsying might also invoke in the 1920s and 1930s.[81] The image marked a temporary adventure under the supervision of a Camp Fire leader or camp counselor.

Camp Fire's Gypsy honors became synonymous with outdoor adventure and skill. For a girl to earn the Torch Bearer, Camp Fire's highest rank, with a specialization in camp craft, she had to earn "Gypsy Honors" through participation in an overnight camping excursion. The candidate took charge of planning and preparing the meals, made several kinds of campfires and cooked biscuits over one of them, erected a tent, slept in it, disposed properly of all camp garbage, and led a treasure hunt.[82]

Gypsy trips were usually of significant distance and duration. One young Camp Fire leader wrote of her backpack trip into the White Mountains of New Hampshire as "becoming a gypsy." On the several-day excursion, the young women cooked outdoors and had to build fires.[83] A "perfect Gypsy Camp" was one far enough away from camp that "you cannot see a single tent or dining hall." At Camp Kiwanis near Boston, the "Gypsy Camp" was within camp boundaries, but girls used it as a base from which to venture out on hikes of ten miles or more and a place where they could work on ranks and honors. It was a site apart from the routine and the younger girls of camp. Although Gypsy treks most often referred to forests, Camp Fire's magazine noted that girls anywhere in America could take such adventures. Camp Fire Girls at the Seattle's Camp Sealth, took sailing Gypsy trips around the islands.[84] Catherine Lee Wahlstrom, member of the National Field Staff and an executive in Battle Creek and later in Pasadena, described "one of the happiest trips of my life, so far . . . taking fourteen girls on a gypsy trip to New York." They left Battle Creek in two cars, visited Niagara Falls, Albany, Atlantic City, Philadelphia, Gettysburg, Pittsburgh, Cleveland, Detroit, and then returned home, "sleeping out every night, rain or shine, in bed rolls, cooking all meals over open fires, with the exception of one memorable feast in an Automat in New York."[85]

Gypsy adventures might be long but not necessarily strenuous. Camp Fire Girl literature maintained that Gypsy trips were more about "lazy hours following a beckoning road where you haven't been before, with never a care nor a plan more tangible than your mood demands for the joy of the hour." The Gypsy stopped when she wanted to bathe her toes at the sandbar or rest in the shade. Their foremost aim was to "give your fancy rein" and to "get away from civilization." Shipping gear ahead or having a cart in which to rest, then, was fine. Saddle horses were appropriate too. Still, the bureaucratic rules governing youth organizations demanded that, despite the maxim to follow the road as it carries you, Camp Fire groups leave their intended route with those at home and be accessible in case of emergency. Gypsying was for the romantic spirit but not to be carried out in a way that led to real danger and vulnerability.[86]

Camp Fire also sprinkled Gypsy-themed activities through the outdoor program. At Cincinnati's "colorful" Romany Day, Camp Fire Girls "dressed in bright bandannas and gypsy garb," for a day hike. They carried "lunch in a bandanna at the end of a stick" and sang "gypsy songs."[87] Gypsy entertainments appeared alongside day hikes and might include fortune tellers, treasure hunts, and "Gypsy carnivals."[88] Fortune-telling was not central to Camp Fire's performance of gypsying, with its emphasis on outdoor adventure, but it added to the fantasy. A young woman or an older girl pretended to be a fortune teller, and a crystal ball might appear as a prop. In these instances, the darker fears of the occult, which fortune-telling has historically elicited, were seldom in play. Camp Fire newsletters portrayed this as a fun extension of the Gypsy stereotype and a way to pretend to know the future.[89] Camp Fire Girls enjoyed suspending disbelief for an afternoon's adventure.

Much that Camp Fire did with the Gypsy theme resembled the American Indian imagery of the founding years. References to camp craft activities regularly blurred the two. As six hundred Grand Rapids, Michigan, girls in Gypsy costume went forth on a two-hour nature hike, their leaders described them as like "a large tribe."[90] Camp Fire also used the same terminology that linked American Indians to primitive nature and beauty. Just as girls dressed as Indian Maidens appeared charming, Camp Fire authors described Gypsy attire as picturesque. Gypsy representations captured the "romantic, picturesque, and wild," and like Indianness, satisfied a temporary "longing for an escape from modernity."[91] Gypsy performances were also like Indian performances, in that they effectually contrasted, and therefore affirmed, the girls' affiliation with the settled, industrial, consumer-oriented world that she would always return to. Moreover, sampling other ethnicities, as bell hooks explains, "becomes spice, seasoning that can liven up the dull dish that is white mainstream culture."[92] Hence, the "picturesque" romance of Gypsies and Indians provided an antidote to the felt dryness of mainstream modern life.

Girls readily adopted the language of Gypsy camping into their counts alongside the Indian imagery. Maine Camp Fire Girls used the Hiawatha meter to tell of the reestablishment of a camp in a new location in the mid-1930s. They alternated between the Indian theme, referring to fellow campers as maidens and leaders as chiefs, and the gypsy theme. As they relocated to the unfinished camp, they referred to it as the Gypsy camp and to themselves as the Hitinowa Gypsies.[93]

Just as Camp Fire recommended reading Longfellow's *Hiawatha* rather than the words of American Indians, Camp Fire recommended poetry and songs about Gypsies with little recognition of Roma people. According to Roma studies scholar Jodie Matthews, this "manufactured authenticity" occurs when non-Romany writers and critics determine that the works done by non-Romany poets capture the spirit of the Gypsy better than those done by those who identify as Romany.[94] Thus the folk song "The Wraggle-Taggle Gypsies," along with a dramatization of the song, and Ethel Reed Jasspon and Beatrice Becker's *Ritual and Dramatized Folkways* offered examples upon which councils might draw. Camp Fire also recommended several gypsy-themed poems. One, Pauline Slender's "The Vagrant," encouraged readers to "leave the dust of the City" to find fairies, Gypsies, and riches in the form of golden cloaks and silver "shoons" in the wilderness. Camp Fire's publication recommended "The Gipsy Trail" by Rudyard Kipling, master of making the colonial narrative of the white man's burden accessible to youthful readers. Camp Fire literature quoted the Kipling poem calling girls to roam "over the world and under."[95] This poem calls the "lass" and "maid" out of her "gorgio" camp, a Roma word for non-Roma, to go with like-minded spirits, to rejuvenate, and wander along trails, roads, and *patterans*. Just as Camp Fire held Longfellow to be an expert on Indians, Anglo poets were taken for the voice of the Gypsy.

The imagery of Gypsy encampments was also consistent with the organization's use of the campfire as a symbol for the hearth and woman's connection to the home. The Gypsy campfire, depicted with women and children around it, is the outdoor hearth in British literature and paintings. Encampments offered "travelling domesticity" that was useful to Camp Fire as well. The idea that the hearth and the associations of homemaking that went with it could be transferred out of doors made Camp Fire's outdoor activities suitable for girls. Unlike Gypsies, however, Camp Fire Girls had settled homes, which legitimated their travel as a temporary excursion and hobby and did not mark them as strangers outside American norms.[96] Just as the Camp Fire maiden did not give up Christianity when she communed with the great spirit, the gypsy Camp Fire Girl did not relinquish whiteness or settledness. The Camp Fire Girl used Gypsy imagery because it invoked the differences between the nomad and the white, middle-class home with its hearth as a symbolic centerpiece.

When girls adopted the Gypsy image, they rarely considered actual Romany people, who immigrated to America primarily from Russia and other Eastern European countries in the late nineteenth century. Most were not recorded as Roma but as immigrants from their country of departure. Working in various "portable occupations and professions" as show people, coppersmiths, fortune-tellers, horse-traders, and basket and furniture makers, they traveled in search of economic opportunity. Native-born Americans shared the European aversion to these traveling strangers and feared them as vagrants reputed to steal chickens and eggs and even snatch children.[97] Camp Fire's Gypsy themes avoided these darker stereotypes most of the time. The Camp Fire Girls' usual lowercase spelling of "gypsy" epitomized how the organization viewed them as part of a fantasy landscape rather than as a specific group of people. Camp Fire literature also commonly used the gerund "gypsying" to indicate a set of practices middle-class girls could undertake or an attitude they could adopt; such usage obscured real people. In these ways, the Gypsy remained "an impression—something vaguely drawn."[98]

Camp Fire occasionally explored Gypsies' association with "criminality and deceit," a theme common in English literature since the sixteenth and seventeenth centuries.[99] When Camp Fire Girls returned to camp following their "gypsy trips," the hikers would "give the gift of the loot they have found to the [other] campers." Camp Fire, then, still associated Gypsies with theft, but the danger was neutralized as the girls' "loot" turned out to be harmless memories of "trees and stars, little trails and roads" as well as the "love of the open, understanding, tolerance, [and] comradeship" gathered along the way.[100]

Camp Fire fiction, too, included chance meetings with Gypsies, often deploying negative stereotypes to drive the plot. The Gypsy encounter in Camp Fire fiction promoted the concept that civilization was a racial trait that Gypsy characters lacked. In one short story, two Camp Fire Girls stay at camp to clean up while their mates go canoeing. They believe a Gypsy girl is living in the woods and stealing their pea plants. They decide to hunt the Gypsy girl down. When they finally meet the girl, who is living in a cave, she is disheveled and dirty but beautiful, "like a Venetian painting." Their adventurous spirits draw the Camp Fire Girls and the stranger together. The girls exclaim that she is a Gypsy "but not really." The narrative thus upholds the racial expectation. The readers and the Camp Fire characters learn that the girl whom they have quickly grown fond of is not really a Gypsy but a runaway with a "gypsy spirit." She has tired of living with her materialistic aunt and is following a wanderer's spirit, just like the Camp Fire Girls.[101]

The Saalfield Publishing Company's Camp Fire Girl fiction series likewise affirms the racial difference. These books, although they bore the Camp Fire Girl name, were written by outside authors who used girls' organizations in their series titles to boost sales to girls interested in reading about adventure. When two fictional Camp Fire Girls meet wandering Gypsies while walking in the woods, one girl affirms that they are "very different from ourselves." Central to their differences is that they do not "have any real homes." Having a home that does not move is a symbol of national belonging. The difference is racial, and education cannot undo it. One Camp Fire Girl explains that the Gypsy, even with education, stays "wild and untamed" since "they haven't got a lot of civilized ideas to hold them in check." She draws a connection to American Indians, saying, "I've heard the same thing about Indians."[102]

Later in the series, an adult male Gypsy attempts to kidnap the Camp Fire Girls for ransom. They will only be safe if he leaves their vicinity or is captured. The kidnapping stereotype, the "most menacing facet of the European Gypsy stereotype," appears in other of the Saalfield Camp Fire novels.[103] The trope reminds the reader that the characters are susceptible children, despite their remarkable autonomy as they camp away from parents with Camp Fire leaders who are only a few years older than they are.[104] Moreover, as adolescents the young women are at risk for sexual exploitation. In 1910 reformers worried that gangs forced young white women who appeared unchaperoned in public into prostitution. Books such as *Fighting the Traffic in Young Girls: Or, War on the White Slave Trade* warned parents about the supposed dangers of allowing daughters to live or work in cities, take public transportation, visit ice cream parlors or restaurants, and congregate in dance halls.[105] Camp Fire fiction emphasized that tough, smart girls could temporarily escape Gypsy kidnappers, but girls' ultimate safety depends on the presence of white, middle-class men who protect them.[106] The trope of the misplaced child—whether she has been snatched or runs away in response to the lure of the Gypsy—reveals anxieties about a society's ability to locate individuals in the proper "class, race, nation or locality," a pressing issue in the early twentieth-century United States, where urban anonymity and burgeoning immigrant populations sparked fears of white slavery. The presence of Gypsies, though a fun fantasy for Camp Fire Girls, was also a marker of the dangers that "a sojourn with the Gypsies," or too much freedom, posed for white, middle-class families.[107] It was important that Gypsy trips be temporary and well supervised.

The Camp Fire Girls tried to foster a timeless and universal concept of womanhood through racial mimicry. Rather than unify, the program feature reinforced the importance of race in the lives of American girls. In the 1910s through the 1930s, Camp Fire Girls were encouraged to "seek beauty" through the ritual and symbolism associated with other supposedly premodern cultures. They made ceremonial gowns, crafted beaded headbands, selected Indian-sounding names, went on "Gypsy trips," and followed Gypsy *patterans*, all to inculcate feminine ideals. Granted, Camp Fire's mimicry destabilized racial taxonomies to the extent that appropriative play highlights the fluidity and performativity of racial categories. Girls—across races and classes—could temporarily adopt traits of those deemed outside civilization. At the same time, it reaffirmed the essence of those racial categories by asserting that there was something elementally different about those classified as others, and it made race part of girls' daily activities. Such practices thus "reinforced and dismantled the concept of 'race' in the same gesture."[108]

But youth rarely reproduce culture exactly as adults intend. Camp Fire's history was one of cultural negotiation. Camp Fire's Indian play, tied up with the promise of what girls could become, engendered boundary crossings, and Camp Fire activities became spaces for trying on racial and sexual identities. Whereas adults consciously deployed the Native feminine body as part of a recapitulation theory for girls that would ensure their health, purity, and service as mothers in industrial America, girls negotiated these messages through their own definitions of modern girlhood.

Meanwhile, girls from marginalized ethnic groups and their communities understood Camp Fire's values and activities through distinct histories. Native girls joined Camp Fire in small numbers, and the organization cast them as curiosities or as needing assimilation to be counted as citizens. Still, those few used the organization to their own ends, layering the meaning of girlhood in twentieth-century America. Their participation articulated a claim to membership in a national girls' culture. They expressed their identities as modern young women who blended Native and assimilative dress and activities. American Indian girls found space to strengthen pan-Indian identity and learn about and share their cultures. As we will see, immigrant, working-class, and African American girls, too, made claims on national belonging through the Camp Fire Girls.

3

"All Prejudices Seem to Disappear"

Race, Class, and Immigration
in the Camp Fire Girls

The founders of the Camp Fire Girls insisted that the organization would appeal universally to girls across class, nationality, race, religion, and ability. The 1914 certificate of incorporation promised to "make available to all girls . . . an educational-recreational program" of feminine character training.[1] It was, in many ways, a bold statement in the 1910s. Camp Fire developed in an American social and political context rife with nativism and racism. The 1910s and 1920s witnessed racial violence in the form of lynchings and race riots, and the resurgence of the Ku Klux Klan targeted not only Blacks but also Catholics, Jews, and immigrants. Jews were considered by many white Protestants to be a separate and inferior racial group, not just a religious group. Many also accused Catholic and southern and eastern European immigrants of being loyal to their countries of origin and to the Pope and thus incapable of being good Americans. At the same time, rising labor militancy sparked national debates, and immigration restrictions took shape as agitators stemmed the tide of southern and eastern European immigration through quota bills. On the West Coast, politicians sought to bar Asian immigrants. Worried that immigrants and African Americans threatened their economic and political supremacy, white, native-born Americans expressed cultural anxiety and looked for ways to stop change.[2] That the Camp Fire Girls provided limited opportunities for national belonging to immigrant girls, working-class girls, and girls from religious, ethnic, and racialized groups during this period is remarkable.

Camp Fire's membership was predominantly white, middle-class, and Protestant, but there were also clubs in synagogues, settlement houses, playgrounds, orphanages, industrial schools, and American Indian boarding and mission schools in the 1910s and 1920s. Although the national headquarters maintained no precise records concerning the racial or ethnic breakdown of membership in its first three decades, national publications played up stories that demonstrated inclusivity. They also highlighted the organization's nonsectarian credentials by noting participation of Catholic and Jewish alongside the more numerous Protestant girls.[3] At a time when the American population was approximately 15 percent foreign born, membership was far from proportional. Still, in 1923, 4 or 5 percent of clubs were connected to settlement houses, and 6.5 percent of Camp Fire's girl members had foreign parentage. Although the ancestral backgrounds of these girls cannot be determined, Camp Fire literature usually referred to European immigrants. It also included a small number of girls of Mexican and Asian background. In addition, several African American Camp Fire clubs existed as early as the 1910s.[4] While some groups mixed girls across class, religious, and ethnic lines, race nearly always separated Camp Fire Girls into separate, not integrated units.

The Camp Fire Girls embraced a pluralistic model of inclusivity in the 1910s and 1920s that was consistent with the efforts of a considerable number of educators and religious leaders to foster tolerance among youth. Camp Fire officials were interested in integrating heterogeneous populations into what they viewed as the American mainstream and in celebrating the "cultural gifts," such as dance and handicrafts, that they saw as consistent with training girls for work, health, and love.[5] However, Camp Fire's inclusion policies reveal the limits of American pluralism. It organized along neighborhood and religious lines, promoted a model of girlhood based on narrow middle-class understandings of gender, and failed to address the legal barriers that Black communities faced. Camp Fire's early inclusion efforts accepted segregation as natural and as consistent with pluralism. Camp Fire moved further to bring immigrants into the mainstream of American life than it did Black girls, but Camp Fire was not as open to all girls as its founders asserted. The organization's adaptations to the color line, especially in Nashville, laid bare how its inclusion policy upheld white supremacy after all.

Organizing Clubs That Mingle Socially

The formation of separate clubs based on race, ethnicity, and religion resulted from neighborhood organizing policies. In the South, Camp Fire faced laws that precluded interracial meetings, but even where no segregation laws existed, Camp Fire Girls joined through their churches or synagogues, schools, or neighborhoods. When these institutions were segregated, so too were their groups. More than happenstance, Camp Fire's policies promoted groups of girls with like backgrounds. A 1914 leadership application urged prospective guardians to organize those girls they knew personally and among families that "mingle socially." "Our experience has shown that the best results are secured by those who know and understand each other," Camp Fire explained.[6]

Camp Fire placed a premium on allowing girls to choose their friends and compose their own communities, and this could lead to exclusion. Luther Gulick praised the "intimate" nature of the "personal friendships" developed in Camp Fire. Early twentieth-century Americans would not have expected such intimacies to cross racial, religious, or class lines. *Wohelo* explained the acceptability of excluding some girls from membership. A leader had written to national headquarters to say that a girl "of good character, good family and one genuinely interested in Camp Fire work was proposed as a new member to a Camp Fire group." After her group had openly discussed her admission, two girls voted against her joining. The guardian hoped to press the matter and ask the girls to withhold their objections, but she wanted advice. "I don't like my girls to be snobbish," she wrote. *Wohelo* maintained, "It seems wisest to have the girls pick each other out so that each Camp Fire shall be a circle of those who like each other and who work together best. . . . You don't pick out your friends in order to be democratic. You pick them out because you like them."[7] Camp Fire, therefore, prioritized the relationships of girls already in the organization at the likely expense of integrated units. These policies and preferences led to separate Camp Fire units that mingled little with people from different social or cultural backgrounds.

Religious-Based Camp Fire Girls

The religious-based units are instructive. In the 1910s and 1920s, Catholics tended to join the Girl Scouts because of the clear duty to God and country in the Girl Scout Promise, but by the 1930s, Camp Fire Girl groups affiliated with Catholic churches increased, especially in Washington, Massachusetts, and in the Midwest, where Camp Fire was strong.[8] Camp Fire also had Jewish groups as early as 1913. They joined through Jewish institutions such as B'Nai-El Temple in St. Louis, Missouri; Young Men's Hebrew Association in Louisville, Kentucky; and the Brooklyn (New York) Council Home for Jewish Girls.

In their separate institutions, girls did similar activities such as performing plays and puppet shows for younger children, creating arts and crafts, and singing. They created Indian-sounding names and gathered at council fires. Such activities were usually separate, though council-wide events brought girls together. One such regional meeting in Spokane, Washington, included over a thousand Protestant, Catholic, and Jewish participants from thirty towns. Together girls sang "Wohelo for Aye"; heard a lecture on "What Makes a Home?"; participated in a flag service; and staged a fire lighting ceremony. The next morning, however, girls were encouraged to worship separately at the various churches and synagogues in Spokane. Similarly, when the Camp Fire Girls kicked off its anniversary observation each March, councils did so with separate worship services in various denominations.[9]

Girls in these religious-based groups, though affiliating separately, nonetheless were brought into a national organization. The groups contributed collectively to larger civic institutions, and were regularly commended in newspapers for their efforts toward unified causes such as national support during World War I.[10] Only gradually, especially following the Second World War, did Camp Fire begin to champion interaction among girls from different backgrounds within the same clubs and councils, but even then, separate groups based on religious affiliation were common through the 1960s.

Camp Fire Values as Universal Values

Even as Camp Fire maintained largely separate clubs for girls from different social backgrounds, its public statements obscured the presence of differences. Early officials framed girlhood as a universal experience. Like colorblindness more generally, pretending that racial, class, and religious differences did not matter resulted in the erasure of social differences that in fact shaped individual girls' experiences. Camp Fire presented a set of middle-class, Protestant, white ideals as if they were equally accessible and useful to all girls.

The organization's publications incorporated the theme of a universal girlhood. In the 1920s, for example, *Wohelo* was renamed *Everygirl's*, a title that affirmed the idea that one set of activities, reading materials, and rituals applied to all. The magazine adopted a sophisticated, modern look, giving up the woodsy art of the earlier *Wohelo*. Still, the magazine's editors promised to deliver "good stories" without "false thrills" and "depict simple, moral living without preaching."[11] In 1925 Camp Fire asked artist Howard Chandler Christy to paint and capture the essence of "everygirl." Not surprisingly, the model of universal American girlhood was a white, middle-class, Protestant Camp Fire Girl. Ruth Stephens had recently moved from Cincinnati to New York and would take a position in the Camp Fire publication office there. Editors stated emphatically that she was chosen not for her glamour or position but "because she is a glorious example of real American girlhood with the light and spirit in her face that comes from following the Camp Fire ideals of Work, Health, and Love."[12] Christy's painting went onto the cover of *Everygirl's* and onto publicity posters across the United States.

The Camp Fire Girls also celebrated the potential of the organization's artifacts, rituals, and symbols to bring together a diversity of American girls. In 1914 the executive secretary of the Camp Fire Girls, Grace Parker, described what she regarded as the egalitarian effect of a grand council fire, the largest of the regional club gatherings. Public spectacles, these events gathered up to a thousand girls from the same region, their families, community members, and occasionally dignitaries. Girls wore their Indian-style ceremonial gowns, decorated with their awards and symbols, for added meaning.[13] Parker reported:

Nowhere have I seen true democracy better demonstrated than during the past few months at Mass Meetings or Grand Councils of Camp

7. In 1925 artist Howard Chandler Christy painted a Camp Fire Girl. Her image was intended to capture the essence of an ordinary American girl. Camp Fire chose Ruth Stephens, a white, middle-class, Protestant girl from Cincinnati, because she represented "real American girlhood." *Camp Fire Girl* by Howard Chandler Christy. Cover of *Everygirl's*, 1925. Reprinted with permission of Camp Fire.

Fire Girls. Girls from every strata of society—from the richest to the poorest—girls of foreign birth, colored girls, blind girls—all meeting on an equal footing as members of one great organization, singing their Camp Fire songs together, working under the same law with the same ideals. Even in a Southern city, where the colored children are segregated—attending separate schools—all prejudices seem to disappear when the forty colored girls—members of two Camp Fires—met with the white girls on the common basis of the Camp Fire Law at a Mass Meeting of the Camp Fire Girls of the City.[14]

As Parker noted, through national rituals like the Council Fire, girls appeared to partake equally and in the same way. Their attire seemingly washed away class and race as the girls earned honors for working toward the same goals.

For their part, some girls found the council fires exciting and unifying. Celia Anderson, a Camp Fire Girl in Portland, Oregon, in the 1920s and 1930s, remembered eagerly anticipating council fires because they confirmed girls' involvement in a larger institutional culture. Although she did not address class and race differences, Anderson noted that "hundreds of girls, all together" would mingle, examine each other's ceremonial gowns to get ideas, and feel part of something larger.[15] The connection to something larger indicated the importance for girls to identify with a national girls' culture, but this early assertion that color, class, and ability did not matter in the Camp Fire Girls evaded hard questions about access and inclusion. The assumption of a single model of wholesome girlhood masked deep division in the organization and U.S. culture.

Class and Belonging in the Camp Fire Girls

Camp Fire's approach to class division and struggle stressed the potential of young people to join the middle class by adopting its standards of health, usefulness, and individual responsibility. Although some working-class individuals rejected the middle-class norms that were offered by organizations like Camp Fire, those that joined for the most part shared Camp Fire's vision of social purpose and self-improvement and were drawn to Camp Fire's promise to channel working-class girls' leisure time toward what adults saw as wholesome forms of adventure. Many families likely hoped to replace daughters' time spent amid the public amusement and sexual expression of dance halls, movies, and amusement parks with camping, athletics, and search for adventure. At the same time, radical labor organizers and socialists sought to empower labor and challenge capitalism. The Industrial Workers of the World, with its view of America as divided between antagonistic haves and have-nots, in fact, expanded to reach the height of its popularity in the 1920s, the same period that Camp Fire was becoming an established part of the American landscape.[16] Despite tensions, the Camp Fire Girls held tight to the promise of American democracy and harmony. Camp Fire leaders hoped to assimilate the daughters of immigrants and laborers. Social uplift meant accepting the "primacy of motherhood and domesticity," a middle-class vision of gender roles that many working-class women rejected out of necessity. In the *Daily People*, socialist writer Jeannette D. Pearl noted this goal, vehemently denouncing the Camp Fire Girls for "making docile slaves" for capitalism. She complained that girls were being trained for modern homes that the working class were not able to afford. The romanticization of drudgery taught girls the "meekness" necessary "to fit in the scheme of things, and to be rendered intellectually torpid so as not to sound the discord." She recommended that children find recreation and direction in the Socialist Sunday School movement instead.[17]

However, Camp Fire believed that teaching girls to participate in community reform would equip them to deal with grievances through government channels. Its literature suggested that the organization's ideals and values bridged class differences. Ida Thurston's *The Torch Bearer*, a 1913 novel endorsed by the Camp Fire board, implies that class status was irrelevant to Camp Fire membership and to character. When a character asks, "What kind of girl is [Camp Fire] for—poor girls—working girls?" an experienced leader explains, "It is for any kind of girls—just girls, you know. Of course, we can't admit any bad ones." The novel echoed Camp Fire's notion that it served a universal girl audience disassociated from class, race, religion, and national background.[18]

Other Camp Fire Girl novels portrayed the organization as a place for cross-class friendships, and one where girls of all classes came to embrace hard work, self-sacrifice, and planning. Margaret Vandercook's 1913 novel, *The Camp Fire Girls at Sunrise Hill*, portrays Camp Fire as diminishing class distinctions and transforming both the wealthy and the poor. Family wealth has spoiled the main character, Betty. Part of the plot involves Betty's redemption through Camp Fire. As the novel opens, she is impatiently waiting for the maid to come and light a fire, which she is not confident she can do herself. Instead, she meets Esther, an orphan whom her parents have taken in as a servant. Esther is a Camp Fire Girl and knows how to light a fire. She inspires Betty to start a cross-class Camp Fire club. In pairing Betty and Esther, Vandercook described Camp Fire as a space where cross-class friendships might flourish. Furthermore, the pairing suggested that wealthy girls had as much to learn from Camp Fire's middle-class values of service and responsibility as poor girls did. In Betty's brother's words, Betty was in danger of "growing up to be more ornamental than useful."[19] Betty becomes more useful and popular as she learns to eschew class privileges. The Camp Fire model of girlhood signaled the superiority of middle-class independence and usefulness. It also prioritized self-reliance for women in terms of self-sufficiency within their homes.

Girls' letters and diaries show that the fictional Betty captured some real life experiences. One fifteen-year-old middle-class Camp Fire Girl, Clarissa, wrote to her mother of how the Camp Fire spirit inspired self-reliance at Camp Sebago-Wohelo. "Some of the girls come from well-to-do families and have never done anything for themselves," she noted. They had begun to do chores and to take care of their own hair because "they feel it is a matter of pride with the other girls."[20] Clarissa's letter suggests that peer pressure within Camp Fire enforced a middle-class model of girlhood, one geared toward developing useful, self-sufficient women who took pride in domestic competence. Both upper- and lower-income girls would learn in Camp Fire to be self-reliant.

Although Camp Fire's leaders imagined that costumes broke down barriers, they did so by enforcing the organization's middle-class standards of utility, modesty, and individualism. Program materials espoused economic frugality and practicality as part of a girl's wise consumer ethic. Camp Fire promoted its fashions as consistent with the dress reform efforts of middle-class feminists in Britain and the United States who called for an end to constricting excesses in women's fashion. Camp Fire urged girls toward modesty and practicality and decried working-class girls' lavish hats, earrings, and high heels. For young working women, dress at this time was, indeed, "a cultural terrain of pleasure, expressiveness, romance, and autonomy."[21] Camp Fire's organizing committee had criticized the "impracticability" of these prevailing styles, calling ready-made garments "cheap and over-trimmed." The pieces "tempt the girl of small means by their showiness and suggestion of 'style,'" Camp Fire complained. Although ready-made garments seemed inexpensive, they were made of inferior materials, needed routine replacement, and, therefore, "drain the pockets." Contemporary fashions were also objectionable for undermining the health of active girls. Vigorous activity required durable clothing and shoes that avoided "strain and weariness upon feet and back" and did not "disable the brain for clear thinking."[22] Hence, Camp Fire commissioned an entire clothing line not just for meetings and ceremonies but also for school, work, swimming, and other activities. The independently operated Camp Fire Outfitting Company sold officially approved Camp Fire clothing: outdoor suits (dark blue serge bloomers or skirts and white blouses) along with hats, emblems, ceremonial gowns, and more. Camp Fire added "service uniforms" of dark blue or black skirts and a white blouse with a red neckerchief during World War I.[23] If girls preferred to make the items themselves, they could buy materials and patterns from the Camp Fire Outfitting Company as well. Although the attire stressed modesty and practicality, one woman who appreciated the physical activity the outfits enabled boasted years later that the bloomer outfits were "very daring costumes, really!"[24]

Despite official assurances that all uniform materials offered "beauty of color, durability and inexpensiveness," the organization placed a considerable financial burden on members. Not only would girls want to buy the uniform pieces, but they also would pay dues and activity fees, and purchase camping equipment, ceremonial costumes, awards, and manuals. Girls paid 50 cents each year in membership dues in the 1910s and $1 by the 1930s. Although 50 cents was a far cry from the $10 that the Chicago Woman's Club charged its members, girls from working-class and immigrant families had little spending money in the 1910s and 1920s. Though middle-class girls often were given spending money from their parents, working girls likely had to skim their pay envelopes for it "in defiance of parental wishes." Camp Fire Outfitting Company catalogs and *Wohelo* advertisements during the 1910s and 1920s show the prices of various items. If a girl bought the basic service uniform of blouse, skirt, neckerchief, and hat along with her ceremonial gown and moccasins, and some necessary camping gear (bloomers, swimsuit, and black stockings), she would pay nearly $20. And she would still need to purchase her magazine subscription (which national headquarters told her was a duty), handbook, Camp Fire bracelet, and honor beads. With those items and additional accoutrements that the Camp Fire Outfitting Company offered such as beadwork kits, individual record books, and sweaters, a girl might easily spend an excess of $50. This was not a small sum at a time when the youngest working girls earned only $4.73 per week, and even army nurses, by way of example, earned only $720 to $960 per year.[25] Camp Fire's official pronouncements indicated that the uniform and extras were not required, but some girls viewed the items as necessary for living up to the Camp Fire ideals.

Indeed, one girl who hoped to live up to the Camp Fire ideal but could not afford the products she deemed necessary to do so described her feelings of inadequacy. Author Margaret Runbeck attended the original Camp Fire camp at the special invitation of Luther Gulick and later gave insight into the class dynamics there. The other children at camp, she noted, "were the daughters of very well-to-do people, and my camping equipment, I must tell you, was a droll series of make-shifts and short cuts." She loved camp until another little girl made her believe that her camping equipment and lack of uniform were inadequate. "I felt perfectly frightful," she remembered. She thought that she "wasn't living up to Dr. Gulick and that I really was a disgrace to camp." She recalled how "for five hours I lived in that little-girl purgatory" of dread until Gulick himself consoled her and assured her that a uniform was not necessary to be useful. Runbeck's story displays how girls might feel pressure to purchase the Camp Fire equipment and how their understandings about class status shaped their relationships once there. Divisions in American culture were beyond the direct control of the adult leaders and even the girls themselves.[26]

The manual acknowledged that affording the activities and costumes might be difficult for some but insisted that most girls could readily earn dues, and maintained that the "Camp Fire Girls is not a charity."[27] Although a few board members took offense at this stricture, most agreed with Luther Gulick, who held that although the Camp Fire Girls should help "the poor and needy," recruitment of girls had to be among "those who can be effective" as leaders in the community. Middle-class leaders would establish reforms to "care [for] those who primarily need help."[28] Throughout its history, the organization emphasized paying one's way. "If she earns the money by her own effort," *Wohelo* insisted, "she will place a higher valuation on it and be worth more to the organization."[29] Camp Fire insisted that girls from orphanages and settlement houses, though poor, were not charity cases but were earning their way by following the Camp Fire Law. They were potential self-reliant Camp Fire Girls so long as they could earn dues. One Camp Fire publication noted that working-class girls themselves would not join "if it were charity."[30] To the end of getting girls to pay their own way, Camp Fire regularly posted in its magazines money-making schemes such as selling subscriptions to the Camp Fire magazine or Camp Fire Outfitting Company blouses.

Paying one's way was deemed meaningful for rich girls as well as poor girls. When Shirley Temple became a member in 1939, Camp Fire's press release made much of how Shirley—despite an income of $200,000 per year in 1942—proudly announced that she had earned her $1 in dues by dusting and cleaning her house for three nights. When she accepted her Camp Fire pin, she said she was "glad to be a Camp Fire Girl" because it meant that she would "have to work hard and learn a lot of new things." Shirley's club leader, Mrs. Margaret B. Sterett, praised Shirley for being "unspoiled," "unaffected," "bright," and having "a fine feeling of what is right." Moreover, Shirley was a committed girl president of her club, who expressed her frustration when she had to miss Camp Fire meetings, even though she missed only two all summer. Like Betty in Camp Fire's fiction, good rich girls exemplified the Camp Fire ideal when they exhibited thrift and a strong work ethic.[31]

Self-support did not preclude giving service to those deemed less fortunate. Camp Fire Girls regularly participated in service projects for orphans and children with disabilities and provided supplies and clothing to World War I refugees. During the Great Depression, Camp Fire Girls practiced direct charity to neighbors, mixing service with social activities. A Camp Fire Girl in Portland, Oregon, remembered that instead of selling Camp Fire candy or doughnuts during the 1930s, which was "too hard to sell in those days," her group spent time taking dinner to hungry neighbors and visiting sick friends.[32] Camp Fire framed its members as service providers and not as recipients of charity. Rather, by participating in fundraisers and service efforts, working-class girls, even those from families with little income, entered the middle-class world of female benevolence. When "very poor" girls "from families of field workers" in Traci, California, participated, they earned their dues by making nut cups for an American Legion Auxiliary Thanksgiving service for hospital patients. The auxiliary paid the girls to make the cups.[33] Since in ordinary circumstances, girls volunteered their time for such activities, one suspects that the benefactresses in the women's auxiliary deliberately came up with a means for the girls to earn money to pay their dues. Very much like charity, the press release painted it otherwise.[34]

Camp Fire Girls' activities disassociated members from poverty in other ways. Some Camp Fire Girls participated in "poverty socials," or "hobo parties," as they were called by the 1940s.[35] Sometimes held as benefits for the club that hosted them, partygoers dressed in rags and won awards for the "worst looking costume," and guests paid "fines" if they did not wear clothing with at least one patch.[36] Guests dined on corn mush, pork and beans, or "food scraps" on wooden plates, drank from tin cups, sat on broken soapboxes, and used newspapers for napkins.[37] Forty-five Camp Fire Girls in Boardmanville, New York, dressed like "ragged urchins" or wore "grandmothers' old fashioned clothes" at their poverty social in 1931.[38] Such events included racial appropriation as well as the trappings of poverty. One Long Beach (California) Methodist Church social was attended by "paupers of every race and nationality, and every walk of life." The "originality in garb" was "the subject of much merriment."[39]

Commonly associated with the superrich of the Gilded Age, these poverty-themed galas appealed to middle-class school and youth groups, social clubs, women's auxiliaries, labor unions, church groups, and granges throughout the country from the 1890s through the 1930s.[40] White Americans generally associated such activities with "individual expression," as the National Fraternal Congress explained, and championed them as wholesome entertainments. Poverty socials and other forms of inversion costumes and appropriative identity play such as cross-dressing and black-face "helped their wearers play with gender, class and social role."[41] Such activities, however, had the effect of emotional distancing and trivialized poverty among middle-class Americans. In the 1890s, Boston residents had used poverty parties to distance themselves from their working-class neighbors. Especially in neighborhoods where geography itself did not mark class lines, paying to attend a poverty party marked class status.[42] Into the 1920s and 1930s, when poverty socials were most popular in the Camp Fire Girls, participating in a poverty party, along with adopting its other middle-class feminine values, was a way that middle-class individuals signaled their distance from the lower classes.

Americanization Honors: "Work among Foreign Girls"

Camp Fire's leadership responded during its first two decades to an immigration peak and a rising tide of nativism that brought about restrictive laws in the 1920s by creating assimilation activities for which girls could earn honor beads. These activities both brought immigrant girls into the organization as full members and encouraged them to adopt Camp Fire values as American values. Over twenty million immigrants streamed into the United States between 1890 and 1920. Regarded as "new immigrants," many of them came from eastern and southern European nations, regions that had been only spottily represented in previous waves, as well as Mexico and Asia. Their children, who made up 21 to 25 percent of American children and youth, became targets of progressive reformers who looked to public schools and other youth-oriented institutions to instill American values.[43] Joining organizations such as Camp Fire became one way that immigrants could identify with U.S. institutions and, especially those from Europe, might claim the privileges of whiteness.[44] Camp Fire was established a year before Congress released the Dillingham Report, with its indictment of recent immigrants for their failure to assimilate. A popular image of the immigrant girl held her to be ignorant of the English language and of American ways because her parents sent her to a religious school instead of her local public school. Rather than condemn immigrants, however,

Camp Fire clubs sought to teach native-born girls about the social and political implications of immigration and to teach immigrant girls American ways. The editor of Camp Fire's publications, Rowe Wright, explained the organization's special role in this national cause: "As yet all who have worked on Americanization have been interested only in adults—in the men who would vote. . . . It is only fitting that the greatest organization of girls in the country should devote itself whole-heartedly to this work among the foreign girls."[45]

In 1919 Camp Fire developed a subsection of patriotism honors titled Americanization. Like most Americanization programs, Camp Fire's sought to make Americans out of foreigners, a process that often "ignored and often derogated the first culture" of foreign-born young people.[46] It also understood the United States to be a nation of immigrants, and therefore supported tolerance and the embrace of some cultural gifts. In 1924, the same year Congress passed the Immigration Quota Act, a critical enunciation of anti-immigration sentiment in the United States, 20 percent of Camp Fire Girls earned at least one red, white, and blue Americanization honor bead, demonstrating girls' commitment to the issue.[47]

Camp Fire responded to the concerns of social reformers that immigrant girls were especially vulnerable to negative influences. Reformers believed that such girls were exposed to urban dangers because employment brought them onto city streets where they witnessed prostitution and crime. At the same time, the daughter of immigrants was thought to chafe under strict rules in her household. Her likely rebellion was thus natural but still needed to be contained. Luther Gulick promoted Camp Fire's usefulness to the nation through "new and better" activity to divert the girl's attention from the "bad dance hall" and to Americanize her in the process. But Camp Fire leaders hoped to do more than divert girls from popular amusements.[48]

Ideally, the immigrant Camp Fire Girl would soak up American values and Americanize others. Several honor activities positioned immigrant girls as mentors to less Americanized immigrants and especially to their parents. Foreign-born Camp Fire Girls could, for example, earn honors by teaching their mothers "the days of the week, how to tell time and count money, and names of nearby streets in English." They were encouraged to teach English to their mothers, fathers, or other immigrants and "direct a newly arrived immigrant family to five helpful American institutions."[49] *Wohelo* printed a play that clubs could use in their Americanization program that demonstrated this process. The script's main character, a Camp Fire Girl from a poor Italian immigrant family, is involved in war service. Through her consistency and patriotism, she teaches her mother, an Old World woman who is skeptical of American public schools and the efficacy of the government to protect citizens, to embrace America. At the end of the play, the mother unfurls an American flag that she has sewed and, in her limited English, shouts, "Three cheers for the American flag."[50]

Camp Fire clubs formed at institutions known for their efforts to help immigrants. Settlement houses and other institutions that served immigrant poor in many different cities adopted Camp Fire for education, recreation, and enrichment. Clubs sprang up, for example, at Hull House in Chicago, Morgan Memorial in Boston, and Bethlehem in Nashville. The Houchen Settlement, founded in 1912 in South El Paso by the Methodist Church, had by 1918 "a full array of 'Americanization' programs, such as citizenship and English classes, Camp Fire Girls, Bible studies, working girls' clubs, and Boy Scouts." Methodist white women ran these activities and hired a Mexican American student helper to assist with the programs for youth.[51] Clubs formed among Japanese American girls on the West Coast in the 1920s in rural areas of California like Yuba City and Marysville as well as in urban locations such as San Francisco and Pasadena. These were not centered in settlement houses but were the product of local Camp Fire council efforts and represented a desire among second-generation immigrant girls to access the popular recreational activities of the modern girl. Often excluded from high school clubs and extracurricular activities, girls flocked to Camp Fire and other girls' clubs organized nationally.[52]

In addition to reaching immigrant girls themselves, the Camp Fire Girls addressed immigration by according responsibility to native-born Camp Fire Girls, who were urged to learn about immigrants and their own immigrant backgrounds. As early as 1914, Camp Fire Girls could earn honor beads by writing "a paper of not less than 1500 words describing present immigration to this country, its advantages and disadvantages, and some of the problems created thereby."[53] Camp Fire's publications encouraged girls to think of the United States as a nation of immigrants. Camp Fire staffer C. Frances Loomis insisted, "Scratch an American and you find a foreigner!" Although some girls were more recent arrivals than others, Loomis maintained, in an erasure of Indigenous people's unique relationship to the land, that, if the theory of the Bering Strait crossing was correct, even American Indians were immigrants to America. Girls, then, examined their backgrounds through the lens of the immigrant nation. They could learn the history and the meaning of the flag of "the country from which [their] ancestors came" and "give the history of five great heroes of your own race."[54] This framing celebrated America as a nation of immigrants even as it prioritized the assimilation of new immigrants.

Certain citizenship activities put native-born girls in the role of mentor. Native-born Camp Fire Girls could earn honors by inviting foreign-born girls to American holiday celebrations, giving a girl English lessons, teaching an immigrant about five great Americans, instructing "a foreign mother or girl how to cook five practical American dishes," teaching American games and songs to immigrant girls, and taking immigrant girls to a museum. While these activities created opportunities for girls of different backgrounds to build friendships, the interactions were arranged along unequal lines. The Camp Fire manual, for example, suggested a native-born girl "adopt as your special charge for nine months, a foreign-born Camp Fire sister" and teach her about the Camp Fire program.[55] Although "sister" invoked parity, the native-born Camp Fire Girl stood in a position of authority. Immigrant girls generally found themselves in the role of student. A separate section of Camp Fire Americanization honor activities addressed girls from immigrant families. It singled them out as needing to learn school rules and city ordinances. They were likewise encouraged to read facts about "great Americans" and poetry by American authors. Lessons on how to cook American dishes and observe American holiday customs rounded out their instruction.[56]

Even though the Camp Fire Girls often situated native-born girls as citizenship instructors, it encouraged a degree of mutual respect that was usually absent from mainstream American political discourse. Camp Fire warned native-born girls, "Never for a minute think that the girls you are learning to know have nothing to give you." Wright emphasized that through sharing experiences and history, both native-born and foreign-born girls "grow into better American citizens."[57] Native-born Camp Fire Girls would teach immigrant girls, but they would also learn cultural gifts such as folk dance and handicrafts from them. Several Americanization honor activities celebrated the retention of traditional customs and called upon immigrant girls to teach them to native-born girls. Immigrant girls earned honors by teaching "five American-born girls three folk dances" of their native country or "one kind of native handiwork to five American girls."[58] Camp Fire clubs held Japanese teas and put together "mock museums" with "curios" from India, China, and Mexico to teach about other cultures.[59] To learn more about a nation from which America was receiving numerous immigrants, the Sunset Hill School Camp Fire Girls in Kansas City, Missouri, performed pageants featuring Polish history.[60] Camp Fire's Americanization program, then, had the potential to produce intercultural sympathies.

The leader of a multiethnic Camp Fire club in Colorado explained what Americanization looked like in her group. When she first "faced fifteen solemn little faces, shading from dingy white to chocolate brown," the girls little understood the Camp Fire Law, though they repeated it after their leaders. Over the months, however, "personalities emerged" as the girls hiked, sang, and put on a folk festival. Although the leader's patronizing tone is palpable in the letter, so is her appreciation of the girls' unique cultural backgrounds. When she taught the folk song Purple Owlet to the girls, she saw "a flash of recognition," and "in a moment the tune was swept away from us in Spanish words of the original!" She also praised the girls' knowledge of folk dances and the Mexican drawnwork with which one girl embellished the dishcloths they had made for a fundraiser.[61] Even as these girls learned the American style of girlhood through Camp Fire, its emphasis on folklore and handicrafts offered space for recognition and mutual exchange.

Folk dance, which was part of a popular movement in American education at the turn of the century, was particularly popular in Camp Fire. As boys' athletics grew in popularity to teach sportsmanlike competition and strength, educators centered on folk dance for girls to promote health, graceful movement, and cooperation. Girls performed folk dances from various European and American Indian backgrounds as entertainments at local halls and informally at campfires and meetings. Educators used it to teach native-born, middle-class girls about other cultures, and it offered a space for immigrants to feel pride in their nation of origin and its traditions. According to Luther Gulick, the United States had recognized immigrants' economic contributions but had not yet "understood, cared for, or even thought about the precious social heritage that the immigrant might give us—a heritage of art, of story, of music, of the dance." The nation was missing out on "the greatest . . . and perhaps the last blending of human stock and also social inheritances." Dance, which he believed young people were innately interested in, allowed children, who might otherwise lose what Gulick viewed as their racial inheritance to urban industrial environments, to appreciate "the old rhythmical movements." Dance, he argued, "must be resurrected and given again to the children as part of their birthright, as a fundamental part of their education." Dancing would not only open up to children "avenues into what is beautiful and noble," but would also lead the way to "a national life far richer, deeper, and more beautiful."[62]

The Camp Fire Girls did not regard all dances as appropriate for its members. Luther Gulick assured the public that Camp Fire did "not by any means advocate an indiscriminate teaching of all the folk dances of all the peoples." "Love dances" of the Middle East were excluded as contrary "to the morals of our civilization." Moreover, selected dances would not have injurious effects on health and posture and would not contradict girls' gracefulness. He wrote that he excluded some American Indian dances because of the bent body posture and the extended crouching positions they required. Despite this critique, Luther Gulick believed that "primitive" peoples, by which he meant Africans and American Indians, were more rhythmically expressive. He attributed especially "complicated rhythms" to central African tribes. He alleged that "to say things over and over in a rhythmical way appeals both to savages and to children; and in complicated ways it appeals to adults." Still, African dances did not appear among Camp Fire's recommendations. Instead, Gulick recommended dances for young people in his *The Healthful Art of Dancing* that originated in Europe. Dances like the Danish Greeting were circle dances where young people joined hands. The Danish Shoemaker's Dance used a double circle and partners. Each dancer performed the motions of making a shoe, such as spooling and pulling thread.[63] Others, like the fast-paced Highland Fling, emphasized individual movement. The folk-dance books of Elizabeth Burchenal, a member of Camp Fire's first council of advisers, also provided descriptions of numerous dances from nations as diverse as England, Hungary, and Portugal.[64] Folk dance was one way that Camp Fire incorporated immigrants into the middle-class model of girlhood. Folk dance championed immigrant cultural gifts and promoted interaction between girls of different European backgrounds.

This level of integration and Americanization rarely applied to African American girls, even those who were among the nearly two million migrants fleeing the South for northern cities in the early twentieth century. To some extent, Camp Fire clubs at settlement houses produced an analogous "northernization" process for girls who were part of the Great Migration, but Camp Fire made no efforts to elevate African American cultural gifts or encourage cross-racial mentorships.

Black Camp Fire Girls

Despite Grace Parker's comment that "all prejudices seem to disappear" when Camp Fire Girls of color met with white Camp Fire Girls at a regional council meeting, the treatment of African Americans more than any other group illustrates the limits of Camp Fire's inclusion model. Although Camp Fire promoted access to its version of middle-class American girlhood for all by promising to include Black girls, organization leaders permitted clubs to be organized along racial lines. In addition, structural barriers meant few Black girls joined Camp Fire. Cross-racial interactions were rare, resulting in few opportunities for the mutual exchange that was built into the immigration honors.

At the initial organizing meetings, Camp Fire's founding leaders did not establish any rules concerning race. They appeared blind to the potential controversy of asserting that Camp Fire was open to all girls. Indeed, Luther Gulick gave a speech at the interracial Southern Sociological Congress (ssc) in Nashville, Tennessee, in the spring of 1912 on the topic of Camp Fire's relevance for the South. Despite one of the ssc's purposes being to solve the "race question in a spirit of helpfulness to the Negro," Gulick's address did not reference African American girls. Instead, he restated that "it is not an organization for rich girls, for poor girls, for working girls nor for girls of leisure hours. It is for all girls, with activities correspondingly elastic to fit all conditions."[65]

Although Gulick ignored the specific needs of potential Black members in his speech, historian Marcia Chatelain notes that Black community leaders sought out their children's participation in national youth organizations to "signal their right to full citizenship." Black women reformers, according to Glenda Gilmore, had long embraced "a constellation of Victorian middle-class values—temperance, thrift, hard work, piety, learning" to "carve out space for dignified and successful lives." Black women leaders in Chicago's Black neighborhoods adopted Camp Fire because its "patriotism, community involvement, and elevation of women's work" offered a way to "foreground a good black girl citizen" and to decrease juvenile delinquency in their community. Indeed, the influential Black weekly the *Chicago Defender* repeated Camp Fire publicity favorably, urging Black families to sign their girls up and help them "to develop the home spirit and make it dominate in the entire community." The Camp Fire Girls "elevated black women's work to the level of science and precision to generate more respect for their labor." For those "African American girls, who may have worked toward the bleak and often inevitable future of working as a domestic as their only occupational position, Camp Fire dignified these acts." These Black leaders refracted Camp Fire's messages through the lens of racial uplift.[66]

One of the first Black Camp Fires was not called Camp Fire at all, but its debut demonstrates the desire in the South, among social workers, for programs for Black girls. The SSC's general secretary, Reverend James E. McCulloch, embarked on a separate program for Black girls called Girls of the Forward Quest on the model of the Camp Fire Girls. It seems likely that he and Gulick would have met and discussed bringing Camp Fire to Black girls in the South during the Nashville SSC conference. McCulloch at first planned to call them Camp Fire Girls. According to newspaper reports, which Gulick claimed were false, McCulloch's effort to do so was rebuffed by "the north." Whether or not Gulick rejected the application of the Black Camp Fire group or asked McCulloch to move more slowly, McCulloch's Nashville Institute for Negro Christian Workers established the parallel organization with Margaret Murray Washington, the wife of Booker T. Washington, and several other prominent Nashville citizens, Black and white, on its board.[67]

In 1913, as McCulloch was working to establish the Girls of the Forward Quest, Gulick responded to the application for membership by an increasing number of African American groups by seeking assistance from individuals concerned about educational and interracial issues. He asked Quaker peace and civil rights activist L. Hollingsworth Wood and African American economist and social worker George E. Haynes "to determine upon a policy for the promotion of the work among colored girls." Haynes, who was also an SSC member, researched Black migration to northern cities and had advanced African American YMCA branches in the South. Beginning in 1910, he was at his alma mater, Fisk University, training Black social workers, many through the Bethlehem Settlement House in Nashville.[68] At Bethlehem, which would form one of the first Black Camp Fires, whites and African Americans worked together to provide social services. The Woman's Missionary Council of the Methodist Episcopal Church, a white women's club, and Fisk University were Bethlehem House's principal supporters. The boards of the M.E. Church, South, and the Bethlehem House were interracial. Donations and volunteers from the Mothers' Community Club, an organization of Nashville's African American mothers, also supported the Bethlehem House.[69]

The advice of Haynes and Wood does not survive, but whatever they said, Camp Fire moved ahead with a white-girls-first policy, recommending "that no attempt should be made for the present to promote Camp Fire work among colored girls especially in the south" and that "colored groups be authorized only in cities where the work has already been established among the white girls."[70] The policy accepted the existence of some Black groups, which would be called Camp Fire Girls, and Camp Fire would, therefore, assert that it provided access to Black girls. The policy, however, barred outreach if white clubs had not already begun in an area and thereby privileged growth among white members.

Some successful Black Camp Fire groups started in the early years despite this discriminatory policy. In states where segregation was de facto rather than de jure, race generally still separated Camp Fire groups, though they sometimes met together at council fires. Black philosopher and educator Anna Julia Cooper started a Camp Fire group in 1912 at M Street School in Washington DC, where she was a teacher.[71] Black Camp Fires were also connected to YWCA's and settlement houses. Black Camp Fire Girls began meeting in New York in the fall of 1912 through the Black branch of the YWCA, and the East Orange Settlement House in New Jersey hosted a Black Camp Fire unit beginning in 1914. Along with a Black group from New York, these girls attended a mixed council fire in 1914 with the region's white Camp Fire Girls. It was probably the council fire that Parker referred to in her report.[72] Before World War I, African American groups met in locations such as Frederick, Maryland; Fresno, California; and Kansas City, Kansas.[73] A Camp Fire leader in Youngstown, Ohio, bragged that of the eight groups in the city, "The best one . . . is one of colored girls with a colored guardian who devotes the greater part of her time to them."[74]

Few differences in these girls' club activities separated them from their white counterparts. Churches and settlements more often sponsored their clubs than those of their white peers, but they held council fire ceremonials complete with so-called Indian music and dancing just as their white counterparts did.[75] In Manhattan, Kansas, Black girls hosted their own benefits and attended camp during a separate session.[76] The Decatur, Illinois, club, connected to the AME Sunday School, called themselves the "Gold Wings Camp Fire Girls." Gold represented "their deeds" and wings their expectation "to soar to the heights of knowledge and love."[77]

In their community work and presence, Black girls devoted time and energy to elevating their communities. For example, the Black Camp Fire Girls of Frederick, Maryland, celebrated Emancipation Day, a Washington DC holiday commemorating the end of slavery in the District of Columbia.[78] Black Camp Fire Girls also, like their white counterparts, participated in civic celebrations. As a Buffalo, New York, newspaper pointed out such events expressed racial pride. And when World War I draftees left for Europe, the *Buffalo Commercial* noted that "colored citizens of Buffalo," including "colored Boy Scouts and colored Camp Fire Girls," gave the "draft contingent a send off that the white folks have seldom equaled." Hundreds marched in a parade to escort the new soldiers to the station.[79] Calling attention to pride in the work of other Black people and connecting it to national service, these Camp Fire Girls were also involved in promoting collective pride and racial identity.

Although Black girls found room for civic engagement in Camp Fire, the color line shaped camping experiences throughout the first six decades of Camp Fire's existence. "The 'local customs' of rural areas that refused integration and the dangers that befell Black children when they did participate in interracial camping" limited Black girls' access. In the 1930s, members of Black women's clubs and elite African Americans established camps for Black girls, broadening opportunities somewhat. The National Association of Colored Girls, an offshoot of the National Association of Colored Women, opened a camp at Lake Storey, Illinois, and in 1947 Annette B. White donated land in the Idlewild, Michigan, region, known as a welcoming vacation spot for African Americans. But these attempts were few and far between, and racial exclusions at camps that catered to white children prevented Black girls from attending. The exception was that some camps opened for a few weeks each year to Black children. In the rare instances when interracial efforts were broached, Black girls often found themselves the solo representative of their race among strangers and "had a rather hard time of it," as one Chicago settlement worker explained.[80]

The contradictory nature of Camp Fire's race policy, wherein a few groups were admitted where white groups were already flourishing, led to revealing problems, especially in Nashville, where the Forward Quest Girls was established. In 1914 Luther Gulick and the Board of Directors authorized a northern Black settlement worker, Lizzie Smith, to start a new Camp Fire club of eighteen Black girls through the Bethlehem Settlement House.[81] Controversy erupted when Smith "boast[ed] publicly" that Black girls met with "the same privileges as White Girls" and that "the color line is not drawn in this organization." In response, McCulloch, bitter that a Black Camp Fire circle would compete with the Girls of the Forward Quest and angry that Luther Gulick was not more supportive of the separate organization, admonished Gulick. Smith's claim, McCulloch wrote, was too bold for Nashville whites. He countered her assertion that African American girls had the same privileges as white girls, and he enjoined Gulick to direct Smith to "transform her organization into the Girls of the Forward Quest."[82] McCulloch now maintained the importance of distinct names as well as branches. "It isn't a question of whether the Negro Girls want to come into the [Camp Fire Girls] Movement," he wrote. "Of course, that is true at present. It will not be true when you work out something distinctive for the Colored Girls."[83] McCulloch was also responding to "repeated objections" by Nashville whites that Black girls met on an equal footing in their separate clubs. Assigning different identities to organizations for people of color was a common practice in Nashville organizations at the time. In 1919, for example, the Nashville YWCA organized a Blue Triangle League, an African American branch, in their city. The women of Nashville considered their YWCA interracial, but the units met separately.[84] McCulloch wanted to follow this more cautious standard that propped up white supremacy.

But Gulick had already told McCulloch that he supported a policy of moving ahead "as cautiously as we may, but nevertheless continuing to authorize the establishment of groups among colored girls when the conditions are promising."[85] Gulick thought Nashville was promising, but McCulloch disagreed, writing, "The Negro Camp Fire Girls organization in Nashville is more likely to give trouble than such an organization anywhere else in the South because they are boasting publicly that they . . . have the same privileges as White Girls. Of course, this alienates your White Girls." McCulloch criticized "the motives that led to [Bethlehem House's] organization" of Camp Fire Girls as "not to the credit of the leaders."[86] He did not elaborate on what appeared to be underlying friction with Bethlehem's leaders regarding their assertiveness, but he presented Lizzie Smith, despite her connections to the Methodist community through the missionary society, as an outsider stirring emotions with claims of equality.

Local white Camp Fire women, some affiliated with the YWCA, protested the presence of this club in Nashville. The YWCA had organized four white Camp Fire clubs, and their leaders argued that the existence of a Black Camp Fire group would deter white members from joining, harming the image and popularity of the organization throughout the South. McCulloch's research found that leaders "would disband immediately if the Negro girls are organized in Nashville." He warned, "We must . . . make up our minds at once whether it is best to have Camp Fire Girls among the white people of the south. If so, you cannot have Colored Camp Fire Girls in the South . . . you will immediately destroy the usefulness of your organization among White girls in the South."[87]

White leaders believed that they were entitled to define the makeup of Camp Fire membership. White Nashville club leader Florence Leigh of the YWCA wrote to Gulick to express her "astonishment" and dismay. She had read in the paper of the Black group's formation, likely through writer D. Wellington Berry's column in the *Tennessean*.[88] She wrote, "The organization of colored groups would be the death knell of the Camp Fire work in the South and is most discouraging to those of us who hoped great things for it."[89] Despite such claims, Nashville was, according to Gulick, "the only city in the South" where such controversy over the inclusion of Black girls in separate groups emerged.[90] And even though it had just adopted a whites-first policy, the board did nothing to remove nor to shore up support for the Black Bethlehem House group.

News releases show that in Nashville separate African American and white clubs continued to meet as the Camp Fire Girls, and Lizzie Smith led the girls at Bethlehem House while awaiting a missionary appointment to Africa until mid-1914.[91] Then, Dr. Haynes's wife, Elizabeth Ross Haynes, took over the group. She was, herself, a Fisk graduate, national YWCA leader, and social worker. Her appointment appears to have reduced the tension in Nashville, where the Black Camp Fire units continued to meet, as did the separate white Camp Fire Girls, through 1918.[92] Reports of the Girls of the Forward Quest continue through 1919 as well.

In fact, work at the Bethlehem House provided a model of Black access to national youth organizations. In 1918 the SSC printed the argument of A. M. Trawick, a white Southern Methodist minister and professor of sociology at Scarritt College in Nashville, insisting that African American boys and girls be included in national Boy Scout and Camp Fire work. He contended that "local patrols must be affiliated with the national movement," and that groups that were not affiliated reduced the benefits of the organizations. He pointed to the work at the Bethlehem House among Camp Fire, Boy Scouts, and other agencies as evidence of the positive impact such youth work could have when young people of color were "recognized as part of the national movement, without limitation or restriction in their membership."[93]

Changes occurred during World War I that led to the eventual consolidation of the groups for Black girls in Nashville into the YWCA Girl Reserves. During World War I, the Bethlehem Settlement House collaborated with the YWCA, and the Forward Quest Girls became affiliated with the Bethlehem House and its war efforts. Although in the 1910s many YWCAs had hosted Camp Fire units, in 1918 the YWCA formed the Girl Reserves, a girl auxiliary. By the 1920s most branches had replaced Camp Fire units with their own programs.[94] Moreover, during World War I Black Nashville women had organized to make items for Black soldiers. They formed the nascent Blue Triangle League; during World War I, they too met at Bethlehem House and other local facilities. In 1920 the league purchased a building and hosted a Girl Reserve program.[95] The *Nashville Banner* announced the organization and first initiation of African American Girl Reserves in early 1920.[96]

In the interwar period outside Nashville, Black Camp Fire Girls' activities and membership grew alongside other social spaces like Black YWCAs. The clubs continued to be markers of racial respectability.[97] Blanche E. King, wife of Illinois state representative William King, led the Oececa Camp Fire Girls of Chicago's south side. It offered a scholarship program to help girls raised in poverty. They invited elite and politically connected Black speakers, including boxer Joe Lewis and journalist and activist Ida B. Wells Barnett, to support and be recognized at Camp Fire events. Leaders met to discuss politics and literature. Chicago's Camp Fire Girls represented Black girlhood at the 1940 Negro National Exposition, which celebrated seventy-five years of emancipation and Black life and culture.[98]

The Camp Fire Girls founders had established an organization that was nominally open to all girls in the 1910s. A bold movement among mainstream, white organizations in the early 1910s, Camp Fire made efforts to minimize the distinctions among girls across class and ethnic lines and to celebrate the cultural gifts of girls from immigrant backgrounds. When Camp Fire reached beyond white, middle-class girls, it served an assimilationist function, assuming that its values—self-reliance, self-improvement, and usefulness—were universally shared as markers of good citizenship. It offered an avenue to national belonging to those who could access and achieve its standards of civic fitness.

Still, Camp Fire's founding in a time when racist discrimination against Blacks prevented their legal organization as integrated groups, and when separate-but-equal was broadly accepted policy, meant that Camp Fire was not open to all girls. The Camp Fire Girls ultimately accepted segregation, despite its discriminatory effects, as consistent with tolerance and democracy. The organization's national scope and political moderation led it to capitulate to local racist patterns. Camp Fire's controversies in Nashville highlight the limits of its version of American pluralism. As the next chapter shows, Camp Fire fared better as it extended its commitment to all girls and its assimilationist function to girls with disabilities.

4

"There Are Lots of Other Camp Fire Things We Can Do"

Disability, Disease, and Inclusion in the Camp Fire Girls

The Camp Fire Girls applied its inclusion policy to girls with disabilities both within the mainland United States and in the territory of the Philippines. Within two years of its U.S. launch, Camp Fire Girls met in U.S. institutions for children with vision impairments, deafness, and limited mobility. In the 1920s and 1930s, Camp Fire was established in the Hansen's disease treatment centers (so-called leper colonies) in the Philippines as well. Although the colonial history of the Philippines resulted in a distinct experience for Camp Fire Girls under treatment, examining these two groups side by side reveals several shared themes with regard to the treatment and expectations of those separated due to disability or disease. These Camp Fire groups provide a lens for examining how age, gender, race, and disability shaped inclusion and advantage. Illness of body and mind have been used historically to mark individuals as different and regulate their movement and access to civil society. Colonial populations have often been regarded as disabled or perpetually childlike with regard to their ability to perform labor and enact modern citizenship.[1] Camp Fire's intervention in educational and medical institutions to bring some of the most marginalized girls into a national youth organization broadened the definition of modern girl citizenship even as Camp Fire's strategies of inclusion continued to mark differences and privileged those girls who could readily make use of the Camp Fire program.

Although children in institutions for the physically disabled in the United States were not feared due to contagion, and they were not removed under force of law as Hansen's disease patients were, they were segregated, institutionalized, and treated as medical cases. Beginning in the early nineteenth century, U.S. institutions for disabled children were established to house and educate blind and deaf children. Children with intellectual disabilities were still generally deemed uneducable, and their families cared for them, or, by the early twentieth century, they could be placed in custodial care "colonies." Indeed, during the Progressive era, overcrowded custodial care rather than instruction and assimilation became routine for those deemed unteachable. "Crippled" children, a broad category that included orthopedic patients as well as children with amputations or postpolio paralysis, usually attended mainstream schools, but they often fell behind due to lengthy hospital stays. Many remained at home, uneducated or informally educated. New institutions for the care of young people with mobility limitations began to appear in the 1900s. Both a benevolent impulse to provide education and care and a practical, custodial purpose drove such institutions. Those that Camp Fire collaborated with also sought to impart moral values, and to train children in academic and practical skills to overcome negative stereotypes that disabled children were "uniquely subject to laziness and moral turpitude." Vocational or homemaking skills, which Camp Fire's lessons supplemented, might provide a route to independent living. Having some independence was especially critical since no laws protected people with disabilities from rampant employment discrimination until the 1970s, and "ugly laws" further prevented people with physical deformities from begging.[2]

The Hansen's disease treatment centers shared much in common with institutions for the disabled. Both were custodial, medical, and, to some extent, educational, and both groups elicited a mixture of contempt and sympathy. Hansen's disease is progressive and, if left untreated, can lead to disability as it affects the nervous system, skin, vision, and cognitive abilities. The United States developed leprosariums to quarantine patients in connection with its imperial foreign policy in the 1890s. In the territories of Hawaii and the Philippines, colonial health officials held patients in colonies distant from population centers to prevent the spread of disease.

Hansen's disease colonies were established on Moloka'i, Hawaii, in 1901 and Culion, Philippines, in 1902. Americans viewed Hansen's disease, incorrectly, as a tropical disease and associated it with primitive cultural practices and poor hygiene. As white soldiers, missionaries, and bureaucrats also contracted the disease, the U.S. Congress established a leprosarium at Carville, Louisiana, in 1917 so that white patients would not be shipped to Moloka'i. By the 1920s, health professionals better understood that Hansen's disease infections could be controlled with injections and that it was not as infectious as once believed.[3]

In the Philippines, strategy shifted toward smaller, less costly facilities that were closer to population centers. Camp Fire groups were in these treatment centers. Although patients were still confined during their treatments, the chance to receive visitors and eventually be released back into the community made these preferable options for patients. Large colonies at Culion and Moloka'i continued, nonetheless, because the United States and colonial health officials were reluctant to discontinue what they viewed as a modern and important health measure.[4] Throughout the 1920s and 1930s, the centers taught the colonial medical practices of hygiene and regimentation, and the tools for useful citizenship beyond the institution's walls. Camp Fire was an ideal agent for such lessons.

Camp Fire advocates professed that the organization's health and hygiene program fostered, for all its girls, the "zest and vigor" necessary for useful citizenship and cheer.[5] On one hand, Camp Fire's emphases on usefulness and health put a premium on fit bodies and implicitly cast doubt on the perceived value of the lives of disabled persons.[6] On the other, Camp Fire's intervention—always imagined to be transformative—was thought to be especially so for ill and disabled children. The Camp Fire Girls served girls with conditions that elsewhere led to their categorization as "defective" and formulated a definition of girl citizen that included them. If mainly in separate facilities, the Camp Fire Girls' inclusion of girls with disabilities set the organization apart. In the same years that Camp Fire expanded to institutions for girls with disabilities and illness diagnoses, the U.S. government restricted immigration of people with perceived disabilities and illness on the grounds that they were likely to be a public charge. Public commentators expressed concern about the supposed degeneration of the

American race, and state eugenic sterilization laws curbed the reproductive rights of the so-called feeble-minded and infirm. As historian Kim E. Nielsen writes, "Physical 'defects,' both scientists and the casual observer increasingly assumed, went hand in hand with mental and moral 'defects.'"[7] While the organization's emphasis on useful citizenship meshed with eugenic concerns, Camp Fire sought to transform girls with disabilities and illness into useful citizens and subjects rather than restrict and exclude them. The model recognized girls' potential—even as it cast them as unfit without Camp Fire's intervention.

Camp Fire in Homes for the Deaf, Blind, and "Crippled"

In its early years, Camp Fire groups formed in a few institutions for children with disabilities. These separate institutions emerged in the mid-nineteenth century in the United States, and many had state funding by the early twentieth century. Their purpose was to develop individuals' skills to function usefully and without "the stigma of dependency."[8] Their emphasis on acceptance and productive living made Camp Fire a good fit. In addition to their presence in a handful of institutions for the deaf such as Manhattan's Public School 47 and the Institute of the Deaf in Malone, New York, by 1914 state institutions for the blind in Pennsylvania, Missouri, New York, and Massachusetts hosted Camp Fire groups, and Camp Fire had printed its manual in braille.

The Camp Fire Girls operated on the assumption that extending a national program to girls with disabilities helped those girls to gain a sense of purpose, behave more like nondisabled peers, and feel a sense of belonging. Carrie Wallace Kearns, principal from 1910 to 1936 of Public School 47, which operated as a day school for the deaf, formed a circle of Camp Fire Girls. She reported that the program "made [her girls] more thoughtful through the study of the law of Camp Fire and it made them so happy."[9] Officials at the famous Lighthouse for the Blind in New York, where Helen Keller was an officer, expressed similar notions. Its founders, Winifred and Edith Holt, advocated on behalf of the blind, getting blind children admitted to New York public schools and teaching vocational skills so that blind people might live independently.[10] The Lighthouse sponsored a Camp Fire club that met twice weekly. The meetings and activities, Lighthouse publicity exclaimed, made "listless, unresponsive children" with vision impairments into warm, genial "comrades." Their "young, sometimes destructive energies" were channeled "into happy, useful outlets."[11]

Camp Fire appealed to these educators, in part, because of its gender-specific programming. Teaching girls to adopt proper feminine behavior was viewed as especially important since "disability has historically threatened prevailing gender norms." "It has often required altering expected dynamics surrounding work and home life as well as bodily interactions with space, objects, and other bodies," writes historian Leanna Duncan. Appropriately gendered behavior prepared a girl to participate in mainstream public and private life, a critical aspect since "her life and livelihood could depend on her winning the love of others to take care of her."[12] Thus, Camp Fire's "wholesome" activities complemented the Lighthouse curriculum of "sewing, cooking, general housework, basket making, beadwork, Braille, musical notation and piano." Blind Camp Fire Girls proudly dressed like Indian maidens, adorned by the rows of beads that they had earned and "strung themselves." Lighthouse officials underscored their accomplishments: "A girl who can help with the family wash or mending is an asset. One who can cook and wash the dishes and then sit down and make music for the family is a veritable blessing."[13]

Camp Fire organizers in institutions for children with disabilities hoped to make children useful in a world that offered few accommodations. Kearns endeavored to prepare the children to be "good, useful citizens of this great country." She believed deaf children were "naturally 'shut-in'" because they lacked the same means of communication that hearing people had. The school, therefore, trained children to read lips and emphasized clear speech. The addition of Camp Fire promoted Kearns's goals by giving "these deaf children another view of life," which made them "broader and wiser and more normal."[14] Such comments represent the benevolent impulse while they also show the reluctance of special education workers to think about, let alone advocate for, structural changes that would put the burden of understanding on anyone other than the deaf individuals. Kearns argued for molding the disabled child, not the society.

The Van Leuven Browne Hospital School for children in Detroit also sought to foster its students' usefulness and established both Camp Fire and Boy Scout groups to do so. Blanche Van Leuven Browne, who herself had limited mobility as a result of childhood polio, started the school in 1907. In a statement that reveals how Jim Crow affected disabled education, the school's bylaws and publicity noted that it would rehabilitate "white children who need its care" and to "make cripples independent and self-supporting" through "schooling and industrial training."[15] Many asylums and schools for the disabled, including those that Camp Fire collaborated with, excluded children of color or relegated them to separate, underfunded institutions.[16] Whiteness, too, was a qualifier of disabled children's fitness for useful citizenship.

For the children who had access to her school, Browne emphasized play to develop self-reliance and overcome negative stereotypes. Indeed, for Browne, limited mobility was only part of the children's struggle. "Invalidism," for most children, was a product of "treatment, environment, and constant suggestion of invalidism," she explained. The hospital school provided children the opportunity to partake in the play activities typically associated with American childhood. Its adoption of Camp Fire and Boy Scouts reflected that commitment to play and normalcy. An article in the Playground and Recreation Association's monthly approvingly emphasized the physical activities at the home, where "every child over twelve knows how to swim," and described the children turning cartwheels, wrestling, and climbing trees.[17] Depictions of children in institutions for the disabled engaged in play foregrounded the ordinariness of their lives.

Browne stressed how her Camp Fire Girls did ordinary program activities. Her children wore "regular uniforms" and took a "lively interest in the prescribed activities." Girls received honors, especially in home economics, just as girls without disabilities did, while Boy Scouts did the signaling, bandaging, and first aid that other Scouts did.[18] A Camp Fire Girl at the Van Leuven Browne House expressed her engagement with the program this way: "Well, we can't go on hikes, but there are lots of other Camp Fire things we can do."[19] Browne, and her girls, focused on what children could do rather than what they could not do. These sympathetic representations challenged negative perceptions of girls with disabilities and created a picture of shared girlhood pleasures and competencies.

Still, the girl's remark that she did not go hiking points to challenges in bringing the program to girls in institutions, difficulties that the girls in the Philippines treatment centers likewise faced. Turn-of-the-century Americans understood forays into nature coupled with healthy exercise to be invigorating for girls. Browne herself noted that fresh air was better than surgeries for overcoming mobility problems. However, excursions to farmhouses and country sites where girls could do nature study and camping were costly, fundraisers time-consuming, and not all girls, in fact, could hike. The Camp Fire Girls made efforts to bring girls to nature, but organizers sometimes resorted to bringing nature crafts to girls. One group made nature terrariums with pinecones and moss that leaders brought to them.[20]

Camp Fire's efforts not only aimed to help disabled girls, but also sought to reshape perceptions about people with disabilities. In this spirit, Camp Fire promoted readings about women with special needs, especially Helen Keller's autobiography and a biography of Elizabeth Gilbert, a blind woman who worked to educate others with vision impairments.[21] Keller's *Story of My Life* reported her struggles to communicate and overcome her childhood "prison-house." Gilbert, girls learned, struggled to be useful as she came of age. She had found that work, and every "place in the world," was closed to her. She grieved over the customary bar to her marrying until she realized "the possibility of giving aid to others through experiments and trials of her own."[22] Such accounts emphasized Camp Fire's values: hard work, self-reliance, and usefulness.

In its portrayals of disabled youth, Camp Fire made connections between what were described as the natural sensitivities of people with physical disabilities and primitive people, presenting some of the same themes that it did in the Indian lore and Gypsy fantasy portions of the program. In the *Guardian*, Camp Fire's magazine for leaders, Keller wrote that girls with disabilities at once needed Camp Fire more than nondisabled girls and had a special primitive connection to nature that made them Camp Fire's exemplars. Its brief forward indicated that "these girls enjoy our nature and camping activities as much as any of us, if not more." Keller depicted people with disabilities, including herself, as authentic representations of the primitive. She wrote, "Until I was seven years old I was a primitive creature." She spoke of animals on her family's farm that served as company and how changed she was when her teacher began to teach her names for things in the natural world. Her disabilities continued to heighten her other senses so that she was able to identify plants through smell faster than many sighted experts. Echoing the Gulicks' concerns, Keller wrote that "modern life" had estranged most other Americans from nature. Women especially, she cautioned, spent too little time there. For her, outdoor activities connected people to "the primitiveness of man and nature." Swimming, she explained, made her aware of the great human struggle to survive. "I am convinced," she told her Camp Fire readers, "that it is my abiding friendship with nature that has kept me unusually healthy throughout my life." The authentic connection to nature that Keller claimed for herself made her advocate Camp Fire's nature study and time outdoors as rejuvenating for able and disabled girls.[23]

Camp Fire's representations of girls with disabilities were generally sympathetic, but they left in place the unstated norm of nondisabled embodiment as a qualifier for full citizen recognition. As Rosemarie Garland-Thomson argues, the cultural images of disabled figures can "simultaneously confirm and challenge the received definition of physical disability as bodily inadequacy." Sympathetic representations of disabled people can help dismantle some negative misperceptions about seemingly disabled bodies. At the same time, those representations reinscribe the category of disability itself, especially in settings where children with disabilities are separated from their peers.[24] The rhetoric of normalcy and ability fed into a discourse that devalued those children who could not perform Camp Fire activities nearly the same way that nondisabled Camp Fire Girls did. Indeed, Camp Fire narrowly promoted its program to those girls deemed capable of conforming to societal norms despite their health conditions, the population that disability studies scholar Sami Schalk calls the "able-disabled." These girls could be expected to forge, and in some cases exemplify, Camp Fire's self-reliant, happy, and contributing girlhood, while girls with intellectual disabilities or severe physical restrictions were beyond Camp Fire's purview.[25] Absence of disability, holding on to health in the first place, was still the surest guarantor of full citizenship.

The simultaneous challenge to and affirmation of categories of disability was likely apparent when girls met across lines of ability. Most of the girls with special needs met in separate Camp Fire groups, so their interaction with the other girls in the local council was limited to special events and service projects. This structural division probably inculcated the idea that consequential differences separated the two groups of girls in daily life. Indeed, when the hearing Ouananiche Camp Fire Girls of Malone, New York, visited the Camp Fire Girls in Malone's deaf school, the newspaper ran a story about the generosity of the hearing Camp Fire Girls, whose presence was a form of charity.[26] Camp Fire promotional material also described such meetings as teaching girls with special needs how to interact in society beyond the institutions for the disabled.

At times the meet-ups could be recognized as beneficial to both. Miss Guy, the guardian of the blind Camp Fire Girls of the Lighthouse School, reported that her club had hosted "seeing girls" and put on a play for them. In return, the "seeing girls" gave lessons in "social dancing" at several Camp Fire meetings. Each group had led an activity. Guy implied that Camp Fire's shared activities helped them identify with the national girls' culture, and worked to break down stereotypes. Guy proudly pointed to the ability of her Camp Fire Girls to dance, play games together, and cook.

Guy, nonetheless, considered the Lighthouse girls' participation in an organization of national scope to be especially valuable to the blind girls' self-image and ability to function in the world beyond the blind school. She reported to Camp Fire's executive board "that Camp Fire work has done that which seemed almost impossible with blind girls,–it has developed in them a sense of social responsibility. Now instead of feeling shut off from *seeing girls* and their activities, they are competing with them for honors in Camp Fire work."[27] Although Guy's comments still assumed "seeing girls" came more naturally to "social responsibility," she broke down stereotypes as she spotlighted similarities. Another report of a meet-up between blind and seeing Camp Fire Girls in Cornwall, New York, exclaimed, "It is splendid to see how the blind girls enter into the spirit of an outing, just like other girls." This observation suggests that not only did girls with vision impairments fully participate in Camp Fire but also that the adult authors expected such an impairment to extend to the girls' emotional capacities.[28]

It was clear that organizers believed that Camp Fire Girls with disabilities gained from spending time with nondisabled peers, but nondisabled

Camp Fire Girls also had lessons to learn. A description of the Lighthouse girls' encounter stated that the "seeing girls" realized that the blind girls' accomplishments rivaled their own and warned that they had better "look to their laurels." That phrase implied that if the blind girls surpassed the "normal" girls, then the "normal" girls had become indifferent to their Camp Fire efforts and would need to step up their hard work to maintain their superiority. In other words, if blind girls succeeded as well as the seeing girls, the seeing girls must be lazy.[29] The girls with disabilities who were successful in Camp Fire became standard setters for all Camp Fire Girls, the implication being that if they could achieve success, certainly Camp Fire Girls without disabilities could do better.

Service was another way that Camp Fire Girls without disabilities learned about difference. Whereas a few Camp Fire Girls would have the opportunity described above to meet peers with disabilities, more commonly Camp Fire literature and press releases rendered girls with disabilities not as fellow members but as the objects of service. Indeed, the inclusion of girls who were in institutions for the deaf, blind, and mobility-impaired exemplified Camp Fire's service to the less fortunate. Press releases, the national magazine, and Camp Fire's annual reports spotlighted these clubs, though few in number, and thereby promoted the service-oriented image of Camp Fire. Individual girls gave charity to peers with disabilities too, raising money to send them on fresh air vacations.[30] Any Camp Fire Girl could strengthen her home and hand craft skills by dressing dolls or making picture books or toys to send to hospitals or settlements, and she earned honor beads if she made "six visits a month for three months to sick in homes, hospitals, or other institutions."[31] Aid to ill and disadvantaged girls was a significant way that American girls gave service.

Camp Fire's outreach to girls in institutions for disabled children was a logical extension of the goals of these institutions to provide belonging and useful skills to children with disabilities. Many of the organizers sought out Camp Fire for its gender-specific training and for the opportunity it provided for girls to fit in and access the national offerings for American children. Such opportunities, even though they were within a discourse that continued to mark disability, shifted negative perceptions about girls with disabilities. They were also a limited privilege, extended to white children in those institutions with an educational focus.

Camp Fire Girls in the Hansen's Disease Centers

Camp Fire programs also appeared in the treatment centers for Hansen's disease patients in the Philippines. Camp Fire framed issues of belonging, civic fitness, and usefulness with regard to these girls in ways akin to how it framed them for girls in institutions for disabled children stateside. Between 1926 and 1937, the Camp Fire Girls, through the aid of Irving Hart, an American businessman and humanitarian living in the Philippines, along with Mary Stagg, an American Methodist missionary, established five Camp Fire clubs at Hansen's disease centers. Hart started several Boy Scout groups as well. San Lazaro Hospital in Manila, once a Spanish fort enclosed by a ten-foot-high wall crowned with steel spikes, was the home of the first Camp Fire circle, the Blooming Flowers. Groups at Hansen's disease regional treatment centers at Eversley Childs Treatment Station at Mandawe, Cebu; Western Visayas Treatment Station, Santa Barbara, Iloilo; Bicol Treatment Station, Legaspi, Albay; and finally Mindanao Central Sanitarium in Zamboanga City, Mindanao, soon followed. Camp Fire groups, as well as Girl Scouts and Boy Scouts, were established outside of the Hansen's disease centers, too, particularly for the daughters and sons of white missionaries and government bureaucrats and for elite Filipino schoolchildren. The Hansen's disease centers, however, bring into sharp relief gendered and racial colonial dynamics and show how Hart and health officials viewed Camp Fire as useful for a larger colonial public health project. Hart's rationale was similar to that of educators who worked with children with disabilities in the United States; he believed involvement in youth organizations would improve the morale and the health of youth with Hansen's disease. The Camp Fire Girls' special emphasis on domestic crafts appealed to him as activities that girls in the centers could do and that would help them cultivate feminine usefulness.[32] Hart started Camp Fire clubs in all the treatment centers excepts Culion, where a Catholic priest prevented its establishment. In each center, Hart supervised and guided the clubs that he established.

8. The "Blooming Flowers" Camp Fire Girls at San Lazaro Leprosarium, Philippines, act out their roles as modern Camp Fire Girls in photographs. They donned white middies with red neckerchiefs and lined up in drill formation. The images portray the girls in Hansen's disease centers as capable of regimentation and control. Courtesy of U.S. National Library of Medicine, Bethesda, Maryland.

Camp Fire in the Philippines was a humanitarian effort that also reflected the colonial context of the Philippines. Part of the Spanish Empire since the 1500s, the Philippines became a colony of the United States in 1898 as a result of the Spanish-American War. Revolutionaries in the Philippines had resisted first Spain and later the United States. They sought independence only to be conquered by an exhausting war against U.S. forces. By 1902 the war had drawn to a close, and Filipino elites who were promised government positions and the benefits of modern nation building—hospitals, schools, infrastructure, and democratic political institutions—collaborated with the U.S. occupation and looked forward to eventual independence. Filipinos became American nationals, neither aliens nor eligible for full U.S. citizenship. Descriptions of Filipina Camp Fire Girls reflected the United States' ambivalent embrace of its colonial subjects. Camp Fire's literature cast the Filipina Camp Fire Girls as, at once, Camp Fire sisters and unfamiliar outsiders. *Everygirl's*, the magazine for Camp Fire Girls, reflected this dual status as Americans and racial others, declaring, "She is one of our American Camp Fires, yet of different blood and race. Meet miss Filipino Camp Fire."[33]

Such attitudes reflect how, as historian Vicente L. Rafael explains, "U.S. colonization of the Philippines was predicated . . . on a policy of benevolent assimilation." This entailed "the domestication of native populations and their reconstruction into recognizably modern political subjects." The United States implemented Americanization efforts on the islands through American schools and in the United States as young male scholars, *pensionados*, traveled to study and returned to assume administrative positions in the Philippines. Youth organizations were also assimilative. Because colonization assumed that native practices were infantile and could be remade through teaching by superiors, youth were ideal targets. Scouts and Camp Fire groups extended U.S. power through self-legitimizing, uplifting actions that blurred the brutality of conquest. As historian Mischa Honeck writes of Moro Boys Scouts of America in the Philippines, the work "opened up a space that permitted imperialists to shed their warrior masculinity and separate themselves from the bloody reality of conquest."[34] Girls were also fitting targets since lessons on domesticity engendered empire. As Camp Fire Girls trained in American home economics, Western bourgeois notions of domesticity crossed borders—an exportable marker of colonial modernity and girlhood.[35]

Hart, a veteran who served in the Third Cavalry for the United States in the Spanish American War and returned to the Philippines after the war as a businessman, exemplified the mindset of "benevolent assimilation." He worked for a Methodist publishing house, printing Bibles and other religious materials in English and native dialects. His knowledge of Filipino dialects, Spanish, and English made him valuable to the civil government when they began moving people with Hansen's disease to Culion Leper Colony, the largest and most isolated of the institutions for patients with Hansen's disease. He then started his life's work to improve the lives of those with Hansen's disease and other disabilities, philanthropic endeavors he supported through constant fundraising in the United States and throughout the Philippines.[36] For men like Hart, a "soldier-turned-scoutmaster," scouting abroad was redemptive through "the 'love' and 'friendship' he received from his boys." Girls filled a similar but distinctly gendered role when former warriors like Hart became protectors to girls. Many referred to him as "Daddy" over the years, a phrase he enjoyed and one that placed him in the role of paternal imperial protector.[37]

In addition to Hart and Stagg, Filipinas, especially former teachers who had been diagnosed with Hansen's disease and were living in the centers, also helped establish Camp Fire. Fé Almendrala (later Alfafara) worked with Stagg to start the first Camp Fire at San Lazaro. Stagg was familiar with the Camp Fire Girls because her church in Pasadena, California, had a group. Stagg later shifted her attention to forming Camp Fire circles among the daughters of missionaries, but Almendrala continued to work with Hart to create Camp Fires at the Hansen's centers.[38] Like the elite Filipina club women who, in partnership with white women, helped establish maternal and child health programs, these women prized teaching Filipina girls an idealized vision of motherhood and domesticity as well as broadened civic roles. These ideals characterized modern Filipina womanhood and Camp Fire adhered to them. These women sought to improve health, morale, and education in the Philippines through their collaboration with Americans, and Camp Fire was a means to this end.[39]

Camp Fire's national magazines showcased the effects of American benevolent assimilation. Filipina Camp Fire Girls acted out their new roles as modern Camp Fire Girls in photographs and news stories. They donned white middies with red neckerchiefs and lined up in drill formation, images that capture the order and control of which Filipina girls were capable. Despite their own tribal traditions, they wore Camp Fire's American Indian–style ceremonial gowns and beaded headbands. In one published photograph, three girls wearing the dresses direct their "determined" gaze, as the editors called it, toward the camera. The text noted the "purposeful way" that the girls worked on their Camp Fire honors and taught their Camp Fire lessons to younger girls. The editor's interpretation of the photographs was important for asserting the possibility that Filipinas were Camp Fire sisters. Anglo-Americans regularly refused to distinguish Indigenous people; American soldiers sometimes referred to Filipinos as Indians or used other familiar racial epithets indiscriminately during the Philippine-American War. Ethnographical photographs of Filipinos in the early colonial period also highlighted primitive attributes, suggesting that assimilation would be challenging. Thus Anglo readers may have seen Filipina Camp Fire Girls dressed as American Indians merely as inferior primitives. The editors believed it was necessary to explain that these were plucky, well-educated, self-reliant Camp Fire Girls. In this way, the photographs and text suggest the permeability of culture and the possibility of transformation under American tutelage.[40]

Although not all Filipina Camp Fire Girls had Hansen's disease, the girls who did were further separated—geographically and metaphorically. Contagion meant isolation, and explanations for the disease reinforced notions that so-called primitive hygiene and cultural practices caused the disease. Camp Fire publicity portrayed the girls in Hansen's centers as patients who, without the youth organization, were sick, deprived, and lonely. This characterization exaggerated the illness. Stagg had noted that except for the guardian who had a lesion on her ear, the girls she encountered at San Lazaro showed no signs of illness. Still, the illness discourse, especially reminders that thoughtful people "shudder at the mention" of leprosy, made the Filipina Camp Fire Girls sympathetic, if strange, figures.[41]

As was true in the U.S. institutions for children with disabilities, the Camp Fire Girls used illness and disability to identify the Filipina children in Hansen's disease centers as special targets for service. Camp Fire's national office determined that despite the organization's usual policy of not offering charity to any members, those girls secluded in treatment centers could not be expected to pay dues. The decision was not entirely unheard of. Camp Fire had encouraged members to raise funds to help send girls with disabilities to the countryside, and publications praised the efforts of local clubs that "adopted" children who could not pay their dues. One club "decided that they would adopt *a little leper girl in the mission at Kwanja, Korea*, make her a Camp Fire Girl, and support her and pay for her treatments until she was cured and allowed to return home."[42] The national office followed suit. In 1932 the national board, "realizing the splendid work" Hart was doing with the girls in Hansen's disease treatment centers, determined that it would "underwrite dues for leper girls everywhere."[43]

The medical environment of the treatment centers was also optimal for a benevolent empire. American colonial agents at Culion, historian and

9. Filipina Camp Fire Girls from elite educational institutions pose for a publicity photograph in their American Indian–style gowns. The caption in the Camp Fire Girls' magazine explained how the girls worked in a "purposeful way" on their Camp Fire honors, underscoring their belonging in the American organization. "News from the Philippines," *Everygirl's*, September 1924. Reprinted with permission of Camp Fire.

medical doctor Warwick Anderson writes, "structured the leper colony as a laboratory of therapeutics and citizenship."[44] Filipino children and adolescents were taken from their families, socialized through white, gendered citizenship practices, trained to regulate their bodies through medical treatment, and encouraged to follow U.S. domestic hygiene regimes. In 1901 the Philippine Commission created a Board of Health made up of American and Filipino bureaucrats. The board opted to quarantine and segregate Hansen's disease patients and established a remote colony at Culion for that purpose. The American occupation government viewed quarantine and isolation as signifiers of modernization. In 1907 health officials held police powers; police had to report anyone suspected of carrying the disease and it was criminal to harbor someone with the disease. By the 1920s, health officials understood the disease better, especially that it was far less contagious than previously believed. Since segregation in facilities was costly and the disease affected relatively few individuals, the Philippines shifted toward more regional treatment centers where patients lived closer to their relatives and family members could visit. In the 1920s and 1930s, patients whose disease was controlled by painful daily injections of chaulmoogra root oil extract were "paroled" and allowed to return to their families. Still, parole required quarantine until a person tested negative for the bacillus for six to twelve months in a row.[45]

Hansen's disease centers were microcosms for training American colonial subjects, and Camp Fire's programming on hygiene and habit meshed with the aims of the Hansen's disease centers to promote modern medical methods and citizenship through the self-regulation of the body.[46] Public health policy taught both hygiene practices and how to relate to modern institutions.[47] Of Culion, which did not have a Camp Fire club but was the largest of the leper colonies in the Philippines, Anderson writes, "Rituals of modern citizenship pervaded the colony." Colony residents elected a mayor and council, and they made their own regulations. Culion's women began voting in 1908 (the earliest female suffrage in Southeast Asia). Police forces made up of confined patients "saw that the town was 'kept in good sanitary condition' and made 'arrests of offenders against their own ordinances.'" Recreation included drama, music, and baseball. And residents worked, though "general debility" prevented self-sufficiency in the colony.

They cooked, cleaned, made dresses, took care of streets, repaired buildings, swept, collected garbage, assisted at hospitals, and carried supplies. Their routines normalized the American ideals of labor, industry, and civic responsibility. Camp Fire Girls added lessons about modern American childhood, in which a girl should be protected, cheerful, and useful.[48]

To learn appropriate behavior of U.S. citizen subjects, the girls did many of the same activities their American counterparts did. Girls played games, drilled, and sang. But girls in the Hansen's treatment centers could not participate in all aspects of the broader Camp Fire program due to their confinement. Although the San Lazaro girls attended a council fire, staying distant from the other participants, permission to go camping and leave the center was rarely forthcoming. In addition, the centers lacked Camp Fire supplies and reading materials. In a report from Iloilo, the leader explained what her girls missed: "Campfire's life has three ranks to attain with honor to be awarded for each rank. None of the members has been promoted to the next rank as the requirements for promotion have not been met by any one of them yet. Besides this, the group is not well equipped with honor beads and other things necessary for the ceremony." Camping was also difficult since under the regulations of the treatment station the girls needed special permission to leave the grounds. Without regular Camp Fire activities, in 1934, of the twenty girls who started the year as Camp Fire Girls, six quit, five were sent to Culion, one was paroled, and fourteen remained active.[49]

Public health officials hailed the Camp Fire program for building the health and happiness of the girl participants and those with whom they interacted. The *International Journal of Leprosy* noted the value of Camp Fire service to sick children as "one of the finest of activities for the younger inmates of leprosy institutions."[50] Numerous reports coming from the Philippines stated that Camp Fire boosted morale and led to faster recovery. Hart cited Dr. Rodriguez, a specialist, who reported that discharges—those who tested negative for the disease after treatment—were highest among Camp Fire Girls and Boy Scouts. Dr. José G. Tolentino explained of the Camp Fire Girls in the Eversley Childs Treatment Station at Mandaue, Cebu, "These girls, as a lot, are the cleanest, the healthiest, and the happiest, in the female section, and what is more is that they have far more and better morale than those outside of the organization. Their membership in this society is, therefore, conducive to their early recovery." Nurse Petra Asibal added that Camp Fire's "hopefulness and cheerfulness together with [its] well regulated mode of living are a necessary help in affecting their recovery."[51]

Not only did health professionals report that the girls with Hansen's disease had improved, but along with Camp Fire advocates, they claimed that Camp Fire Girls improved the morale of other patients. Dr. C. Gavino, chief of the San Lazaro Hospital, cited Camp Fire as producing good conduct and order among the children, and "keeping up the morale of the rest of the female patients of this Institution."[52] The director of health in the Philippines thanked Hart for his service, noting that the Camp Fire Girls in treatment centers with Hansen's disease "have not only improved their own health, but have been encouraged to do kind acts of helpfulness towards the other inmates."[53] Whether or not such accolades exaggerated Camp Fire's efficacy (and one suspects that they did), they demonstrated the organization's reputation for building model colonial girl subjects—respectable, influential, and useful to the colonial project. Colonial administrators viewed the girls as performing useful labor for the institution by providing a calming spirit and behavioral standard.

Officials in the Philippines and Hart himself also viewed Camp Fire Girls in the hospitals and treatment centers as a tool to bring a dissatisfied and at times unruly population under control. Unrest was a challenge at Culion; its disturbances attest to the resistance of people with Hansen's disease who were quarantined by force. The most significant disruption was a rebellion at the Culion colony in response to a 1927 ban on the marriages of people with Hansen's disease. About eight hundred young men stormed the women's dorm, and about two hundred young women fled the quarters with them. Colony police, made up of the residents, tried to stop them.[54] Hart was quick to point out that former Camp Fire Girls at Culion did not participate in the rebellion. Although Culion did not have active Camp Fire clubs, many who had been Camp Fire Girls at other treatment centers, especially San Lazaro, had been moved to the colony. Although Hart was sure that Camp Fire Girls, too, "have their sweethearts," he declared Camp Fire values responsible—and presumably their adoption of the modern regulatory state—for their absence in the rebellion. "To the credit and the honor of the Camp Fire Girls and the Boy Scouts not a ONE OF THEM joined the rebels or took any part in it," Hart declared.[55]

More ordinary transgressions, as authorities saw them, included pregnancies out of wedlock and attempts to run away, and here too Camp Fire Girls were ideal colonial subjects.[56] Hart believed that the seven laws of Camp Fire were "especially applicable for leper girls." He continued, "Such things as indiscretions, breach of discipline, or immorality, is conspicuous by its absence, for, up to the present time, not ONE of the leper Camp Fire Girls, in ANY of the leper colonies, have so far forgotten themselves as to be led astray." Hart specifically pointed out that none had become mothers "except those that are married." Colonial administrators regarded low birth rates to be a cost saving for the government since those born in institutions were cared for at government expense.[57] Nurses, too, pointed out that Camp Fire Girls were obedient. Dr. Juan Goitin declared the Camp Fire "experiment" a success. "Before our Scouts and Camp Fire Girls were organized we had trouble with patients running away. Now we have virtually abandoned our guards[, but] have never had a Scout or Camp Fire Girl try to leave the station. Instead they bring in their friends from the outside who are suffering from the disease." By contrast, Culion—where the priest would not allow Camp Fire to form—reportedly struggled with unwanted (at least by the authorities) pregnancies and had to transfer girls to other centers for uncooperative behavior. Hart believed that if he had been allowed to establish a Camp Fire group at Culion, "Much of this misery and degradation could have been avoided." Girl Scouts, which the priest was trying to establish instead, was no substitute, according to Hart. Former Camp Fire Girls who had been transferred to Culion regarded the Girl Scouts as a "wild lot" and wanted nothing to do with them.[58]

Despite the levels of social control they faced, the girls generally responded with favor and wrote appreciatively of Hart's efforts and of Camp Fire. When the priest at Culion refused to sanction Camp Fire Girl membership, declaring it to be an attempt to draw girls out of the Catholic Church—despite the thriving clubs and lack of controversy at other treatment centers—girls at Culion, who were familiar with Camp Fire, defied him. Nearly one hundred of the young women attended a meeting with Hart at Culion in 1934. The Bureau of Health had sent him to establish the Camp Fire Girls and the Boy Scouts, but the priest threatened the girls with not being allowed to take communion if they attended the Camp Fire gathering. According to Hart, the former Camp Fire Girls who had been transferred to Culion from other centers "donned their old Camp Fire uniforms" and informed the Mother Superior that, as "REGISTERED Camp Fire Girls," they "could not attend the meeting unless they were properly uniformed."[59] Although Culion did not establish a Camp Fire club, these girls demonstrated that their affiliation mattered to them.

Girls also wrote letters to thank Hart, which he forwarded to Camp Fire headquarters. A guardian at Zamboanga, who was also isolated there, wrote calling Hart "Daddy," the nickname that bespoke both affection and the paternalistic relationship that Hart forged. "Really Daddy, Camp Fire had taught me many wonderful things," she said. "At night when I go to bed and think over all I have done during the day, joy and contentment crowd out all sorrows that beset me. It may not be much that I have done, perhaps only a word of encouragement for someone, or a smile for another, yet all these give an inward feeling of joy which makes me think that I am not a useless person, a 'living dead,' as some people call us."[60] For her, the Camp Fire circle had brought a greater sense of purpose. Hart also regularly wrote how the Camp Fire Girls "were very glad indeed to see me" and described the entertainments through which they feted him.

Still, occasional tensions surface in his letters. In 1940 he wrote in frustration, for example, that the girls and leaders did not write to him, sometimes for years at a time.[61] Moreover, Hart could be controlling in his efforts to protect the girls. He regarded the Camp Fire Girls with Hansen's disease as "MY Camp Fire Girls" and introduced them as such when a new president took over Camp Fire in 1937.[62] The guardians, too, he regarded as his girls, despite their age and professional status (several of the leaders, whom he also referred to as "girls," were teachers).[63] Gender and illness shaped dependence, and the nickname "Daddy" indicated that.

In the mid-1930s, his overprotective tendencies were in full force when his first and favorite group at San Lazaro planned a dance. The hired musicians had tried to cheat the club out of fees. The band was double-booked and did not show up for the dance but demanded full payment for a second, alternative date. The girls wanted to hold the dance anyway and so agreed to the questionable terms. Hart was livid and declared that the dance could not be affiliated with Camp Fire. Although Hart was probably correct that the musicians were taking advantage of the girls, he was also unwilling to let the guardian and the girls decide. When the group held the dance anyway, Hart removed their Camp Fire banners. The leaders and girls were so angry they threatened to "resign en masse." But when Hart refused to accept their resignations, they stayed with the organization. These Camp Fire Girls treasured their club. They told Hart that they "had to write to you as we did" because they lacked any way to register their anger and had so little control over their situation. The dispute over a business transaction reflected the broader colonial and gendered lines of authority in the 1930s American Philippines.[64] Hart appears as a paternal figure trying to protect his ill girls. As targets of U.S. benevolence, they had little sway over their group's choices.

World War II took an extraordinary toll on the Camp Fire Girls in the Philippines. The Japanese occupation resulted in the abandonment of patients at treatment centers. They struggled without assistance to get food, and the disease worsened for many. At Culion, only 1,800 of the 5,000 patients remained at the end of the war. Most had starved or fled. Girls became sicker during the Japanese occupation. One young woman wrote to Hart, "Daddy, it breaks my heart to tell you, that I have become an advanced case. That is why I have hesitated to write you." Advanced stages of the untreated disease brought disfigurement, hampered mobility, ulcers, and blindness. She requested, "When you come to the colony don't look at me any more, but I shall be at the side-lines looking out at you."[65] Hart's first guardian at San Lazaro, Fé Almendrala Alfafara, died during the war of starvation. Hart's American colleague, Mary Stagg, who had helped establish the first Camp Fire unit, was beheaded by the Japanese for her efforts to hide fugitives from the Japanese and to help wounded soldiers and allied supporters. Hart was incarcerated at the hospital at Santo Tomas Prison Camp, one of several sites where Americans were confined during the war, but he emerged committed to rebuilding his humanitarian work.

Despite being seventy years old in 1946, Hart tried to rebuild the Camp Fire Girls and the Boy Scouts in the treatment centers with varying degrees of success. As part of an international relief effort, Texas, California, and Washington Camp Fire Girls sent his groups relief supplies. Clubs in the treatment centers continued to function into the 1950s, but the Philippines national government adopted the Girl Scouts as a nationally recognized girls' organization, and references to Filipino clubs disappear from Camp Fire materials and the press by 1957.[66]

Camp Fire Girl officials in the United States promised to train girls to be useful, healthy citizens. The Hansen's centers' promotion of modern medical methods through the self-regulation of the body and modern citizenship practices of civic engagement meshed with girls' citizenship training methods. Given the influence of the hygiene movement of the early twentieth century and the racial recapitulation theories of G. Stanley Hall, with their emphasis on health, fitness, and transcendence to a superior human existence, the girls marked as disabled both in the United States and in a colony of the United States had a unique relationship to the organization. Camp Fire's claims of success in making these girls, deemed exceptionally marginal, happy and useful elevated the organization's worth among all girls. Messaging suggested that Camp Fire could be transformative for even the girls with the greatest health deficits.

The Camp Fire Girls' early pluralistic model led to separate clubs within institutions for the disabled (especially in schools for the blind and deaf). These groups received sympathetic coverage within Camp Fire, which tried to shift negative perceptions. Camp Fire publications countered stereotypes that disabled girls lived miserable, downtrodden lives by emphasizing girls' participation in the same Camp Fire program that nondisabled girls prized. At the same time, the organization reflected the popular image of people with disabilities as needing charity and as worthy of full citizenship only after proving their capacity to "be happy" and "give service." The attention that the girls with disabilities gained because they had disabilities also reaffirmed the difference itself. They were targets of service but rarely equal Camp Fire sisters. Camp Fire framed girls with disabilities as recipients of aid and nondisabled Camp Fire Girls as having a duty to help the less fortunate. This made the latter more complete citizens and diminished the citizen responsibilities of girls with disabilities.

World War II would further affect Camp Fire and the way Americans thought about the inclusion of children with disabilities and other groups. The return of veterans with disabilities increased the sympathy of many Americans toward people with disabilities, as did the success with which people with disabilities had entered the wartime workforce. World War II would further alter the landscape of possibility for civil rights and inclusion within Camp Fire.[67]

5

"Worship God"

The Camp Fire Girls, Antifascism,
and Religion in the 1940s and 1950s

During the Second World War, many youth leaders attempted to create as
normal circumstances for children as they could. The freedoms of American
childhood were after all powerful symbols of the war's deeper meaning.
However, wartime needs propelled girls into new roles and responsibilities, many that "challenged society's juvenile labels and gendered biases."
Many playgrounds and camps closed for the duration, and girls took on
domestic and agricultural labors instead.[1] At the same time, leaders found
the essential feminism of Camp Fire's founding remarkably adaptable to
the political demands of America at war. Girls served their nation through
feminine work like food conservation that, though traditional, broadened
their claims to civic participation. Thus Camp Fire officials assured girls a
greater civic role through militarization, even as they affirmed a conservative gender ideology. Wartime Camp Fire Girls identified as patriotic
citizens and worked for victory.

How the Camp Fire Girls mobilized during World War II evinces both
the ways in which war influenced the understanding of civic fitness and,
more broadly, how it affected girls' experiences. Camp Fire officials conceived their clubs, and girlhood itself, as powerful contributors to military
morale and success. During both the First and Second World Wars, Camp
Fire refashioned the rhetoric and justification of its program activities to
meet the needs of the U.S. government's wartime agenda. Girls' worlds
were militarized as Americans came to see military aims and ideals as their

own. Martial symbols became appropriate for civilian institutions, public discourse, and popular culture.

Militarization, which often pervades American society during wartime, is of particular interest to feminist scholars. It historically privileges values coded masculine and suppresses debate on women's issues.[2] The ultimate national service, for example, is often said to be a soldier's willingness to fight and die for his country, a form of service women were deemed incapable of until recently. Such service boosted African American men's claims to greater citizenship privileges after the Civil War, for example, while women's rights lost ground. During the First World War, suffragists knew better and worked for both the war and the vote, solidifying their political claims by virtue of their wartime contributions. Camp Fire Girls had contributed to the food conservation campaign and shored up morale with skits.

During World War II Camp Fire Girls again exhibited their patriotism and got behind the war effort. Girls adopted military names and images that signaled their patriotic commitments. Instead of the Indian-sounding names typical since 1910, groups called themselves the Victory Blue Birds (Highland, California), for example.[3] Similarly, at a Quincy, Massachusetts, day camp shared by the local Camp Fire Girls and Girl Scouts, girls named their units after the women's military branches. The ten-year-old girls were called "Waves" after the Women Accepted for Voluntary Emergency Service (Navy); the eleven-year-olds were "Spars" for the women's Coast Guard units. The next age group called themselves "Waacs" for the Women's Army Auxiliary Corp, and the senior campers adopted the masculine-sounding title of "Marines."[4] Camp administrators sold war stamps every morning at registration, and a large percentage of campers invested regularly.[5]

At the same time, national youth leaders worried over the creep of fascism into youth organizations and attempted to curb rigid militarism. American youth organizations differentiated their patriotism from the nationalism of fascist countries by emphasizing individualism and spiritual values. Like many leaders of American youth, Camp Fire officials turned to God and democracy to buffer girls through the hard times. In 1942 the Camp Fire Girls added two words to the Camp Fire Law: "worship God." The national council, composed of delegates from all local councils, inserted this new marker of citizenship before the other pledges—to glorify work, maintain health, and be happy—suggesting it was foundational.

"Worship God" reflected a broad cultural shift. Historian Kevin Schultz explains that a "tri-faith vision," or religious pluralism that embraced America's Protestants, Catholics, and Jews, "took center stage in the shadow of European totalitarianism in the 1930s. By World War II, it had become America's standard operating procedure," one further strengthened after the war by the "public religiosity demanded by the Cold War" as politicians connected atheism and communism.[6] Religion became a more central marker of patriotism even as public assertions regarding respect for diverse faiths increased. Indeed, the addition of "worship God" embraced the three religions but ostracized those who did not practice any faith; this exclusionary practice existed alongside the new respect accorded Catholicism and Judaism as American religions.

At the same time, the war challenged older concepts of race and racism, undermined the study of eugenics, and brought new attention and commitment to inclusion in educational institutions. Camp Fire's vision of the democratic girl citizen embraced both antifascism with its antiracist implications and anticommunism with its racist denunciations of civil rights activists. Its leaders were also complicit with the incarceration of Japanese American Camp Fire Girls and willingly accepted ongoing patterns of discrimination during the war years. The Camp Fire Girls grappled with changing concepts of inclusion and gradually began to revise its policies that had permitted segregation, though full development of integration and reevaluation of its assimilationist model of girlhood would not occur until the 1960s, and then unevenly.

In the Camp Fire Girls, wartime brought a partial reconceptualization of girlhood. On the one hand, the organization invoked girlhood innocence and charm as symbols of American values, and reinscribed girls' and women's traditional connection to domesticity and nurture. On the other hand, Camp Fire officials who had called girls to public service since 1912 found an outlet in war contributions. Although militarism had some power to transform women's roles, forcing Americans to recognize women as citizens with civic responsibilities, its innovations ultimately hewed to gendered expectations. Images of girlhood spurred protective emotions that limited girls' claims to civic equality. Girls serving their country, though significant, still were supportive and subordinate to those who made the "ultimate sacrifice."

"Training Our Youth for Democracy": Antifascism and Camp Fire

As the threat of fascism in Europe grew, Camp Fire officials, too, professed concern about the turn that youth organizations at home and abroad were taking toward regimentation. In the United States, worries about fascist and authoritarian personalities led many psychologists, sociologists, and educators to argue that fighting prejudice was critical to a democratic American future.[7] But the large marches and discipline of the Hitler Youth, Nazi Germany's compulsory youth organization, appealed to some youth leaders. Some 4-H leaders, for example, wanted to emulate the ritualistic performances. In Great Britain, too, some Girl Guide and Boy Scout leaders admired the strength and discipline of young people in fascist organizations.[8] Camp Fire leaders echoed the desire to prepare girls to serve as patriotic citizens but wanted to protect them from nationalistic extremism.

To this end, Camp Fire's national council invited historian and women's rights advocate Mary Ritter Beard to address the 1940 meeting, less than four months after France had fallen to Nazi forces, and to help lay concrete plans for Camp Fire Girls' work in support of the allies. She warned against the threat of fierce nationalist identities: "Native leaders of young people, fascist at heart, may be a more serious peril to our democracy than alien Trojan horses or Fifth Columnists." Alluding to the Hitler Youth, but also speaking to the nationalistic tendencies of voluntary youth organizations in the United States and around the world, Beard commented that activities that strengthened "bodily vigor" and "group friendships" served "evil" as well as "pure" ends. She cautioned against "leaders whose ultimate intentions are for regimented youth, in the interest of a non-democratic law and order." Beard believed France was an example of what tragedy could befall democratic institutions, and she referred to France as "Nazified before [Germany's] machine rolled into his own land." She argued that before the war French youth leaders cooperated with and copied Hitler Youth tactics of regimentation and stern discipline and had, therefore, sowed the seeds of their own destruction.[9]

National director Lester Scott had made similar pleas to youth leaders to avoid extreme nationalism. He, too, decried that "young people in many countries abroad, with which we are all too familiar today, are trained through regimentation. A leader's one ideal is the indoctrination of the young people under his influence with one narrow propaganda of blinding racial patriotism with its consequent curtailment of the potentialities of the individual." To this, he added adamantly, "We don't want that sort of thing for our young people."[10] Thus Camp Fire officials broached mobilizing American girls with caution.

Camp Fire's board of directors committed Camp Fire to "the training of our youth for Democracy," calling actual practice in democratic methods in youth organizations "paramount for our defense and for the progress of the world." The board encouraged leaders to allow girls to share their input at meetings and to talk about the Bill of Rights and other aspects of America's democratic history. Such practices would differentiate Camp Fire from youth organizations in fascist Europe and guarantee the strength of American democratic traditions.[11] This argument cast Camp Fire's ordinary meetings and activities as essential to the war's larger purpose. Scott urged local group leaders to "carry on" with their groups; abandoning them for the seemingly more momentous work in factories would only undermine democracy. Consistent leadership would foster the "strength of fibre," and the "physical, mental and spiritual health" that "will save, and is saving, the great democracies today."[12]

Girls at War

While maintaining that youth programming was essential to democracy, the Camp Fire Girls also responded to the U.S. government's call for all citizens to do their part for victory, especially once the nation was drawn into the war. Organizers highlighted the military significance of the Camp Fire Girls. They worked closely with government agencies to ensure work was not duplicated. After consulting child psychologists and educators, Camp Fire promoted specific activities for its members that would involve them in the government's campaign to enlist the home front in the war effort. Camp Fire extended the war work children were doing through their schools. The Schools at War campaign, run by the U.S. Department of Treasury and the Office of Education's Wartime Commission, encouraged educational institutions to involve children in saving, serving, and conserving. Young people saved money to purchase war bonds and stamps, volunteered in victory gardens and on poster drives, conserved and collected metals and fats for national defense, and helped their communities with childcare needs as women entered the defense factories.[13] Camp Fire officials stressed not only how the Camp Fire program was already conducive to war work, but also the ways that war work educated girls as useful citizens beyond the war. Each activity, leaders argued, developed organizing skills, cooperation, and other life skills. Most important, the efforts taught girls to recognize the larger significance behind tedious or ordinary work.[14] Summarizing Camp Fire's aims during the war, Martha F. Allen, then Camp Fire's assistant to the national director, said that Camp Fire's recreational program had always been an "aid to emotional stability" for youth. It would continue during the war to train girls for "responsible citizenship in a democracy" through "a war activities program which would give the girls an opportunity to serve according to their capacities."[15] Camp Fire officials refashioned the everyday program activities to help win the war, maintaining a separate set of goals for female citizenship and providing an outlet for girls to be useful during the crisis.

In its war work, the Camp Fire Girls continued to reflect the traditional associations of girls and women with cooking, household chores, and childcare. Girls' knowledge of nutrition, marketing, food preparation, and even household repair would be put to a useful purpose. "Fortifying the Family" was Camp Fire's annual project for 1942, and it encapsulated the organization's philosophy regarding the connection between girls' home craft activities and war service. Girls could start by making at least one meal per week so that their mothers would be available for war work outside the home. They could offer services such as babysitting to other women to free them to do more difficult war work as well. Doing additional chores assisted the objectives of military victory and national strength.[16] Girls collected supplies for soldiers. One Providence, Rhode Island, group demonstrated gender solidarity as they sent beauty kits filled with soap, nail polish, emery boards, talcum powder, and hand lotion to women in the armed forces.[17]

10. Camp Fire Girls from Central Puget Sound pose while working in a World War II Victory Garden. The girls are wearing Camp Fire attire and have the Service for Victory insignia on their sleeves. Courtesy of Camp Fire Central Puget Sound, Seattle, Washington.

Camp Fire offered a direct alternative to training girls to work in the defense industry. Between 1935 and 1943, the National Youth Administration (NYA) trained older teenagers to replace men in the defense industry. Initially, this included girls as well as boys. However, some factories complained, and a perception developed that girls took too long to train and did not take their work seriously. As a result, the NYA agreed to place only those girls who were at least eighteen years old in defense industries.[18] Camp Fire's plan, then, by encouraging girls to help adult women access industry war jobs, filled a gap in defense preparation even as it kept girls out of industrial spaces.

Even though Camp Fire's efforts kept girls out of factories, militarized domesticity still took girls beyond the confines of the home. Girls took to the streets to gather consumer pledges from neighbors who promised to buy wisely and to conserve clothing and household items.[19] In addition,

Camp Fire recommended that girls not only plant victory gardens of their own but also work as farm aids and establish canning co-ops with the help of federal agencies like the Agricultural Extension Service and the Farm Security Administration.[20] The Colton, California, Camp Fire Girls were typical. The group gave conservation demonstrations to encourage rationing compliance, offered free sugarless cookie samples, and marketed their honey, syrup, and molasses-based recipes in the community.[21]

A Dallas group of thirteen- and fourteen-year-old Camp Fire Girls made childcare for the war effort their special project. They had wanted to do "something more than just buy war savings stamps," and as Camp Fire publicity noted, "They had intelligence and energy to invest in a real job." They brought in fourteen more girls and, in late 1943, with their leader's guidance, conducted a childcare course using an outline prepared by the national organization. They studied children aged two to six and collected games, pictures, and ideas. Then they began going two at a time to the Silverstein Day Care Center to work directly with children. "Soon each girl could take a group of eight or ten children and plan her own programs for a whole day and thus relieve the older women for other work." The girls worked one day per week all summer. Their work extended beyond childcare to refurbishing the nursery, mending toys, and sewing baby dresses. To get others interested in the work, the girls wore their blue and white pinafore-style uniforms with the service for victory shield on the left sleeves of their blouses to school each Monday. "With eighteen girls appearing in crisp pinafores," their leader explained, "you can imagine the conversation that went on, and other girls were aware that they were having a wonderful time." Lest outsiders fear that Camp Fire was all work, Camp Fire's publicity affirmed that companionship and fun, as well as commitment to serve, kept this Camp Fire group going.[22]

Camp Fire's traditional concern about girls' health also continued during the war and took on new national defense overtones. Group leaders who taught nutrition won public commendation for making "a real contribution to the present and future strength of the nation!"[23] Likewise, even though many camps closed during the war to preserve resources, organization leaders insisted that outdoor activities and those camps that remained open served the girls' mental and physical health needs and, therefore, the national defense. Camp represented a particular version of American childhood; health, youthful vigor, and the freedom of the outdoors signified American identity. They promised to "build morale and health" and were in line with the Youth Committee on Civilian Defense guidelines urging as many youngsters as possible to attend camps. Children needed to step "away from the strain and stress of world events" and strengthen their bodies for future service. Camp life itself remained largely unchanged by the war overseas. Woodcraft, fire building, exploring trails, overnights, star lore, and nature handicrafts prevailed.[24]

National Camp Fire officials used images that invoked girlhood to advertise the war effort and sell war bonds. *Camp Fire Girl* explained, "There's something about a Camp Fire Girl—in her red, white, and blue service costume, pigtails and grin—that makes the great American public dig deep into pockets and purses to buy that extra bond. She seems to signify what we're fighting for—and saving for."[25] Camp Fire Girl Rebecca G. Morris agreed, noting that she believed she and her friends "were walking posters of allegiance" in their "navy blue skirts topped by white blouses and red triangular neck scarves."[26] Indeed, pictures of innocent childhood and family life underscored how Americans perceived the war as a defense of the home and its traditional division of labor, and not just a war against fascism. Fathers were protectors, soldiers, and breadwinners. Women pitched in when needed. Girls and women were symbols of the way of life for which men and women volunteered and contributed.[27]

The image that Camp Fire promoted of the pigtailed girl was an emblem of white, pre-pubescent femininity. Although the organization would, by 1946, feature interracial photographs in its magazine, wartime representations privileged white, middle-class girlhood as the symbol of youthful innocence. Depictions of Camp Fire Girls busy at work for the Red Cross or the Salvation Army, and tending babies, showed white girls doing their patriotic duty for the war effort. They supported a noncontroversial image of girlhood worth fighting for.[28]

Such campaigns were effective. In 1944 Camp Fire's national council could boast that Camp Fire Girls' war bond sales of $2,340,000 purchased a fleet of 1,200 army ambulances. Such triumphs occurred through the grit of individual Camp Fire Girls. For example, two Trenton, New Jersey,

Camp Fire Girls "installed themselves" outside city hall, hitting up city commissioners and the mayor.[29] Roslindale, Massachusetts, girls helped sell nearly $20 in war stamps, attended a "War Bond" party at the YMCA, and marched in a United War Fund Parade despite bitterly cold weather.[30] Author Rebecca Morris, calling her group "ruthlessly patriotic," explained that her Ohio club scoured the neighborhood to collect scrap metal, aluminum, and rubber bands.[31] The assistance of women's groups did not hurt either. In Massachusetts, women's auxiliaries of the American Legion Post and Veterans of Foreign Wars opened booths for war bonds and stamp sales to assist Camp Fire in their goal of funding the ambulance fleet.[32]

Girls displayed pride in their accomplishments. A Boston area Camp Fire group recorded in its scrapbook that one of the group's first accomplishments was earning money for victory bonds by selling greeting cards. They had received a certificate signed by the national executive director of Camp Fire, Martha Allen, and presented the receipt for their bond to a council office delegate at their council fire.[33]

The Camp Fire Girls taught its members to identify with the democratic values associated with the war effort. Articles in the bulletin advised leaders of how best to connect citizenship honors to egalitarian goals. Commentaries directed leaders to address "the rights of others," teach "the democratic way of living," and allow girls to plan and make group decisions. While recognizing that a leader might sometimes need to assert authority, she was expected to encourage free expression of ideas and foster consensus.[34] Camp Fire urged leaders to broach lessons on inclusion and tolerance. Highlighting the special place of the next generation to usher in a prejudice-free era, Camp Fire Girl published girls' voices. One teenage Camp Fire Girl extolled the inclusive promise of America. Her grandparents had immigrated to the United States and found advantages such as "no class distinction," equal opportunity for the children of immigrants, and an open educational system. Her essay invoked aspirational American values to which Camp Fire increasingly turned attention during the war.[35]

As the war neared its end, Camp Fire officials argued that to sustain America's eventual victory, they needed to build an environment where peace could flourish. To do so, Camp Fire Girls would extend this framework of tolerance to learn about and connect with "foreign neighbors."[36]

An international outlook, which made some appearance during World War I as Camp Fire Girls paid tribute to American allies and sent gifts to suffering European families, became an integral part of the Camp Fire experience during the 1940s and grew in importance in the 1950s. Even as the Cold War intensified, Camp Fire imagined that through pen pals, folk dance, and sending gifts abroad, girls could promote tolerance and understanding between nations.

Incarcerated Japanese American Camp Fire Girls

In 1942 the U.S. government removed over 120,000 Japanese residents and American citizens to makeshift assembly centers and then to incarceration camps (so-called internment camps) in response to racist suspicions following Japan's attack on Pearl Harbor. More than three-fourths of the detained were under twenty-five and about a quarter were school children.[37]

The Camp Fire Girls worked upon request from the War Relocation Authority (WRA) to bring programming to the camps where girls with Japanese ancestry were held.[38] The WRA's aim was both to disrupt Japanese ethnic networks and to "encourage[e] evacuee identification with groups typically American in concept." These groups included the Camp Fire Girls, YWCA, YMCA, Boy Scouts of America, Girl Scouts of the USA, and the American Red Cross. The WRA policy also, knowingly or not, took advantage of an entrenched practice of girls' club organizing within Japanese American communities. Girls had already been participating in youth clubs that they created, and they joined the national affiliated ones.[39] In the Pacific Northwest, most Camp Fire groups were segregated along lines of ethnicity and religion. Christian congregations and some Buddhist temples in Japanese American communities had their own Camp Fire circles with Japanese American leaders and the aid of white women from local councils.[40]

Thus when the confinement of Japanese residents and Japanese American citizens began, Camp Fire was among an array of activities and groups that the WRA supported to "[carry] out the general aims of Americanization."[41] National Camp Fire director Martha Allen noted in 1942 that the Japanese American girls and leaders who had been Camp Fire Girls wished to continue the program during the detention. "Their continuous request for our program," Allen wrote, "stimulated the War Relocation Board to approach us." Camp Fire had already chartered several groups in the relocation centers; this formalized the link.[42]

White and Japanese American youth leaders hoped that they could help Japanese American girls assume as much normalcy as possible despite their detention, but their actions still made them complicit in the historic denial of freedom. As historian Yoosun Park asks, "What might have happened had social workers and social work organizations definitively opposed mass incarceration" rather than having "facilitate[d] the process?"[43] The reality was, however, that local Camp Fire executives tried "to help the girls carry on."[44] In Klamath Falls, Oregon, local Camp Fire leader and member of the Catholic Daughters of America Azita Kennedy, for example, helped establish a Camp Fire group at Tule Lake Relocation Center in the summer of 1942.[45] Women detainees who were familiar with the program stepped up to lead clubs, and Camp Fire prepared others to guide groups by sending the *Guardian* magazine with its tips and ideas and offering a correspondence course that leaders could enroll in from inside the barbed wire.[46]

In addition to pursuing the seven crafts, Camp Fire Girls in the camps engaged in an array of patriotic activities, such as war stamp drives, holiday parades, and studying democratic processes, which were internment camp staples.[47] Camp Fire Girls at Heart Mountain Relocation Center in Wyoming elected officers, hosted parties, and even hosted a roundtable with a boys' group with the title "Attitude toward Cooperation."[48] By 1944, as an increasing number of young people were being released to colleges and community work programs, the Camp Fire Girls, Girl Scouts, and Boy Scouts at Heart Mountain went camping near Yellowstone, outside the barbed wire. The *Topaz Times* explained to its readers that such adventures were "not for pleasure but part of the national training program." So intertwined were definitions of youth citizenship and service with camping and self-reliance that the community activities department permitted the trek and the WRA funded it.[49] At Granada Relocation Center, also known as Amache, in southern Colorado, too, youth organizations offered "opportunities to travel beyond the barbed wire."[50] No doubt these young people appreciated this opportunity to get away, but they must have

11. The Camp Fire Girls and Girl Scouts of the USA established clubs in the Japanese internment camps as a way to ameliorate girls' situations. Here members of both groups participate in memorial services for soldiers from Heart Mountain, Wyoming, who died in the war. The Camp Fire Girl is laying a wreath before the community gold star service flag. Henry Ushioka, Heart Mountain, Wyoming, December 8, 1944, War Relocation Authority Photographs of Japanese-American Evacuation and Resettlement, no. G-807A, Bancroft Library, University of California, Berkeley.

also experienced the other aspects of Camp Fire—lessons about service, tolerance, and democratic decision-making—with a degree of irony.[51]

Worship God

The values of wartime also led Camp Fire's leadership to turn greater attention to the spiritual values that the organization supported. At the time of its founding, Camp Fire's leaders avoided a religious statement in the Camp Fire Law. Despite founder Luther Gulick's background in a missionary family and Camp Fire's typically Protestant emphasis on usefulness, traditional Christian worship was not the organization's focus. Youth worker Ernest Thompson Seton and the Gulicks instead wove into Camp Fire a broad spiritual ethic symbolized (a "Great Mystery") by the campfire. It invoked the entire history of humankind and the original wonderment about human origins, which Seton regarded as "the first thought of true religion."[52] They had not abandoned Christianity. Instead, they found in Indian imagery a means to worship in a symbolically universal, nonsecular way.

The first Camp Fire guidebook also made no explicit mention of religious activities within churches or synagogues, but within two years Camp Fire began to offer honor beads for religious activities under the category of patriotism. Camp Fire connected religion and civic participation, a shift that was strengthened during and after the Second World War. Girls earned honors for activities such as teaching in or belonging to a church, tabernacle, or religious settlement; attending religious services; describing the lives and accomplishments of religious leaders or missionaries; and "commit[ting] to memory one hundred verses of the Bible or an equal amount of other sacred literature."[53] However, there was no pledge to worship god, and these honors were among numerous civic options.

In 1916 Camp Fire's board had rejected implementing a category of honors called religion and ethics. Although critics complained about a lack of cooperation with the organized religions, the board did not want to be in a position of needing to interpret church doctrine.[54] The manual printed in 1917 instead included a broad reassurance to mainstream religious groups: "Camp Fire needs the church, and the church finds in our organization a most attractive means by which its spirit can be brought into larger daily service. Camp Fire is religious in spirit and purpose." Although Camp Fire carefully separated itself from "responsibility for doctrinal instruction in religious life," it assured potential members that organization values prepared girls to receive instruction in and live out their spiritual values.[55]

At the same time, Camp Fire willingly affiliated with religious groups such as the YWCA, the Board of Sunday Schools of the Methodist Episcopal Church, and the Episcopal Church's Girls' Friendly Society. The Young Ladies' Mutual Improvement Association (YLMIA) of the Church of Jesus Christ of Latter-day Saints also adopted Camp Fire's awards and honors, though Mormon women fitted them to their purposes in what became the Bee Hive Girls.[56] Religious leaders believed that the Camp Fire program was consistent with and helped promote girls' interest in religion. A joint pamphlet put out by Camp Fire and the Episcopal Girls' Friendly Society explained, "These activities are often just the same as those already in use in the G. F. S., but the Camp Fire symbolism and system in many cases give them special appeal."[57] As a result, a growing number of churches adopted the Camp Fire Girl program in the interwar period.

Camp Fire was less popular with the Catholic Church, though many local Catholic groups did emerge. Catholics regularly supported establishing Girl Scout troops because that organization required girls to make a clear statement of devotion to God, and some accused Camp Fire of harboring "a worship of nature rather than a reverence for God." The Girl Scouts had cooperated since the 1920s with local Catholic officials and with the National Catholic Youth Organizations Federation since its founding in the 1930s. The executive committee of Camp Fire, lacking this firm relationship with the Catholic church, reported that negative publicity caused problems for Camp Fire in several locales.[58] Lester Scott noted that during the 1930s, in some places (as we saw in Culion, Philippines), local Catholic churches kept Camp Fire from girls.[59]

Thus although Camp Fire leaders viewed the organization as promoting spiritual development, they separated its educational commitments from those of churches and synagogues until World War II. The persistence of Catholic criticism and, more importantly, the fusion of patriotism and worship during and after the war led to a shift. Liberal progressives disassociated themselves from ungodly fascists and communists through religious devotion, and Camp Fire leaders merged religion with patriotism. In this context, Camp Fire made explicit its religious position and connected the "alignment of good Americanism" with membership in one of the dominant Judeo-Christian faiths. The so-called tri-faith commitment rested on American assumptions that democracy could not survive without a deeply felt religious faith, especially one premised on individual human dignity.[60]

Thus in the 1940s the organization turned greater attention to religious worship as a marker of citizenship. Prefiguring by more than a decade the addition of "under God" to the Pledge of Allegiance, which President Dwight Eisenhower suggested to Congress in 1954 to set the United States apart from the communist threat, Camp Fire's national council rewrote the Camp Fire Law in 1942 to begin with "worship God." Future Camp Fire Girls would worship God before they sought beauty, gave service, pursued knowledge, held onto health, glorified work, or were happy. The organization asserted an ongoing commitment to nonsectarian ideals, but it increasingly sought the approval and involvement of three major religious groups: Protestants, Catholics, and Jews. Although Camp Fire's board championed tolerance toward diverse forms of religious worship and encouraged girls to participate in the churches or synagogues that were consistent with their family backgrounds, the organization now promoted a narrow definition of spiritual experience. It focused on recognized mainstream religious structures, marginalized atheist families, and thoroughly entwined civic participation with organized religious experience.[61]

Its tri-faith commitment followed a trend in American life. As a commentator on American religious life, Will Herberg, would soon note, Americans practiced a "civic religion" wherein religious identification as a Protestant, Catholic, or Jew was itself a way of belonging in American culture or subscribing to core values. Separate beliefs within the overarching principle of Judeo-Christian faith affiliation gave ethnically diverse Americans "an identifiable place in American life." Herberg argued that broad religiosity mattered more than daily practices or doctrine, an inclination that may have made it easier for Americans to accept the connection of a secular organization like Camp Fire to their places of worship. Indeed, Herberg's America was reflected in Camp Fire's own statistics. He found that 95 percent of Americans professed a belief in God, that 68 percent identified as Protestant, 23 percent as Catholic, and 4 percent as Jewish. Of those, about 68 percent regularly attended church or synagogue.[62] Camp Fire's constituency skewed more heavily Protestant. In a 1946 study of a cross-section of American Camp Fire groups, Camp Fire found that approximately 79 percent of its members were Protestant, 13 percent Catholic, less than 1 percent were Jewish, and the remaining were either other or not known.[63] By embracing the three major religions, Camp Fire signaled a consensus that religious diversity should be tolerated. At the same time, Americans scorned a lack of religious affiliation, and the exclusion of Buddhists, Muslims, Hindus, Sikhs, and others from public representation suggested that these adherents, even when native-born, were foreign.[64]

The first step Camp Fire took to make its spiritual values visible came in 1941 in response to the growing power of Catholics and to the demands of American pluralism. The national council added a preamble to the Camp

Fire Law, which girls would recite when they joined the organization. Mirroring the Girl Scout and Boy Scout oath, Camp Fire Girls would say, "It is my desire to become a Camp Fire Girl, to serve God and my country, and to follow the law of Camp Fire."[65]

Although most council members voted to add the preamble, the move was not without controversy. Several council members noted that the addition might undermine Camp Fire's inclusion policy. Camp Fire's national president, Karla V. Parker, expressed concern that such an oath's focus on "my country" might exclude immigrants and that it might even be a way for nonnaturalized girls to pledge loyalty to a foreign nation. Parker asked what nonnaturalized immigrant girls might say and mean when they said "my country." Gertrude Pettijohn Frary of New York expressed her concern that a religious statement would deter girls from nonreligious families from ever joining. Not only would such girls be deprived of Camp Fire ideals, but they would not be exposed to the spiritual aspects already within Camp Fire. Several council members underscored the importance of the separation of church and civic institutions. Despite such critiques and the group's secular origins, the amendment passed as council representatives asserted their belief that spiritual values already ran through Camp Fire and that the preamble simply articulated this to outsiders.[66]

Camp Fire's shift also responded to the growing power of Catholics in America. Council representatives hoped that Catholics and other critics would endorse Camp Fire, but the preamble was not enough for these critics. One council member noted that the preamble was a way to reach "a great area outside our present constituency that is not satisfied at present."[67] Despite the addition of the preamble, the youth division of the National Catholic Welfare Conference (NCWC) was among those dissatisfied. Director Lester Scott had met with its assistant director, Father Paul Tanner. He indicated that the preamble was an improvement, but believed Camp Fire would be "more readily acceptable to the Catholic Church" only when "a phrase mentioning the name of God were incorporated into the law itself."[68] Camp Fire's board of directors had hoped that formal backing from the NCWC would increase membership among Catholics. The organization was, after all, competing against the Girl Scouts, which had received formal approval of their program in 1941.

Scott reported to the national council that only a "forthright" move, such as adding "worship God" to the law itself, would end conjecture about nature worship in Camp Fire and bring Catholic support. The national council, therefore, debated the separation of church and civic agency again in 1942 as members considered adding a line to the Camp Fire Law. An emotional debate followed. Most believed that worshiping God was already a sincere, unstated part of the Camp Fire experience. They had no objection to the addition. Some feared that the Catholic groups would continue to discriminate against Camp Fire despite the change. Leaders in the Boston area council voiced again the concern that the change would hinder diversity. They also declared that while they all desired to worship God, "they believed no freedom to worship him would exist unless the freedom not to worship him was implied." The amendment's advocates, however, like national vice president of the Camp Fire Girls and long-time member of the board of directors Dr. Joseph Raycroft, successfully silenced the opponents when he called the disagreement an "emotional reaction" and asserted that all council members philosophically backed the change. The amendment passed with the support of about three-fourths of the local councils.[69]

Reception of the change among the membership and the public was chiefly positive. For example, Margaret Lee Runbeck, a Camp Fire Girl in the 1910s, was pleased that "worship God" had been moved to the top of the Camp Fire Law.[70] A local leader in San Bernardino pointed approvingly to the law as evidence of the organization's inclusivity despite how it left out those who did not worship. "It is with good reason that the Camp Fire Law begins with 'Worship God,'" she declared. "All races and religions are embraced by this group and our members learn to respect the rights of those holding different beliefs, while exercising their own freedom of worship."[71] Guardian associations discussed the importance of the new line, and the addition was also discussed in church sermons and became the theme of special vesper services.[72] In wartime America, local newspapers and local council bulletins echoed the new emphasis on religion and the revised law. Local events such as the Winneconne, Wisconsin, council's "Go-to-your-own-church day" were increasingly popular. The council believed that the experience gave "appreciative expression of the

12. Camp Fire leader and her family, along with other Camp Fire Girls from East Baton Rouge, Louisiana, attending church in uniform. During and after World War II, when worship in Catholic, Protestant, and Jewish congregations became a marker of citizenship, girls earned citizenship honors for their participation. Courtesy of the East Baton Rouge Parish Library.

fact that in America the people are free to worship God as they wish and can attend church services of their selection."[73] Catholic Blue Birds in Oceanside, California, all attended communion together at Saint Mary's Star of the Sea Church as Camp Fire girls and women merged their faith and civic participation.[74]

The Camp Fire Girls continued to solidify religious collaborations. By 1944 Camp Fire sought membership in the United Christian Youth Movement and the Committee on Religious Education of Youth for the International Council of Religious Education (ICRE), important Protestant conferences. The organization followed Father Tanner's advice to revise its pamphlet "Camp Fire and the Church" to include advice from religious leaders who worked with Camp Fire in their communities. It also began separate brochures for Protestant, Catholic, and Jewish groups.[75] The national board of directors appointed a Religious Policies Committee in

1948, made up of current board members, ministers, priests, and rabbis, to implement religious programming. In choosing the personnel of the committee, Camp Fire's president sought the advice and guidance of such national religious bodies as the ICRE, the NCWC's youth division, the Synagogue Council of America, the American Association for Jewish Education, and the National Jewish Welfare Board. Its purpose was to ensure that as "spiritual concepts" were made to "permeate the whole program," the organization did so in sound and sensitive ways.[76] The committee would "study and improve existing relationships and methods of work with the three major faiths and . . . develop and establish basic policies for guidance of the national staff and local councils. The committee would also advise on program materials to keep them sound from a religious standpoint." One result was more inclusive practice. According to the new national director, Martha Allen, Camp Fire needed to revise the book on ceremonials as there was "nothing suitable for Jewish girls," who might object to oaths and rituals outside the synagogue. Allen hoped that the committee's "proper guidance" would prevent local councils from dealing with religious concerns in ad hoc and harmful ways.[77]

Its report led the national council to adopt an official statement urging councils to be sensitive to differences in religious observance when planning spiritual observances at camps, developing menus for public functions, and scheduling places and times for citywide events.[78] It formulated ways that each religious group could incorporate its practices into ceremonies. Protestant girls might include a minister's invocation or the singing of hymns. Catholic girls might "include . . . a devotion to the Blessed Virgin Mary." And Jewish Girls might mark Jewish holidays by holding council fires.[79]

A major outcome of the religious policy committee's work was the publication of three pamphlets promoting Camp Fire's development among religious institutions and explaining to group leaders how to integrate faith practices into the club. Each of the three pamphlets, first published in the early 1950s, begins with a statement titled "The Importance of Religious and Spiritual Values in the Camp Fire Program." Following a note on the diverse composition of the Religious Policies Committee and the general membership, the pamphlets state, "The National Council of Camp Fire Girls believes that spiritual development is essential to a healthy, wholesome

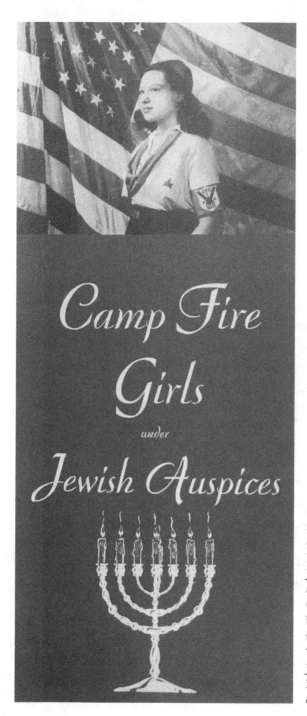

Camp Fire
Girls
under
Jewish Auspices

13. Attention to religious faith and to a (limited) diversity among members—Protestant, Catholic, and Jewish—increased during and after World War II. Camp Fire printed separate brochures for each faith tradition. Camp Fire Girls, "Camp Fire Girls under Jewish Auspices," ca. 1950. Reprinted with permission of Camp Fire.

personality and recognizes the importance of the church and synagogue and of religious experience and teachings in the life of a girl." They explained how each aspect of the Camp Fire program taught "ethical living" and "an appreciation for God's world." Next the pamphlets asserted Camp Fire's promotion of "the right to freedom of worship," not merely by respecting "the right of every girl to practice her own religion" but by encouraging "her active participation in her church or synagogue."[80]

Next, the pamphlets addressed the girls of the three major faiths separately but with a unifying message about gender roles. Aside from the religious terms used to identify the groups and whether they worshiped at church or temple, the essential religious values were portrayed as the same. The committee sought to highlight the common ways that religious belief supported the American way of life. Learning "the qualities of gentleness, kindness and high ideals" and acquiring "interests and experiences needed in building a home that is wholesome, happy, efficiently managed" supported "Christian virtues" suited to Protestant and Catholic girls. Although the pamphlets for Jews did not promote "Christian virtues," Camp Fire repeated that, in Judaism, "homemaking is one of woman's major responsibilities." Therefore, Jewish girls would also "acquire those interests and experiences needed in building a home that is wholesome, happy, [and] efficiently managed."[81] Despite the recognition of three distinct faith traditions, Camp Fire's religious pamphlets, in effect, sponsored one model of American girlhood across faiths.

In addition, the national council granted religious groups the right to organize girls under their own leadership and gave them power over their use of the program. Not all Camp Fire officials supported the policies that gave religious institutions more independence. As Hattie Smith of the Boston council argued, the policy would lead to greater segregation among Camp Fire groups as the tradition of joining through separate institutions would intensify. Indeed, religious groups would make their own determination as to whether girls of different faiths would be admitted to their clubs. Moreover, churches and synagogues could compel the Camp Fire Girls in their flock to join through the church or synagogue rather than through a neighborhood or school group.[82] Although opportunities to learn about religious groups outside one's background existed, as when several fifth grade non-Jewish Camp Fire groups visited Temple Bethel in San Bernardino, California, for a tour and discussion of Jewish beliefs with the rabbi, the basic structure discouraged girls from forming deep cross-faith friendships.[83] Allen maintained, however, that religious groups needed to have greater latitude to supervise the programs under their auspices, lest they split from or avoid Camp Fire entirely. The Latter-day Saints' YLMIA, she pointed out, had started its Bee Hive Girls via an early collaboration with Luther Gulick. Allen contended that the Mormon girls would have been Camp Fire Girls—and that Camp Fire would have had a relationship similar to that between the Boy Scouts and the Latter-day Saints—had the Church not been "denied the privilege of organizing Camp Fire groups under its own auspice." Instead, the YLMIA had selected a different name and altered the program; Allen called it Camp Fire "distorted over the years." She hoped that by offering religious institutions more control, Camp Fire could stay in closer connection to them and exert more sway over their programming for girls.[84] Camp Fire could draw new members by allowing religious institutions to adopt the program. This opinion winning the day, Camp Fire's marketing urged churches accordingly to adopt it for their youth programs.[85]

As Camp Fire sought new members by collaborating with the three faiths, its framework for articulating religious obligations through civics and service continued. Camp Fire continued to include the religious honor activities in the citizenship and patriotism sections of the manual. Across the faiths, Camp Fire recommended similar civic-religious activities: participating in religious services, learning about religious beliefs, and volunteering in church work.[86] Although the Camp Fire Girls remained predominantly Protestant, Catholic and Jewish girls now saw their institutions valued and reflected.

Beginning in the 1940s and accelerating under Allen's direction in the 1950s, Camp Fire solidified its relationships with various religious communities. In the minds of most Camp Fire officials, this could be done by emphasizing the freedom *to* worship, and welcoming girls from the three major religious groups in the United States furthered inclusive policies by affirming diverse faiths. Camp Fire lauded the work of its religious policies committee for bringing about "greater sensitivity on the part of Camp Fire

Girls and their leaders to the religious observances of those of differing beliefs" and for providing religious leaders with unambiguous, accurate information about "the spiritual and ethical values of the Camp Fire Girls program."[87] Although Camp Fire promoted greater interest in the three major religious groups, girls affiliating with religions outside the mainstream would not have seen their faith and beliefs represented. The freedom not to worship and the principle of separating church and state—or, here, religion and civics—were discounted. Although a few women on the national council had raised these concerns, those who favored the majority position of associating citizenship with mainstream religious worship drowned out alternatives. "Worship God" was inclusive enough to include Catholicism and Judaism as mainstream, but it left little room for others.

As World War II neared its end, Camp Fire began to emphasize how its victory projects could be carried out in the name of peace.[88] The war against fascism had awakened a mainstream conversation about challenging prejudice. Girls had taken on new roles during wartime. If they had fallen back on a familiarly gendered division of labor to do so, the war indelibly altered American gender roles as well, and in the postwar period Camp Fire Girls would renegotiate them. Fighting prejudice at home was also important, and Camp Fire enlarged its commitment to combat racism. Dorothy Scully, the managing editor at Camp Fire's national magazine, explained the ways that the war had also increased the need for Camp Fire, and Americans generally, to improve "mutual understanding and respect" among diverse Americans. World War II, she said, was a "re-purchasing" of "the ideals of liberty and justice." In this context, the time was ripe for leaders to call on girls "to understand and appreciate their neighbors, of whatever color, creed, or national origin" for a stronger, more unified nation. In particular, she urged social organizations such as Camp Fire to "introduce a needed leaven of reasoned understanding, tolerance and appreciation for the contributions of some less socially-favored groups" in communities where racial prejudice seemed high.[89]

6

Being a "Homemaker—Plus"

Gender and the Spiritual Values of the Home

In March of 1945, as Allied victory in Europe seemed certain, Camp Fire officials redirected the program toward peacetime concerns and to meeting the "profound changes in [girls'] personal and social lives in the postwar world."[1] Camp Fire's new woman executive director, Martha Allen, soon cautioned that what "civilization" needed most was "attitudes and skills which nurture rather than . . . those which destroy." This was women's domain, and Camp Fire would inculcate it. Vaguely echoing the founders, she maintained, "Woman by virtue of motherhood and her long experience and training in nurture of the race has on the whole developed greater capacity for compassion and greater skill in human relationships than has man."[2] Camp Fire's national magazine, therefore, declared that even at the launch of the atomic age, "homemaking remains one of women's major responsibilities." Despite its recognition that increasing numbers of women were entering the professions, Camp Fire insisted, "The majority of girls prefer a home and children to any other career." The organization's leadership pledged to continue to develop girls' "skill in home management." Recognizing, however, that the war had brought girls and women into greater participation in democratic life, the leadership also promised to "help girls to develop a greater capacity for sympathy, forbearance, tolerance, [and] understanding," qualities it deemed necessary in a tense world.[3]

Although the politics of World War II turned greater attention to how Americans defined democracy and inclusion, the discourse around universal girlhood changed little. The founders' legacy was flexible in the hands of Camp Fire's national leaders, who turned opportunities to revise the founding mission for a new generation into a recommitment to distinct gender roles. Girls' citizen roles continued to revolve around their useful service through nurture, giving, and care. Camp Fire's leadership continued to find the founders' use of traditional roles to justify women's public participation practical as they argued that girls' and women's influence was much needed in the stressful times of the Cold War; the Gulicks' essential feminism still held sway at midcentury.

The immediate post–World War II period is not renowned for feminism. As historian Elaine Tyler May demonstrates, white, middle-class American families, in search of security amid the dual threats of atomic war and the global spread of communism, turned homeward, reinventing separate spheres ideology for the twentieth century in an attempt to contain the anxieties of the Cold War age. To tame "potentially dangerous social forces" such as rising divorce rates, working mothers, sexual precocity among teens, and juvenile delinquency, American "public policy, personal behavior, and even political values were focused on the home."[4] Cold War discourses normalized and affirmed the nuclear family predicated on heterosexual marriage and male authority. "The inward-tending domestic front of the cold war taught good white girls to practice 'containment on the homefront' by fending off their boyfriends' advances, and the family kitchen was utilized by Richard Nixon as a 'weapon' against the Russians in proving American superiority," writes historian Whitney Strub.[5]

Yet the Victorian separate spheres that elevated motherhood and gloried in mothers' moral sway had lost currency. By the 1940s, a growing antimaternalism infected American culture, signaled by works like Philip Wylie's *Generation of Vipers*. The mom, a white, middle-class woman of middle age, no longer garnered respect and influence by virtue of having given birth and having raised children. The mothers of America sensed that the basis of their social value was slipping even as the Cold War discourse instructed them to invest in it.[6] Given this contradiction, Camp Fire's leadership studied the founding ideals for a means to honor women's traditional roles while embracing each girl as an individual. Members of the board and council incorporated greater liberal individualism but refused to diminish the central role of the home in girls' education.

The Camp Fire Girls' national leadership reflected the contradictions that characterized American women's lives in the 1950s, paving the way for the women's liberation movement in the late 1960s and 1970s. Women's magazines offered inconsistent messages, portraying women as homemakers while presenting a cornucopia of career and volunteer choices beyond the home. Wage-earning women were on the increase, and they shaped labor unions and the peace and civil rights movement in the 1950s. Active also in civil defense brigades, PTA, and more, their activities continued to find justification through the maternalist arguments that formulated women's civic participation as an extension of their feminine roles. The girls who were asked to buy into a feminine mystique that saw motherhood and domesticity as women's surest path to fulfillment also shaped their lives anew by attending college, working in greater numbers, and searching for personal enrichment. Many adult women raised their daughters for broader roles, and many who were homemakers when their children were young opted for new life paths once their children grew.[7]

Even as Camp Fire stressed tradition and promised to raise girls "to become mentally and physically healthy and capable homemakers," it introduced a range of possibilities. Homemaking itself was increasingly portrayed as a career demanding "unique capacities and skillful preparation." Camp Fire, however, also cautioned that, with approximately three hundred thousand American lives lost during the war, many girls would not find husbands or that they might marry injured veterans and need to be the primary or secondary breadwinners. Thus Camp Fire took seriously its responsibility to help girls understand "the dignity of work" and how "the community can be a woman's home." In addition to assuring girls that civic participation was appropriate for girls and women, girls learned that jobs outside the home would not threaten their "peculiar" feminine character. She would find outlets for her feminine skills. The organization enlightened girls to various vocational options and the requirements needed to find jobs in appropriate fields.[8]

For their part, girls' postwar Camp Fire experience was a mix of broader horizons and messages about feminine gender choices. Girls still enjoyed camping and outdoor picnics, which remained a centerpiece of programming. So too did service projects, which brought girls into their communities and even into the international sphere as they sent care packages abroad and wrote to pen pals. Weekly club meetings included these activities, planning Red Cross projects, rehearsing entertainments, and learning how to run a meeting by electing officers and planning events. They continued to integrate the Indian imagery as a historic part of Camp Fire, choosing names and producing beadwork. One Camp Fire Girl recalled that this element differentiated Camp Fire from Girl Scouts and made it feel like the more outdoorsy of the programs, even though much of what she did was oriented toward the home. Baby care classes and "charm" lessons made regular appearances at girls' meetings. Camp Fire's oldest girls spent extra time thinking about their futures, planning the homes they hoped to have someday, learning about marriage, and pondering college as they planned collegiate wardrobes. Friendships sustained their commitments to the program as the girls they knew through their clubs were often the ones with whom they went to birthday parties, met for "Nancy Drew book clubs," and watched American Bandstand on television.[9]

Restating the Founders' Plan

The Camp Fire Girls was under new and, for the first time, female leadership in the postwar period. Martha F. Allen, national director from 1943 to 1966, took over the top post from Lester F. Scott after serving two years as his assistant. Allen's perspectives on women's roles embodied the cultural contradictions long evident in Camp Fire's philosophy and in postwar America. Allen, a single, professional woman who understood independent women's struggles, offered particularly candid, clear-sighted observations on gender discrimination. Nonetheless, her writing and direction expose her easy acceptance of the biological essentialism of Camp Fire's founders.

Martha Allen was born in Cherokee, Alabama, in 1906 and grew up in the small Mississippi town of Iuka near her large extended family. She was the only daughter and the youngest of three children. As a child, Martha faced divergent expectations. By her own account, her mother "assumed without question" that she would marry, while her father assumed that she "would do something else." She only learned to cook as an adult, having been raised in a well-to-do home with a cook. Her father, who owned a gravel company, paid her to work in his office during the summertime. She "kept time sheets for employees and fashioned myself a business executive." While she enjoyed business, she thought of becoming a missionary to help people, an idea her aunt, a Sunday school teacher, suggested to her. Although a belief that spirituality was essential to youth development influenced her career, she settled on social rather than religious work. Allen graduated from Mississippi State College for Women in 1928 and earned her master's degree in Latin at Columbia. She taught English and Latin in Mississippi public schools and at All Saints College for five years before working for the Board of Public Welfare of the District of Columbia in the 1930s. Soon after that, she worked for the Federal Resettlement Administration and the Farm Security Administration in the United States Department of Agriculture, where she worked on housing, public health, and community home management projects, including handicrafts programs. In Cincinnati, she worked with the daughter of Camp Fire's president on a woodcraft and weaving class for low-income tenants. Through this connection, her name came to the attention of the board of directors, who were awaiting Scott's retirement. Reversing forty years of male leadership, the board specifically sought a woman for his replacement.[10]

Allen's early interests in business and social work came together in directing Camp Fire. Personally, she believed that she had "rather inadequate preparation" for the job she filled, and that observation helped shape her priorities for girls. She had trained to be a teacher in part because there were few opportunities for girls to experiment with potential careers. Thus of especial interest to Allen was helping "girls find out what they can do most happily and effectively and to give them some opportunities to sample a variety of things so that their ambitions can be based on real understanding of themselves rather than on fancy, daydreams and other people's ambitions." As useful in this regard she cited the range of activities in Camp Fire's seven crafts and the Torch Bearer specializations for older girls. These ranged beyond homemaking to social leadership, business, health, and music. Allen, however, worried that too few girls became Torch Bearers and that the organization was not adequately reaching girls on this point.[11] What she viewed as contemporary American women's uncritical acceptance of domestic restraints troubled her. The trend among girls "to get a husband at the earliest age possible," she believed, obstructed women's education and robbed the nation of the ability to solve social problems intelligently.[12]

Along these lines, Allen regularly qualified her praise for domesticity. In 1954 she assured girls and leaders, "We do not wish to overemphasize homemaking as the only satisfying career, thereby creating a sense of failure in those who do not achieve it." Rather, the decisive factor was whether a woman "accepts herself as a woman and . . . has developed her mind and talents." She assured *Camp Fire Girl* readers, "Deep satisfactions are to be found in any career," and "those qualities which she might have used for the benefit of a family of her own can be used for a wider circle."[13] Certainly, this description suited Allen's career.

Still, she led Camp Fire in its look backward to the founders, echoing their rejection of both "the clarion call of the feminist" who misdirected girls away from the home and the conservative "overly sentimental lullabies about home and family life."[14] She characterized the founders' views as a satisfying compromise between feminism and conservatism. Despite her background and interest in creating opportunities for girls, Allen placed homemaking at Camp Fire's center. She differentiated the Camp Fire Girls from the Girl Scouts, saying, "Our program is different. Throughout our history we have had a definite and unchanging conviction that home making is a CAREER and that woman's talents in this capacity should also be used for community betterment, that the welfare of children everywhere should be one of her concerns."[15] Allen portrayed the founders' maternalist vision as one that continued to offer postwar girls and women a pathway to their pursuit of fulfillment. Generations of studies by "men particularly," Allen complained, had portrayed women as either inferior or superior, leaving women "dissatisfied with [their] lot and confused about how to change it." Allen believed that the founders had answers. They had lived through a time of rapid change "as woman began to play her new and freer role," and had resolved "that woman's maternal feelings should be brought to bear on the problems of humanity as well as on those of her own family."[16] Like the Gulicks before her, Allen found in maternalism a logic that elevated traditional feminine roles and extended them to the public arena.

Despite the Camp Fire Law's injunction to "be happy," the girl's own pursuit of fulfillment, if it did not stem from homemaking, figured little in

Camp Fire's postwar pronouncements. Only in 1963 did Allen specifically use the term "fulfillment," and when she did, she said that girls needed to learn to balance it with "society's need of her in the reproduction and preservation of the race." The women who were "at peace with themselves as women and as human beings," she insisted, "harmonized these two demands." Camp Fire did not advise girls how to achieve this balance within the patriarchal social structure.[17] Rather, leaders held "Homemaker—Plus" roundtables, where women in the community spoke to girls about their interests beyond homemaking. Vocations were introduced as a way to be well-rounded. With homemaking clearly at the center, girls were free to add other interests.[18]

Perhaps Allen saw homemaking as a way to save girls from the anguish of struggling for success on an unequal playing field. She wrote, "Any woman who pursues a career outside the home whether she be married or single will encounter discrimination." She did not, however, counsel confronting discrimination or the laws and customs that allowed it, but urged women not to become resentful: "If she allows herself to be embittered by this and if she concentrates on beating men rather than getting the best out of herself, she will become hard and highly competitive and while she may become expert in her chosen field, she will be damaged as a human being."[19] Thus, despite Allen's recognition of constraints facing girls, she framed confrontation and competition as antithetical to women's nature, leaving few ways out of the bind she described.

Camp Fire Debates Its Objectives

Indicative of these contradictions, between 1952 and 1955, under Allen's lead, Camp Fire's national staff, local councils, and national council worked to revise the statement of objectives outlined in the 1914 articles of incorporation. Three years of debate over various drafts reveal how white, middle-class women, who predominated as delegates at local and national Camp Fire council meetings, perceived women's roles and girls' training for them. National leaders like Allen were willing to adopt language that recognized girls' employment and education opportunities. Other leaders, especially at the local level, sought to resuscitate a glorified version of motherhood and homemaking. Their pushback resulted in debate over language and ultimately a statement that bound girls to home and family. Targeted for change were several original objectives now deemed outdated. For example, Camp Fire's "endeavor to devise and put in use ways of measuring and creating standards of woman's work" and attempt to "understand . . . the newer economic relationships into which women are coming" were dropped on the exaggerated grounds that women had already moved into the workforce and nearly all fields. Leaders now believed that the aim of fostering "intimate relations between mothers and daughters" was too narrow and they replaced it with one that valued the relationship between fathers and daughters equally. Camp Fire would, therefore, help "to perpetuate the spiritual ideals of the home and to strengthen the ties within the family" rather than only with mothers.[20] Meanwhile, the emphasis on spiritual values further cemented Judeo-Christian faith in Camp Fire's programming.

The earliest drafts included assertions of female "initiative" and "self-reliance" as well as a commitment to citizen duties beyond the home. Specifically, girls would continue to improve American democracy through women's historic "contribution . . . in the field of human relations." However, the final statement, after three years, several drafts, and local councils' assertions that the spiritual values of the home be front and center, reaffirmed gender distinction and girls' connection to nurture rather than her individuality. In particular, Camp Fire's new statement pledged to "encourage in every girl: the application of her religious, spiritual, and ethical teachings to her daily living; a love of home and family that grows as she grows; [and] pride in woman's traditional qualities—tenderness, affection, and skill in human relationships." National service via "deep love of her country, the practice of democracy, [and] readiness to serve" were also maintained along with emphasis on friendship and belonging, camping and outdoor activities, and finding "beauty, romance, and adventure in the common things of daily life."[21]

Over two years, women and men on local council boards considered draft proposals. Many criticized the suggestions for lacking emphasis on girls' and women's unique citizen contributions. They brought their ideas to debate at the two annual national council meetings, including a three-hour session in Omaha in 1953 and another in Kansas City in 1954. The national president of Camp Fire, Martha D. Hunter, then near sixty years old, opened the 1954 meeting with a conservative position. She asserted, "In spite of woman's emancipation into other careers . . . her true role in life will be that of wife and mother. This, more than anything, will bring her satisfaction and joy."[22] One national council delegate expressed her similar concern that American women did not appreciate themselves as women; she wanted a stronger statement about the "dignity of woman-hood" to encourage Camp Fire Girls to value traditional women's roles. Others called for an assertion that Camp Fire would "perpetuate the ideals of the home." They contended that the phrase "contributions of women" was worded too "loosely" and wished to narrow it to "the particular con-tribution of women to the home and community."[23]

The final statement was personal and individual. The onus was on the Camp Fire Girl personally developing "pride in woman's traditional quali-ties," her "tenderness, affection, and skill in human relationships." The early draft's call for societal attitudes regarding women's work to change—a demand Luther Gulick's essential feminism had also made—disappeared from the final version. The final statement also dropped terms like "self-reliant," which the interim draft had included, for its association with mas-culine individualism. "Ability to take care of herself," which still suggested responsibility but seemed a toned-down version of adult independence, replaced them. Similarly, "[developing] individual interests" became "inter-ests and hobbies she can do with others, and alone," stressing the need for girls to develop their interests in relation to what others would like to do.[24] After three years of negotiations over the meaning of Camp Fire, the national council voted unanimously to approve the new statement.[25] It incorporated changes, but the founders' gender ideology still prevailed. The new objectives looked backward and attempted to restore a vanishing concept of the home as the source of women's identity.

Girls' Responses to the "Homemaker—Plus" Campaign

Camp Fire's focus on the home as the center of women's orientation reflected how domestic values were accorded importance during the anxious Cold War years of the mid-1950s. For their part, girls tried to navigate new roles within the narrow definition of womanhood that adult leaders offered. Some enjoyed the domestic focus, while others joined the organization for outdoor activities and to be with friends.

Camp Fire staff understood that girls were grappling with questions about how to fulfill themselves and use their talents. *Camp Fire Girl* author Beatrice How recognized that "very often a girl is dissatisfied with her role as a woman." Rather than work for social change, How believed the Camp Fire leader's job included "help[ing] girls find satisfaction in being women and doing women's jobs." She doubled-down: "Boys and girls are not the same in everything." Noting that many "partnership ventures" require a division of labor, How wanted girls to accept that "family life is one of these" and that girls would take the domestic part.[26] The Camp Fire Girls, then, continued to offer the idea that tedious domestic tasks could be elevated through the elective honor program. Recalling Luther Gulick, a regional director wrote that beads "served to dignify" the work and play of the Camp Fire group. Girls, she said, did not find "much fun, doing the dishes at home alone the first month, but the flame colored beads received at the ceremonial brought a sense of unseen companions—the other group members at similar tasks—to the hitherto lonely job of dish washing."[27]

Even as Camp Fire's national staff insisted that "the majority of women will find their happiest career in 'being a homemaker—plus,'" Camp Fire's public statements suggested that girls were challenging the message of domesticity. Programming department staffer Eleanore Korman, who stepped down from her position, as she said, to spend more time homemaking, noted with dismay that "running a house, even with modern equipment, seems a dull life" for many teenage girls. Her solution was to make the world of homemaking seem more appealing to girls. "Our girls need to increase their understanding of the word 'homemaker' in order to accept positively their future careers," she wrote. "'Homemaker' can include the world, and a little more, if we only let it." Although Korman included broad tasks like fostering international understanding, most of her examples significantly narrowed "the world." Korman noted, "We sometimes read in the newspapers about a woman who attends college with her children, or even with her grandchildren. These women often use many ingenious ways to fit their studies into their schedules as homemakers. Sometimes they are preparing themselves for careers upon which they will embark when their children are grown." Although Korman admired such women, her own take on "homemaker—plus" put her public and career ambitions aside during the years she had children at home. (No such sidelining was asked of Boy Scouts.) Although Korman remarked that some women succeeded with both a career and a family, she advised leaders, "Your girls will want to know what preparations they can make today for the eventuality of their continuing work after raising a family."[28]

For the career-oriented, Camp Fire's magazine introduced vocational training in ways that entrenched stereotypes about women's career interests. In 1950, tucked in among articles devoted to quilting and rock gardens, was an article on job awareness for the girl who would not go to college, would "probably marry young," and who desired work for a few years in respectable employment. The author, Clara Lambert of Camp Fire's program department, suggested factory jobs for such young women. Of their benefits, she wrote, "A girl interested in clothes and people ... [could] find satisfaction in working where dresses are being made." Moreover, like Camp Fire, unions carried on educational programs and summer camps, enabling girls to "get as much out of life as possible." Nurseries and flower shops were recommended for those who liked gardening. Domestically inclined girls with administrative ability could go to work in hotels and inns. Hospital trainee, telephone operator, salesgirl, receptionist, printer, stenographer, typist, bookkeeper, and caterer filled out the list of recommendations. More entrepreneurial girls might follow their talents and open a small business. For example, girls who enjoyed fashion might learn to design and manufacture children's clothes, and a girl who "loved to fuss with her hair" might take a beauty course and manage her own shop.[29] With its career suggestions, Camp Fire presented the contradictions of 1950s American womanhood. Girls were encouraged to imagine themselves as workers, but only for a limited time and in segregated female jobs.

Girls' responses to the focus on domesticity varied. Homemaker and Citizenship were the most popular specializations for older girls earning their Torch Bearer rank, Camp Fire's highest level.[30] An Oakdale, California, Camp Fire Girl enjoyed working for beads across the categories, noting, "I loved checking off what I'd done in my little book and turning it in to the leader to sign off and ordering the beads and just feeling that sense of accomplishment." There was an unstated competition among girls in the group to see who could earn the most beads.[31] Clearly, many girls appreciated the homemaking aspect of the program. In Scottsbluff, Nebraska, one girl dressed as a homemaker at the group's future careers workshop.[32] Some girls combined homemaking with their interest in entrepreneurship. In Blaine County, Idaho, a Camp Fire group established a babysitting co-op. The girls took a home economics course to increase their employability in childcare and homemaking.[33] Mary Alice Beard, a Blue Bird in the 1950s, recalled that her favorite memories of Camp Fire included making "angel cookies from slice and bake cookie dough" and crafting "Blue Bird pouches" out of light blue felt. Once she became a Camp Fire Girl, she appreciated learning from a volunteer mom "the 'proper' way to cook and serve to guests" at a formal dinner party. A daughter in a farm family, she was stunned to see that a high-society dinner meant that one poured the butter off the vegetables. It seemed to her at the time to be a colossal waste of calories. (The anecdote is a reminder of how "homemaking" lessons were grounded in class-based norms.)

Homemaking lessons overlapped with outdoor activities. Mary remembered that she learned "how to cook almost anything by wrapping it in aluminum foil and throwing it into the campfire."[34] Indeed, outdoor cooking continued to be one of the staples of Camp Fire training, blending the domestic arts with outdoor adventure. Girls not only learned to make foil-reflector ovens and "hobo-stoves" from tin cans, but also to lash logs together into makeshift tables, create dishwater drainage systems, and dig fire pits to dispose of garbage.[35] Girls learned to plan menus, shop, select and use utensils, and cook and clean up safely. Camp and picnics made these domestic skills more fun.

Girls' Desires: Outings and the Outdoors

Some girls plainly preferred other activities to homemaking. One woman recalled in an interview that making her ceremonial gown revealed to her that "I had neither the skill nor patience for sewing." Similarly, Barbara Himmelberger grouped homemaking among the "many new skills" that she learned in Camp Fire but recalled the field trips around the city, camping, and hikes as her most meaningful Camp Fire experiences.[36] Camp Fire provided engagement and activity, which varied depending on the leader's skill and sense of adventure; in any case, girls made clear that Camp Fire was more than learning domestic skills. As a Pennsylvania Camp Fire Girl told her leader, she had spent a good deal of time at home with little to do before joining Camp Fire, but once she entered, "everything is different." She found the club connected her to public life in her community, which was "the most friendly and wonderful place to be."[37] A survey of Chicago-area alumni whose Camp Fire involvement ranged from the 1920s through the 1990s also indicated that homemaking was not a favorite Camp Fire memory for most. Of the sixty-two women who responded, nearly half reported that their fondest memories were of camping. Not one woman said that training in domesticity or "learning to cook an egg four different ways" (an actual honor bead activity), was her favorite part.[38] Camp Fire Girls across the United States echoed this love of outdoor adventure. One San Diego girl noted, "There is nothing in Camp Fire or, in fact, I might say in my life, that I would prefer to talk about than Camp Wolahi," her summer camp near San Diego.[39]

Most of all, girls wanted to be outside with their friends. A 1946 survey showed, "The nine most popular activities are those in which the girl is active physically out of doors in a group of her companions." Among the top six listed were: "going to a girls' camp," "going on an overnight camping trip," and "cooking out of doors."[40] A 1954 report reiterated that 90 percent of girls said they liked camping best of all.[41] Camp Fire did not always meet girls' desire along these lines. A 1961 study showed, "Ninety-five per cent of girls who join Camp Fire Girls do so because they want to do things out-of-doors. Many are disappointed because these activities don't materialize."[42] The annual report that year indicated that only 40 percent of Camp Fire Girls had actually attended a resident, day, or group camp in the preceding year.[43] The low number speaks to the fact that many leaders found homemaking activities easier to teach. Camping took a great deal of preparation, not all councils operated camps, volunteer club leaders often lacked supplies or were not comfortable with group camping, and some parents refused to let the girls sleep away from home.[44] The expectation for outdoor activity and the actuality of homemaker training meant that the program did not always deliver the adventure girls expected, leading to retention problems among the older girls.

"Charm All Your Own": Keeping Older Girls

Even as Camp Fire emphasized homemaking for future middle-class wives, it underwent a demographic shift in the 1940s and 1950s. Though Camp Fire was originally designed for adolescents, the organization increasingly appealed to younger girls. Blue Birds, the youngest Camp Fire Girls, were the fastest-growing segment in the 1950s, and by 1963, Blue Birds made up just over 40 percent of Camp Fire's girl members, up from 10 to 20 percent of members in 1928. Girls were most likely to drop out during their middle school years, though those who stayed in until high school tended to finish the program. According to one leader, who had led a group from Blue Birds through Horizon Club, "The young junior high miss feels she has outgrown her Camp Fire sisters." She explained, "The girls become interested in boys now, if not before, and they feel very sophisticated."[45] Girls concurred. Even in a town where, as one former Camp Fire Girl recalled, everyone was in Camp Fire, as girls got older it was seen as a bit babyish and not fashionable. Many members would stop wearing their uniforms and identifying vests and beads to school when they reached junior high.[46]

Camp Fire tried to cater to the junior high age girl's sense of herself as grown up to address this issue. Some local councils and clubs started forming separate junior high groups. In 1949 the Eastport, Maine, Camp Fire Girls split their members into two groups to recognize junior high age girls separately from the fifth and sixth graders. These girls received a distinctive uniform that signified their greater maturity (a "teenage looking blouse," a skirt, and a new red tie) and were offered different programming. They would no longer focus on the seven crafts alone but on cultivating peer relations, skill in associating with boys, and community service. National headquarters officially adopted this junior high program in 1962 when it announced new age divisions and ranks. Following a trend that had been gaining attention among educators and child experts since the beginning of the twentieth century, Camp Fire officials further broke down adolescence into more distinct age stages. There were four divisions of Camp Fire Girls: the youngest Blue Birds were seven and eight; the regular Camp Fire Girls were nine, ten, and eleven; the Junior Hi Camp Fire Girls were twelve and thirteen; and the Horizon Club girls (first formed in 1941) were fourteen to eighteen. The ranks of Trail Seeker, Wood Gatherer, and Fire Maker in the regular Camp Fire Girls program were made to correspond with grade level rather than to individual accomplishments.[47]

As the Blue Bird segment grew, so did the presence of mothers. Although numerous mothers of Camp Fire Girls had been present as guardians (with daughters as apprentices) from the outset, there had been a dual emphasis on recent college graduates who were near equals. By the 1950s, a majority of leaders were Camp Fire Girls' mothers. A 1967 survey indicated that mothers became involved primarily to lead their daughters' clubs. Thus the same parental authority that dominated in other aspects of girls' lives almost always characterized group meetings.[48]

The changes brought something of an organizational identity crisis. Camp Fire emphasized spiritual values in the home and, as described above, included some career and leadership training, but its messaging to older girls now promised relationship advice and beauty, dieting, and fashion tips. Attracting a man was seen as an essential step in the formation of a home, after all. Whereas Camp Fire's references to appearance in the early twentieth century had most often addressed how a girl's outer self reflected her inner character, attention shifted to outer beauty as a route to greater happiness through heterosexual relationships. This was not entirely new. *Everygirl's*, the magazine for girls published in the 1920s and 1930s, included a beauty column that covered hair care, nutrition, and related topics. One article had offered girls advice on how to find "beauty in household tasks" and recommended vigorous housework as a method of weight control.[49] But by the 1940s, Camp Fire had developed a more complete beauty and poise program called "Charm All Your Own." Purportedly to "help teen-agers develop good taste in the selection of their clothes" as well as to "add to personal security and poise," the program connected girls to the commercial world of fashion and stressed making the appearance and personality attractive.[50]

Following guidelines for attire that matched her coloring, figure, and personality, in one exercise a Camp Fire Girl developed her personal fashion "blueprint." She drew a sketch of herself, described her personality, and then detailed her ideal wardrobe. Personality was revealed through style, and *Camp Fire Girl* recommended girls visit wholesale dress houses, designers, and look at *Vogue*, *Seventeen*, *Mademoiselle*, and *Junior Harpers* for self-expression ideas. Girls could help each other by offering "criticism of each other from an impersonal point of view," an exercise that was not likely to boost anyone's self-esteem. In New York, as advertisement for Camp Fire and for the spring fashions, a Staten Island department store posted the best "blueprints" from a local group in the window. This group, underway with their study of fashion and beauty, also held a fashion show, visited a beauty parlor "to study different hairstyles," practiced giving each other manicures, and filmed their progress on posture improvement.[51]

"Blueprint for Beauty" was part of a larger reevaluation of Camp Fire's health program. The founders had designed health craft to "bring so much more zest and vigor to the business of living."[52] The new model still maintained that health was "one of the necessities in realizing the purposes in our lives," but its focus shifted. Health was dropped from the seven crafts, incorporated instead into other portions of the elective honors. Immunizations, for smallpox as well as diphtheria, tetanus, and pertussis (combined in one shot in 1948) and polio in 1955, were listed as examples of good citizenship. Moreover, Camp Fire abandoned the old health chart in favor of a new "Charm Chart" in 1946. Rather than a "prosaic tabulating of baths, toothbrushings and food intakes," which girls neglected and then hurriedly filled in "after several days with not too good memory," as physical education director Flora M. Frick observed, the new chart was a personality and appearance quiz. Copying the self-assessment trend in women's and teen magazines, twenty-seven questions about cleanliness and manners followed: "Is your inner charm reflected in smooth, clear skin? . . . Can you say 'No' and mean it, when candy or other sweets tempt you before a meal? . . . Do you carefully avoid attention-getting mannerisms, such as loud talking, interrupting others, etc.?" Girls calculated a score that indicated if they were "fairest of them all," "lovely to look at," "average type," "droopy," or "help, help." *Camp Fire Girl* called this "a language she understands." Frick insisted that it was more inspiring "to make ourselves over into something better" than to "writ[e] down how many times we washed our hands."[53] One leader wrote how the charm charts worked won-

14. Camp Fire Girls Charm Clinic, 1958. Camp Fire Girls took charm lessons. Here an adult models posture and grace. Developing a feminine posture was deemed a necessary skill for girls who wanted to achieve the "Homemaker—Plus," Camp Fire's term for well-rounded women who contributed to the community. Courtesy of the East Baton Rouge Parish Library.

ders with her girls. She noted her joy in "seeing Fatty Patty knuckle down to the charm chart and emerge looking beautiful; or noticing how Little Miss Fussygossip learns to control her tongue."[54] Insisting that the focus on fashion and outer beauty was "not being frivolous," Ruth Teichmann, Camp Fire's associate director of programming, explained that "good grooming guides" helped each girl "forget herself because she knows she appears well," a comment that revealed how outer appearance had replaced health as the foundation for civic fitness.[55]

Girls learned that beauty was a project they could work on just as they developed home and camping skills. Camp Fire Girl Gladys Mae Jackson, from Lincoln, Nebraska, earned her Torch Bearer rank with a homemaker project in charm that took up 1950s idealized femininity. She created a recruitment skit for high school–aged Camp Fire Girls that featured a Camp Fire group learning how "to make yourself more attractive to others." In her sketch, the girls learn from hairdressers to match hairstyles to their face shape. Turning to fashion and the body, the skit explains, "We are going to show . . . how figure defects can be helped by concentrating color in different places." One character in the skit enthusiastically adds, "Then we are going to take up personality—that's something we can always work on." Other characters express interest in etiquette and improving posture to exhibit feminine "grace." The skit was not the only part of Gladys's project. She also taught younger girls to do nature-rubbing art and worked at her church's charity, but her final undertaking was to "make a personal appearance analysis" of herself and her clothes. She wrote that her best features were her hair, eyes, and teeth and that she had sought her home economics teacher's advice on how to accentuate these features best. "Since my hair is red, my eyes dark brown and my skin predominantly tan—no freckles—I should wear clear red lipstick, or lipstick with a slightly orange cast," she wrote. "My powder should be cream or slightly tan. At my age I do not need rouge, but when I do it should match the lipstick."[56]

Although Camp Fire Girls no longer followed the rigorous health charts, Gladys detailed her strict skincare regimen and wrote a special section on blemishes, explaining her routine of washing, applying alcohol and zinc ointment, and never picking or squeezing her skin. She followed the advice of experts and friends. She took to heart the guidance of a hairdresser who told her that "for my type of face I should always keep my temples covered." One of her friends "told me that I would be much prettier if I smiled more, so I am taking her advice." And her home economics teacher helped her to plan a wardrobe based on her bodily proportions rather than comfort and durability alone. Tall and thin, she would "wear contrasts, large figures and large plaids," but "wouldn't dream of wearing vertical stripes." She cut out pictures from fashion magazines and catalogs to illustrate the ideal fall apparel for school, parties, and church. Writing as if for a *Seventeen* magazine fashion spread, she opined that "for all-around school and sport wear, [headscarves] are a must."[57]

Posture was important to Gladys as well. She believed it provided a window into personality and health. Women needed to walk straight while avoiding excessive displays of confidence. She typed out excerpts from Janet Lane's popular "Your Carriage, Madam!" with cautions such as "The domineering, self-satisfied woman, draws back her head, throws out her chest and sails down the street." Gladys noted how young women should monitor their bodily movement to project "beauty" and "general ease." She copied an entire page of instructions on how to sit properly that included, "Perhaps the worst single thing you can do to spoil your looks is to let your knees spread apart" since "your whole body settles into a squat." The sitter looks like "either a scrub woman or a geometry problem," depending on her size, Gladys observed through Lane's words.[58]

After posture, Gladys addressed the regulation of her speech, noting that "a low musical voice is an excellent thing in a woman." Gladys worked for two years with a speech coach who taught her "about correct breathing, enunciation, pronunciation, articulation and projection." She explained, "I used to be one of those mile-a-minute talkers who rattle on from one subject to the next, while the infortunate [sic] victim tries to get away." She learned to slow down and "be more deliberate." One guesses that her public speaking lessons were valuable in her future career as a university president. Teenage Gladys, however, wrote, after nearly twenty-three pages on outer appearance, posture, and voice, one brief paragraph about her internal character and its outward expression: "I have made an honest effort at being kind. I try to be sincerely interested in other people, and to keep the Golden Rule—'Do unto others as you would have them do unto you.'"[59] Gladys was not alone. As historian Joan Jacobs Brumberg explains, twentieth-century American girls became increasingly concerned with body projects, highly individualistic efforts to regulate the body. Parents, home economics teachers, and girls' leaders supported these projects because good looks and proper feminine appeal were important for social success.[60] These highly individualistic projects were a far cry from the socially engaged aspirations of the Progressive era in which Camp Fire got its start.

The importance of exercise also shifted away from its pleasures and health benefits to an outer focus on girls' figures. In *Camp Fire Girl*, gym proponent and beauty advice author Terry Hunt wrote that although "glamour starts . . . with . . . interest in other people, alertness, [and] enjoyment of many things," it also depended on body shape and size. Hunt promised, "Whatever the figure fault that bothers you, it can be corrected with the proper exercise." She urged Camp Fire leaders and girls to "start right now—individually or as a group—to check the figure faults you'd like to correct," assuring readers that they would see "wonders" in one summer's program. A list of exercises followed for general and specific flaws in the hips, lower abdomen, arms and back, thighs, calf and ankle, and height. While the exercise recommendations were reasonable—half an hour three days per week of bending, stretching, and leg lifts—the emphasis was now on exercise for appearance's sake, and the long list of faults would all but guarantee a young woman could identify one. Moreover, the suggested indoor activities were a far cry from the grandeur of the early days when Luther Gulick called on girls to walk a hundred miles in a month, not to fit into a ball gown but to prepare for "the business of living."[61]

The fitness focus mirrored national concerns about the physical fitness of American youth. President Eisenhower established the President's Council on Youth Fitness in 1956 to combat the ill effects of America's increasingly sedentary lifestyle. Martha Allen had attended the president's conference on young people's physical health that year and pledged Camp Fire to do its part to improve the health of American youth. She urged more camping opportunities and complained that while competitive sports, one of the conference's focal points, existed for exceptionally gifted youth, there was "very little for the average boy and almost none for the average girl."[62] Along these lines, advice could be measured. *Camp Fire Girl* warned leaders not to press children and young women to diet, citing research that diets can damage a teenager's or child's health if not properly supervised by a medical professional.

But even as Camp Fire cautioned its readers, its publications set out other reasons to reduce. "The attractive figure is usually easier and cheaper to clothe," editors observed, adding, "Who wants to participate in a fashion show if she's overweight—or underweight? And doesn't appearance rate high in the first interview for a job?"[63] Articles in *Camp Fire Girl* demonstrated a perception that girls were uninterested in athletic activity and had to be coaxed into exercising with promises of boyfriends and flawless figures. The national Horizon Club program advisor, Eunice Brunst, told leaders to persuade older girls "to pursue individual sports through the approach of glamour, popularity and their basic desire for admiration." She advised leaders to discuss with their girls the social benefits of being skilled at an activity. For example, if a boy asked a girl skating, her skill would increase her enjoyment of the outing and presumably her chances at romance. The magazine explicitly advised discussions around "how the sport ties in with personal appearance."[64] Such guidance reminded leaders and girls that appropriate feminine appearance mattered for self-fulfillment. Beauty was a prerequisite to marriage, a respectable career, and to being a "homemaker—plus," and it could be achieved through hard work.

Activities with Boys and Science

Beauty and homemaking were part of the heteronormative training Camp Fire Girls received in the postwar period, but so was direct interaction with boys. As noted, Camp Fire leaders thought girls lost interest in the program as their interest shifted toward dating. Dr. Rosemary Lippitt, writing for Camp Fire, advised that boys might be appropriately integrated into activities, even among Blue Birds. The key was to involve them just as girls started to show romantic interest in them: "Are [the girls] keen to talk about boys among themselves? . . . Do their books, scarves, jackets . . . have boys' names scrawled on them?" These indicators suggested girls were ready for boy-girl activities. Although most Blue Bird and Camp Fire leaders in the late 1950s still did not think boy-girl activities should have prominence in programming, a majority of leaders of older girls said they planned to integrate boys into club events regularly. (Only 32 percent actually did so.)[65]

Camp Fire magazines published ideas for making the adjustment. Lippitt suggested a range of activities, from building projects to social gatherings, insisting that girls would, as a result, "find it easier to meet [boys] in more purely social situations." If "Joan's older brother knows how to set up tents in a hurry" or "June's brothers have always loved swimming and can help set up the waterfront," then they should be invited to share a skill. By inviting boys as teachers, Camp Fire recreated expectations that boys were active and knowledgeable and that girls were passive spectators who could rely on boys to do mechanical or manual labor for them. And, more far-reaching, inclusion of boys would help the girls improve their social skills for the dating scene.[66] Such advice enshrined heteronormative expectations as it reaffirmed gender stereotypes. Indeed, girls practiced their dating and flirting skills at Camp Fire outings. A scrapbook notation indicated that Oklahoma City Camp Fire Girls enjoyed a boy-girl hay ride and that one girl "kept getting her feet mixed up" with those of a boy. The scrapbook author noted that she was "sorry I can not report what went on in the rear of the rack," but that "everyone had a swell time."[67]

The reverse relationship, with girls teaching boys new skills, appeared only rarely in Camp Fire publicity, and these also affirmed gender conventions. The January 1954 cover of *Camp Fire Girl*, for example, featured three teenaged girls and two boys, all apron-clad, making a dessert together in a 1950s suburban kitchen. The girls are in charge, frosting cupcakes and smiling, but the boys, dressed in florals and ruffles, appear to avoid the labor. With a sly grin, one boy helps himself to a soda while the other leans over to breathe the aroma of the fresh-baked cakes. The image subtly mocked the notion of girls as instructors, and the photo credit, which mentioned that the girls might have found some less feminine coverings of "denim and burlap" for the boys, further made the role reversal seem ridiculous. *Camp Fire Girl* editors may have approved of the playful cross-gender performance enough to put it on the cover, but they also signaled that it was humorously outside the norm.[68]

Another way that Camp Fire headquarters sought to stay relevant to older girls was through science education, but this was often reduced to a way to meet boys in *Camp Fire Girl*. In 1946 Camp Fire established a science category for honors called "Frontiers Craft." Frontiers craft focused on physical science and its practical applications. Responding to fears after the Soviet Union launched Sputnik in 1957 that the United States was falling behind other nations in science as well as the hope among educators that science could be a vehicle to new careers and international cooperation, schools and youth programs strengthened science education

15. Boy-girl activities increased in the 1950s as Camp Fire experimented with ways to retain older members. Usually, boys taught girls science or outdoor skills. Here the gender role reversal is depicted as humorous. The teenagers giggle as girls teach boys to bake. Cover of *Camp Fire Girl*, January 1954. Reprinted with permission of Camp Fire.

for boys and girls.[69] Some Camp Fire leaders, like founding field worker Edith Kempthorne, believed that science activities were crucial for girls "to keep up with boys."[70] Indeed, one girl earned honors for explaining the operations of her home heating system and her family's heating bill.[71] The Camp Fire manual suggested that girls lacked natural interest in science, but that knowledge of it would help them talk to boys. "A girl who doesn't know anything about football or baseball is out; so is the girl who can only look coy when a boy explains a radio or some mechanical gadget to her. Don't be on the outside," *The Book of the Camp Fire Girls* cautioned.[72]

Camp Fire literature regularly drew a careful line separating a natural curiosity for biology and observation seen as appropriate for girls and the turn toward physics and chemistry of the atomic age. Camp Fire messaging implied that girls should not be pushed toward systematic study or traditional laboratory research. One article extolled women scientists but dwelled upon their exceptional quality. Educator Evelyn Goodenough Pitcher wrote, "I do not think that many of us know many Madame Curies, nor many women physicists or engineers or mathematicians," she explained. Women were "more interested in people, in personality, and in themselves or the self" while men were more interested in "facts, abstractions, things, and ideas," she reasoned.[73] Frontiers craft never became one of the most popular honors, but steady interest gave the new frontier craft program "secure popularity" by 1953.[74] One girl recalled that the inclusion of science, math, and careers "encouraged girls to have a well rounded experience" beyond homemaking.[75]

Sex Education and Marriage Training for the Older Camp Fire Girl

Beyond frontiers and charm, Camp Fire officials turned cautious attention to the romantic and sexual relationships of their older girls. Abandoning the old euphemism "What a Girl of Her Age Needs to Know about Herself" for new ones, Camp Fire encouraged leaders to answer "her difficult personal questions . . . the questions about which so many adults are so very tongue-tied." Such appeals for candor were significant, despite the avoidance of the phrase "sex education." One 1961 article in *Camp Fire Girl* read:

> Only about 50 per cent of our girls get any kind of adequate answer for their many questions in their own homes. The great bulk of our young people still get what they need to know from friends their own age. This, in spite of the fact that all of our leaders in child development and education, all of our religious leaders, all of our leaders in the field of youth development agree that young people should have a responsible, loving, frank, full empathetic kind of relationship with responsible adults on some of these basic questions.[76]

The author hoped that if girls got this valuable information in Camp Fire, the organization would be meeting their needs and their interest in belonging would be strengthened.

Sex education was blended with baby care lessons. When Roslindale, Massachusetts, Camp Fire Girls held an infant care course for late junior high age girls, the girls needed permission slips, which assured parents that the registered nurse who directed the course would handle delicate information "with wisdom and tact," to participate. It urged parents to keep in mind "that we would all rather have the girls learn such facts in a wholesome intelligent manner" than to pick them up "wrongly from their misinformed schoolmates and from poor movies."[77] It is unknown how many girls attended or what material was deemed age-appropriate, but during the 1940s and 1950s the sex education programs that were gaining broader support usually included information about girls' maturation, menstruation, and fetal development (though not always how the woman got pregnant). Courses regularly covered gendered personality expectations within heterosexual marriage and gendered divisions of labor as well. Adults wanted youth to be "interested—but not too interested" in heterosexual sex.[78] The Boston area council agreed with the national office that some information about reproduction was necessary for older girls and that Camp Fire clubs were appropriate spaces to disseminate it.

In addition to offering sex education, *Camp Fire Girl* hoped leaders would caution girls about "going steady." One *Camp Fire Girl* contributor saw going steady as an innovation that young people created to deal with an overly complex social environment, but she worried that a girl loses out when she becomes too deeply involved with one person. She fails to meet others and marries "before she knows who she is."[79] Boy-girl activities, she suggested, promised some reprieve from the trend of going steady and helped girls establish relationships with boys founded on friendships. But Camp Fire literature was also explicit about training girls for marriage, noting how the growing "number of broken or unhappy family situations in America" might be countered if Camp Fire and other organizations could prepare young people to understand the opposite sex. Activities where youth worked cooperatively and solved problems together prepared them for "the test of marriage and family building."[80] To this end, girls in Oshkosh, Wisconsin, had a date etiquette session with a group of boys where they tackled such topics as "conversational icebreakers, manners, and what to wear for different kinds of dates."[81] Other councils held "Date with Dad" dinners to provide lessons on dating etiquette.[82] Such daddy-daughter dances and dates evidenced a new "social meaning of the father-daughter relationship" as necessary to the sexual and emotional maturity of girls in a heteronormative pattern of development.[83]

Marriage-centered activities and discussions came to take up more time as Camp Fire leaders tried to interest older girls. One leader, who said that she had lacked practical knowledge when she entered marriage, coordinated a marriage project for her Horizon Club. Girls created a set of make-believe husbands at one meeting by writing "vital statistics" on index cards (mythical name, age, job and salary, savings, major financial obligations, hobbies, personality, and number of children the family would have). One husband card read: "George Bates, Age—31, Job—bookkeeper—$75.00 a week, Bank account—$2,500 (this sounds hopeful doesn't it), Buying house and furniture, owns car, hobby—photography, Personality—calm, methodical, neat, Expecting first child in three months." At the next meeting, the girls drew cards. (It is not clear if the sixteen-year-old girl imagined that she was thirty or if she figured she was pairing with a much older man.) "[Each girl] then made out her budget in line with her husband's income." She selected a hypothetical apartment from the local newspaper and even visited some flats to experience what it would be like to be a prospective buyer. Next, the girls discussed which electrical appliances they would purchase and why, ways to pare family expenses in case of emergency, the cost of starting a family, and how to create a food budget. The food budget lesson led this group to the important conversation on "men and food," especially "how to interest a hitherto 'meat n' potatoes' man in salads, vegetables and fruit [and] the importance of a good breakfast." Finally, the club hosted guest speakers who offered "beauty tricks and tips," "facts and fancies about home furnishings," instruction on "how to dress well on a budget," and counsel on how to meet the "spiritual needs of a family."[84] Lessons about wives' consumer roles and the creation of an accepting mindset toward heterosexual marriage and its conventional division of labor, then, were at once part of citizen training and a strategy for retaining older girls.

Throughout the 1950s, Camp Fire still promised to make girls useful. The exact meaning of that usefulness shifted as did the political and cultural concerns facing American girls. The 1950s brought greater educational opportunities for girls, more professional opportunities beyond the home, and new exposure to science. To a degree, Camp Fire officials recognized the need, as they had since the 1910s, to revise the program materials to prepare girls for a new world where they would be involved in political life, sports, and careers. Older women at national headquarters and in local councils, however, held fast to an older feminine ideal that placed home-making at the center of female life. The cultural valorization of motherhood was fading, but Camp Fire leadership continued to subscribe to a model of femininity based on maternalism. As in the past, Camp Fire organizers understood the impulse to nurture as plausibly extending beyond the immediate home. Camp Fire's literature and programming indicated that girls could add external sources of fulfillment to their homemaking duties and that they had a responsibility to the community and the world. But the homemaking role remained primary.

7

"Prejudices May Be Prevented"

Race, Tolerance, and Democracy in the 1940s and 1950s

Even as the Camp Fire Girls reentrenched homemaking skills as keys to girls' success in the postwar era, the Cold War called girls to take up new citizenship roles. Challenging prejudice became a goal of the postwar Camp Fire Girls. Rather than merely emphasize the essential feminism it promoted in other areas of programming, the Camp Fire Girls also asserted the potential of youth organizations to shape democracy. Endowing children with the responsibility for the future of democracy and national strength, youth leaders often identified children as innocents as yet untouched by the harmful sentiments of racism. In their speeches and articles, Camp Fire leaders expressed the belief that if they could develop in children ideals of tolerance and cooperation, a democratic future could be assured. Camp Fire's new Committee on Intercultural Policies and Practices explained, "Camp Fire deals with girls during the ages in which right attitudes are developed and in which prejudices may be prevented." By developing enlightened policies and practices, the committee asserted Camp Fire's ability to "lessen existing tensions within the organization and in the community."[1] The organization gradually enacted policies that challenged prejudice and supported inclusion. Legacies of local control, however, stood in the way of integration in many councils.

Cold War Civil Rights

National director Martha Allen noted that the Cold War required of children the same citizen roles developed during the First and Second World Wars, but she also argued that the times demanded new training: "We must also recognize without hysteria the tragic fact that atomic war is a possibility and give thought to how we can best prepare girls physically and emotionally to go through such an eventuality with the least hurt."[2] Camp Fire published a pamphlet, *Camp Fire's Part in Defense*, to this end. Its suggestions, such as "learning emergency cooking, making neighborhood maps," and using "play-situations to help younger children develop confidence under unusual circumstances," incorporated Camp Fire activities in the new context.[3] Camp Fire understood such lessons as shoring up "the spiritual and emotional needs of children." Belonging to a group, learning to be resourceful and skilled, experiencing the value of real service, and releasing "tensions through play, fun and friendship" were essential to combating the anxieties of the atomic age.[4]

The "struggle between the ideals of democracy and totalitarianism of all varieties, especially communism" presented additional challenges. Allen urged the Camp Fire Girls to do more to prepare youth. "An organization which seeks to train girls for citizenship cannot ignore this struggle or operate on the assumption that if we teach children to tie knots, build a campfire and give service, all will be well," she stated. Since Camp Fire Girls would learn primarily "by our words and especially by our examples," she sought to heighten the organization's democratic practices, particularly related to inclusion.[5] Allen believed that the best vehicle for combating communism was an inclusive, antiracist, democratic system. "If democracy could be made 100% effective in the United States," she wrote, "I don't believe it would be possible to convert a single American citizen to communism. Whenever we fail to practice democracy we hand the communists powerful propaganda weapons to use against us," she concluded.[6]

Allen's statement captures the Cold War civil rights imperative in the United States. In the competition with the Soviet Union for the hearts and minds of people around the world, the U.S. foreign policy need to counter images of American racism led many leaders to voice a commitment to civil rights. After all, the international press reported on the repeated occurrences of foreign dignitaries being turned away from American hotels and restaurants due to their skin color. Other racist events in the United States, such as Emmett Till's 1955 murder and the Little Rock high school desegregation battle that began in 1957 also made headlines.[7] Moreover, the African American campaign during World War II for "Double Victory" against Nazis abroad and racism at home, as well as the revelations of the horrors of Hitler's death camps, had led more Americans to renounce eugenics and other forms of racism.[8] The tri-faith movement, too, which Camp Fire had embraced in the 1940s, "helped soften the ground for the civil rights movement."[9] Acting on behalf of and through girls, Camp Fire officials could do their part to address inequity and shore up democracy.

Camp Fire's approach was two-pronged. First, Camp Fire's national council pledged to live up to its inclusion promises. Its postwar plan listed as a top goal "striv[ing] to give girls of all minority groups an opportunity to participate fully in such character-building and recreational programs as ours." Camp Fire continued to view its character-building recreation and education model as ideal for all girls. Second, Camp Fire's antiprejudice lessons focused on white, middle-class girls learning about communities of color. In materials and group activities, officials promised to "train girls of the majority group to understand and respect the accomplishments, native capacities, personal dignity and socio-economic problems of minority groups within our country."[10] The objective called on white girls to learn about their peers. Camp Fire recognized who its primary members were and that they had a responsibility to address prejudice.

Camp Fire Voices Antiprejudice Ideals

Although it continued to recruit girls through racially and religiously separate groups, Camp Fire was among a growing cohort of educational institutions that began to rethink race, tolerance, and segregation. In its antiprejudice efforts, the Camp Fire Girls was in line with other youth organizations that reflected upon and gradually implemented change. Girls' groups, especially, outpaced many educational institutions and comparable private groups to assert the need for and begin to implement change. The YWCA's teen auxiliary and the Girl Scouts, which like Camp Fire had supported separate but equal policies in their early years, moved to include Black girls and women "in the mainstream of association life." At the council and club level, these organizations moved toward integration, though their progress, like Camp Fire's, was uneven. The Girl Scouts' first fully integrated triennial conference was not until 1969, almost twenty years after its first desegregation steps had begun. The Boy Scouts of America and 4-H, similarly, had stated policies of openness, embracing "citizenship as a set of practices that were egalitarian and accessible," while allowing segregation and privileging white members. Boy Scouts allowed local councils to decide if and how they would admit African American boys and men until 1974, when the National Association for the Advancement of Colored People (NAACP) sued the Boy Scouts for its racial barriers.[11]

One of the first visible shifts was Camp Fire's public statements and marketing. "Do you really believe that all persons have value in God's sight?" Allen asked group leaders in *Camp Fire Girl*. "If so, you will help to bring the enjoyment and the benefits of the Camp Fire program to all girls in your community who want it—Negro girls, foreign girls, Jewish, Protestant, Catholic, the poor and the rich alike," she wrote. "We can make friends for democracy and render an essential service by making democracy work at least in our own organization."[12] Images of girls from different racial and cultural backgrounds began to appear in its publications. Sketches and drawn silhouettes in the 1944 and 1946 printing of the manual included a few that are ambiguous, resembling Asian and African American girls, and pictures in *Camp Fire Girl* increasingly included African American, Asian, and Latina girls. A May 1946 "Picture of the Month" winner, for example, featured a multicultural group of girls delivering their contribution of "Bibs for Babies" to a Netherlands Aid Society representative.[13] Gertrude Whiting's 1945 painting "A Prayer for Peace" similarly captured a racially diverse set of Camp Fire Girls standing around a globe. The art memorialized Franklin Delano Roosevelt and was used in Camp Fire's campaigns for international friendship. When *Camp Fire Girl* reported on a Boston high school group's 1947 Tea Party, it highlighted the presence of both Black and white girls to underscore the organization's inclusive ideals.[14]

Expert voices also appeared in Camp Fire materials to urge group leaders to counter prejudice. In one 1949 article, Ethel J. Alpenfels, associate professor of education at New York University, detailed the process of breaking down racial prejudices. Unlike some commenters who cast children as racial innocents, she acknowledged children could harbor prejudice. She insisted that adults were responsible for teaching them alternate ways of thinking. "Unpacking prejudices" consisted of identifying the biases that

16. World War II brought increased challenges to American prejudice. The Camp Fire Girls responded with more inclusive imagery in its publications. Here a mixed-race group of Blue Birds from Trenton, New Jersey, deliver a care package. *Camp Fire Girl*, May 1946. Reprinted with permission of Camp Fire.

existed in one's community, recognizing that they existed in the Camp Fire group as well, and working as a group to dismantle those stereotypes. The next step, meeting people from different backgrounds, promised to keep prejudices "unpacked." She readily admitted the complexity of teaching tolerance, recognizing that even young people might dislike one another for a multitude of reasons other than bias. The challenge was to "get youngsters to know enough people of English, or Negro, or Methodist backgrounds in order to teach that we can dislike some without being prejudiced against all of them." In addition to raising awareness about the prevalence of stereotyping, she addressed what she saw as cliques forming along racial or ethnic lines within integrated clubs. "If girls of one national, economic, or racial background tend to cluster together and form little cliques, you may have to work out various ways of choosing partners for trips, for committee work, or for games." Alpenfels expected leaders to step in and assign partners, forcing girls to work with girls from different backgrounds. This might be disconcerting to girls from racialized groups, who may be inclined to band together for security, but it would disrupt the practice of exclusion by girls of the dominant race. In the process, Alpenfels hoped that stereotypes would disintegrate.[15]

Finally, Alpenfels explained that racially homogenous communities might have even more trouble "unpacking prejudice" than diverse communities but that Camp Fire could provide an opportunity to challenge racial isolation. Diverse communities had experience working through tensions and bridging cultural divisions. "If, however, your community happens to be one in which all the citizens belong to one race or even to one socioeconomic group, then your problems become much more difficult and your responsibility more urgent," she wrote. Challenging the developing sociological discourse that cast communities of color as underprivileged, Alpenfels called the all-white neighborhoods "under-privileged" because "no Chinese, no Mexicans, no Negroes live (or are allowed to live) there." Cross-cultural experiences within Camp Fire, even if infrequent, could challenge this disadvantage. Girls could "visit other communities, bring in speakers and discussion leaders from all races, religions, and nationalities." These speakers, she advised, should be invited to talk on general topics. Understandings of common humanity could not be forged when people of color were asked to speak only about their ethnic or racial groups. "If, however, you bring a Chinese girl to speak, it is wise not to have her talk about what it means or feels like to be Chinese. Rather let her talk about a common problem or demonstrate a skill in which she is talented," Alpenfels explained. She also suggested reading literature that would present people that the girls would not typically meet in another way.[16]

Thus in its official publications, Camp Fire recommended tactics for confronting stereotypes and prejudice. In another example, in 1951 Camp Fire's director of membership registration, Gail Montgomery, urged leaders to tackle racism when they saw it in their groups. "You can do something about prejudice," she said. If anyone in the group used a derogatory term, for example, group leaders should immediately address it and discuss the negative impact of prejudice. She also encouraged Camp Fire members, speaking to the predominantly white women and girls in the organization, to expand their friendship circles. If they had no friends from a "minority group," she encouraged them to go into the community and meet some more diverse friends.[17] Although individual groups were free to do as little or as much "unpacking" as their inclination led them to, both Alpenfels and Montgomery placed the responsibility of unpacking prejudice on the shoulders of white, middle-class girls and women.

Camp Fire Examines Policies and Practices

By 1952 the leadership's concern about inclusion in the organization resulted in a national council resolution at the annual meeting in New York City in favor of inclusion. Camp Fire pledged to "consciously increase its efforts to carry out our already stated membership policy" and to live up to its articles of incorporation promise of being "available to all girls." This was two years after the development of the religious pamphlets for Protestant, Catholic, and Jewish Camp Fire Girls, and two years before the *Brown v. Board of Education* ruling that declared that "separate educational facilities are inherently unequal." In 1953, to move forward, Camp Fire appointed the National Committee on Intercultural Policies and Practices "to study our progress in interracial and intercultural practices and to develop specific techniques to guide board and committee members, leaders and staff."[18] The committee's report was completed in 1955.

Although the committee's analysis of the organization's demographic makeup was less than systematic, it found that local custom and de facto segregation had determined Camp Fire club membership. At a time when Camp Fire's make-up in a cross section of its councils was over 98 percent white, the report on diversity in Camp Fire found that although some councils, "due to the general climate of the community and sometimes largely due to conscious and intelligent effort," had made great inroads against segregation and discrimination, others had not "given the matter much thought." And some were "frankly hesitant in view of local customs." It concluded, "In no Council that we know of, do we have a membership that fully reflects the diverse cultural groups in the community."[19]

Some regions—Camp Fire noted its councils in the Pacific Northwest, Northeast, and Midwest—were far ahead of southern councils in the degree of integration their membership experienced. Scrapbook photographs of girls from various councils in California show integrated memberships. Girls expressed hope. One twelve-year-old, Black Missouri Camp Fire Girl reported her view that Camp Fire's democratic policies demonstrated the strength of America: "To me [democracy] means you can join any organization you want to, join the clubs and go to the church you want to." Her white peers echoed similar sentiments, explaining that Camp Fire exemplified democracy because "we can all go to the churches we want and we can join our own organizations."[20]

Diversity went by different definitions across Camp Fire clubs. One former Camp Fire Girl in Elmhurst, Illinois, recalled that her late 1950s Camp Fire club, which was established among children from her school and a few additional friends, had what she understood as tremendous religious diversity. Lutherans, Presbyterians, Catholics, and Methodists were among them. She learned the word "ecumenical" in Camp Fire, she recalled. The club also had girls of different economic means and nationalities, but all were white.[21] For her, other factors than race and ethnicity signaled diversity. Staten Island's Camp Fire Girls represented religious and ethnic diversity too. The group, "composed of girls of many nationalities and of the Catholic, Protestant, and Jewish faiths," participated in an interfaith group. They had hosted a "brotherhood program" in 1949, inviting their parents along with representatives from schools, churches, religious groups, and community and civic organizations to a banquet. The diverse representatives from various social agencies included Black and white pastors and representatives from the local Jewish organization. A guest speaker from the Staten Island Council for Democracy spoke on how children could lead the way for adults to better practices of "brotherhood."[22] Diversity could signal the breakdown of religious barriers as well as racial ones.

By 1955 some groups took the initiative to challenge racial segregation as well, doing outreach and raising awareness. A midwestern council reported that it successfully operated a camp on a nonsegregated basis, and an eastern city recorded its considerable efforts to increase participation among racialized groups in leadership and promote cross-cultural activities and integrated events.[23] However, without strong national backing and commitment of resources, when they met with community resistance these fledgling groups faced an uphill battle. Celia Anderson, a mid-1950s Blue Bird leader in Fort Collins, Colorado, found some of the better-off, white community members stigmatized her group after she admitted a few poor and Mexican American girls. The parents of white girls in the community opted for their daughters to join the Girl Scouts, where the more affluent and white girls were, after the Camp Fire circle had opened up to the new members.[24] The local council had little ability to challenge such entrenched prejudices.

The Committee on Intercultural Policies and Practices also noted sporadic interracial events in the South. Black Camp Fire Girls "in a supposedly very prejudiced neighborhood," which unfortunately Camp Fire did not identify, invited a white group to an entertainment at their church. The white group attended and later reciprocated. In another unnamed community, an integrated group wished to hold a skating party at a roller rink that excluded Black people. The group refused to have the party until the roller rink changed its policy, which it did. The rink's old policy unraveled as more and more integrated groups beyond Camp Fire sought use of the facility.[25] Newspapers also occasionally noted the interracial activities of Camp Fire Girls in their communities. In Tyler, Texas, where clubs were segregated, an African American group invited the white Camp Fires to a fundraising carnival. Although donating to the Black girls' benefit mirrored the donations ladies' clubs made to support African American clubs in an earlier era, it still brought Camp Fire Girls together across the color line.[26]

Still, uninformed and racist practices stymied inclusion attempts. Segregation resulting from neighborhood, church, and school-based organizing was the reality in all of the locales. The efforts at outreach in some Camp Fire councils were "awfully clumsy," in the words of one consultant; many leaders seemed uncertain about how to proceed or gave up at the first sign of resistance. One group, for example, embarked on an interracial camping program but "completely folded up" when one mother objected.[27] In Camp Fire's councils where racially integrated clubs did exist and more racially inclusive ideals might be expected, insensitive customs continued. At an Eastport, Maine, Camp Fire Halloween party, costume contest awards went to two girls dressed as a Black woman and man. They wore blackface and tattered clothing, earning them the honor of "funniest."[28]

The report also explained how segregated groups formed. In one unspecified Pacific Northwest council, a membership extension program focused on churches and schools. The Committee on Intercultural Policies and Practices reported that in neighborhoods where the schools included students of varying religious beliefs and racial origins, the Camp Fire Girl membership was "intercultural and interracial." Where the extension targeted churches, the result was clubs consisting of girls from "one religious idea or one racial group." Therefore, when Japanese and Japanese American girls in the council joined Camp Fire, they joined through a Buddhist temple and were not in integrated groups. "Neighborhood pattern[s] of housing and community interests" were also reflected in the council's leadership. While this particular council was dissatisfied with the situation and hoped to make greater inroads to interracial membership and increase racial diversity on the local board, its report still concluded that the current situation was "natural" because it developed out of what council representatives believed were individual choices. Indeed, laws did not mandate such separation, and families from marginalized ethnic groups and religions often sought solace in separate community-based organizations. Camp Fire's neighborhood organizing policies nonetheless reinforced racial separation.[29]

In the South, African American participation increased during and after World War II through segregated clubs. A regional report from the Atlanta Council described outreach to the African American community in the 1950s. The Atlanta Council remarked that two of its best-functioning districts served five hundred African American girls. The council boasted the presence of an African American field director who had been employed with Camp Fire since 1948.[30] Still, this outreach remained on a segregated basis. In 1958 the Atlanta Council operated four girls' day camps, three for white girls and one for their Black members.[31] Here Camp Fire followed an early twentieth-century pattern wherein white women in the South supported progressive, ameliorative racial politics, often working through interracial conferences to improve Black facilities and institutions even as they defended segregation and white supremacy. Although these white benevolence efforts became more politicized in the wake of the *Brown* decision in 1954, with fewer moderate white Southerners using the humanitarian language of the earlier generation, efforts to support separate Camp Fire clubs for Black girls persisted through the 1950s.[32] White women's clubs regularly sponsored Black Camp Fires units. In Oklahoma the Seminole Business and Professional Women's Club sponsored a Black Camp Fire club, and in Abilene, Texas, the Albany Study Club, a white women's group, paid for the dues of the Black girls' club and bought the curricular books for its leaders.[33] White newspapers lauded the work of African American Camp Fire Girls, presenting a picture of shared but separate service commitments. As if to convince readers that the girls were worthy of a day at camp, the Corsicana, Texas, paper lauded the Black Camp Fire Girls and the group's leadership, pointing out the number of girls who had earned rank, listing their talents in handcraft and needlecraft, and presenting their community service accomplishments.[34] Camp Fire's challenges to racism rarely challenged the color line. Many whites supported better facilities and inclusion for Black people but adhered to the idea of separate but equal and did not want Black and white children to meet together.[35] Tyler, Texas, youth organizations expressed such ideas symbolically when, in the mid-1950s, they participated in the city's annual holiday parade. Black and white Camp Fire Girls and Boy Scouts marched but did so in separate units, with the white youths stepping out first.[36]

One southern Camp Fire official lamented, "I am not really satisfied sometimes in my heart about the way we handle our Negro program since, in so many ways, it is separate."[37] Elsewhere, a draft of the committee's report noted that in one locale, a Black council operated separately from the main council even though national leadership considered them to be one unified council. Indeed, newspaper reports from Texas in the 1940s regularly reported on separate Black councils. In 1946 over a dozen "leading Negro citizens" formed the Waco Black Council, for example. The white Waco Council of Church Women largely funded it. Although the group was folded into the main Waco Council in 1950, its clubs continued to meet separately as "Negro Camp Fire Girls."[38] In many instances, such African American clubs were separated from the white council to set their own policies and often raise their own funds separate from the community chests that provided for the whites.[39]

"A Great Deal of Margin for Local Customs": Camp Fire Accepts Segregation

Despite Camp Fire's plan to study race, the national council sought to avoid controversy at the local level. Local councils received the recommendations of the Committee on Intercultural Policies and Practices, but there was little pressure to change. The guidance was "not mandatory, but rather a method of suggesting ways in which this [race] question can be approached." The national council assured segregationists that "there is a great deal of margin for local situations, local needs, and local customs." A male Texas representative at the national council meeting said that he approved of the committee recommendations because it makes "known to everyone that we are concerned" but would not "alienate the love and affection of people who really have a serious problem about this matter." He argued for a gradual approach to establishing local racial policy committees to avoid the appearance that the executive was forcing councils to integrate.[40] Thus when the suggestions went to local councils for extending their programs more fully into communities of color, they focused on further study, establishing local committees on intercultural practices, appointing local boards that reflected local diversity, and consulting with civic leaders with experience on intercultural issues. The committee did not ask councils to desegregate. Phrases like "as far as possible" peppered throughout the recommendations and acknowledgment of "widely varying" local standards reminded leaders to use caution when pushing for change and to move only as rapidly as local custom permitted. While these reminders may have promoted cautious progress, they also provided a rationale for stalling.[41]

The trepidation with which Camp Fire responded to resistance was born out of awareness of the costs of controversy. There was danger in the 1950s that those on the right, who sought to delegitimize liberal efforts, would brand the organization radical, and that civil rights commitments would lead to charges of communist infiltration. American conservatives, from the White Citizens' Councils to governors and justice department officials, labeled integration a "communist disease" brought about by outside agitators seeking to destabilize the United States. The Girl Scouts faced harmful allegations from the Illinois chapter of the American Legion in the early 1950s that communists had influenced its leadership, in part due to its embrace of antiracist speakers and writers.[42] Massive white resistance made efforts at integration costly in many national education organizations. In 1956, two years after *Brown*, southern segregationists forced the national Parent Teacher Association to back off from a statement in support of integration.[43] In this context, Camp Fire moved forward gradually, but the prioritization of white girls and their families was clear.

Even as Camp Fire made diversity and inclusion claims, the national headquarters neglected to conduct, and perhaps quite purposely avoided, systematic analysis of its demographic makeup. At the national council meeting in November of 1955, the same year that Camp Fire published its pamphlet on intercultural practices and policies, Allen proudly remarked that Camp Fire was becoming more inclusive. Still, she noted, no statistical information on the membership's religious or racial groupings existed. Thus Allen based her assessment on anecdotal reports from field staff.[44] While limited resources may have prevented Camp Fire's national office from conducting a more systematic analysis, the absence of this data meant that Camp Fire could assert inclusivity without accountability. National headquarters would not have to confront white supremacy in the organization, a move that might have undermined its popularity in Camp Fire strongholds like Texas and Oklahoma.

Persistent Segregation in the 1960s

Camp Fire's national council and staff repeatedly championed inclusion, passing a similar resolution to that of 1952 again in 1961. Organization leadership pledged again to teach girls to work with others from diverse backgrounds. Allen pledged that national headquarters would work to create "a membership in step with the growing population and one inclusive of all groups" and called on local councils to do the same. Explaining that Camp Fire had to prepare girls for the real world, Allen pointed to the inadequacy of segregated groups in training girls for the future: "Even though we adults often find it hard to accept diversity we must understand that never in the lives of the young people with whom we work today will they live and work exclusively with people 'like themselves.' Failure to give them opportunity *now* to experience diversity is to cripple their ability to adjust to the realities of the modern world."[45] But national Camp Fire officials still refrained from forcing groups to integrate, letting local leaders pursue their own course.

Another Camp Fire leader tried to guide an integrated group in Washington State's Tri-City region in the mid-1960s. Like Celia Anderson, who had faced the prejudice of community members a few years earlier, her story from the eastern Washington region reveals the impact of Camp Fire officials' unwillingness to challenge local customs or to offer meaningful support to those who did. With previous Camp Fire experience as both a girl and leader, Sonia Littrell accepted her local council's request that she admit Black girls to the group she started for her daughter. The Tri-City region was embroiled in controversial busing efforts to desegregate the public schools at the time. Littrell thought that taking part in the social changes would be good for the girls and never anticipated, she said, the obstacles she would face. Although the Camp Fire publications offered some advice to leaders on how to confront stereotypes in their groups, Littrell was not aware of them. Neither local nor national officials prepared Littrell to deal with local prejudice or the cultural differences within her group. She faced each obstacle in isolation. Desertion by the few white girls who had initially enrolled in the club signaled the first troubles. All but two, one of whom was Littrell's daughter, stopped attending after the arrival of the new members, and soon the other white child dropped out as well, leaving Littrell's daughter and three African American girls. As Littrell's daughter recalled, the four became best friends, going to birthday and skating parties together, but the departure of the other white girls was a stark reminder of the white supremacist values in the community.[46]

In addition to losing members, Littrell's group faced blatant discrimination in the wider community. She described one occasion when she took her integrated group and her younger daughter out for ice cream. An elderly couple "literally hissed" in their faces. Similarly, the group asked local merchants to hang Camp Fire publicity posters in store windows. When the Black girls made their requests, shop owners turned them down, but when Littrell's daughter returned with the same request, businesses welcomed her and granted their permission. In her words, Littrell "wasn't sure what to do," and Camp Fire offered few practical tools for dealing with the situation into which they had asked her to enter. In Washington no laws prevented Black girls from being fully included; customs and prejudice, though, were no less rigid. She did have some community support from the children's teacher, an African American woman whom Littrell commended for helping her understand the problems she faced, but she did not credit her local council or national headquarters with much assistance.[47]

Littrell, nonetheless, discussed race as best she could with her group of girls. She did not discuss the actions of the storeowners, but she did discuss skin color and tolerance with her club when the girls themselves broached the topic. When her youngest daughter exclaimed in surprise upon meeting her Camp Fire sister's friends, "You're all Black!" Littrell diffused the tension as best she knew how by saying, "So what? You are all pink." When the face of one "assertive" young girl relaxed, Littrell believed that her comment had helped establish an environment of understanding and acceptance. She remembered other conversations with the girls about how skin color did not matter in determining character. On one occasion, however, she recalled that her telling her Blue Birds they could be whatever they wanted to be when they grew up was met by one Black girl's comment that she would probably be poor. In retrospect, Littrell believed that this could have been a lesson, but at the time, she had not known how to handle such a sensitive remark.[48]

The parents of the Black Camp Fire Girls had little extra time or money to devote to Camp Fire. When her girls could not afford to pay for dues or special activities, she either paid for them herself or they went without. This problem was not unique to Littrell's group. Council reports from the South also noted that Black girls often fell behind in dues payments.[49] Littrell recalled asking the local council office for their assistance in outfitting her girls in uniforms. Her frustration mounted as they told her to watch the thrift stores, and she became wary of asking.[50] Camp Fire's leaders recognized the importance of challenging racism for democratic education, but its councils lacked the resources and commitment to challenge structures of white supremacy in local councils.

In 1961 the Camp Fire Girls had been responding to the demands of the Civil Rights movement for over a decade with promises of further integration and access. It nonetheless prioritized its middle-class membership, signaling the leadership's assumption that middle-class girls were the citizens that Camp Fire most needed to develop. Camp Fire's leaders defended the strategy: "The administration of Camp Fire Girls, Inc. . . . makes no apologies for the fact that its membership comes largely from the middle class which constitutes the greatest segment of American society, for if this group is not trained for responsible leadership, society is in danger."[51] Thus while Camp Fire's publications voiced concerns about prejudice and racism, Camp Fire's outreach and interracial policies fell short of challenging white supremacy within the organization. Despite its rhetorical commitment to equity and tolerance, Camp Fire accepted that local customs would prevail in club membership, lauding integrated groups where they existed and accepting segregation where it existed. The organization aimed to make Camp Fire available to *all* girls even as it accepted segregation. Because segregated groups did at least the minimum of making Camp Fire available to all types of girls, the organization maintained its claims to inclusivity, as it had done since its founding, without pushing for integration in communities where there might be white resistance.

In 1914 Grace Parker had declared, "Nowhere have I seen true democracy better demonstrated than . . . at Mass Meetings of Camp Fire Girls." Parker insisted that "all prejudices seem to disappear" as girls all met "on equal footing as members of one great organization."[52] Camp Fire pursued a mainstream liberal racial and ethnic agenda that associated tolerance and cooperation with democracy. Camp Fire provided some spaces that brought together diverse girls, but local pressures and philosophical contradictions, especially the privileging of white, middle-class girls as future leaders, tempered its commitment to tolerance. As it had in Nashville in 1914, Camp Fire's leadership in the postwar period asserted ideals of inclusion and equity in publications and resolutions but then backed away from them. Needing money and members, Camp Fire officials did not believe that they could "rock the boat" and maintain an organization with a national base. Since the definition of inclusion itself was open to multiple interpretations, acquiescing to local practices alleviated tensions in the short term.

During the 1940s through the 1960s, tension between Camp Fire's aspirational ideals and the realities of local pressures and its internal philosophical conflicts persisted. About the same time that Littrell was struggling with her integrated group in Washington State, however, Camp Fire embarked on a major outreach project, the Metropolitan Critical Areas Project (MCAP), to extend its membership to nontraditional members, particularly girls of color and children with disabilities. MCAP consultations, which began in 1962, would usher in more tangible changes.[53]

8

"The War on Poverty Is Being Waged by Camp Fire Girls"

The Metropolitan Critical Areas Project

The 1960s and 1970s were a turning point for Camp Fire. In response to issues of equity raised by the social justice demands of the long civil rights movement and to threats to funding and overall youth member-ship, the Camp Fire Girls would reevaluate the structure and function of the organization yet again. In 1962 Camp Fire began to engage with antipoverty programs, and the lessons that its leaders learned redefined the organization's purpose. Newspapers noted that "the War on Poverty is being waged by Camp Fire Girls" and detailed how Camp Fire now battled delinquency and "explosive unrest" as it brought its program to "Negroes, Mexican-Americans, migrants, Indians, Puerto Ricans, mentally disturbed children and others."[1] Camp Fire's national leaders rethought their promise to serve "all girls." National executive director Martha Allen spoke in earnest of moving with speed "toward full integration within our own ranks" and of the organization's responsibility to bring "opportunities for life-enriching experiences" to "more minority groups and economically and culturally deprived girls."[2] Camp Fire's efforts led to a new organiza-tional structure in 1975, with multiple programs that served not only girls but all youth from birth to twenty-one. Youth across these programs were known as Camp Fire kids.

The centerpiece of Camp Fire's outreach was the Metropolitan Critical Areas Project (MCAP), a three-year, federally funded effort to reach girls in America's urban centers. Camp Fire was the first youth organization to receive such funding. Through MCAP, organization leaders began to identify the structural changes that were needed if the organization wanted to reach girls beyond its narrow, white, middle-class demographic. The story shows how Camp Fire responded to rapid social change and how working-class families, especially those of color, continued to struggle. It is a story of successful study and adjustment by white community leaders who identified barriers to inclusion. Camp Fire's national leadership, with a handful of local leaders, pioneered a new course through experimentation and commitment to inclusivity. Youth membership became more racially representative as a result. In 1968 white youth were 90 percent of the total, but by 2004 white youth made up just under half of the membership and Latinx and Black youth had risen to over 30 percent.[3] But it is also a story of failure. Although Camp Fire's leadership began to decenter white, middle-class models of leadership and recreation, the broad suburban memberships' embrace of the new aims varied. White women remained disproportionate in the organization's leadership, and Camp Fire's membership and national reach began to decline in the 1970s. Moreover, Camp Fire's well-intentioned hope for urban transformation through values and behavioral change, one that the federal program architects with whom they collaborated shared, remained unrealized. The MCAP strategy and philosophy, based on the sociological theories of urban Black pathologies that animated federal delinquency programs, worked to reify those understandings while doing little to undo urban inequalities.

The program reports of the MCAP candidly assess the strengths and limitations of Camp Fire's outreach efforts in the 1960s and include numerous anecdotes and statistical data about the girls and their parents. Although filtered through the eyes of the predominantly white, middle-class women who ran these projects, the reports provide a window into the experiences of urban, low-income girls who joined Camp Fire, and they illuminate the structural barriers that girls of color faced. Occasionally judgmental, local leaders' appraisals also offer a sense of the extent to which urban and low-income girls found the Camp Fire program worthwhile. Those girls who went to camp, for example, enjoyed it enough to return. Yet Black girls at camp saw few Black counselors and, therefore, expressed uncertainty about their own opportunities to lead. The choices low-income girls and girls of color and their families made come through in these reports, offering a glimpse into their hopes—Camp Fire provided them with opportunities and status—and their resistance to an imposed middle-class model of girlhood. Girls and their families became agents who reshaped Camp Fire.[4]

A Changing Youth Agency Landscape

Youth organizations confronted membership challenges in the 1960s and 1970s. Between 1970 and 1974, Camp Fire's youth membership fell by over one hundred thousand. If trends continued, leadership feared Camp Fire would be unable to operate as a national agency. Camp Fire first noted that membership growth was not keeping pace with the baby boom population increase in 1956, and its membership first dipped in 1964. Following a brief rebound and an all-time peak of 633,101 in 1970, membership plummeted despite a recruiting campaign. The Boy Scouts and Girl Scouts faced similar obstacles. Youth leaders blamed the rising numbers of white, middle-class working mothers, increased commuting, a higher divorce rate, and growing mobility among American families for exacerbating a decline in adult volunteers. In addition, by the late 1960s the oldest baby boomers were reaching their twenties, and although Camp Fire served children of the baby boom through the 1970s, it could no longer count on a growing youth population.[5] One southern California council reported that as the baby boom waned, several local elementary schools closed, and although it was doing outreach in previously untapped communities of color, new members there barely offset the boomer losses.[6] No less significant, youth leaders noted a trend nationwide among youth away from joining traditional organizations. A new "sophistication" among young people whose coming of age was shaped by the civil rights movement, anti–Vietnam War protests, and the counterculture movement led them to eschew the conformity and obedience that they associated with youth organizations.[7]

Competition for limited funds for nonprofits posed additional challenges. The Camp Fire Girls and other youth agencies had depended on united funds and community chests for support at the local council level since the 1920s, but such support was diminishing by the mid-1960s.[8] A 1966 Camp Fire study observed that in most of its districts, united funds were "in a precarious position." These community fundraising agencies were seeing an increase in budget requests with which their own annual fundraising endeavors could not keep pace. Believing character-building organizations could be self-supporting, many united community chests were less willing to pay for them. That Camp Fire competed with the Girl Scouts, and girls' organizations together were allocated only 33 cents for every dollar given to boys' organizations, made its situation more difficult. Councils turned to dues, sales, and other fundraising efforts, including government grants, as a new source of money. In the 1960s these grants favored action in low-income neighborhoods of American cities, so Camp Fire adapted.[9] It tapped into these resources and, in the process, redefined its mission.

Camp Fire and the War on Poverty

Political responses to the 1960s social movements remade the American urban landscape: white flight depleted inner cities of vital resources; punitive policies provided funds for police surveillance of Black communities; and a growing colorblind rhetoric challenged the egalitarian, race-conscious programs that had blossomed from civil rights activism. Meanwhile, the prevailing economic injustice and the expansion of law enforcement in inner cities led to urban unrest and also pushed youth to demand greater rights to free speech and the ballot.[10] Private foundations and government programs aimed to contend with "the problems of juvenile delinquency and poverty among low-income people of color," especially in America's cities. Programs to stop crime, beginning with John F. Kennedy's 1961 Juvenile Delinquency and Youth Offenses Control Act, sought to address, in Attorney General Robert Kennedy's words, "youth unemployment, poor housing, poor health, inadequate education, and the alienation of lower-class communities and neighborhoods." Lyndon Johnson's Economic Opportunity Act, part of the War on Poverty, would soon call for "community action organizations to plan and administer programs to provide economic opportunity for the deprived with special emphasis on young people who are out of school and out of work." This was followed by the Law Enforcement Assistance Act, which poured federal money into community surveillance and policing.[11] Camp Fire collaborated with the federal government to provide a softer, less polarizing response to urban challenges.

Before 1960, Camp Fire had made limited outreach efforts to girls outside the white middle class. As previous chapters discuss, it drew few girls from communities of color, American Indian reservations, settlement houses, and migratory farmworker camps. In 1962 Martha Allen called on the national council to "find ways to serve more girls." She insisted, "We must experiment and innovate and find ways to include more girls from the inner-city, from the underserved, unserved, undeveloped neighborhoods."[12] The national council voted to step up efforts to reach "culturally deprived" girls, a term sociologist Frank Riessman popularized, and applied for federal grants to do so.[13]

Camp Fire would tap into federal programs that were built upon the assumptions that animated Assistant Secretary of Labor Daniel Patrick Moynihan's 1965 report "The Negro Family: The Case for National Action." Moynihan theorized that Black children in urban centers were caught in a "tangle of pathology" that drove them to lives of crime. While Moynihan supported liberal policies to alleviate race-based income inequalities and increase social services' efficacy, he blamed "broken families" and their poor choices, against which recent civil rights measures could make little headway, for racial inequality. Camp Fire's MCAP, like other demonstration projects called for by the Kennedy and Johnson administrations, emphasized behavioral change: teaching discipline to Black youth and poor children, developing their "work personalities" to make them employable, offering them home economics instruction, and "expos[ing] them to the values, norms, and ways of speaking in dominant society."[14] MCAP fit this format and offered Camp Fire's foundational model of personal growth and middle-class character formation. Youth organization leaders believed in the plasticity of youth and bought into the idea that "societal reforms could be enacted through personal changes."[15] Such efforts were well-intentioned but did little to transform those systems that led to joblessness and inequality, ignored existing institutions established by Black adults for Black children, and reified the association of Black and urban youth with criminality.[16]

Indeed, the plan to bring middle-class organizations to urban centers was a more preventative social program than the police surveillance that would characterize later anticrime efforts in cities, but it showed long-lived middle-class presumptions. Although a few Camp Fire consultants challenged the language of cultural deprivation, arguing that educational disadvantages and cultural coherence were distinct issues, Camp Fire organizers regularly assumed that poor people were ensconced in ghetto cultures that white, middle-class reformers could disrupt and replace by bringing to children their version of character education. Both the MCAP plan and Moynihan's famous report in effect blamed family structure and neighborhood cultures rather than social and economic systems for poverty and crime. Although Camp Fire organizers pledged to move beyond their middle-class roots, they remained stuck fast when they spoke of disrupting urban culture to bring "children out of the dailyness [sic] of their lives[,] of the cycle of fear, boredom, and failure" and into a world "of fun, activity, and feelings of achievement." The statement showed an ongoing belief that middle-class programs of personal growth were the solution to urban poverty and racial struggle.[17]

Selecting MCAP Sites

The MCAP pilot began in 1962 in New York, Baltimore, Washington DC, and the Roxbury area of Boston.[18] Camp Fire then received grants totaling $204,211 from the Children's Bureau's division of Health, Education, and Welfare to further develop its program in Boston and Washington DC and establish one in Detroit. It received another grant of $25,000 from the Office of Juvenile Delinquency and Youth Development to develop a leadership training guide. These federal funds incentivized private nonprofits to create demonstration projects to test new delinquency prevention and control techniques. Nine more cities (Albuquerque, New Mexico; Bakersfield, California; Baltimore; Buffalo, New York; Dallas; Minneapolis; Pasadena, California; Phoenix; and San Francisco) soon became involved in MCAP through various state and local grants, and the Los Angeles Camp Fire Council gained a National Institute of Mental Health grant to pursue connected aims. Federal grant monies for study and experimentation lasted through the summer of 1967. By that year, 8,751 girls had participated in MCAP groups.[19] Most were from low-income families with parents who worked in semiskilled trades, service industries, cleaning services, and mechanical careers. Median income differed by city but was between $3,800 and $5,688 per year. In Detroit one-quarter of the girls' families received some kind of welfare aid. Not all councils broke down the membership by race, but the Boston area council did, and its MCAP membership of around 60 percent Black girls was not unique.[20] Most projects targeted upper-elementary through high school girls, but the Los Angeles project provided the Blue Bird program to elementary school girls. In addition to urban outreach, MCAPs served a migrant camp near Bakersfield, California, and the Yaqui town of Guadalupe, Arizona, near Phoenix.

A national Camp Fire advisory committee selected the urban neighborhoods from among those that met grant parameters. These were communities not served by other youth programs. Their proximity to long-established Camp Fire councils with well-functioning professional staffs and day and resident camp facilities made them likely to succeed in the action research project. Moreover, the cities had university social science research centers with which Camp Fire could partner, a necessary feature since federal funds required the involvement of social workers and delinquency experts.[21] The neighborhoods, though characterized as having a "lack of space for play" as well as some "deterioration" and "overcrowding," also had stable middle-class communities adjoining them and successful civic agencies with which Camp Fire also cooperated.[22]

MCAP leaders defined the cities as multiracial and deliberately sought to establish groups that were "heterogeneous across racial, socio-economic and ability lines." Many had growing African American populations.[23] The Greater Boston Council, for example, chose Boston's recently completed Cathedral Housing Project and the Shawmut neighborhood in Boston's South End for its diverse Syrian, Lebanese, Chinese, Puerto Rican, Polish, and Southern-white residents. Detroit's Davison and Cleveland neighborhoods, which included African American youth and the children of Polish immigrants, made up Camp Fire's target area in that city. Its greatest membership was within the Charles Terrace Housing Project and its surroundings.[24] Reports described the Washington DC neighborhood of the thirty-third census tract, the target area in the Potomac Area Council, as "heterogeneous," with a large nonwhite population.[25]

Integration was limited, however, and the groups continued to reflect the demographics of the neighborhoods served as they had historically in

Camp Fire. In New York City's Bedford-Stuyvesant, groups were made up of Puerto Rican and African American girls from the Roosevelt Housing Project, reflecting the neighborhood's population.[26] Similarly, in Baltimore Camp Fire failed to construct mixed-race groups because of the paucity of white children in the target neighborhood. The flight of white families from city centers to the suburbs in response to Black migration had left behind an aging white population. Between 1940 and 1970, for every one Black family that arrived in northern cities, two white families left. As a result, in Baltimore few white families with young children remained so the Camp Fire Girls served a community that was 85 percent African American.[27] In Detroit, despite its postwar reputation as a model city for racial progress, Camp Fire met Black families on the economy's margins in segregated and substandard neighborhoods. Detroit's white community, which was nearly 80 percent Roman Catholic, used parish schools to maintain insularity and racial boundaries. Since Camp Fire was working with public schools and other public agencies, few white girls joined the Detroit groups. In this way, the segregation of Detroit's schools persisted in Camp Fire's groups despite its aim to integrate.[28]

Los Angeles's MCAP produced some integrated groups but also groups that reflected the segregation of many Los Angeles neighborhoods. As the city's economy and population ballooned after World War II, its entertainment, aerospace, and automobile industries favored white workers, but communities of color, segregated due to redlining, housing covenants, and white flight, were the fastest-growing populations. A major metropolis with nearly 2.5 million people in 1960, Los Angeles was being transformed from a majority white city to majority nonwhite in the 1970s and 1980s.[29] The demographics of the Camp Fire groups matched the makeup of the elementary schools and their neighborhoods. For example, a mixed group met in central Los Angeles's multiracial Magnolia school; the school population was 50 percent Mexican-American, 25 percent African Americans, 13 percent Asian or other, and 12 percent white. Latinx girls predominated at the east Los Angeles school, and African American girls did at 111th Street School in Watts, the southern central section of Los Angeles where many Black migrants had settled since the 1940s. In addition, the beatnik community of Venice, California, was part of the Los Angeles MCAP, as was San Pedro, with its naval families and fishing community of Portuguese and Yugoslav families.[30]

Recruiting Local Leaders and Volunteers

Camp Fire's national staff, almost entirely white when they undertook the project, increasingly acknowledged a need to diversify. To their credit, the antidelinquency programs of the Kennedy and Johnson years prioritized "indigenous leadership," which meant that social programs would involve local people, and Camp Fire resolved to meet this standard.[31] Allen worried, however, that Camp Fire's recruitment efforts would meet resistance because its white, middle-class leaders, local and national, "[represent] the power structure" and that the organization had historically taken a "colonial" approach to the poor. To counter this reputation, MCAP planners developed different strategies. In Detroit, MCAP hid its affiliation and advertised for leaders who wished to help disadvantaged girls, without naming Camp Fire explicitly.[32] For effective outreach Camp Fire hired Dr. Eva Schindler-Rainman, a faculty member at UCLA School of Education, Extension, and consultant on community organizing, to create a series of seminars to set the project's tone and write a manual for MCAP staff. She had experience mobilizing volunteers in low-income neighborhoods with racialized minorities. She could link sociologists and educators, many with research and activism experience in communities of color and among children with disabilities.[33] Schindler-Rainman invited activists and sociologists to Camp Fire's training seminars for fresh perspectives on how class and cultural barriers had limited the access of girls to Camp Fire's programs.

These consultants urged Camp Fire staff to move past their model of training girls for middle-class respectability. African American educational sociologist Mozell C. Hill, who served as a state consultant on desegregation policy during the 1960s, urged Camp Fire leadership to interrogate its capacity for effective outreach in Black communities.[34] Camp Fire staff and leaders were, he noted, "overwhelmingly middle class in their outlook." They gave priority to "cleanliness, good manners, correct dress and address—quiet and soft-spoken but 'good' speech, social conformity, and respectable reputations." He believed that due to their vantage point, council leaders could expect push-back from poor Black communities and social activists.[35] Manuel Diaz from Mobilization for Youth, a New York City demonstration project initiated by Henry Street Settlement, also cautioned that middle-class youth workers tended to focus on personal change by offering a "cornucopia of programs" without challenging structural encumbrances. Middle-class volunteers too often assumed, he said, that the poor are "simply waiting to be served." Camp Fire, he argued, had to transcend this model of "social work colonialism that has alienated the helping professions from the low-income population and minority groups." He suggested collaborating with community leaders and agencies that were already trusted and established.[36]

Schindler-Rainman also underscored the need to harness the local community's resources and not simply import leaders.[37] She recommended tactics such as sending Camp Fire leaders to meet local people at laundromats, issue advocacy associations, and health centers. The method mirrored those of the New Left's Economic Research and Action Projects and the Student Nonviolent Coordinating Committee during what was dubbed the Freedom Summer in 1964.[38] In Los Angeles, Camp Fire officials opened an office near University of Southern California and held coffee hours to train local leaders. They also identified middle-class organizations in communities of color such as the National Council of Negro Women (NCNW), as key partners who, as teachers, secretaries, and professionals, would share attitudes about civic engagement and women's organizing, and would have contacts in their communities. Schindler-Rainman called on Camp Fire's staff and volunteers to rely on local people's ample experience organizing and assisting neighbors, expertise that did not neatly fit Camp Fire's usual definition of leadership. Recruiters would have to translate local community strengths into positions within the organization.[39]

Using these tactics, Camp Fire brought on board women of color as project directors at several sites and recruited many volunteers from the local communities. But the organization struggled to retain the women of color in the project director positions. One who served as project director for the duration of the grant was Boston Council's Ione Vargus. Trained at the University of Chicago, later the first Black dean at Temple University, she was a social worker with the Boston Housing Authority before coming to Camp Fire. The daughter of an army colonel, she had been educated in integrated schools in Medford, Massachusetts, but faced explicit racism when she was denied school social worker positions. Like Vargus, many middle-class women of color in Camp Fire were previously held back due to racial discrimination. Vargus shared the view of national headquarters that Camp Fire was a means to transform communities. By training the girls and local volunteers as leaders, she explained, "you can see the change as these girls take hold in the community." Unlike Allen, who had made "integration within our ranks" a goal, Vargus sought better educational resources whether or not clubs were integrated.[40]

Other women of color were recruited but did not stay. In Washington, the Potomac Area Council's African American project director, Haroldean Ashton, was a recent graduate of Howard's School of Social Work. Los Angeles's director was a Nisei social worker, Tetsu Sugi. She was a UCLA graduate with a master's in social work from University of Pittsburgh. She had worked for the Church Welfare Bureau in Los Angeles before becoming involved with Camp Fire. Both women left Camp Fire after about a year's work and white women replaced them. Later reports offer no reason for either woman's departure, but evidence suggests personal and professional reasons. Sugi's mother died in 1968. She may have left to care for her mother. Ashton likely found a better job in what would be a long social work career in camps and education (and ultimately as an Episcopal rector). In January 1968 the New Jersey State Department of Education employed her as an educational specialist.[41] The final report of the Potomac Area Council indicated, however, that local bias about MCAP may have frustrated Ashton's efforts and hastened her departure. The local council, early on, viewed MCAP as a temporary project that diverted resources from the suburban backbone of the organization. Ashton's office at a church in the target neighborhood placed her in proximity to her Camp Fire Girls, but offered her little opportunity to interact with the regular council staff.[42] The white woman who replaced her as head of the Washington DC program was Dr. Shirley McCune, a member of the Social Research Group at George Washington University. She would later serve as an American Association of University Women officer and on the commission that drafted Title IX gender equity guidelines in 1972.

McCune's report describes the extraordinary emotional labor, or what she called "investment of self," required of project directors, which may also have contributed to some early leadership departures. Directors handled a wide range of responsibilities involving a variety of stakeholders, including the adult volunteers, families and girls, Neighborhood Youth Corp enrollees, graduate students involved in the research, and the council's disparate members. The multiple demands could be "depressing and discouraging." So, too, was "the need to affect optimism even in the face of very discouraging circumstances." "This 'giving of self,'" McCune lamented, was "not always balanced by adequate return in satisfactions."[43] One imagines that the work was exhausting, and especially so for the women of color who could not escape the racism that intensified the difficult conditions.

In addition to project directors, Camp Fire successfully recruited volunteer group leaders from local families. MCAP adopted Schindler-Rainman's methods to make contacts through school personnel, churches, settlement houses and neighborhood centers, neighbors and friends of the project leaders, housing project staff, recreation department staff, Volunteers in Service to America (VISTA) enlistees, and child welfare agency staff. The group leaders reflected their communities, with Black, Asian, American Indian, and white women serving. Half of Detroit's volunteers were Black women.[44] The Maricopa (Phoenix, Arizona) Council recruited twenty-two "indigenous" leaders for the MCAP in Guadalupe, a Yaqui and Mexican American village of about five thousand people. Nearly all of the women had been Camp Fire Girls at the same Guadalupe elementary school when they were children.[45] Ashton and McCune did not provide a breakdown of the racial background of Potomac's leaders but noted that they were all local women. They ranged from age seventeen to fifty-six, including a mix of middle-class women of color and several who occupied a more marginal socioeconomic status. Three were attending Howard University, Washington DC's historically Black university, but several had not finished high school.

These women demonstrated pride in their Camp Fire affiliation by carrying their Camp Fire books and displaying Camp Fire training certificates "prominently in their homes," but they also resisted suburban leadership styles and carved out new methods. For example, they preferred cooperative leadership patterns. They wanted to colead rather than take sole charge of a group of girls.[46] These choices would later inform Camp Fire's 1970s restructuring.

Despite some success recruiting local volunteers, challenges persisted across MCAP sites. Constant attrition due to "family and health problems," job changes, and "the lack of the necessities of life" prevented continuity of leadership. In Los Angeles, where many of the target area girls were from Spanish-speaking homes, mothers had limited command of English and they may have believed that they were less capable leaders. In Boston, Detroit, and Los Angeles, Camp Fire supplemented the local leadership with outside volunteers and paid staff.[47] A mix of local women of color and white, suburban Camp Fire women, then, brought programming to girls in MCAP neighborhoods.

White Leaders in Communities of Color

Because women of color were hard to retain in director positions and as volunteers, Camp Fire relied on white women of varying skills. Among the leaders who proved to be strong allies in the communities they served was project director Lola Beth Buckley, a white social worker and Detroit YWCA director, who led Detroit's MCAP. Born in Houston, Buckley was thirty-nine years old when she assumed the role of project director. She became well known in the community, meeting people where they were: at laundries, putting out their trash, and at ball games. She attended PTA meetings, block clubs, church services, neighborhood councils, and nationality group meetings. Buckley also used MCAP to connect families with available services in the community, not just those Camp Fire provided. Detroit's MCAP recruited twenty leaders from the target area and twenty-nine from outside the area through these processes.[48]

During the summer of 1967, Buckley's response when racial injustice led to violence just four miles from the Detroit MCAP neighborhood underscores her personal investment in the Camp Fire families in the city. She lived between two areas of heavy disturbance. She maintained communication with Camp Fire families via telephone and through contacts in the neighborhood. Since many families lacked telephones, some women were already tasked with disseminating information. Her immediate goal was ensuring that Camp Fire Girls could get to camp, but she also sought to use Camp Fire resources to aid families. When several families asked for help to move temporarily out of the area, Buckley used her network to rehouse two families. Two days into the violence, she went into the conflict areas to help locate missing persons and connect people to services. Camp Fire Girls had relatives whose homes had burned, and one local Camp Fire leader died due to underlying health problems: when the buses stopped running, the family could not reach the hospital. In the aftermath of the unrest, the Detroit Camp Fire Council continued to help. The camp housed girls whose relatives were burned out or faced other housing problems, and the suburban groups in the council gathered supplies for their peers.[49]

Whereas urban unrest led to deepened outreach efforts in Detroit, in Los Angeles it prompted at least one white Camp Fire leader to pull back. When an urban rebellion broke out two summers earlier in Watts, the MCAP included two "all Negro groups," one near the center of the conflict in the Watts area and another near the northeastern boundary of the area known as South Central. A white female staff member there reported her fear of working in Black neighborhoods, and the local office altered her schedule to ensure that meetings and Camp Fire activities did not keep her in the city past dark.[50]

In other instances, white, middle-class norms prevented many of Camp Fire's staff and volunteers from connecting with local volunteers. For example, project directors encouraged new leaders to attend leaders' association meetings. These meetings consisted overwhelmingly of the most active, white, middle-class women within the local Camp Fire councils, and they often gathered at suburban sites. Most MCAP recruits did not attend because the cost of transportation and lack of babysitters made it difficult.[51] In addition, several women noted that the "class room atmosphere" of these sessions discouraged participation. Local working-class women, especially women of color, did not "feel necessary, important or welcome."[52] McCune observed that a "common Camp Fire Girl culture existed in that leaders tended to be alike." These middle-class women practiced an "educational model" and "behavioral styles" that "were more like teachers than other helping professionals." Their tendency to lecture and to instruct alienated those who were more attuned to what one director called "charismatic leaders" who used connections, persuasion, and personal appeal to lead. Local volunteers wondered if and where they fit in the broader organization.[53]

A similar cultural disconnect occurred when national Camp Fire resource people came to MCAP volunteer trainings and presented activity examples as if middle-class pursuits were universal. They presumed local women had prior knowledge of Camp Fire programming. For example, one representative instructed local Detroit leaders on how to take a "penny hike." She told the group that the children decide that heads or tails will direct them to go right or left, and then a child flips a coin. Some had never heard the phrase "heads or tails" so could not carry out the activity.[54] Despite training to raise awareness that such information is cultural, some local Camp Fire representatives remained tone-deaf in their approach. In one African American community, a local leader was livid when Camp Fire's staff sent "a beauty specialist . . . to her group [who] knew nothing about the care and the treatment of Negro hair."[55] The observations within MCAP reports point to the ways women of color pushed back against white expectations and standards and to how the white project directors amplified those concerns.

The white women's reports also demonstrate that many learned as they rolled out Camp Fire to new communities. With self-reflection, these women began to adopt methods to combat their cultural exclusivity. Local leaders, for example, were instructed to verify understanding as they taught new activities. Manuals were redesigned in a three-ring workbook style instead of the authoritative text of the past, and universal stick figures replaced photos of white girls. In addition, to offer volunteers greater flexibility, Camp Fire adopted new leadership models such as coleaders for groups and "floating" leaders who supported different groups in the council based on need.[56] Councils provided transportation to leaders' association meetings outside of target neighborhoods, and they redefined these meetings, calling them seminars, workshops, and task groups so the benefits to the leaders were more evident.[57] Some local volunteers began attending meetings, especially those held in their own neighborhoods. Some even attended Camp Fire board meetings as they became acquainted with the people in the organization. Schindler-Rainman noted that in South Central Los Angeles, locals called for greater autonomy, requesting "politely, but firmly" that she not attend a volunteer session since "they could handle their own meeting."[58]

The Experiences of MCAP Camp Fire Girls

Camp Fire's MCAP leaders selected girls "who appeared to need group experiences" for the first cohort, but how leaders identified those in need reflected the program's roots in juvenile delinquency prevention and the cultural biases of the professionals they consulted. Camp Fire worked with school principals and teachers, who assessed girls' school performance and their relationships to peers and adults.[59] In the Potomac area, referrals also came from clinics for the "mentally retarded," the church, and welfare personnel. The Los Angeles Council offers a case study on how the markers for "who appeared to need group experiences" varied by ethnic background. Although there were exceptions, the behaviors of Latina girls that brought attention from teachers and led to their selection for group work were traits such as being "quiet and overlooked," "immature," and "overprotected by mother." In contrast, the teachers of the African American girls selected for MCAP noted characteristics such as being too "playful," "aggravate[ing] others," "aggressive," "sneaky," or "too bossy, stubborn, [and] talkative."[60] Groups, then, often gathered girls based on prevalent behavioral stereotypes. After the establishment of the initial groups, MCAP organizers allowed groups to grow organically. New members joined through friendship circles and church and community agency contacts. In Baltimore, VISTA volunteers recruited additional girls.[61]

Despite fears that girls and their mothers would reject Camp Fire as too middle class, those girls who were invited to join for the most part did. In the Los Angeles pilot, the project director ended up with groups that were too large when none turned down the opportunity to join.[62] In Detroit, too, groups grew as friends and siblings sought to join. A fourth-grade group widened to forty girls, more than the leader believed she could effectively lead. But she did not want to turn anyone away. MCAP recruited better among older girls than did its suburban counterparts. While the average age of MCAP girls in Detroit was still just under twelve years, the number of junior high and high school–aged girls was proportionally larger than in the council at large, which was predominately made up of elementary school girls' groups. Although Camp Fire leadership feared that urban Black youth would resist the white-led organization, the youth found in Camp Fire avenues to serve in the community, participate in "girl talk," and host status-increasing events like dances and carnivals. The day-to-day activities rarely took place under the supervision of white leaders; local people ran the meeting and local girls populated the clubs.[63]

Still, retaining girls was a challenge. Older girls sometimes clashed with leaders. The Potomac report noted that girls were looking for role models, and neither the local mothers nor the white Camp Fire staffers fulfilled their idea of a mentor. These girls also regularly hid their Camp Fire affiliation from non–Camp Fire peers. Although McCune did not explain why, they may have found the association with middle-class values out of step with the radical Black politics in their communities. Nonetheless, most girls who joined the program stayed for at least an additional year, indicating that they and their families did find value in it. The program in Washington DC retained 82 percent of the original girls through to the end of the project in 1967.[64] Detroit's program was less successful, but still 59 percent of the girls who came to Camp Fire continued, at least sporadically, through the program's three years. When girls did leave, their reasons were similar across MCAP areas—their families moved away, they had to help with chores and babysitting, they disliked girls in the group, or they lacked spending money for dues and activities.[65] As girls matured, the "money demands, priorities of home housekeeping tasks, [and] the 'little girl' image of Camp Fire Girls" compelled many girls to quit.[66] In some instances, a girl's departure signaled deep family and school troubles. The mother of one Los Angeles girl who left the program did not want her to live at home and reported her as incorrigible to court officials. After a juvenile hearing, the girl entered foster care in another section of the city. A few others had been expelled from school and one was pregnant. Camp Fire's report merely stated this as a reason for her departure as if no one considered that a girl who was pregnant might continue her activities. While Camp Fire project directors acted as intermediaries, putting girls into contact with social services in their communities, local volunteers did not address pregnancy or abuse with their girls. The Detroit report noted that local volunteers believed that speaking about such problems in front of the other girls was unacceptable. When the pregnant teen's Camp Fire group dropped her, for example, no follow-up conversation occurred within the unit.[67]

To accommodate girls with more quotidian needs, Camp Fire adopted new membership policies. In traditional suburban groups, meetings were usually limited to girls of the same grade level and their leaders, but MCAP showed the need to adjust this practice. Detroit MCAP girls often brought younger siblings, whom they babysat, with them to meetings, and leaders came to recognize that younger brothers and sisters "were accepted as part of group life." Parents and older siblings came along for events too.[68] The strict age and grade levels were neither necessary nor useful. MCAP leaders created space for cross-age networks. In one group, a twelve-year-old Detroit girl had difficulty relating to peers her own age, but she was a "tremendous help" to a group of seven- and eight-year-old girls. This unconventional model permitted the girl to engage more meaningfully. Instead of strict grade-based groups, Detroit program staff built upon "friendship patterns" regardless of age and allowed siblings to join together.[69] Boys' appearance at ordinary meetings shifted practice too.

The girls' mothers assisted with meetings and joined field trips when they could take children of different ages and genders with them. Soon Detroit MCAP groups included boys on field trips as mothers and older sisters looked after them. To the surprise of program staff, boys were "happy to be part of the activities."[70] In addition to the little brothers, high school MCAP girls in Detroit worked alongside boys from other social agencies on a Camp Fire–sponsored service project. In San Francisco, too, where the MCAP Camp Fire Girls built upon a Ridge Point Church youth outreach program at Hunter's Point, boys were already involved and continued to be as the church partnered with Camp Fire.[71] The inclusion of boys, made official in the 1970s, was already well underway in MCAP. Camp Fire officials recognized their exclusion as one of several traditional practices that had hindered outreach to low-income girls and so adopted more flexible group structures.

MCAP groups also adapted by finding new meeting spaces, though they faced significant challenges in finding safe ones. MCAP groups met at schools, recreation centers, housing project community rooms, and churches, and rarely in women's homes the way suburban clubs often did.[72] Still, discrimination and sub-par community buildings could make MCAP meetings difficult. Detroit's junior high girls met at a recreation department center near their school. The staff there, however, continually disparaged the MCAP girls, comparing them negatively to a Girl Scout club that was better behaved. Neighborhood boys and girls that the Camp Fire Girls knew interrupted meetings frequently with "window breakage and foul language." Leaders minimized interruptions by moving to an upper floor to reduce schoolmate encounters. Another Detroit group, this time an elementary school club, did not have a classroom or lunchroom to meet in, so they met at a store-front church, "a poor choice" because "it was in a neighborhood where a group of young adult men came to a bar." Verbal street harassment of the "girls kept a number of them away." They moved to a funeral home, but this unnerved the girls. They finally moved to a church yard, but they could only meet when the weather was nice.[73]

Aside from structural changes, girls in MCAP participated in the activities for which Camp Fire was known. They sold candy, joined service projects, and held carnivals. Girls indicated through surveys what their favorite aspects of the program were. The youngest girls favored play activities such as games and creative arts, whereas girls over twelve preferred trips and "self-development," especially "girl talk." The oldest girls liked to discuss personal and social issues and sought activities that led to community prestige, such as community dances and raising money to attend regional Horizon Club conferences. The girls also excelled at candy sales and displayed their sales award certificates where others could see them. The opportunity to work with community adults offered the older girls a professional network they relied on when seeking jobs and volunteer work.[74]

MCAP groups performed extensive community service. The list included: holding parties for younger children, babysitting at PTA meetings, helping senior citizens, cleaning up playgrounds, distributing information about community programs, and making gifts for children's hospitals.[75] One leader noted that "the most deprived girls" were most likely to request projects "to help 'poor kids.'" Detroit MCAP leaders were especially proud of their teenagers' participation in a preschool vision testing program. Fourteen girls and boys went door-to-door to tell Detroit neighbors about a free program to have young children's eyes checked with the Detroit Society for Prevention of Blindness. The teenagers taught their neighbors to fill out registration forms and convinced reluctant adults of the test's worth.[76]

Girls were motivated to improve their communities through their service projects. When elementary school girls planted flowers at a housing project for old people, they "said that they had never planted them for their own family apartments and asked if they could have some seeds and plants for that also." They also held a penny carnival that was the largest neighborhood event held in the housing project area for many years. Its proceeds funded future recreational activities in the neighborhood. (Despite the welcoming community activity, someone called the police during the carnival, stating incorrectly that a large gathering of Black people indicated that a riot was forming. MCAP reported this neighborhood surveillance as if it were a humorous anecdote.)[77]

Girls also stayed in Camp Fire because their parents approved of its activities. An overwhelming 92 percent of Detroit parents interviewed thought Camp Fire had been useful for their daughters.[78] Undoubtedly their support was wrapped up with respectability politics. As sociologist Elizabeth Higginbotham notes, the strategy of respectability politics has had special significance in the Black community since the nineteenth century. Black women joined organizations to advance racial equality and emphasize the qualities they shared with white, middle-class women. Camp Fire symbolized access to the middle class and to equal participation in its opportunities for girls. Although the strategy became increasingly controversial in the 1960s as Black liberation activists pointed to its failure to address systemic racism and to its premise that failure to perform respectability is grounds for inequality, many still found respectability politics to be an essential tactic in the creation of viable models of womanhood, gaining access to opportunities, and preserving safety.[79] Some parents hoped Camp Fire might keep their daughters away from young people who they thought were bad influences, and some noted that the girls made new friends that parents regarded as respectable.[80] Mothers believed that girls underwent positive behavior and attitude changes. They indicated, for example, that girls got along better with siblings. Forty-three percent of the Detroit mothers who were interviewed mentioned such personal transformations in their Camp Fire daughters.[81] These mothers saw Camp Fire as a convenient and useful tool for supervising and providing extra-curricular activities to their daughters.

From MCAP leaders' perspective, too, girls' attitudes improved, but some behavioral issues persisted. Although these problems likely occurred more or less often in the suburbs as well, MCAP leaders associated them with urban, racialized youth. Reports identified tardiness of girls (and their mothers) as a perennial problem. In addition project staff disclosed that MCAP girls occasionally stole and misused supplies.[82] Overall, however, MCAP leaders recorded that their Camp Fire Girls fought less, ridiculed and teased less, and generally exhibited less "general friction" and "rude-ness to each other."[83] After a district-wide integrated event, one white adult reported that a "Negro girl who 'never plays with white kids'" had announced that she "never had so much fun!" The adult saw this as proof of Camp Fire's transformative power. Others reported that girls became leaders in their groups and classrooms and learned to talk things out.[84]

Occasionally white leaders noted self-reflectively that changes in man-ners were not indicative of positive social transformation. One leader in the Dallas County Council recognized that middle-class etiquette simply for its own sake did not appeal to girls and should not be prioritized. A poem she penned mocked the project chairs who "come to teach the darlings the things I hold most dear. I think they should say 'thank you,' and also 'if you please.'" To the instruction in propriety, the poem's Camp Fire Girl retorts, "Shoo fly, don't bother me" and insists that in Camp Fire "I am somebody." For this white adult leader, middle-class manners were not prerequisites for being "somebody." The poem valued girls' sense of belonging and identity, accepted differences in language norms, and pro-tested white, middle-class leaders' thoughtless interventions.[85]

In addition to social skills, the parents identified cultural literacy as crucial for their daughters' success. Most of the mothers found that the program "gave girls opportunities to 'go places' and 'do things they couldn't otherwise do.'"[86] The leaders concurred, reporting that girls' "experience levels were so limited, in little things like using a needle, riding a bus, going around a revolving door, eating in a restaurant, walking to the library, going downtown shopping, and electing officers" that many first experienced these situations during group activities. Detroit girls took trips to museums, the zoo, Greenfield Village's historic parks, the theater, and the city's Fourth of July fireworks display.[87]

Camp Fire's model of female citizenship remained tied to domestic competence, something MCAP families desired for their daughters too. Indeed, the mothers valued "the typical female role type activities," including skills in cooking, sewing, nutrition, budgeting, and home decoration and maintenance. Although these activities may be seen as simply promoting middle-class values, the parents and girls said it provided girls with a broader view of the world. Years later, one Black woman who lived in a foster home in the 1960s recalled that Camp Fire involvement "instilled in myself" a sense of belonging as well as "confidence, self-esteem, pride, and a host of other wonderful qualities." She added that, for her, no other space offered these same opportunities.[88]

Parents also valued "personal health and grooming" and "family-life education." Although the report did not define family-life education, in the 1960s and 1970s educators used the term to encapsulate themes that promoted "responsible decision-making," including sex education, and physical, sociological, and mental health. Several MCAP mothers associated family-life education with avoiding teenage pregnancy.[89] Although the reports did not record girls' responses to sex education, MCAP surveys indicated that the girls valued "girl talk" that addressed dating and family life in an informal way. As Camp Fire Girls had in the organization's first decade, these girls learned, through group conversations, "what a girl of her age needs to know about herself."

Although meetings, dances, parties, and service were staples across Camp Fire groups, the girls contested some traditional aspects of the Camp Fire program. They were not interested, and neither were their volunteer leaders, in American Indian symbolism or Indian names. MCAP staff reported these had "no or little reality" for these girls and women. One MCAP report maintained, "Attention should be given to other alternatives which may have more relevance for inner city girls."[90] Although Camp Fire made no move to abandon Indian lore at this stage, leaders recognized that throughout the organization many young people preferred to honor their own heritage and began adopting a choose-your-own identity policy that reflected a girl's ancestry or religious practice. The 1971 issue of *Camp Fire Girl* explained that young people were making dashikis and "Spanish ponchos." Undoubtedly, the admission of boys to Camp Fire also hastened a choice to broaden ceremonial attire beyond the Indian gown, which boys would not be expected to wear.[91] Although many white suburban groups continued to rely on the Indian imagery that had been a distinguishing feature of the organization since its founding, the practice gradually lost its centrality.

Likewise, MCAP girls rarely earned beads for specific achievements through the traditional honor program, and when they did earn beads, they rarely sewed them on the traditional Camp Fire vests or gowns. Although one Camp Fire report concluded that urban girls of color were not interested in the beads, their lack of involvement may have been due to expense. Beads and vests had to be purchased. Some showed an early interest that waned when the girls found out they had to pay for the "awards." One asked tellingly, "If we earned them [the beads], why do we have to pay for them?" In addition to cost, honor activities and sewing beads into designs required time and attention at home, and leaders noted that the girls "were not able to carry through to the point of completing the necessary work or keeping the complete records which permitted them to earn honor beads."[92] Earning beads was, therefore, not a central part of MCAP, and Camp Fire officials came to accept that it could take a back seat to alternate initiatives.

The Hidden Costs of Camping

As Camp Fire expanded to include new groups, central program elements such as camping—including day camp and resident sleepaway camp— were also reevaluated. Working with MCAP girls and their families shed new light on structural barriers to inclusion in Camp Fire that had long been ignored. Camp Fire leaders noted that the MCAP made them aware of many hidden costs of camp. Still, MCAP staff remained committed to offering outdoor activities. Indeed, the consultant Mozell Hill had identified camping as relevant for modern girls. Not only did it get urban girls out of crowded cities, but they also experienced independence from parents. Moreover, since camp fostered "experimental thought and action," it was vital, Hill argued, for advancing women's political and social freedoms.[93]

17. By the 1970s, Camp Fire Girls dressed in costumes that were meaningful to their culture. Some still chose the American Indian imagery. Camp Fire Girls Sacramento—Yolo Council Records, MS0002. Courtesy of the Center for Sacramento History.

Hill pointed out, however, that camping was often not available to urban, Black children due to racial and religious exclusion and expense. Most camping remained private and organized by racial, ethnic, and religious groups into the 1960s. Summer vacation spots used "the code phrase 'restricted clientele'" to discriminate against African Americans and other marginalized groups. Moreover, although Jewish and other European immigrant groups began to build camps in the 1920s, few African Americans established camps, leaving them without youth camping opportunities as the twentieth century progressed. Before the 1960s, few organizations provided integrated camping. Although the Communist Party and other left-wing organizations had taken up interracial camping in the 1940s as part of a broader critique of racism in public spaces, these camps—hardly mainstream—were subject to anticommunist surveillance and attacks in the 1950s. Even in the YMCA, one of the first mainstream organizations to integrate camping in the 1940s, less than half of its urban chapters offered integrated camping experiences, and these chapters were concentrated in the Northeast and upper Midwest. Scouts and Camp Fire Girls followed the Y's lead but did so in few areas until the 1960s. Then, in the 1960s and 1970s, responding to the 1964 Civil Rights Act, leaders of organizational camps across the country admitted children of color into formerly all-white camps.[94]

Although camp appealed to some MCAP girls and their families, communities of color lacked familiarity with the camp industry and its processes. This kept many from participating. In Southern California, where the *Los Angeles Times* funded robust "camperships" in 1966, the San Gabriel Council's MCAP sent 125 girls to Camp Wasewagan resident camp.[95] In Detroit, however, MCAP leaders struggled over three years to build interest in camping. Families had little "understanding of the value of such an outdoor experience" and some thought their daughters should not be away from home.[96] Parents alluded vaguely to safety concerns regarding unfamiliar environments. As cultural geographer Carolyn Finney explains, for many Black people, the woods are associated with lynching. Even though positive stories of nature may moderate fears, trepidation about "white spaces" may persist and keep Black people from entering what may be "hostile white terrain."[97]

Girls themselves often had mixed feelings about going to camp. Many "were frightened about outdoor 'night noises,'" did not want to use outdoor toilets, and shared their parents' apprehension about unfamiliar environments. In addition, some MCAP girls had been "to other camps for 'poor kids,' as they said, and most had had poor experiences." The Camp Fire reports did not detail what the children experienced, but other scholars note that "braving racist slurs at a mostly white camp" was not high on the agenda of nonwhite youth.[98] Some MCAP leaders concluded that "the concept of camping in residence as a primitive experience may not be valid" for girls in urban communities of color. They sought other kinds of outings, like visits to college campuses, "for fun, camaraderie and cultural enrichment."[99] But like Hill, most Camp Fire women remained committed to camping as a core Camp Fire activity, even if they needed to re-think policies and persuade the families of urban, low-income girls.

Convincing parents was a major MCAP task. Camp brochures, which described a camping philosophy of building self-confidence and skills in the outdoors, perplexed low-income families of color with their descriptions of camp nicknames and photos of girls carrying firewood and doing archery.[100] Struggling with varying degrees of literacy, busy parents also found unfamiliar terms confounding. Both day and residential camp offerings, with their varying fees, were listed, and brochures assumed the reader knew the difference. Different due dates for registration and camper fees required further decoding. It was likewise difficult and time-consuming for families to obtain forms, medical examinations, transportation, and proper camp clothing if they chose to send a child. The Detroit final report explained that MCAP staff and volunteers spent approximately fifteen to twenty hours per camper to convince parents and help them prepare their daughters for their first trip. In essence, for the unfamiliar, figuring out a trip to camp was the equivalent of a part-time job.[101]

Camp costs were significant for low-income MCAP families. Day camp at one New York site in 1964 was $10 for eight days of camp and transportation, and prices for resident camp ranged from $19 to $50 for one week.[102] Although "camperships," or agency-funded scholarships, existed, as did Office of Economic Opportunity (OEO) Tap funds, pamphlets rarely mentioned them or explained how to claim one. Families relied on information passed along by Camp Fire staff. Even after parents became aware of camperships, few women sought them out for their daughters. They may have been reluctant to ask for charity or may not have been that interested in sending their daughters away for the week. Even after girls were awarded assistance from a special gift fund or the OEO, some parents turned it down. In Detroit, three of seventeen such girls signed up only to cancel.[103]

Many parents lacked the time required to get their daughters ready for camp. One said she was too busy to get together "all that stuff you need," referring to registration paperwork and physical examinations.[104] The stuff also included equipment, bedding, towels, luggage, and transportation.[105] Although suburban, middle-class families might easily spare a bedroll for the week, low-income families shared bedding at home. If a departing daughter took a comforter, her siblings would have none. Even when sisters camped together, camp rules required each girl to have her own bedroll.[106] In the third summer, MCAP staff worked with United Community Services to hold a clothing drive so girls would have bathing suits and summer jackets. Goodwill loaned luggage, and the council's special gift fund allocated additional supplies to girls.[107] Even when provisions could be had, another hidden cost was the lost labor of an older daughter who looked after younger siblings and did housework.[108]

Camp Fire women worked hard to get girls to camp. In Detroit, unrest during the summer of 1967 further disrupted the preparation process, but Camp Fire staff persevered. For girls scheduled to attend camp the weekend after the uprising began, medical exams were interrupted as offices stayed closed, and many families still needed to make last-minute clothing and equipment purchases. The unrest disrupted the U.S. mail, delaying families' Aid to Dependent Children checks. Worse, neighborhood stores had been burned or remained shuttered. The project director and the school community agent made personal contact with each family to help girls make the trip, getting them the necessary supplies and shuttling them to nurses. For those girls returning from a week at camp, the Detroit council hired special buses with armed guards to deliver girls directly to their homes rather than to the designated pick-up point because snipers were still active in Detroit as the bus headed home.[109]

Because many MCAP girls had never been on a picnic or cookout, let alone to a seven-day sleep-away camp, volunteers focused on building girls' interest. At first during outdoor activities girls "were annoyed by the wind blowing their papers and by the mosquitoes." They went on day hikes and then some dusk hikes. They grew accustomed to the sounds of the outdoors, and leaders taught them about insect repellent. Over time, some girls even became fledgling nature scientists. According to one account, Detroit girls had read that "mosquitoes were attracted more to darker skins." They "check[ed] this out by counting mosquito bites after a trip" and found the science lacking. The same group took a snow day trip to Camp Wathana, fifty miles from Detroit, and many of the mothers came along to help; gradually, "a new picture came to them" of camping as fun.[110]

Reportedly, girls who went camping enjoyed it. The generally candid Detroit report noted, "There was little evidence that either the white or Negro girls from the Metropolitan Critical Areas Project felt left out at camp," and that despite a few problems with cleanliness and with stealing (the reports remind the researcher of stereotypes that followed these girls to camp), the MCAP girls adjusted well. One strong indicator that girls enjoyed their camp experience is that many opted to go again. A high number of returnees spoke to their enjoyment, and many encouraged peers to attend. Some MCAP girls expressed interest in doing the counselor-in-leadership training program for older youth, but they were unsure if they were eligible since "they hadn't seen any Negros in this unit." Camp Fire pledged to hire more Black counselors, but the observation indicated both girls' interest in camp and the limits of Camp Fire's perspective on whether or not they "felt left out."[111]

The Hidden Costs of Camp Fire

Financing for individuals and therefore for groups, too, was a challenge even for regular programing. Outreach to girls with limited resources for dues, uniforms, and ordinary field trips stretched the organization. Historically Luther Gulick pledged that Camp Fire would be an army, not a charity, and although that model had shifted with the move toward social service, Camp Fire still sought to instill self-reliance. While some councils waived dues or accepted smaller payments than the usual dollar for MCAP members, most MCAP leaders argued that families wanted to pay and were insulted if they were not asked to do so. Camp Fire adapted rules but rarely changed them. In San Francisco, for example, dues payments might be delayed until a candy sale, but the girls earned the money.[112] The question of charity aside, Camp Fire's MCAP leaders learned a great deal about the hidden costs—beyond dues—of running the program. They found costs to be higher in low-income city centers than in the suburbs because suburban, middle-class families subsidized the program as they offered volunteer service and transportation, allocated space in their homes, and purchased supplies and tickets. These taken-for-granted costs were on top of those that leaders expended on their membership dues, books, and transportation to various meetings and trainings. The Detroit leadership estimated that the cost to volunteer was about $50 per year.[113]

MCAP leaders and girls cobbled together funding and supplies as best they could. Councils held clothing drives and MCAP girls sold the items at rummage sales.[114] Suburban clubs gathered crayons, pencils, and paper to share with Camp Fire peers in the metropolitan program, continuing the long tradition of white, middle-class girls serving those they deemed less fortunate, and the project offices had additional supplies on hand upon club leaders' request.[115] Camp Fire also bridged the gap by collaborating with other community agencies. In Detroit, for example, the American Friends Service Committee helped finance group expenses and trips. Private businesses, service clubs, unions, community groups, and individuals also donated. MCAP girls often received free tickets to attend circuses, ballets, zoos, and sporting events with their Camp Fire clubs. But not all businesses opened their doors, and leaders noted that girls spent time planning activities that many in the group could not afford. One MCAP leader explained that they seldom confronted money problems openly during group meetings.[116] Leaders instead handled these situations one-on-one, but they were not always aware of each girl's financial need.

Uniforms were a special concern because they connected girls to the larger national organization and gave them a sense of belonging, but they were expensive, and community chests often refused to cover dues or uniforms. Sometimes MCAP staff received donations of uniforms, but rarely enough for an entire group. The leaders of groups would divide up the donation so that each girl would receive part of a uniform, leaving no one with the whole ensemble. The Camp Fire tie became the "significant symbol of membership" for which project offices paid.[117] Although some councils developed membership funds, the issue of ordinary costs was never fully resolved.[118]

Camp Fire's work in urban areas during the 1960s awakened leaders to issues of inclusion that were formerly invisible to organization founders and staff, who had pledged to serve all girls but operated on a narrow, middle-class model. MCAP illustrated that the Camp Fire program, with its offer of opportunities for service, fun, and adventure, appealed to girls across racial and economic lines. Without resources and strategic planning, however, it would not be available to girls outside the middle class. (Grant funds ended in 1967.) It was now evident that hidden costs in camping and ordinary programming made accessing the organization's features too difficult for low-income, urban families. In addition, a group structure that relied on a mother who was not gainfully employed taking care of a group of same-age girls within her home was increasingly outmoded for middle-class women as well as their lower-income counterparts. In response, Camp Fire went beyond MCAP and undertook a reexamination of its structure and function in the 1970s to ensure that it could reach all girls.

9

"It's a New Day"

Camp Fire's Reckoning and
Restructuring in the 1970s

The challenges of the 1960s awakened Camp Fire leadership to the need for deeper change. In 1967 local councils transitioned MCAP girls into regular Camp Fire programs. Although retention of MCAP girls was uneven, Camp Fire's leadership reckoned with the lessons learned through MCAP, brought in a new director, and restructured the organization to continue to reach diverse girls moving forward. In 1975 it launched the New Day program. The phrase recalled founder Charlotte Gulick's signal to campers at Lake Sebago each morning in 1910. "This is a new day!" she called as campers arose and greeted the sunrise. Her words had signaled Camp Fire's newness as an organization "quite unlike any there had ever been for girls."[1] When organization leaders repeated it in the 1970s, they invoked multiculturalism and the rise of second-wave feminism. The New Day program empowered local councils with "the maximum freedom to organize" in response to unique community needs, and each council was responsible for bringing youth into efforts to improve social conditions through social justice or other forms of volunteer work.[2]

American women's increasing calls for women's liberation brought about new definitions of girl citizenship, and the organization's admission of boys meant that Camp Fire would define youth citizenship and not girl citizenship alone. In 1963 executive director Martha Allen still understood girl citizenship training to be about "harmonizing" the demands of "women's own need for personal fulfillment" with "society's need of her in the reproduction and preservation of the race." She retired in 1966, and the new executive director, Hester Turner, exclaimed instead that "Today's girls will be tomorrow's executives, workers, wives, and mothers in a society that offers equal rights to everyone." She called out inequality in funding for girls' organizations, identified sex stereotyping as a barrier akin to racial oppression, and critiqued the assumption that the place for girls and women was in the home.[3] As Camp Fire admitted boys, its purpose shifted from fostering beautiful and useful womanhood to helping youth, regardless of gender, "to realize their potential and to function effectively as caring, self-directed individuals responsible to themselves and to others."[4] The gender-neutral purpose focused on the individual and extended to boys the responsibility to care.

Allen had overseen the launch of MCAP and Turner, an accomplished career woman, replaced her during its transition. The board of directors recruited Turner when she was the dean of students at Lewis and Clark College in Portland, Oregon. A lawyer with a doctorate in education, a delegate to the 1965 White House Conference on the Status of Women, and a divorced mother of four (the first mother to head the organization), she had enrolled her twin daughters in an Oregon club that helped them to flourish despite their visual impairment. When Turner publicly praised the organization for its disability inclusion efforts, she was tapped for the directorship. In addition to her equity focus, Turner would also attempt to put the organization on a sounder business footing through various efforts, including moving the headquarters from New York City to Kansas City in 1977.[5] Turner brought commitments to gender equity and to equal access for youth with disabilities to the position that would characterize the transition away from MCAP.

The Transition from MCAP to Mainstream Camp Fire

It became necessary to transition away from MCAP in the late sixties for a variety of reasons. One had to do with the disappearance of outside funding, another with a lack of commitment to the program in absence of those resources. Efforts to create a smooth transition followed different pathways in the various cities, depending on local commitment and levels of alternative funding. Grant funds for MCAP ran out after the summer of 1967 just as social welfare funding, especially that for community action programs that connected local nonprofits to federal funds, gave way to law enforcement spending. In fact, Camp Fire continued to support antidelinquency measures even as they were tied to juvenile justice, piloting several programs in the 1970s and 1980s in juvenile detention centers, but these were on a small scale.[6] Some councils had additional united community funds to continue projects in high-poverty areas. Others merged their MCAP groups into suburban councils, which cobbled together funding from united funds, product sales, local membership dues, and fundraising efforts.[7]

Many of the metropolitan projects lost members during the transition. Detroit and Los Angeles councils, despite plans to continue, lost organizing momentum. In Detroit, MCAP staff worked with the local council to provide a transition in which local colleges would collaborate with Camp Fire to keep the groups running. But since funds were short, many paid MCAP staff crucial to its operation found other jobs before the new effort got off the ground. Moreover, because of the uncertainty about continuity, leaders made no attempts to create new groups for girls during the last year of the project. And although the volunteers in local groups were becoming more diverse, few local people were in positions of authority in Camp Fire to continue building.[8] In Los Angeles, careful planning went into introducing the MCAP girls to the broader Camp Fire program. But as paid staff left, local volunteers could not be found to replace them. Following one recruitment meeting with seventy-two mothers, only eleven were willing to colead or assist. No mother committed to lead a group by herself. The Los Angeles project staff turned to friends of group workers and local leaders with experience. Los Angeles staffed all but one of the existing groups, but the new leaders were not as tied to the neighborhood or group as mother-leaders typically were. Of the ninety-three girls in Los Angeles remaining at the end of 1967, about one-third left during the transition summer. Although many moved away, following patterns consistent throughout MCAP, over ten percent left because they had no leader. By 1968 only six of the eleven clubs still met, with one more continuing within a non–Camp Fire agency.[9] Such losses were typical of the transition period.

During the transition period, MCAP councils discussed next steps—whether their MCAP groups could be folded into traditional Camp Fire councils and whether those councils were able to afford ongoing support. Many local councils rethought their purpose. In Washington DC, where some members of the local board and staff had initially regarded MCAP as "a short term project that was 'special,'" transition planning led to tensions over the allocation of resources. Potomac area leaders noted, "Staff and resources of the suburban areas were already stretched to a critical point, and any diversion of staff would mean losses" for Camp Fire's traditional strongholds. Many Potomac council members deemed Camp Fire to be primarily an educational enrichment program for middle-class girls. Still, local board members appreciated the "substantial amount" of positive media attention that resulted from participation in the low-income project, and they wanted this to continue. Board members recognized the potential marketability of a reputation for social sensitivity, concluding that MCAP "established" Camp Fire "as one of the more 'alert' social agencies in the community." To that end, the board continued MCAP-style efforts to serve low-income girls and "entered into a new phase as a community oriented agency," with more collaborations with other agencies and churches.[10] The Potomac area was not unique in its board and council's struggles to agree on a direction. A Camp Fire headquarters study observed that many local councils viewed the MCAP as a special temporary program and not a core Camp Fire feature.[11] This lack of recognition made necessary a formal restructuring with multiple program options if Camp Fire was going to continue to reach new communities of girls.

The MCAP experiments provided new opportunities for small pockets of girls in metropolitan centers, but more notably, they changed the structure and nature of the Camp Fire program itself as organizers experimented and found new ways of operating. In the process of community organizing, Camp Fire's leadership came to recognize the value of whole-family involvement (including boys), organizing across strict age boundaries, and the cultivation of new forms of leadership, and saw them as necessary reforms to the entire program. The challenges and opportunities of MCAP led to more choices and greater flexibility, qualities that characterized the New Day program and Camp Fire's restructuring in the 1970s.

"It's a New Day": From Reckoning to
Restructuring in the Seventies

The metropolitan projects had awakened those in Camp Fire who sought to serve more girls and had provided opportunity for experimentation, but structural barriers remained. Detroit leaders' main takeaway was that "the National and local councils should study the traditional group structure of Camp Fire Girls to see if there are alternative ways in which the organization can effectively serve the needs of today's girl."[12] According to the Potomac Area Council report, MCAP had "raised issues of policy that had not previously been questioned. Issues such as membership procedure, financial investments of leaders, the emphasis upon district organization of Camp Fire Girls, and the assignment of staff members gained new perspective and meaning for the Board."[13] In 1972 Camp Fire embarked on another self-study. The resulting New Day program embraced the spirit of experimentation and inclusivity these MCAP reports called for. Flexibility in membership—extending age groups, including boys, and counting as members children touched by the program rather than just those in traditional groups—became a Camp Fire hallmark in the 1970s and 1980s and has continued to define how the organization reaches young people. Camp Fire became a multiprogram organization that prioritized local autonomy to serve diverse community needs. It extended new programs to racially marginalized communities, low-income youth, and young people with disabilities.[14]

As Assistant National Executive Director Carol Bitner explained, the New Day program meant that councils reexamined their organizational structures and added people (paid and volunteer) to "build in multiple program delivery capability." In the past most councils had been structured uniformly. Now each council focused on its specific jurisdictional needs. Local boards and program committees assessed community needs through market research and developed program directions to match them. Local executives and staff carried out the specific directives adopted by their boards. Councils developed such programs as camps for preschool-age children, outdoor skills training, post–high school recreational and vocational development classes, athletic leagues, tutoring, and confidence-building and leadership workshops. A variety of meetings, seminars, task groups, and forums for leaders and others involved in program delivery replaced the classroom-like leaders' associations. These assemblies supported not only middle-class women's networks but all leaders, to "facilitate activity planning, communications, training and skill-building" and to gather new perspective regarding administration of the council. Camp Fire also replaced the national council with a national congress that gave local councils, now corporate members of Camp Fire Girls, more proportional representation. Local councils had greater accountability and capacity to create community-specific programs. For the first time, Camp Fire was designed around multiple "girls' life styles and needs" and not one universalizing, middle-class model.[15] Its diversity statement committed all councils to maintain "openness and welcome all persons regardless of race, religion, sex or national origin, mental or physical disability, economic status, etc."[16] These policy changes indicated a greater commitment to actual diversity and not just an openness to low-income girls of color who subscribed to middle-class values and customs.

Multiple program types were soon underway. In Oakland, California, unemployed sixteen- to twenty-year-olds received training for jobs at summer camps; in Bethel, Alaska, Indigenous children were enrolled in a water safety program; in Washington DC, special programs served youngsters on parole; in Seattle, working parents utilized a child-care program; and in Tulsa, Oklahoma, American Indians were targeted for Camp Fire outreach.[17] The New Day program extended services to girls with physical and mental disabilities. The Everest School for youth with intellectual disabilities such as Down syndrome sent twenty-eight girls aged ten to twelve to summer camp under the supervision of special education teachers. They camped alongside their "normal peers" and participated in the usual camp program of swimming, hiking, boating, arts and crafts, dramatics, and singing.[18] Such activities became widespread in the 1970s as the disability rights movement intensified demands for access to basic children's activities.

Programs serving youth with physical and intellectual disabilities, which the Children's Bureau and National Institute of Mental Health had required of programs receiving grant money, grew out of MCAP as well. MCAP

18. Camp Fire's New Day program allowed local councils to develop programs based on community need. The 1970s saw an extension of Camp Fire services to youth with disabilities. *Camp Fire Leadership*, Spring 1975. Reprinted with permission of Camp Fire.

focused on girls with "inadequate social adjustment; reduced learning capacity; and/or slow rate of maturation."[19] However, Camp Fire and social work literature also blurred the categories of children of color from low-income groups and those with intellectual disabilities. In Detroit 47 percent of the elementary school-aged girls in MCAP were designated as physically or mentally handicapped.[20] Sociologist Meyer Schreiber, addressing an MCAP seminar, explained that the intellectual disabilities of the MCAP girls were mild or moderate. Although these girls may have included some with neurodevelopmental disorders, lower-income girls from racialized communities were frequently labeled with mental disabilities. Schreiber explained that the children that Camp Fire served appeared "normal in the physical sense but function as mentally retarded." Schreiber continued, the "greatest concentration" of these children "is among minority groups residing in city slums." Schreiber attributed their problems to a range of environmental factors such as prenatal care, premature birth, and other health factors but did not exclude earlier twentieth-century eugenic explanations. "Factors of inheritance of intelligence are undoubtedly significant," he remarked. Camp Fire offered social support for these families with children with real or perceived disabilities. Schreiber noted that considering "the lack of community facilities; the limited opportunity for social companionship for the child; the burden of constant care and supervision and financial stress due to various urgent needs, prolonged dependency, and limited capacity for self-support," the Camp Fire Girls alleviated the solitary pressures on families of raising children with real or perceived disabilities.[21]

Although Camp Fire served some children with programs in separate institutions, MCAP also mainstreamed some with perceived intellectual disabilities by placing two or three girls labeled slow together in larger groups.[22] Sometimes Camp Fire staff placed girls with perceived mental disabilities with a younger age group, disrupting the strict age distinctions common in the traditional program. Organizers stressed that for girls with disabilities, "the program activities were essentially the same" and included things like singing and hand crafts.[23] Mixed groups were not always successful. Local leaders reported teasing as a problem among older girls, who used their peers with intellectual disabilities "as scapegoats for all that went wrong." Yet these leaders also reported that dealing with "retarded girls" was far less challenging than coping with "the very aggressive normal ones."[24] Camp Fire's staff concluded that girls with intellectual disabilities benefited by learning to do new things and being expected to have a greater degree of independence while the nondisabled children grew in awareness of what their peers with disabilities could do.[25]

Girls with more severe challenges joined Camp Fire in segregated facility-based groups. For example, the children's unit at Buffalo State Hospital, once known as the Buffalo State Asylum for the Insane, asked Camp Fire to start an MCAP extension for the fifty children with mental disturbance diagnosis there. A hospital staffer was a longtime Camp Fire member and helped facilitate the program. Some of the girls got to go to residential camp and all attended a day camp.[26]

Camp Fire's experimentation within MCAP made its way into the organization's new structure in the 1970s. Services for children with disabilities and their families was one of the many local needs that councils identified for impacting their communities.[27] By 1981 over four thousand girls with physical or mental disabilities participated in Camp Fire clubs, camps, or other programs.[28]

Camp Fire maintained that Blue Birds, Camp Fire Girls, and Horizon Club were still the "bread and butter" of the organization but that councils were being asked through New Day programming to add different kinds of "jam."[29] As Camp Fire expanded its programming to fulfill multiple purposes and suit communities' needs, it became more inclusive and offered an example of structural change.[30] Although external factors such as the legal requirements of the Civil Rights Act to prohibit segregation drove some reforms, leaders also engaged in critical inquiry into exclusionary organizational practices.

Camp Fire Boys

While the structural changes in the organization were substantial, to many outside observers the most substantive change of the 1970s was the admission of boys. The board of directors initially recommended that Camp Fire admit high school–age boys in 1971. The national staff cited "requests from high school students for co-ed organizational options and evidence that co-ed programs are preferred by many high school students" as reasons for the inclusion of boys. Turner later noted that many boys had found Boy Scouts "too militaristic, too organized, [and] too demanding." Camp Fire offered them, as it had girls, "freedom to choose activities." In 1971 the national council voted in favor of the measure and added a provision to allow either men or women to lead Camp Fire clubs. They claimed "the spirit of 'liberation' movements" called for "utilizing the best skills wherever they are found" and pointed out that the "women only rule" was based on the false stereotype that only women could be effective role models to girls.[31] Camp Fire began to use the name Camp Fire, Inc., instead of Camp Fire Girls in 1973. In 1975 the New Day program officially incorporated boys across age groups, and groups for young boys, called Blue Jays, began cropping up across the country. Like many of the other structural changes, the gender-neutral policies and broad age span first came into place in MCAP as organizers experimented by partnering with other agencies where boys participated and by allowing little brothers to tag along.

Camp Fire also admitted younger children. With the New Day program, the youngest regular club members were six years old, and Camp Fire also reached preschoolers in special community programs. By the 1980s, Camp

Fire had initiated an age class below Blue Birds called Sparks to meet the needs of families who wanted to provide a coeducational organizational experience for their preschool and kindergarten-age children.[32] Lowering the age limits to membership opened Camp Fire to an age group that no other youth agency was then serving. One Sacramento mother said she enrolled her six-year-old boy in Blue Jays because he could not join Cub Scouts until he was eight and they did not want to wait.[33] Thus the age and gender inclusivity had the potential to bring in new members.

Regarding boys, however, reporters quipped that the Camp Fire Girls had "switched smoke signals," using the organization's traditional Indian imagery to mock the entry of boys: "Sitting cross-legged around the camp-fire now—right there next to the young ladies—will be Camp Fire Boys."[34] But Camp Fire articulated the change in second-wave feminist terms. When its new issues-focused magazine appeared in 1971, it included the National Organization for Women's call for women to work in active "part-nership with men" to bring about their own equality. Camp Fire signaled its commitment to forge that partnership with the admission of boys. Camp Fire also moved away from the heteronormative program planning that had characterized boy-girl activities in earlier decades. Rather than encouraging boy-girl activities to ensure harmonious marriages, Camp Fire noted the importance of "enriching platonic relationships" for fun and learning "mutual respect."[35]

A new gender-neutral statement of purpose that challenged Camp Fire's history of gender stereotyping accompanied the New Day rollout. Camp Fire pledged to aid individuals in realizing their potential and refashioned its older ideals such as woman's spiritual connection to the home to encompass "the development and preservation of spiritual and ethical values; [and] the realization of the dignity and worth of each individual." The new statement also affirmed the importance of "self-reliance, initiative, and a positive self-image" for boys and girls.[36] Articles in the leadership magazine targeted sex-stereotyping. For example, the national magazine prompted club leaders to ask themselves:

Do I build into the program nontraditional female activities such as self-defense, bike repair and carpentry, in addition to the usual cook-

19. In 1975 Camp Fire admitted boys across all age groups. Boys had begun attending meetings and activities during the Metropolitan Critical Areas Project, and Camp Fire adjusted to meet the needs of more families. Camp Fire, Annual Report, 1977. Reprinted with permission of Camp Fire.

ing and sewing? . . . Do I say, "When you grow up to be a mother (or wife) . . ." excluding the possibility of another life style? . . . Do I reinforce the myth that a female must have either a career or a family, while a male is expected to have both? . . . Do I allow the girls to constructively express their anger at appropriate times, or do I have them always "appear" pleasant and internalize any negative feelings?[37]

Camp Fire literature no longer advised bringing in men to do heavy tasks. In making a birdfeeder, even the youngest Camp Fire Girls would now be taught to hammer.[38] New recommendations for choosing Camp Fire nicknames encouraged "strong, active, adventuresome names" and observed "what they call themselves is important to their self-concept."[39]

Camp Fire faced resistance to the admission of boys in some locations. In Sacramento, members and leaders told the press that they "felt like they would like it to remain an all girl club." Some members believed that recreational-educational programs should train boys and girls in different ways.[40] Not all councils adopted gender-integrated groups. Many chose to offer separate groups for boys. In 1977, for example, most reported the addition of separate boys' groups within the traditional program and the rewording of publications to include "all youth."[41] Like the girls' groups, boys' groups met weekly, participated in typical field trips, service projects, and crafts—though one mother noted a particular affinity for projects that featured hammering. When asked why the groups were sex-segregated within the organization, the mother and leader explained the boys "like playing with boys. To them, at this age, girls are just 'blech.'"[42] Such statements demonstrate how the new gender-neutral approach at the national level lived alongside older gender stereotypes about acceptable boy and girl behavior at the local level.

Nationally, growth in boys' clubs were sluggish; the core clubs for youth nine to thirteen were particularly resistant to change. Not only did some women leaders resist admitting boys, but also ample recreational alternatives for boys of this age group already existed. In 1979, although 70 percent of Camp Fire councils included boys, they were only 9 percent of youth members. In 1986 boys were still only 14 percent of traditional club members.[43] Gender desegregation moved much slower than did the simple admission of boys. Turner recognized that change would be slow, laughing that many "boys probably don't appreciate what we're offering; they're not that liberated."[44]

Sometimes the girls resisted. At a Horizon Club conference in the early 1970s, a girl chided, "Why would any boy want to join Horizon? It's a girls' club." A boy in the room defended himself and the social and leadership opportunities the organization offered to him with, "We joined the club because it was the natural thing to do."[45] Girls also expressed a desire for all-girl spaces. When girls had been surveyed in 1957, a majority indicated a desire for an occasional boy-girl activity, but a report noted, "There seems

20. Camp Fire literature changed in the 1970s to depict girls of color and children doing a broader range of activities. Camp Fire expected girls to hammer and not to call on their fathers and brothers for help. *Camp Fire Leadership*, Spring 1975. Reprinted with permission of Camp Fire.

to be a desire for groups composed of girls only." In 1957 Camp Fire adults thought that the primary purpose of boy-girl activities was preparation for heterosexual dating and marriage, noting that what "may be a surprise to the men in this audience is that girls have many interests other than boys!" Girls wanted all-girl spaces to "let their hair down" and be free from competition with and scrutiny from boys.[46] One former California Camp Fire Girl recalled, "I remember being happy that there weren't boys around. . . . It gave you that chance to not be self-conscious about having a boy around and not worrying about how you acted around them. . . . You knew that it was okay to be just a little girl . . . out playing and being dirty and whatever and just giggly without that feeling that the boys were around."[47]

Despite such resistance, Camp Fire was the first in the youth services market to forge a broad coeducational plan. The Girl Scouts, which also faced membership struggles during the 1970s, responded to the feminist movement by reaffirming the organization's operation for girls and by women. Girl Scout leadership briefly considered admitting boys at its 1975 triennial conference. Proponents thought it would keep older girls in the organization longer and that boys and girls would learn better how to interact with one another. One Girl Scout declared that boys had better join and learn to cook because "they might not have us (to do it for them)."[48] Opponents of the move, however, won the day by arguing that boys were not "knocking down the doors to get in" and that "an all-girl" organization was "essential in a society" where women's roles were changing.[49] Meanwhile, the Boy Scouts of America had opened its Explorer Scouts to older girls, despite not having any women on their program staff, but most of its programming remained closed to girls. To assert women's liberation while forging an alternative path of fostering interaction between boys and girls, Camp Fire adopted the long-range plan of being "the *coed* youth agency in the United States."[50] Camp Fire stood uniquely poised to serve a niche of coeducation across a broad swath of age groups.

By the 1980s and 1990s, more groups were gender-integrated. Although some groups were reluctant to accept boys into formerly all-girl groups, many councils carried the spirit of the New Day forward and created options for boys. When historian and Camp Fire member Barb Kubik's sons joined in Washington State, the family chose Camp Fire over other youth-oriented programs because, as Kubik explained, she appreciated its inclusiveness, and "I just wanted my sons to learn some of the skills that I had learned in Camp Fire and have some of the same opportunities." The Tri-City elementary school club that the boys participated in was made up of different age groups, a feature common in clubs by then. When the family moved to Vancouver, the oldest boy, then in high school, continued with his Tri-City Horizon Club group. Through long commutes and independent work, he earned his Wohelo award.

The younger boy was in elementary school at the time, and several clubs welcomed him. "The problem came when he entered middle school," Kubik notes. "His former leaders and their kids weren't going on in Camp Fire, and he was left afloat. We simply could not find a club who would welcome him." Fortunately, the council had a Teen Club program, one of the innovations that had grown out of giving councils more local autonomy. Although the club was mostly girls, the older ones understood that he was a kid without a neighborhood club, "and they welcomed him with open arms." The projects at the Teen Club befitted Camp Fire's goal of involving youth in improving the social conditions in their communities. Each grade level had a representative on a teen board that planned council-wide service projects, social activities, and craft projects. Kubik's son developed a service project in partnership with the Clark County YWCA to aid its domestic violence shelter. Despite the traditional clubs' reluctance at the middle-school level to admit boys, the local council had created meaningful opportunities for boys in the program.[51]

Councils Respond to the New Day:
"Slaying Dragons" or Resisting Change

There was little overt resistance to the other New Day program require-ments among council leaders. However, some councils struggled to make change happen in the face of outside hostility, limited funding, and hes-itant volunteers. On the whole, local leaders appreciated the ability to experiment and serve their communities as they saw fit.[52] Many expressed enthusiasm for their increased advocacy role. They saw their units as "slay-ing dragons," referring to urban problems, and they found rewarding their enhanced relationships with other community agencies. Most councils acknowledged the need for expanding access to low-income children and those of color, and many described a new earnestness in pulling together to achieve these goals.[53]

Even when local councils supported diversifying the membership, at times outsiders resisted equality. In Pomona, California, Camp Fire's local headquarters were the target of racial violence when its board followed the MCAP lead by responding to community needs. Pomona was changing from majority white to majority Black in the 1960s. The predominantly white board started Camp Fire clubs in the local public schools and hired more diverse personnel. Connie Turner, the first Black woman to serve as district director for the area, successfully recruited Black children. Then someone threw a Molotov cocktail into the Camp Fire building, destroying council records and gutting the building's interior. A police spokesperson attributed the attack to the local "high school's race problem" because racially motivated fights had erupted in two schools in the weeks before the bombing. But local Camp Fire leaders attributed the arson not to the high school students but to white supremacists, "outsiders," they said, who were "not happy that Camp Fire was serving black people." The case was never solved, and Camp Fire relocated its local headquarters, though a teen center in a portable trailer continued to operate in the space.[54] Although this extreme response to inclusion was rare, it is a reminder of the real risks that girls' groups ran as they sought change.

A more common problem was council reluctance to make transformative change. Councils tended to add new programs, such as a separate group for boys or measures to bring low-income children to camp, rather than fundamentally change the traditional practices to which they were accustomed. About a quarter of local directors commented that the traditional members of their councils "resist change" and "prefer the traditional program." One director noted that she was "not sure club leaders really care" about the new program and that the council was likely to do its own thing. Councils noted uncertainty about how to extend New Day programming and maintain traditional programs without new resources. Indeed, councils accustomed to recruiting among suburban girls did not see clearly who their potential new members were or how to reach them.[55] As Hester Turner recalls, one of the organization's strengths, its longtime members who started as girls and later led groups and councils, was also a barrier to change. For longtime members, "there was so much nostalgia," she noted, "that it was difficult to change some things." They "couldn't see why we couldn't do it the way we used to do it."[56]

As a result of the lack of funds and the reluctance to overcome resistance, the New Day program had mixed results. It succeeded in redefining the gender distinctions that had been at the heart of the founders' vision of girls' programming. The efforts also put Camp Fire squarely on the side of inclusion and diversity across class, race, and ability lines. But the problems concerning resources and the fact that core constituents came from white, middle-class communities that did not share the same social justice commitment meant that Camp Fire lacked unity of purpose. Separate, parallel programs too often served different portions of the community without bringing them together. In an interview many years later, Turner noted that "the New Day program tried" to demonstrate the significance of Camp Fire and bring in boys and girls. "We really were trying to find some way to be a force in society."[57] The New Day program had created greater autonomy in all areas of programming and management, but the Camp Fire leadership found that this was at the expense of organizational identity. By 1986 organization professionals commented, "There is a perception within the Camp Fire movement that we're not sure what we stand for or what quality can reasonably be expected."[58]

Camp Fire continued to struggle to reach and maintain new members. It was not the only organization to contend with declines in these years. Across the board, American membership and participation in a broad range of civic organizations, from labor unions to parent-teacher associations, declined in the 1970s and after. Individual forms of leisure and technologies displaced many of the early and mid-twentieth-century community social networks.[59] Despite Camp Fire's efforts to adjust and reach different groups of girls, its youth membership declined in the 1970s, with only a minimal increase in the 1980s. The Girl Scouts, facing similar membership drops, also increased council autonomy and deepened inclusion efforts. That these moves led to growth in Girl Scouting and a small increase in Camp Fire during the 1980s suggests that the choices were sound. By contrast, the Boy Scouts had a brief period of diversification, but conservative board members steered that organization toward narrow, reactionary definitions of moral character and strict enforcement of national policies. A decades-long membership slide followed.[60]

Camp Fire struggled for other reasons as well. It went into the 1970s with fewer members and less name recognition than either Boy Scouts or Girl Scouts. In addition, in 1986 Camp Fire's leadership found that the organization's transformation to a multiservice agency "require[d] a greater depth of management expertise" than volunteers possessed and that limited resources hindered the success of both the traditional and innovative programs. The number of traditional Camp Fire clubs and the number of councils declined from the 1970s into the 1980s. In part, mergers of councils were strategic, but the geographic range of the organization decreased as well. In the same fifteen years, Camp Fire went from over 370 councils and associations to 299, with 10 more pending dissolution due to lack of financial resources, volunteers, and professional staff. Camp Fire was, by the mid-1980s, more diverse and attuned to social justice but less prominent as a national organization.[61]

With MCAP and the New Day program, Camp Fire questioned its historically white, middle-class model of girlhood. MCAP had made Camp Fire's white, middle-class leadership aware of the need for structural changes, and New Day marked a break from the rigidity of old practices. The national office abandoned the strict gender ideology and the racial segregation that had characterized the organization from 1910 through the early 1960s. Until the 1960s, the organization's language was more inclusive than the reality of the largely white and middle-class Camp Fire experience. In the 1980s, however, the tension between the traditional club program and the alternative delivery methods persisted, and the two competed for diminishing resources at the local level. Likewise, although diversity had increased, Camp Fire's leadership noted that the organization's volunteer and professional staff were still overwhelmingly white and middle class. This was especially true in the traditional club program, and white members continued to regard the alternative modalities, where children from racialized groups predominated, as "less" Camp Fire.[62] Even as local control and autonomy permitted diversification, in some councils traditionalists dug in their heels and supported narrow, middle-class programming at the expense of other types. By the 1970s, youth leaders recognized that service solely to white, middle-class girls in suburban units was too limited. Camp Fire's different constituents—alumni nostalgic for the youth programs of the 1950s and early 1960s, national employees with degrees in sociology and education, social workers in low-income communities, middle-class mothers who sought out programs that connected them to their communities, lower-income families who found a venue for civic action and advocacy, and girls from many different backgrounds—did not all agree on what constituted girls' needs and desires. The resources necessary to serve them all well were not available as the federal War on Poverty's social welfare focus gave way to new attitudes and policies: punitive intervention in communities of color, deregulation, and trickle-down economics.

Camp Fire would eventually define itself as an organization committed to what a more recent CEO, Cathy Tisdale, calls "radical notions of inclusion." Small enough that its leaders did not need to appease conservative boards, Camp Fire in the twenty-first century created inclusive curricula for youth programming and minimized its focus on traditional clubs.

The organization would largely avoid LGBTQ+ rights controversies that troubled the more well-known Girl Scouts and Boy Scouts beginning in the 1980s. This was not due to any timidity in adopting inclusive policies.[63] In fact, for those who were watching, Camp Fire moved further against inequality, injustice, and exclusion in the twenty-first century than other mainstream youth organizations. The challenges of the 1960s and 1970s produced membership adjustments that were the product of need but that also reflected broader societal changes and established a new tradition and trajectory for Camp Fire to serve all youth.

Epilogue

An All-Gender Organization
for the Twenty-First Century

Camp Fire's founding framework of essential feminism carved out new civic responsibilities and opportunities in physical culture and camping for girls and women based on their supposed inherent feminine character. It proved remarkably flexible through twentieth-century challenges, including the Progressive era, Depression, two world wars, and the early Cold War. But changes in American culture and politics—especially those brought on by the civil rights movement, second-wave feminism, and shifting youth cultures—challenged the maternal rationale for girls' civic responsibilities. Those changes brought new attention to how Camp Fire had failed to serve all girls. Camp Fire's Metropolitan Critical Areas Project and New Day program revealed the insufficiency of a recreational education program designed for middle-class girls to meet the complex needs of a diverse American population. Though it has struggled to articulate a core identity, Camp Fire has deepened its commitment to diversity, equity, and inclusion since the 1970s. New Day marked a break from the strict gender ideology that the Camp Fire Girls sponsored from 1910 through the early 1960s, and its MCAP challenged its traditional adherence to middle-class femininity.

Recent Camp Fire CEO Cathy Tisdale comments that Camp Fire's ongoing diversity, equity, and inclusion work is consistent with its history: "In 1910 Camp Fire offered the radical notion that young girls had as much right to camp in the woods as young boys. That young girls could shoot an arrow from a bow and guide a canoe across a lake as well as a boy. That girls had as much to contribute to society as boys. In an era when the norm was to teach young women about 'managing hearth and home' and 'baking that perfect loaf of bread,' Camp Fire changed the conversation."[1] Tisdale's statement captures how, despite their gender essentialism, the Gulicks expanded girls' opportunities. To their credit, they saw girls as capable, strong, intelligent, and creative at a time when many reactionary voices condemned the new opportunities women were enjoying. Camp Fire's founders believed that to ensure modern industrial society retained a measure of beauty and romance, modern girls and women needed a "new relation to the world" that would bring an ethic of care, cheerfulness, and charm to civic life. Herein lay the girl's usefulness to the community and the nation. Although essential feminism had drawbacks, reinscribing traditional feminine associations with home and hearth, it also brought girls and women greater opportunity to participate in politics, education, reform, and, because strength and health would assure women's ability to contribute in those arenas, athletics and camping.

Camp Fire provided a framework for ushering girls' useful contributions into public arenas. During the first and second world wars, it offered a uniquely feminine version of home front mobilization. Described as a domestic army, Camp Fire Girls had an opportunity to serve their country and maintain the nation's morale even as they projected a reassuring gender stability. The visibility of girls' contributions cast war itself as an effort to protect innocence, families, and healthy childhoods. The Camp Fire Girls expanded roles in ways that were nonthreatening. But in the postwar era, Camp Fire's girl citizenship model had a braking influence on the gender shifts of the World War II era. Camp Fire women lauded the Gulicks as visionaries and reaffirmed their conservative gender essentialism. Indeed, their revival of Progressive era justifications for women's rights nearly four decades after Camp Fire had first framed those ideas was reactionary. Camp Fire now contained women's choices. The "homemaker plus" made room for the girl who was interested in careers, politics, athletics, business, and other activities outside the home but told her that those activities were secondary to her identity as a future homemaker. Even though women's expanding roles in the postwar workforce suggested that this was an outdated model, older women in local councils held fast to it for their girls. Until pressed during the 1970s to address sex stereotypes, Camp Fire adults were content to train girls for this middle-class Progressive era model of "beautiful and useful womanhood."[2]

At the same time, most Camp Fire officials ignored how its programming, even when its ethic appealed across race and economic lines, was not widely accessible. Antiprejudice efforts during and after World War II targeted white girls with lessons on how to be more tolerant, but most Camp Fire clubs remained segregated. Institutional structures depended upon volunteer mothers, girls' social proximity to their leader, and a common understanding of character-building ideals, a model that limited outreach largely to suburban neighborhoods. As girls joined within their neighborhood, church, and school, lines of race, ethnicity, and economics remained unchallenged. Divisions based on social group and cultural background remained very much a part of Camp Fire in the postwar period.

The founders believed that girls across time, as well as class, race, religion, and region, experienced girlhood in the same way. By including "all girls" in the certificate of incorporation, leaders for half a century contended that the organization bridged the social and cultural divisions among girls, but in this Camp Fire did not fulfill its own vision. American Indian and Gypsy imagery helped compose a timeless, cross-cultural portrait of girlhood, but it obscured serious social and political inequalities among members. Moreover, engaging in Indian play when Indigenous people themselves had faced land theft, genocide, and forced assimilation at the hands of the dominant culture was one more appropriation that, however well intentioned, solidified cultural hierarchies. Camp Fire associated primitiveness and proximity to nature with Native peoples for white people's benefit and pleasure and largely ignored the Natives themselves—aside from a few consultants and girls in assimilationist institutions. At the same time, Camp Fire's shared experiences of ceremonials, camping, literature, and writing fostered a sense of belonging to national culture, and this sometimes transcended race, ethnicity, class, and physical disability. Clubs and councils had the potential to bring girls together, but local pressures and the privileging of a white, middle-class membership were longstanding barriers to inclusivity.

The landscape of youth organizations has changed in the twenty-first century. For one, Camp Fire, which became the first coeducational national youth organization in the 1970s, shares the coeducational designation. Boy Scouts of America narrowly opened to girls when its Exploring branch began admitting girls in 1971; it opened to girls at all program levels in the late 2010s. In 2019 the Boy Scouts changed the title of its main program to Scouts BSA and allowed girls to earn the rank of Eagle. Although the elementary school–aged Cub Scouts is gender-integrated, most older members meet in troops separated by gender. The Girl Scouts remains a single-sex organization, now unique among American youth organizations and in the minority among them globally.

Internationally, the World Organization of the Scout Movement (WOSM), which is open to all-boy and coeducational groups, officially admitted girls in 1977, even though many national scouting organizations remained closed to girls. Nations have addressed coeducation variously. For example, Sweden, a coeducation leader, combined its organizations in 1960 and has mixed gender groups. In the United Kingdom, coeducation was voluntary from 1991 to 2000, when newly organized groups were required to accept girls. According to WOSM, by 1990 about half of scouting organizations included girls, though some national organizations had girls meet in separate groups under the same umbrella organization, as Scouts BSA currently does.[3] Since 2016 the World Association of Girl Guides and Girl Scouts (WAGGGS), of which the Girl Scouts is a member, admits organizations where scouting is coeducational alongside the more traditional single-sex girls' groups. The member organizations are required to be "open to all girls and young women without distinction of creed, race, nationality or any other circumstance," a potentially far-reaching promise.[4]

Camp Fire has also been a pathbreaker for LGBTQ+ youth. Indeed, Camp Fire has moved beyond the original notion of dichotomous cisgendered coeducation; Tisdale refers to it as an all-gender organization. Camp Fire was also one of the first youth institutions to include sexual orientation in its inclusion statement, adding it in 1993.[5] In 2021 Camp Fire's expansive inclusion statement welcomes "young people and adults of all abilities and disabilities, experiences, races, ethnicities, socio-economic backgrounds, sexual orientations, gender identities and expressions, religion and non-religion, citizenship and immigration status, and any other category people use to define themselves or others."[6] One small way that Camp Fire recognizes gender diversity is that staff and executives list their pronouns in their email signatures to "affirm our belief that every individual has the right to define their own identity."[7] In addition, Camp Fire hosts inclusion, LGBTQ-friendly, and other themed camps.[8] Camp Fire's LGBTQ-specific Camp sessions in 2018 and 2019 in rural Oklahoma were in demand, explains diversity and equity consultant Ben Matthews, "because there's not a lot of access to programming around LGBTQ+ identities" in rural areas of the South and the Midwest. For Camp Fire's more traditional camps, national headquarters has provided LGBTQ+ awareness training for camp staff to afford campers greater information privacy. At any camp, a child may, in the tradition of choosing camp names, call themselves something new, and camp staff will not share the name with family members. Youth who may not have disclosed an alternative gender identity to their families can live authentically at camp by using a name that accords with their identity.[9]

Camp Fire's acceptance of LGBTQ youth has outpaced peer organizations. After two decades of controversy, the Boy Scouts began admitting gay Scouts in 2013, openly gay adult leaders in 2015 (though the national left it up to local troops and councils to select leaders that reflected the community's values), and transgender Scouts in 2017. Girl Scouts of the USA deals with the "placement of transgender youth . . . on a case-by-case basis." If the family, school, and community recognize the child as a girl and she "lives culturally as a girl, then Girl Scouts is an organization that can serve her in a setting that is both emotionally and physically safe."[10] Camp Fire's approach of accepting all genders embraces greater gender fluidity.

Despite its leadership in opening spaces for LGBTQ+ youth and growth in some segments, Camp Fire's scope and reach have declined in the twenty-first century. Several of the councils where I originally did research in the early 2000s no longer exist. In 2019 Camp Fire reached just over 187,000 youth across twenty-five states and 1,300 program sites. Fifty-seven percent of youth involved in Camp Fire are female, 42 percent are male, and 1 percent identify as gender nonconforming. Its members more closely approximate the American demographic makeup, with a racially and ethnically diverse staff and youth that crosses socioeconomic lines, than at any point in its history. Still, organization leaders note, it is hard to be really inclusive when Camp Fire operates in only half the states.[11]

Camp Fire did not ask children to pledge a duty to God, which the Girl Scouts and BSA do, in its early years, and it continues to operate as a nonsectarian organization. Although a few traditional clubs choose to include the Camp Fire Law, with its "worship God" opening in meetings and on websites, the law is not an official required part of Camp Fire in 2022. History and current expectations occasionally clash. Many camps display artwork or banners made by previous campers. Such banners may "still have the Camp Fire Law," Matthews explains. At one rural Oklahoma camp, such a banner covers a lodge wall, and some young people have expressed discomfort with its presence. Indeed, many Oklahoma youth select Camp Fire camps because they are among the few that are not faith-based in the area.[12] Camp alumni, however, often hold Camp Fire traditions dear, and they desire to maintain their history and traditions at their former camps. Camp Fire's diversity, equity, and inclusion measures seek to honor Camp Fire alumni experiences while guaranteeing that youth have safe spaces to forge their own identities.

Along these lines, Camp Fire has reconfigured many of its old symbols and activities. Some elements, such as the watchword Wohelo for work, health, and love, continue to be used as the name for the organization's highest service achievement award. The award recognizes wide-ranging projects in personal development, leadership, and advocacy. Recently, a teen completed over 180 hours of public education service at the U.S. Botanic Garden; another worked with young children to develop an enthusiasm for the outdoors and conservation.[13] The name Camp Fire is also the same, but it no longer recalls a primitive hearth. It symbolizes "light[ing] the fire within" young people as they "develop interests, skills, commitments, or qualities that give [their] lives purpose."[14] Although some councils still offer traditional clubs, most Camp Fire youth do not meet in the home of a child's mother each week after school but encounter Camp Fire's curriculum through summer camps, day camps, after-school programs that include workshops and classes, and leadership institutes. There are only twenty-three club programs, serving over three thousand youth. The organization partners with other agencies. In 2020 Camp Fire delivered its program at schools, Boys & Girls Clubs, and YMCAs.[15] Activities center on helping children thrive as they figure out their talents and interests, their "spark." Camp Fire tries to cultivate youth-adult partnerships that support young people's ability to express themselves and take leadership roles, emphasizing their ability to do this now, not just in the future.

Camp Fire's national leadership listens to young people's voices, and provides them with an outlet for civic action. The website explains, "Camp Fire is not only for young people but by young people. We include young people in Camp Fire's decision making through youth councils on both the national and regional levels."[16] Camp Fire, the first major national organization to include youth on its national board in the 1970s, seats young people at the table for discussions of diversity, equity, and inclusion. Indeed, youth have been responsible for pushing forward antiracist initiatives, ending cultural appropriation, and fostering LGBTQ+ equity. As the program consultant for diversity and inclusion explains, "Campfire really wants to provide a space for youth to do what they want to do. And right now, a lot of that is activism around environmentalism or activism around Black Lives Matter or activism around LGBTQ+ issues."[17]

Camp Fire executives are keenly aware that definitions of inclusion and diversity that youth workers formulated in the twentieth century must change to fit twenty-first-century needs. It is not enough to tolerate groups separated by religion, race, or economic status. Although children may continue to experience Camp Fire with others from their neighborhood or school community, Tisdale insists that in Camp Fire children work with others from diverse backgrounds. In the days following George Floyd's murder, the current CEO, Greg Zweber, wrote to express solidarity with Black youth and Black families, calling out the ways that the organization's "own color-blindness may have kept us from speaking up on issues of race." He continued, "We believe it absolutely shapes our experiences, and claiming to not see color can harm us and stop us from addressing the inequities we know exist."[18]

Camp Fire also supports children with physical and intellectual disabilities. Camp inclusion coordinators, staff members trained in special education, assist children with ADHD, autism spectrum disorders, and children with physical mobility limitations to participate fully in the programs. Their aim, as they put it, is to provide the resources necessary for each child to discover and develop their spark.[19] This philosophy has been incorporated into a three-year grant awarded to ten Camp Fire councils to make capital improvement projects on their camps. In the work of tearing down the old dining hall at the Minnesota camp, Tanadoona, and deciding what the new one would look like, for example, Camp Fire included many youth voices. They urged the adult planners to radically reenvision facilities. Not only is the new building disability accessible, but also the bathrooms and showers are gender neutral, providing all campers and staff with spaces where they can access privacy when they need it. When the majority of camps were built, before 1975, adults were not terribly concerned about children's privacy. Now, camp staff looks at how to rearrange schedules and make other structural shifts to ensure that a level of privacy is available to anyone who wants it.[20]

Finally, Camp Fire's national headquarters has moved to discontinue the use of Indian-like ceremonial costumes. In 2020 a handful of clubs still perpetuated the traditional club programing, mainly under the direction of ardent alumni. Youth wear a ceremonial gown or vest as part of the Wohelo ceremony. The ceremonial costumes, however, have increasingly reflected the youth's own traditions, and many wear the ceremonial attire of their faiths rather than a traditional Camp Fire costume to honor their identity. Many councils have, on their own, met with tribes in their region and apologized for appropriative practices, and the vast majority of councils have discontinued them after education and reflection. Youth, too, have demanded that the practice be changed.[21]

Today's Camp Fire leaders note that Camp Fire officials have a responsibility to interrogate elements of the program, for which "we now understand the context and see how the commodification of indigenous culture by Camp Fire have caused harm." In 2020 Camp Fire National Headquarters empowered a task force made up local and national staff and alumni, and consultants from outside the organization. In 2021 Camp Fire published guidelines for councils to assess their current practices and to replace the appropriative symbols, imagery, language, names, and rituals. As Matthews explains, the core activities are still enjoyed and carry the same function, but these need not rely on harmful appropriation. Matthews offers the example of naming: "We still allowed youth to name themselves. We had moved past the [Indian] name book at the council that I was at. So, they named themselves things like Razor Scooter or Watermelon.... They named their clubs as well. We had the Honey Bun Dreams." Likewise, Camp Fire may still include rituals such as the council fire, but the young person's own cultural symbols will replace ceremonial gowns. Camp Fire is also working through local councils to make formal apologies to Native American tribes and to ground future relationships in respect.[22]

This book has reviewed, often critically, the Camp Fire Girls' definition of girl citizenship in the twentieth century and evaluated its stated commitment to serve "all girls" against the reality of its segregated groups and ideal of usefulness unfortunately influenced by eugenic philosophy. Throughout the twentieth century, the Camp Fire Girls adopted a liberal-leaning educational model that aspired to tolerance and democratic citizenship. However, it held on to traditional attitudes about the home and family even as it encouraged girls to take on increasingly public citizenship roles. On the one hand, this empowered girls, but Camp Fire failed to challenge, or even really recognize until the 1960s, the limits of the middle-class gender spheres that it promoted.

The Camp Fire Girls was part of an expanding national youth culture that, throughout the twentieth century, provided Camp Fire Girls with shared experiences and rituals that connected them to others in their neighborhoods and beyond. At any given time in the twentieth century, Camp Fire reached about 2 percent of American girls.[23] For those who participated, Camp Fire offered a space for cultivating friendship, adventure, and their own ideas. Into the twenty-first century, Camp Fire alumni continue to testify about the relationships developed and life lessons they picked up through the organization. One recalls "so many practical life skills learned ... all concealed behind the 'value' of a bead. It was one thing to have a parent teach you how to do something, but entirely different when you had to figure out how to earn it." Another recollects that Camp Fire was a "safe haven of just female friends," and that those friendships were "entwined with the songs we sang" and "with the legends of the summer camp."[24] A core group of girls endorsed Camp Fire's message of giving service and developing unique feminine characteristics. Some also added personal meaning to Camp Fire's universal girlhood. Camp Fire has been both a symbol of American girlhood and a genuine forum for girls. The meanings girls gave to their experiences helped to shape Camp Fire's vision of girlhood. In the process, twentieth-century girls themselves helped to define American womanhood.

Notes

Introduction

1. Edward Marshall, "Girls Take up the Boy Scout Idea and Band Together," *New York Times*, March 17, 1912, 3.
2. Luther Gulick, "Camp Fire Girls and the New Relation of Women to the World," address, National Education Association, Chicago, July 1912, 10–11, CFNH. For a discussion of the concept of an American race, see Bederman, *Manliness and Civilization*, 25, 179; and Gerstle, *American Crucible*, 17, 22. Viewed through the eyes of Theodore Roosevelt, the American race retained the superior "blood" of those supposed races that had formed the British race, with the additional asset of having forged a new character through conquest on the frontier. Bederman posits that when Americans talked about race, they also talked about an imagined evolutionary process toward "civilizations," a stage beyond savagery and barbarism that only white people were imagined to have attained. Many spoke of civilization as itself a racial trait. Gender, or sexual, differentiation was, for turn-of-the-century Americans, a marker of civilization and race.
3. Edward Marshall, "Girls Take up the Boy Scout Idea and Band Together," *New York Times*, March 17, 1912, 3.
4. Luther H. Gulick, "Essential Feminism," manuscript, ca. 1910, CFNH. On maternalism, see Koven and Michel, "Womanly Duties"; and Ladd-Taylor, *Mother-Work*, 3–11. On motherhood as a familial and civil act, see Plant, *Mom*, 6.
5. Dorgan, *Luther Halsey Gulick*, 124. See also "5 Questions with Camp Fire CEO Cathy Tisdale," Brand Channel, March 15, 2018, https://www.brandchannel.com/2018/03/15/5-questions-camp-fire-cathy-tisdale/.
6. For a discussion of Luther Gulick's political naivety, see Wallach, "Luther Halsey Gulick," 333–34. On Camp Fire's conservativism, see Inness, "Girl Scouts, Camp Fire Girls, and Woodcraft Girls," 7, 90; S. Miller, *Growing Girls*, 32; and McCallum, "Fundamental Things," 45–66.
7. Two works that address youth organizations across time are Proctor, *Scouting for Girls*; and Foley, "Meeting the Needs of Today's Girl."
8. Gerstle, *American Crucible*, 5, 7.

9. Luther Gulick, "Camp Fire Girls and the New Relation of Women to the World," address, National Education Association, Chicago, July 1912, 10–11, CFNH.

10. For a discussion of the universal language about youth, see Honeck, *Our Frontier Is the World*, 166; and Alexander, *Guiding Modern Girls*, 9.

11. For a discussion on hybrid spaces, see Honeck, *Our Frontier Is the World*, 14.

12. Judith Butler contends that marginalized groups can alter the meanings of social categories, such as gender, by subtly subverting them. Butler, *Gender Trouble*, 25–34.

13. S. Miller, "Assent as Agency."

14. Camp Fire Girls, *Book of the Camp Fire Girls* (1912), 4; and *Book of the Camp Fire Girls* (1914), 9.

15. On the development of separate children's and youth cultures, see Mintz, *Huck's Raft*, 196–97, 253; Fass, *Damned and the Beautiful*, 119–167; Rotundo, *American Manhood*; and Rodgers, "Socializing Middle-Class Children." For specific examinations of girls' cultures, see McRobbie and Garber, "Girls and Subcultures"; Forman-Brunell, "Girls' Culture," 325–27; Mitchell and Reid-Walsh, *Girl Culture*; Forman-Brunell and Paris, *Girls' History and Culture Reader*; and Weinbaum et al., *Modern Girl around the World*, 1–23. For a discussion of the emergence of a teenage girls' culture focused on consumer culture, see Schrum, *Some Wore Bobby Sox*. For discussion of girls of color, see Chatelain, *South Side Girls*; Matsumoto, *City Girls*.

16. Austin and Willard, introduction to *Generations of Youth*, 3. See also Demos and Demos, "Adolescence in Historical Perspective"; and Kett, *Rites of Passage*, 144–72, 217–43.

17. Hunter, *How Young Ladies Became Girls*, 393–94; Weinbaum et al., *Modern Girl around the World*, 13–14.

18. For a discussion of the extension of a protected childhood in the late nineteenth century, see Zelizer, *Pricing the Priceless Child*, 56–72.

19. Paris, *Children's Nature*, 8; and S. Miller, *Growing Girls*, 5.

20. G. N. Rosenberg, *4-H Harvest*, 6.

21. Honeck, *Our Frontier Is the World*, 7. For discussion of masculinity and the Boy Scouts of America, see also Jordan, *Modern Manhood and the Boy Scouts of America*; Hantover, "Sex Role, Sexuality, and Social Status"; Macleod, *Building Character in the American Boy*, 29–59, 292–96; Mechling, *On My Honor*, xx; and Mechling, "Male Gender Display at a Boy Scout Camp."

22. Buckler, Fiedler, and Allen, *Wo-he-lo*, 83; "Relocation."

23. Report of Camp Fire Work for 1913, January 20, 1914, box 11, folder 3, LHWP; and Buckler, Fiedler, and Allen, *Wo-he-lo*, 84.

24. Macleod, *Building Character in the American Boy*, 278.

25. Buckler, Fiedler, and Allen, *Wo-he-lo*, 3, 83. See Pendry and Hartshorne, *Organizations for Youth*, 35; Camp Fire Girls, Annual Report, 1926, 4–5, CFNH; and Camp Fire Girls, Membership Count of Camp Fire Girls, 1930, CFNH.

26. Camp Fire Girls, Annual Reports of the Camp Fire Girls for 1923, 1924, 1929, and the Semi-Annual Report of the General Department for 1932, CFNH; Choate and Ferris, *Juliette Low and the Girl Scouts*, 168; Rosa Esposito, information specialist, Girl Scouts of the USA, email correspondence, April 27, 2005.

27. Camp Fire Girls, *Book of the Camp Fire Girls* (1925), 65–73; and *Book of the Camp Fire Girls* (1933), 64–71. In 1962 the Wohelo Award became Camp Fire's highest achievement. On girls going on to lead their own groups, see C. Frances Loomis, "Camp Fire Girls" (report on her review of the Camp Fire program), ca. 1936, CFNH.

28. See, for example, "Post Scripts"; and "Presidency."

29. L. Gulick, "College Camp Fire Girls."

30. Addams, *Twenty Years at Hull-House*, 119–20.

31. Camp Fire Girls of Rhode Island, Grand Council Fire Souvenir Program, Providence, November 10, 1925, box 1, folder 27, CFCEM; and Camp Fire Girls, *Book of the Camp Fire Girls* (1914), 67.

32. In comparison, Alexander notes that Girl Guide archives in the United Kingdom privilege a specific narrative of girl emancipation and racial cooperation. The collections obliterate narrative challenges (Alexander, *Guiding Modern Girls*, 12). Boy Scouts of America, though it has recently become more transparent, historically limited access to its collections and placed many files off-limits to researchers.

33. On the concept of the able disabled, see Schalk, "Ablenationalism in American Girlhood," 39–40.

1. "Preparing for Sex Equality"

1. Luther Gulick, "How the 'Camp Fire Girls' Are Preparing for Sex Equality," *Oregon Daily Journal*, July 6, 1913, 55; Luther Gulick, "The Social Program," notes, Lansing MI, December 2, 1913, CFNH; and Minutes of Conference Called to Consider Ways and Means of Doing for Girls What the Boy Scout Movement Is Designed to Do for Boys, New York, March 22, 1911, revised, April 7, 1911, Board Minutes, 3, CFNH.

2. Kessler-Harris, *In Pursuit of Equity*, 5–6, 8–9.

3. Luther Gulick, "Essential Feminism," manuscript, ca. 1910, 2, 3, CFNH. For a discussion of how early twentieth-century feminists made claims to equality based on group difference, see Cott, *Grounding of Modern Feminism*, 6; and R. Rosenberg, *Beyond Separate Spheres*. Although individual equal rights feminists objected to this view that men's and women's roles were distinct, they were in the minority among early twentieth-century reformers.

4. Luther Gulick, "Camp Fire Girls and the New Relation of Women to the World," 1, 4, CFNH.

5. C. Gulick, "What the Camp Fire Girls Stand For."

6. Dorgan, *Luther Halsey Gulick*, 114–15; Langdon, *Book of Words*. On Langdon,

see Glassberg, *American Historical Pageantry*, 77. On the British Boy Scouts, see Honeck, *Our Frontier Is the World*, 39.

7. Minutes of Conference Called to Consider Ways and Means of Doing for Girls, New York, March 22, 1911, 2, CFNH; "Memorandum Concerning Camp Fire Girls," 1912, CFNH.

8. Buckler, Fiedler, and Allen, *Wo-he-lo*, 21, 30–31.

9. Buckler, Fiedler, and Allen, *Wo-he-lo*, 20.

10. For a discussion of the Girl Scout program, see Tedesco, "Making a Girl into a Scout," 23, 27.

11. Dorgan, *Luther Halsey Gulick*, 115; Luther Gulick, address, Committee on Organization of an Association for Girls, March 11, 1911, 2, CFNH.

12. Woolman served with Charlotte Joy Farnsworth, Dr. Anna Brown, Katherine Duer Mackay, and Catherine Leverich on the Committee on Organization. Mackay and Leverich were influential forces in founding the Girls' Branch of the Public School Athletic League of New York City. Additional women worked on this committee over the following weeks. The men's advisory committee consisted of Gulick, Howard S. Braucher, Farnsworth, Lee Hanmer, Langdon, West, Virgil Prettyman of Horace Mann School, William McAndrew, and Dr. Gaylord White. Seton, Samuel Dutton, and Daniel Beard continued to serve as consultants from time to time (Buckler, Fiedler, and Allen, *Wo-he-lo*, 27).

13. Minutes of the Camp Fire Girls Organizing Committee, New York, April 7, 1911, Board Minutes, 8, CFNH; and Minutes of a Conference between Representatives of the Girl Scouts of America, the Girl Guides of America, and the Camp Fire Girls of America, June 6–7, 1911, 2, 3, CFNH.

14. See press release in "Society Planned for Girls Like the Boy Scouts," *Wichita Daily Eagle*, April 8, 1911, 12.

15. Minutes of the Camp Fire Girls Organizing Committee, May 10, 1911, 1, 2, CFNH.

16. Report of a Meeting of the Committee on Organization, New York, September 27, 1911, 2, CFNH. For more discussion on the unique visions of girls' organizations, see S. Miller, *Growing Girls*, 17–27.

17. Rothschild, "To Scout or to Guide?," 118.

18. Bradt, "New Patriotism," 182. See also Cordery, *Juliette Gordon Low*, 212–13. When Low approached Lisetor-Lane to consolidate, Lisetor-Lane refused and instead threatened to sue, believing until she died that Low had lured troops away from her organization and stolen her title as founder. Sims, "Juliette Gordon Low," 381.

19. See Minutes of Conference Called to Consider Ways and Means of Doing for Girls, 2–4, CFNH; Luther Gulick, address, Committee on Organization of an Association for Girls, March 11, 1911, 3, 4, CFNH; and Buckler, Fiedler, and Allen, *Wo-he-lo*, 20–25. On the Manhattan Trade School for Girls, see Leake, *Vocational Education of Girls and Women*, 282–83, 285–86, 288. For Woolman's work on home economics, see Camp Fire Girls, *Handbook for Guardians* (1924), 7.

20. Bradt, "New Patriotism," 180; Buckler, Fiedler, and Allen, *Wo-he-lo*, 77–78.

21. Buckler, Fiedler, and Allen, *Wo-he-lo*, 3, 34–35, 65, 81, 83. Camp Fire would incorporate again in 1914 in New York as it worked out its governance structure. By comparison, there were over forty thousand Girl Scouts in 1919 and eighty-two thousand in 1920 (Cordery, *Juliette Gordon Low*, 255).

22. John Dewey and G. Stanley Hall especially influenced the Gulicks. See Dorgan, *Luther Halsey Gulick*, 60–70. For more on early twentieth-century educators' focus on the "whole child," see Arboleda, *Educating Young Children in WPA Nursery Schools*, 7.

23. Luther Gulick, "Symbolism and the Camp Fire Girls," manuscript, ca. 1912, 1, 9, CFNH.

24. Luther Gulick, "Woman's Program: Camp Fire Girls," manuscript, n.d., 1, CFNH.

25. Luther Gulick, "Camp Fire Girls and the New Relation of Women to the World," 4, 9, CFNH; and Luther Gulick, "Patriotism and the Camp Fire Girls," address, Annual Meeting of the Camp Fire Girls, September 1, 1914, 5, CFNH.

26. Luther Gulick, "How the Camp Fire Girls Are Preparing for Sex Equality," *Oregon Daily Journal*, July 6, 1913, 55; Luther Gulick, "Symbolism and the Camp Fire Girls," manuscript, ca. 1912, 9–10, CFNH; and Camp Fire Girls, *Book of the Camp Fire Girls* (1912), 25. For a discussion of how women's early twentieth-century friendships were regularly depicted as shallow or fleeting, see Rosenzweig, "'Another Self'?," 357. For a contemporary perspective that girls lacked loyalty, see Hetherington, "Playgrounds," 958; and L. Gulick, *Efficient Life*, 30–32.

27. Luther Gulick quoted in Buckler, Fiedler, and Allen, *Wo-he-lo*, 95. See also Dorgan, *Luther Halsey Gulick*, 11, 16, 115; and Dewey, *School and Society*, 53.

28. Page, *Socializing for the New Order*, 7, 22–24. For a discussion of progressive education, see Noble, *Progressive Mind*, 59–61.

29. Luther Gulick, "Camp Fire Girls and the New Relation of Women to the World," 7, 8, CFNH; Luther Gulick, "Recreation and Youth," address, Academy of Political Science, New York, April 19, 1912, 3, CFNH.

30. Kloppenberg, *Uncertain Victory*, 43.

31. For a discussion of the arts and crafts movement, see Lears, *No Place of Grace*, 59–96.

32. C. Gulick, "Message to Mothers from Hiiteni."

33. On mother-daughter relationships at the turn of the twentieth century, see Rosenzweig, *Anchor of My Life*. Rosenzweig finds that, despite new sources of tension, mothers and daughters were, by and large, "mutually supportive" (6, 134).

34. Dorgan, *Luther Halsey Gulick*, 15. Luther describes his conversations with Hall in Luther H. Gulick to Family, January 29, 1898; and Luther H. Gulick to Harriet Gulick Clark, May 29, 1898, Springfield; Charlotte describes the relationship in Charlotte V. Gulick to Family, June 8, 1898, Springfield: box 14, GFP.

35. For a discussion of Hall as a progressive educator due to his child-centered and scientifically oriented pedagogy, see Cremin, *Transformation of the School*, 102–4.

36. Hall, "From Generation to Generation," 250, 253; Hall, *Adolescence*, 624, 633, 644. For a discussion of Hall's influential writings on female adolescence, see DeLuzio, *Female Adolescence in American Thought*, 108–20.

37. Bederman, *Manliness and Civilization*, 25, 104–5.

38. Luther Gulick, "Camp Fire Girls and the New Relation of Women to the World," 10–11, CFNH.

39. Hall, *Adolescence*, 624, 643.

40. Hall, *Adolescence*, 638–39.

41. Luther Gulick, "To the Girls and Women of America," *Evening Mail*, April 21, 1917.

42. Gulick, "To the Girls and Women of America," *Evening Mail*, April 21, 1917.

43. Count of the 240 Mile Hike, Madrona Camp Fire Girls, June 1915, CFNH; "The Strenuous Life," address, April 10, 1899, in Roosevelt, *Works of Theodore Roosevelt*.

44. L. Gulick, *Healthful Art of Dancing*, 25, 28, 133, 157. For a discussion of girls' athletics, see Borish, "'Interest in Physical Well-Being,'" 63–64, 71; and Cahn, *Coming on Strong*.

45. Camp Fire Girls, *Book of the Camp Fire Girls* (1914), 25. A paragraph from Ellis's "Studies in the Psychology of Sex" appears on the cover of *Wohelo: A Magazine for Girls* 5, no. 7 (January 1918): 101. It describes how knowledge is transmitted from one generation to another as a torchbearer passes a torch. From this, Camp Fire took the name Torch Bearer for its oldest girls; they were supposed to pass their knowledge to younger girls. For attitudes toward sex education, see Ellis, *Studies in the Psychology of Sex*, 6:56–58, 530; and DeLuzio, *Female Adolescence in American Thought*, 126, 127.

46. Camp Fire Girls, *Book of the Camp Fire Girls* (1914), 27.

47. Celia Anderson, interview by author, January 28, 2004; "A Camp Fire Girl's Memory Book," scrapbook fragments of Lock Haven Normal School, Lock Haven PA, July 6, 1923, CFNH.

48. "A Camp Fire Girl's Memory Book," scrapbook fragments.

49. Ethel Gulick, Sebago ME, to Cara Fisher Gulick, July 8, 1914, box 17, GFP.

50. Mrs. J. Verity (Hattie Hyland) Smith, fragment in ledger, 1919–21, box 2, folder 67, CFCEM. Kellerman was a swimmer, an actress, and a pioneer in synchronized swimming. She was arrested in 1907 for indecent exposure when she wore the one-piece bathing suit to a Boston beach.

51. *Frances Pass Diary*, August, 3, 1922, Schlesinger Library, Radcliffe Institute, Harvard University, Cambridge MA.

52. Smith, fragment in ledger, 1919–21, box 2, folder 67, CFCEM.

53. Paris, "Adventures of Peanut and Bo," 63. See also Smith-Rosenberg, "Female World of Love and Ritual"; Solomon, *In the Company of Educated Women*, 99–100; D'Emilio and Freedman, *Intimate Matters*, 191–93; and Horowitz, *Power and Passion of M. Carey Thomas*, 64, 239–40.

54. Clarissa Fairchild to her mother, June 28–29, 1912, Sebago ME, transcript, CFNH.

55. O'Leary and O'Leary, *Adventures at Wohelo Camp*, 108, 111.

56. Ruth Case Almy, scrapbook [near South Bend IN, ca. 1910], annotated ca. 1982, CFNH.

57. S. Miller, *Growing Girls*, 197.

58. Lombardo, *Three Generations, No Imbeciles*, 7–8; and Glenna, Gollnick, and Jones, "Eugenic Opportunity Structures," 282.

59. To Luther Gulick, from Mother, January 15, 1914, Battle Creek Sanitarium, box 17, GFP; and Dorgan, *Luther Halsey Gulick*, 8.

60. On eugenic feminism, see Seitler, "Unnatural Selection." Seitler argues, as does Louise Newman, that eugenics and feminism were coterminous and mutually supporting. Newman, *White Women's Rights*. See also Nadkarni, *Eugenic Feminism*, 5, 33; and Ziegler, "Eugenic Feminism." On the difference between "positive" and "negative" eugenics, and Charlotte Perkins Gilman's views, see Davis, *Charlotte Perkins Gilman*, 300.

61. Charlotte Gulick to Louisa Gulick, November 6, 1892, Springfield MA, box 13, GFP; and Charlotte Gulick to Louisa Gulick and the Gulick sisters, November 19, 1892, Springfield MA, box 13, GFP.

62. J. Schultz, "Crossing the *Pali*," 211.

63. Journal of Sidney Gulick, January 3, 1882, box 9, GFP.

64. L. Gulick, *Efficient Life*, 30–32. See also L. Gulick, "Will to Be Cheerful."

65. Wallach, "Luther Halsey Gulick," 91–92.

66. G. N. Rosenberg, *4-H Harvest*, 103–4.

67. Monthly Health and Thrift Charts of the Camp Fire Girls, 1920s, folio box 6, CFCEM.

68. Camp Fire Girls, *Book of the Camp Fire Girls* (1933), 67.

69. Camp Fire Girls, Annual Report, 1924, 16, CFNH.

70. Monthly Health Charts, folio box 6, CFCEM.

71. *Frances Pass Diary*, July 8, 1922, Schlesinger Library, Radcliffe Institute, Harvard University, Cambridge MA.

72. Brumberg, *Body Project*, 30.

73. Camp Fire Girls, *Book of the Camp Fire Girls* (1912), 11–12; and Camp Fire Girls, Annual Report, 1922, 3, CFNH.

74. Camp Fire Girls, *Vacation Book*, 7–9.

75. See Nash, *Wilderness and the American Mind*, 141–60; Schmitt, *Back to Nature*, 12–19; Schrepfer, *Fight to Save the Redwoods*, 13–17; and Norwood, *Made from this Earth*, 49–53.

76. C. Gulick, "How Camp Fire Girls Are Being Educated in Babycraft," 125.

77. Camp Fire Girls, Annual Report, 1923, 13; and Camp Fire Girls, Annual Report, 1924, 16, CFNH. Statistics on camping do not specify whether trips were made with family, the Camp Fire group, or another institution.

78. Historical Count Book of Camp Shawnequa [NY], 1917, CFNH.

79. Department of Outdoor and Health Activities of the Camp Fire Girls, Analysis

and Summary of Camping Reports Sent in by 112 Class A Camp Fire Camps, 1927, CFNH.

80. Ethel Gulick to Cara Fisher Gulick, July 5, July 8, and August 1914, Sebago ME, box 17, GFP.
81. For a discussion of girls embracing masculine activities, see V. B. Brown, "Golden Girls."
82. Ethel Gulick to Sidney Gulick, April 25, 1915, Oberlin OH, box 17, GFP.
83. Ethel Gulick to Leeds Gulick, July 12, 1914, Sebago ME, box 17, GFP.
84. Luther Gulick, "Camp Fire Girls," address, annual meeting of the National Board, Camp Fire Girls, February 9, 1912, 44, CFNH; and C. Gulick, "Message to Mothers from Hiiteni."
85. Plant, *Mom*, 11–12.
86. Charlotte Gulick to Harriet Gulick Clark, May 29, 1888, Springfield MA, box 11, GFP.
87. L. Gulick, "Camp Fire Girl Movement and Education," 700; and Luther Gulick quoted in W. Lane, "Camp Fire Girls," 321.
88. See Stage, introduction to *Rethinking Home Economics*, 4–9; and Rury, "Vocationalism for Home and Work."
89. Luther Gulick, "Camp Fire Girls," address, annual meeting of the National Board, Camp Fire Girls, February 9, 1912, 46–47, CFNH.
90. C. Gulick, "Message to Mothers from Hiiteni," 4.
91. Luther Gulick quoted in W. Lane, "Camp Fire Girls," 321.
92. Camp Fire Girls, *Book of the Camp Fire Girls* (1912), 15–16.
93. Camp Fire Girls, Annual Report, 1922, 3, CFNH.
94. Camp Fire Girls, *Book of the Camp Fire Girls* (1912), 12, 15.
95. Scrapbook of the Hinhan Maidens, Springfield MO, 1930, CFNH.
96. Celia Anderson, interview by author, January 28, 2004.
97. Clarissa Fairchild to her mother, June 28–29, 1912, Sebago ME, CFNH.
98. Thompson, *West By Northwest*, "My Life: Introduction and History."
99. *Frances Pass Diary*, June 30, 1922, and August 13, 1922, Schlesinger Library, Radcliffe Institute, Harvard University, Cambridge MA.
100. Ethel Gulick to Cara Fisher Gulick, July 5, 1914, Sebago ME, box 17, GFP.
101. Luther Gulick, "Patriotism and the Camp Fire Girls," 2, CFNH.
102. Camp Fire Girls, *Book of the Camp Fire Girls* (1914), 40–42; and Pratt Institute, *Notable Women of Modern Times: A List for Camp Fire Girls* (Brooklyn: Pratt Institute Free Library, 1913), CFNH.
103. Luther Gulick, "The Modern Girl Needs," manuscript, CFNH.
104. L. Gulick, "Camp Fire Girls," 47.
105. Camp Fire Girls, *Book of the Camp Fire Girls* (1914), 17.
106. Charlotte Gulick to Admont Clark, ca. 1909, box 16, GFP.
107. Luther Gulick, "Camp Fire Girls and the New Relation of Women to the World," 6–7, CFNH.

108. Camp Fire Girls in a suffrage parade appear in "Suffrage Parade Is Biggest Event Held in Kentucky," *Lexington Herald*, May 7, 1916, 1; in *Buffalo Sunday Morning News*, May 24, 1914, 54; and Hazel Murray, "The Town Beautiful," manuscript, 1915, CFNH.

109. Camp Fire Girls, Annual Report, 1922, 4, CFNH.

110. Kennedy, *Over Here*, 53.

111. Luther Gulick, Annual Report of the President, 1917, 17, CFNH.

112. Elshtain, *Women and War*, 4, 9. See also Kennedy, *Over Here*, 30–31; and Steinson, *American Women's Activism in World War I*.

113. Anna Howard Shaw quoted in "Our Foreign Camp Fires."

114. Luther Gulick, Annual Report of the President, 1917, 17, CFNH.

115. "Annual Report of the Camp Fire Girls," *Wohelo* (December 1918): 172.

116. Luther Gulick, Annual Report of the President, 1917, 20, CFNH.

117. Luther Gulick, Annual Report of the President, 1917, 18, CFNH.

118. Luther Gulick, "To the Girls and Women of America," *Evening Mail*, April 21, 1917; Camp Fire Girls, *Book of the Camp Fire Girls with War Program* (1917), v–xviii.

119. Kennedy, *Over Here*, 60–62, 105, 151.

120. "Slacker's Dream."

121. "What Camp Fire Girls Are Doing," *Wohelo* 6, no. 6; and Camp Fire Girls, Annual Report, 1918, 172, CFNH.

122. See, for example, "What Camp Fire Girls Are Doing," *Wohelo* 6, no. 1; and "Sparks from the Camp Fires."

123. Buckler, Fiedler, and Allen, *Wo-he-lo*, 221–22.

124. Buckler, Fiedler, and Allen, *Wo-he-lo*, 154. On Frances Gulick, see Dumenil, *Second Line of Defense*, 121.

125. C. Gulick, "What the Camp Fire Girls Stand For."

2. *"Wohelo Maidens" and "Gypsy Trails"*

1. Camp Fire Girls, *Book of the Camp Fire Girls* (1914), 16.

2. Ortner, "Is Female to Male as Nature Is to Culture?," 84. On the affinity between American Indians and nature, and between women and nature, see also Schrepfer, *Nature's Altars*, 156.

3. Deloria, *Playing Indian*, 101–3, 113. See also Strong, *American Indians and the American Imaginary*, 127–41.

4. Van Slyck, *Manufactured Wilderness*, 51.

5. "Girls Present Cinderella," *South Bend Tribune*, June 20, 1940, 30. A Black cast had recently performed *The Mikado*.

6. Lott, "Love and Theft," 23.

7. Bird, introduction to *Dressing in Feathers*, 4.

8. Van Slyck, *Manufactured Wilderness*, 197–98.

9. Luther Gulick, "Symbolism and the Camp Fire Girls," ca. 1912, 2, CFNH.

10. Van Slyck, *Manufactured Wilderness*, 207.

11. Buckler, Fiedler, and Allen, *Wo-he-lo*, 71; "Treasure Trails of Indian Lore"; and "Newsyviews of Camp Fire Girls." On the Carlisle Indian School, see letter to Commissioner of Indian Affairs, Washington DC, from M. Friedman (Superintendent), Carlisle PA, August 23, 1912, carlisleindian.dickinson.edu/documents/camp-fire-girls-organization.

12. Newman, *White Women's Rights*, 117, 125.

13. Seton quoted in Van Slyck, *Manufactured Wilderness*, 172.

14. "Our Heritage from the American Indians."

15. Bird, introduction to *Dressing in Feathers*, 4. See also Hinderaker, "Translation and Cultural Brokerage," 358, 365; and Lyons, *X-Marks*, 1–2, 8, 24. For an example of tepid Indigenous support for the Camp Fire Girls, see Untitled editorial, *American Indian Magazine*.

16. Deloria, *Playing Indian*, 123.

17. Eastman, *Indian Scout Talks*, 106, 109, 123, 148–49.

18. Ella Deloria, "Gamma, Religion," Untitled Ethnographic Notes Manuscript, Dakota Ethnography, box 2, Ella Deloria Archive, American Studies Research Institute, Bloomington IN. I am grateful to Susan Gardner for sharing this quote. See also P. Deloria, *Playing Indian*, 121–22.

19. Ella Deloria, "The Wohpe Festival," unpublished manuscript (1928), i, Ella Deloria Archive, American Studies Research Institute. See Gardner, "Subverting the Rhetoric of Assimilation," 15–16, 27–28.

20. Seton, *Woodcraft Manual for Boys*, 24–25.

21. Camp Fire Girls, *Book of the Camp Fire Girls* (1912), 4, 19.

22. Mary Gentry Paxton, Scrapbook of Kashingo Camp Fire Group, Grandview MO, 1915, CFNH.

23. Camp Fire Girls, *Book of the Camp Fire Girls* (1912), 19.

24. Luther Gulick, address, Committee on Organization of an Association for Girls, March 11, 1911, 5, CFNH.

25. Putney, *Muscular Christianity*, 158.

26. Scrapbook of Camp Shawnee, Grandview MO, 1922, CFNH.

27. The Count of Cawemaco: Camping in the Western Maine Council, 1930–36, CFNH.

28. C. Gulick, "What the Camp Fire Girls Stand For."

29. Van Slyck, *Manufactured Wilderness*, 188.

30. Seton, *Two Little Savages*, 489; Luther Gulick, "Symbolism and the Camp Fire Girls," ca. 1912, 8, CFNH; and Camp Fire Girls, *Book of the Camp Fire Girls* (1914), 18–19.

31. Van Slyck, *Manufactured Wilderness*, 187.

32. For a discussion of youth and transitional identity, see Fass, *Damned and the Beautiful*, 5. For a discussion of how identities are intersubjective, contested, and created, see Lyons, *X-Marks*, 37–39. Lyons also discusses cultural hybridity within colonial structures (95–102).

33. Lears, *No Place of Grace*, 11, 38; Van Slyck, *Manufactured Wilderness*, 99.

34. West, *Growing Up with the Country*, 102–17.

35. Seton, *Birch-Bark Roll of the Woodcraft Indians*, 16–17; Camp Fire Girls, *Book of Camp Fire Girls* (1912), 19–20; Luther Gulick, "Symbolism and the Camp Fire Girls," ca. 1912, 2–3, CFNH; Scrapbook of the Hinhan Maidens, Springfield MO, 1930, CFNH; Summer Count Book of the Sebago-Wohelo Camp Fire Maidens, South Casco ME, 1912, CFNH.

36. Summer Count Book of the Sebago-Wohelo Camp Fire Maidens, South Casco ME, 1912, CFNH.

37. San Joaquin County Camp Fire Girls, Camp Minkalo Count, 1919, CFGSTK.

38. San Joaquin County Camp Fire Girls, Camp Minkalo Scrapbook, 1922, CFGSTK.

39. Summer Count Book of the Sebago-Wohelo Camp Fire Maidens, South Casco ME, 1912, CFNH.

40. San Joaquin County Camp Fire Girls, Camp Minkalo Count, 1919, CFGSTK.

41. Eastman, *Indian Scout Talks*, 123; Camp Fire Girls, *Book of the Camp Fire Girls* (1914), 80; and L. Gulick, "Ceremonial Gown."

42. Stedman, *Shadows of the Indian*, 92.

43. Scrapbook of National Camp Fire Girls Training Course, Ames IA, 1914, CFNH.

44. Summer Count Book of the Sebago-Wohelo Camp Fire Maidens, South Casco ME, 1912, CFNH.

45. Summer Count Book of Sebago-Wohelo Camp Fire Maidens, South Casco ME, 1912, CFNH.

46. Scrapbook of National Camp Fire Girls Training Course, Ames IA, 1914, CFNH.

47. Luther Gulick, "Ceremonial Gowns," ca. 1915, 8, CFNH.

48. Minutes of the National Board of Directors and Executive Committee of the Camp Fire Girls, January 28, 1925, and February 18, 1925, New York, CFNH.

49. Mechling, "Male Gender Display at a Boy Scout Camp," 140–41.

50. For discussion of sexual stereotypes of Native women, see Gutiérrez, *When Jesus Came, the Corn Mothers Went Away*; and Plaine, *Colonial Intimacies*. In *White Women's Rights*, Newman describes white female reformers' insistence that American Indian girls could be made respectable (117–18).

51. Camp Fire Girls, *Book of the Camp Fire Girls* (1914), 16; "Incidents of Indian Life at Hampton"; see also C. Gulick, *Shul U Tam Na of the Camp Fire Girls*.

52. Lyons, *X-Marks*, 23; Cobb, *Listening to Our Grandmothers' Stories*, 115–16; and Lomawaima, *They Called It Prairie Light*.

53. "All-Indian Camp Fire Girls' Group." On the Yakima Christian Indian Mission, see Kirk and Alexander, *Exploring Washington's Past*, 15; and McAllister and Tucker, *Journey in Faith*, 324. On Yakama dress, see Paterek, *Encyclopedia of American Indian Costume*, 236. In the 1990s, the Yakima people renamed themselves Yakama.

54. Parker, *Phoenix Indian School*.

55. "Camp Fire," *Phoenix Redskin*, May 13, 1933, 9–10.

56. "Camp Fire," *Phoenix Redskin*, October 6, 1934, 1.

57. "Campus News," *Phoenix Redskin*, November 12, 1932, 2.

58. "Camp Fire Meeting," *Phoenix Redskin*, March 5, 1932, 3.

59. "Overnight Hikes," *Phoenix Redskin*, April 23, 1935, 1.

60. Meyers, "Following Indian Trails."

61. "Paper to Feature Local Camp Fire," *Phoenix Redskin*, November 17, 1936, 1.

62. For a discussion of how Indigenous women constructed modern identities, see Cahill, *Recasting the Vote*, 93.

63. Begay, "Modern Indian Girl," *Native American* 30, no. 5; and Begay, "Modern Indian Girl," *Native American* 30, no. 11.

64. "Camp Fire Activities," *Phoenix Redskin*, November 10, 1934, 3.

65. "Camp Fire Girls Hold Last Meeting," *Phoenix Redskin*, May 4, 1937, 1; "Camp Fire," *Phoenix Redskin*, October 6, 1934, 1.

66. Lomawaima and McCarty, *To Remain an Indian*, 73–75.

67. "Camp Fire Activities," *Phoenix Redskin*, December 1, 1934, 1.

68. "Na-a-si-lid Camp Fire Hike," *Phoenix Redskin*, October 13, 1936, 4.

69. "Na-a-si-lid Camp Fire Meeting," *Phoenix Redskin*, October 20, 1936, 1.

70. Bloom, "'There Is Madness in the Air,'" 102.

71. Lomawaima and McCarty, *To Remain an Indian*, 64, 73–75.

72. For a discussion of changing ideas about Indian play, see Lieffers, "Empires of Play," 31–56.

73. Following Jodie Matthews, I use the term "Gypsy," acknowledging that it is a problematic term used by non-Romani groups to create false representations of Romani culture. The stereotype of the "Gypsy," however, found in literary and visual forms is what the Camp Fire Girls drew upon, rarely acknowledging actual Roma or Romani cultural practice. See Matthews, *Gypsy Woman*, 3.

74. "Autumn Council Fire."

75. Berry, *Screen Style*, 108. For a discussion of the suntanning craze, see Peiss, *Hope in a Jar*, 150–51.

76. For a discussion of orientalism in fashion, see Antle, "Surrealism and the Orient," 15. On Greenwich Village fashion, see Blanco F. et al., "Peasant Blouse," 28. See also Hoganson, *Consumers' Imperium*, 90.

77. Kopper, *Virginia Woolf*, 46.

78. Hancock, "The Symbolic Function of the Gypsy Myth," 106–7. On desire and loathing, see Bahba, *The Location of Culture*, 118. In the United States, the Roma have faced laws that permit states and counties to regulate "roving bands," resulting in repeated evictions.

79. Brown and Heintz, "Gypsying Both by Sea and Land," 7, 17.

80. Hancock, "Symbolic Function of the Gypsy Myth," 106, 108, 109.

81. Matthews, *Gypsy Woman*, 29, 35, 37; "Autumn Council Fire."

82. Camp Fire Girls, *Book of the Camp Fire Girls* (1933), 75, 181.

83. Z. E. Wells, "White Mountain Gypsying."

84. Brown and Heintz, "Gypsying Both by Sea and Land."

85. "Miss Wahlstrom Greets Camp Fire Groups," newspaper clipping in Scrapbook, May 18, 1937–May 1, 1942, SAC-SB.

86. Rankin, "Gypsying," 280.

87. "Chatting with the Campers," *Cincinnati Enquirer*, July 20, 1930, 75.

88. A. Wright, "Grand Rapids Gypsies"; and "Girl Campers," *Cincinnati Enquirer*, July 18, 1937, 61.

89. Matthews, *Gypsy Woman*, 146.

90. A. Wright, "Grand Rapids Gypsies."

91. Matthews, *Gypsy Woman*, 74, 95, 112.

92. hooks quoted in Matthews, *Gypsy Woman*, 70.

93. The Count of Cawemaco: Camping in the Western Maine Council, Scrapbook, 1930–32, CFNH.

94. Matthews, *Gypsy Woman*, 108–9.

95. "Autumn Council Fire"; "Vagrant"; and Kipling quoted in Rankin, "Gypsying," 280–81.

96. Matthews, *Gypsy Woman*, 74, 95, 185, 186, 188; Regina Bendix quoted in Matthews, *Gypsy Woman*, 112.

97. Sway, *Familiar Strangers*, 27, 39. See also Reinhardt and Ganzel, "Farming in the 1930s: Gypsies"; Stephens, "American Gypsies"; and Heimlich, "Gypsy Americans."

98. Matthews, *Gypsy Woman*, 97, 125.

99. Cressy, *Gypsies*, xiii.

100. Brown and Heintz, "Gypsying Both by Sea and Land," 17.

101. R. Wright, "On the Trail of the Gypsy," parts 1 and 2.

102. Stewart, *Campfire Girl in Summer Camp*, 87, 90, 92, 130; and McCallum, "Fundamental Things," 64.

103. Philip Landon quoted in Matthews, "Back Where They Belong," 138.

104. For a discussion of girls' series fiction, see Inness, introduction to *Nancy Drew and Company*.

105. Bell, *Fighting the Traffic in Young Girls*, 68, 71–72, 282.

106. Stewart, *Campfire Girl's Chum*.

107. Matthews, "Back Where They Belong," 141–43.

108. Matthews, *Gypsy Woman*, 57.

3. *"All Prejudices Seem to Disappear"*

1. Certificate of Incorporation of the Camp Fire Girls, New York, 1914, CFNH.

2. Higham, *Strangers in the Land*, 134, 166, 278, 285. L. Gordon, *Second Coming of the KKK*, 2–4.

3. The earliest study of Camp Fire's racial demographics is from 1946, surveying nineteen towns with Camp Fire clubs. It found that 98.7 percent of members were white, less than 1 percent were Black, and less than 1 percent were other or unknown. The groups surveyed included those with segregated councils such as Tulsa, Oklahoma; Beaumont, Texas; and Wichita Falls, Texas. See

Camp Fire Girls, *They Told Us What They Wanted: Report of the Camp Fire Girls Program Study*, 1946, CFNH. The next demographic report, the 1968 "Survey of Service," included 177 councils, or 28,767 groups. The areas are not specified, but this was a little less than half the clubs nationally. Ninety percent of Camp Fire's groups were entirely white; 5 percent were entirely Black; 3 percent were entirely Mexican American; 1 percent were Asian; and less than 1 percent were listed as other. Of the 28,767 groups surveyed, 3,720 were integrated. Only 3,168 of the groups surveyed were considered "groups with members from low family incomes." See Membership in Minority and Poverty Areas in "Working Papers: Background Information on Camp Fire Girls," Minutes of the National Council of the Camp Fire Girls, Annual Meeting Minutes, Scottsdale AZ, November 8–11, 1968, 2, CFNH. For an example of publicity about inclusion, see "Budget Drive of Camp Fire Girls Tuesday," *Great Falls (MT) Tribune*, October 23, 1927, 13.

4. Buckler, Fiedler, and Allen, *Wo-he-lo*, 83. On foreign-born girls, see Camp Fire Girls, Annual Report, 1923, 13, CFNH; "What Camp Fire Girls Are Doing," *Wohelo* 6, no. 1. At least one club in Colorado in 1937 included several girls from Mexico, one from Japan, and several native-born girls (see Buckler, Fiedler, and Allen, *Wo-he-lo*, 269).

5. Fass, *Outside In*, 9; and Selig, *Americans All*, 2, 6–7, 71.

6. Enclosure in Camp Fire Girls, *Book of the Camp Fire Girls* (1914).

7. L. Gulick, editorial, *Wohelo*, 7; and "Camp Fire Is for Our Best Friends."

8. Hoxie, *How Girls Can Help Their Country*, 3.

9. "Camp Fire Girls Show Handicraft," *Brooklyn (NY) Times Union*, June 21, 1934, 16; "Look for 1000 at Council Fire," *Spokesman-Review* (Spokane WA), March 13, 1932, 58; and "National Camp Fire Week to Be Celebrated," *News-Messenger* (Fremont OH), February 24, 1932, 2.

10. "Young Women Given Opportunity to Help in United Work for Yanks," *Wisconsin State Journal* (Madison), October 29, 1918, 2.

11. Camp Fire Girls, Annual Report, 1926, 14–15, CFNH. See also Palladino, *Teenagers*, 21–24, on *Everygirl's* and the Girl Scouts' *American Girl*. Although by 1926 *Everygirl's* had thirty-eight thousand readers, it operated in the red. Despite its title and attempt at mass appeal, *Everygirl's* was defunct by 1933. The magazine faced competition from the Girl Scouts' *American Girl* at the same time that family budgets were taxed by the Great Depression so that they were unwilling to pay the extra dollar for a subscription. Camp Fire's top editor left *Everygirl's* to work for the Girl Scout magazine. The publication that remained, the *Guardian*, targeted leaders rather than girls, though it maintained the same universal ideals. The *Guardian* became *Camp Fire Girl* in 1944.

12. "Howard Chandler Christy Paints One of Us."

13. Camp Fire Girls, *Book of the Camp Fire Girls* (1914), 60; and newspaper clipping, *Boston Sunday Post*, April 14, 1933, box 1, folder 25, CFCEM.

14. Grace Parker, Report of the Secretary to the Board of Directors of Camp Fire Girls, May 14, 1914, box 11, folder 3, LHWP.

15. Celia Anderson, interview by author, January 28, 2004.

16. For a discussion of working-class men in the YMCA, see Winter, *Making Men, Making Class*, 5, 65. For a discussion of working-class girls' rejection of middle-class values, see Peiss, *Cheap Amusements*, 162–63. For a discussion of growing labor radicalism, see Higham, *Strangers in the Land*, 176–77.

17. Jeannette D. Pearl, "Organizing Children: Boy Scouts, Campfire Girls and Little Rebels," *Daily People* (New York), April 7, 1912, 8.

18. Thurston, *Torch Bearer*, 14.

19. Vandercook, *Camp Fire Girls at Sunrise Hill*, 73.

20. Clarissa Fairchild to her mother, June 28–29, 1912, Sebago ME, transcript at CFNH.

21. For a discussion of working-class women's fashions, see Peiss, *Cheap Amusements*, 64.

22. Report on Business Which Needs Attention, Minutes of the Camp Fire Girls Organizing Committee, January 18, 1912, 92, and April 3, 1912, 121, CFNH.

23. Camp Fire Girls, *Book of the Camp Fire Girls* (1912), 35; Camp Fire Girls, *Book of the Camp Fire Girls* (1914), 73; Buckler, Fiedler, and Allen, *Wo-he-lo*, 60, 192–93; and Camp Fire Girls, *Book of the Camp Fire Girls* (1917), x–xi.

24. Mrs. J. Verity Smith, "This Is Your Life Region I," address, Council Fire, probably Boston, 1955, box 1, folder 39, CFCEM.

25. Camp Fire Girls, *Book of the Camp Fire Girls* (1914), 16. For a discussion of children's spending, see Jacobson, *Raising Consumers*, 72. On the Chicago Woman's Club, see Remus, *Shopper's Paradise*, 19. For labor statistics, see *Bulletin of the United States Bureau of Labor* 23, no. 96 (September 1911): 414, https://fraser.stlouisfed.org/title/3943/item/477667.

26. Runbeck, "Our Camp Fire Law."

27. Camp Fire Girls, *Book of the Camp Fire Girls* (1914), 71.

28. Luther H. Gulick, "Camp Fire Is an Army, Not a Hospital," in *Written Thoughts: Wapa* 3 [1915], 2, CFNH. For a discussion of those leaders who viewed Camp Fire as more philanthropic, see Buckler, Fiedler, and Allen, *Wo-he-lo*, 108–10, 132; and Ethel M. Towner to the Board of Directors of the Camp Fire Girls, March 29, 1915, New York, box 11, folder 1, LHWP.

29. "Question of Dues."

30. Thurston, *Torch Bearer*, 14.

31. In 1942 *Life* magazine reported Shirley Temple's average annual income: "Speaking of Pictures: Shirley Temple Grows Up," *Life*, March 30, 1942, 8–11; "Shirley Temple Becomes a Camp Fire Girl," press release from 20th Century-Fox, October 1939, transcript in Shirley Temple file, CFNH; Margaret B. Sterett to Camp Fire Girl, Inc., February 28, 1949, New York, in Shirley Temple file, CFNH.

32. "Camp Fire Will Have Party Tonight," *Santa Maria (CA) Times*, October 20, 1934, 3; Celia Anderson, interview by author, January 28, 2004. The Great Depression

affected Camp Fire's membership but not dramatically. By the 1930–31 school year, retention was stable, but the registration of new clubs and new members had declined. By 1932 membership had fallen by only a thousand members overall. National headquarters was dropping girls and groups due to lack of payment. The report noted that "bank failures were the reason for non-payment of dues" in many communities. The girls had the money for dues but the banks were closed, and the groups could not access group funds. Other girls were falling behind. Camp Fire Girls, Semi-Annual Report, 1931–1932, CFNH.

33. "Camp Fire For All."

34. The girls' work for their dues mirrors how federal New Deal programs prioritized work-relief over direct aid during the Great Depression. See Kennedy, *Freedom from Fear*, 173–77.

35. See, for example, "How to Do It without Money."

36. See "Division News," 329.

37. Fluck, "Was ist eigentlich so schlecht daran?," 286.

38. "Camp Fire Girls Activities," *Times Herald* (Olean NY), March 23, 1931, 4.

39. "Let the Poor Rejoice," *Long Beach (CA) Press*, September 9, 1904, 8.

40. Summers, *Gilded Age*, 118; and A. R. Wells, *Social Evenings*, 100–102.

41. National Fraternal Congress of America, Proceedings, Atlantic City NJ, 1934, 388 [online]. By the 1950s, college fraternity members in the South used the same logic to reinforce "notions of Greek[-organization] privilege amid the increasingly diverse postwar student body" (James, "Political Parties," 66–67). For a discussion of gender, race, and class boundary crossing, see B. Gordon, *Saturated World*, 119–20.

42. Deutsch, *Women and the City*, 51.

43. On children and families of immigrants, see Mintz and Kellogg, *Domestic Revolutions*, 86–87; Macleod, *Age of the Child*, 5; Fass, *Outside In*; Berrol, "Immigrant Children at School"; Tyack, *One Best System*, 229–55; and Tyack, *Seeking Common Ground*, 26–29, 53–56, 73–79.

44. Roediger, *Working toward Whiteness*, 8–9.

45. R. Wright, "Makers of America," 212.

46. Berrol, "Immigrant Children at School," 55.

47. Camp Fire Girls, Annual Report, 1924, 16, CFNH.

48. Hahner, "Practical Patriotism," 120.

49. Camp Fire Girls, *Book of the Camp Fire Girls* (1933), 53.

50. Hahner, "Practical Patriotism," 117–19, 127.

51. On the Houchen Settlement, see Acosta, García, and Orozco, "Settlement Houses."

52. For a discussion of Japanese American girls' clubs, see Matsumoto, *City Girls*, 5, 13, 18, 43, 45. Newspaper coverage of Japanese American Camp Fire Girls includes, for example, "East Bay Camp Fire Girls," *Oakland (CA) Tribune*, April 4, 1937, 29; "Japanese Camp Fire Girls Sing Christmas Carols," *Sutter County (CA) Farmer*,

January 3, 1930, 7; and "Camp Fire Girls Grand Council Here Tonight," *Pomona (CA) Progress Bulletin*, December 2, 1927, 7.

53. Camp Fire Girls, *Book of the Camp Fire Girls* (1914), 42.

54. Camp Fire Girls, *Book of the Camp Fire Girls* (1914), 42; C. Frances Loomis, "Fostering International Friendship and Understanding through Recreational Projects in the Camp Fire Girls Program," *Quarterly Bulletin for International Institute, Young Women's Christian Association*, 1935, CFNH.

55. Camp Fire Girls, *Book of the Camp Fire Girls* (1933), 52.

56. Camp Fire Girls, *Book of the Camp Fire Girls* (1933), 53.

57. R. Wright, "The Makers of America," 212.

58. Camp Fire Girls, *Book of the Camp Fire Girls* (1933), 53.

59. "The Camp Fire Girl Afield."

60. R. Wright, "Makers of America," 212.

61. Buckler, Fiedler, and Allen, *Wo-he-lo*, 268–70.

62. L. Gulick, *Healthful Art of Dancing*, 6, 28, 30, 185–86.

63. L. Gulick, *Healthful Art of Dancing*, 38–41, 141–42, 228–29.

64. Burchenal, *Folk-Dances and Singing Games*; Burchenal, *Dances of the People*; and Burchenal, *Folk-Dances from Old Homelands*.

65. McCulloch, *Call of the New South*, 9, 261.

66. Chatelain, *South Side Girls*, 130–31, 137, 139. For a discussion of Black, nineteenth-century reformers, see Gilmore, *Gender and Jim Crow*, 3.

67. On the Girls of the Forward Quest, see Florence Wilson, "Movement to Develop Right Living among Negro Girls," *Nashville (TN) Banner*, November 29, 1913, 31; and "Afro-American Cullings," *Kansas City (MO) Sun*, January 31, 1914, 2. The South Nashville Mothers' Community Club financed the Girls of the Forward Quest, and Bethlehem House Settlement Workers supervised the club (Methodist Episcopal Church, *Ninth Annual Report*, 268). On McCulloch and the institutions he led, see Andersen, "Cooperation for Social Betterment." Andersen notes that the Institute for Negro Christian Workers was a short-lived ecumenical organization that sought to train Black reformers to spread Christianity in the Black community.

68. On Haynes, see Parris and Brooks, *Blacks in the City*, 23–26, 77–78; and Report of Camp Fire Girls Work for 1913, January 20, 1914, box 11, folder 3, LHWP.

69. Mitchell, "George Edmund Haynes"; Leon, "Bethlehem House, Nashville." On the Camp Fire club at Bethlehem House, see D. Wellington Berry, "Of Interest to Colored People," *Nashville Tennessean*, February 1, 1914, 14.

70. Report of Camp Fire Girls Work for 1913, January 20, 1914, box 11, folder 3, LHWP.

71. Washington, introduction to *A Voice from the South*, xxvii.

72. "East Orange Social Settlement Work," *New York Age*, April 16, 1914, 8; "Camp Fire Girls in Council," *New York Age*, June 25, 1914, 8.

73. "Celebrate Emancipation Day," *News* (Frederick MD), August 6, 1914, 5; "Fink-Smith Plans Big Athletics for July 5," *Fresno (CA) Morning Republican*, July 1, 1915,

15; "City News," *Kansas City (MO) Sun*, August 14, 1915, 5; and "Colored Camp Fire Girls Meet Today," *Decatur (IL) Herald*, June 4, 1916, 27.

74. "What Camp Fire Girls Are Doing," *Wohelo* 6, no. 1.

75. "City News," *Kansas City (MO) Sun*, August 14, 1915, 5.

76. "Camp Fire Girls End Encampment," *Morning Chronicle* (Manhattan KS), August 21, 1924, 1.

77. "Colored Camp Fire Girls Meet Today," *Decatur (IL) Herald*, June 4, 1916, 27.

78. "Celebrate Emancipation Day," *News* (Frederick MD), August 6, 1914, 5.

79. "Colored Selects Start for Camp," *Buffalo (NY) Commercial*, August 3, 1918, 10.

80. Chatelain, *South Side Girls*, 145–47.

81. Notes from a clipping originally enclosed in letter, Florence Leigh, Nashville YWCA, to Luther Gulick, February 5, 1914, box 11, folder 1, LHWP; Methodist Episcopal Church, *Fourth Annual Report*, 375, says that fifteen girls actually joined.

82. Copy of James E. McCulloch to Luther Gulick, January 20, 1914, in Luther Gulick to L. Hollingsworth Wood, January 29, 1914, box 11, folder 1, LHWP.

83. James E. McCulloch to Luther Gulick, January 29, 1914, Nashville TN, LHWP.

84. For more on the African American branch of the YWCA in Nashville, see Bucy, *Women Helping Women*, 42–48.

85. Luther Gulick to James E. McCulloch, January 24, 1914, New York, box 11, folder 1, LHWP.

86. James E. McCulloch to Luther Gulick, January 20, 1914, Nashville TN, box 11, folder 1, LHWP; and James E. McCulloch to Luther Gulick, January 29, 1914, Nashville TN, LHWP.

87. James E. McCulloch to Luther Gulick, January 20, 1914, Nashville TN, box 11, folder 1, LHWP.

88. D. Wellington Berry, "Of Interest to Colored People," *Nashville Tennessean*, February 1, 1914, 14. Berry was later secretary of the National Negro Board of Trade and listed as faculty of stenography at Tennessee Agricultural and Industrial State Normal School.

89. Florence Leigh to Luther Gulick, February 5, 1914, Nashville TN, box 11, folder 1, LHWP.

90. Luther Gulick to Dr. George E. Haynes, February 9, 1914, box 11, folder 1, LHWP.

91. Methodist Episcopal Church, *Fourth Annual Report*, 375.

92. It seems likely that Lizzie Smith accepted a missionary assignment, but Elizabeth Ross Haynes may have opted to appoint a new leader to diffuse the tension. D. Wellington Berry, "General News of the Colored People," *Nashville Tennessean*, July 26, 1914, 10.

93. Trawick, "Play Life of Negro Boys and Girls," 361–62.

94. On how the YWCA's initial collaboration with the Camp Fire Girls and the Girl Scouts shifted to support for its own Girl Reserves, see Bucy, *Women Helping Women*, 28–29.

95. Hull and Wynn, "Blue Triangle YWCA." See also Bucy, *Women Helping Women,* 42–54.

96. "Activities of Colored People of Nashville," *Nashville Banner,* February 29, 1920, 36; "Activities of Colored People of Nashville," *Nashville Banner,* March 14, 1920, 37.

97. Chatelain, *South Side Girls,* 138–39.

98. Chatelain, *South Side Girls,* 141–42.

4. *"Other Camp Fire Things We Can Do"*

1. Nielsen, "Helen Keller and the Politics of Civic Fitness," 269; and Imada, "A Decolonial Disability Studies?," n.p.

2. Altenbaugh, "Where Are the Disabled in the History of Education?," 713; Nielsen, *Disability History of the United States,* 89, 118, 135–36; Diokno, *Hidden Lives, Concealed Narratives,* 12; Duncan, "'Every One of Them Are Worth It,'" 331, 343.

3. Moran, *Colonizing Leprosy,* 7, 8, 11, 19. Hansen's disease was still incurable until doctors developed sulfone treatments in the late 1950s.

4. Moran, *Colonizing Leprosy,* 133–34; Escalante, "American Public Health Policy on Leprosy," 101–2; and Gealogo and Galang, "From Collection to Release," 179–82.

5. Luther Gulick, "Symbolism and the Camp Fire Girls," ca. 1912, 10, CFNH.

6. For this insight regarding contemporary issues, see Malaquias, "'Usefulness' Is Not a Measure of Human Worth."

7. Nielsen, *Disability History of the United States,* 100, 109–10, 117.

8. Freeberg, *Education of Laura Bridgman,* 10, 13.

9. Carrie Wallace Kearns quoted in James E. West, "Need of Leadership for the Youth of America," ca. 1918, 22, CFNH.

10. Lighthouse International, "A Look Back at Two Forward Thinkers."

11. Grace Parker, Report of the Secretary to the Executive Committee of Camp Fire Girls, March 12, 1914, box 11, folder 3, LHWP; and "Tells of Its Work for Blind Children," *New York Times,* May 24, 1914, 23. The Lighthouse also had Boy Scouts. See "New York Association for the Blind," 183–84; and Rogers, "New York Association for the Blind."

12. Duncan, "'Every One of Them Are Worth It,'" 345, 347.

13. "Tells of Its Work for Blind Children," *New York Times,* May 24, 1914, 23.

14. Kearns, "Problem"; and Kearns quoted in West, "Need of Leadership for the Youth of America," ca. 1918, 22, CFNH.

15. Watson, "Wonderful Career of a Cripple," 70, 72–73.

16. Nielsen, *Disability History of the United States,* 122–23. Duncan notes that the bylaws at the Van Leuven Browne home permitted only white children, but two American Indian children appear in the records. Additional information about them is not known. Duncan, "'Every One of Them Are Worth It,'" 334.

17. "Recreation for Crippled Children."

18. "Boy Scouts and Camp Fire Girls."

19. Quoted in Grace Parker, Report of the Secretary to the Executive Committee of Camp Fire Girls, March 12, 1914, box 11, folder 3, LHWP.

20. "Redeviva," *Great Falls (MT) Tribune*, March 11, 1923, 17; and "Outdoor Craft for Blind Camp Fire Girls Who Cook," *Kenosha (WI) News*, February 23, 1923, 3.

21. Pratt Institute, *Notable Women of Modern Times: A List for Camp Fire Girls* (Brooklyn: Pratt Institute Free Library, 1913), CFNH.

22. Keller, *Story of My Life*, 3; and Martin, *Elizabeth Gilbert and Her Work for the Blind*, 70, 74, 79.

23. Keller, "Nature Has the Power."

24. Garland-Thomson, *Extraordinary Bodies*, 16.

25. Schalk, "Ablenationalism in American Girlhood," 39–40.

26. Scrapbook of the Ouananiche Camp Fire Girls, Malone NY, 1914–15, CFNH. No further description of the visit is included.

27. Grace Parker, Report of the Secretary to the Executive Committee of Camp Fire Girls, March 12, 1914, box 11, folder 3, LHWP.

28. "Cornwall-on-Hudson Camp Fire Girls."

29. "Candle Light and Ideals," 8.

30. "Outdoor Craft for Blind Camp Fire Girls Who Cook," *Kenosha (WI) News*, February 23, 1923, 3.

31. Camp Fire Girls, *Book of the Camp Fire Girls* (1913), 57, 60.

32. Irving Hart to Dr. E. D. Aguilar, August 16, 1934, Manila, CFNH.

33. "News from the Philippines."

34. Honeck, *Our Frontier Is the World*, 137.

35. Rafael, *White Love*, 53–55.

36. "Missionary Work in the Philippines," *Oregon Daily Journal*, February 28, 1909, 41; "Irving Hart to Leave for Philippine Post with Leper Colony," *Statesman Journal* (Salem OR), March 8, 1950, 5; "Daddy Hart, Famed Worker among Filipinos, Seeks Funds," *Honolulu Star-Bulletin*, June 8, 1951, 14; "Wealthy Man Sought to Build Hospital," *Indianapolis (IN) News*, August 8, 1951, 25; "Essex Junction," *Burlington (VT) Clipper*, April 6, 1901, 8. Hart also established the Philippine Band of Mercy, which aids children with facial and cranial abnormalities to gain treatment.

37. Honeck, *Our Frontier Is the World*, 142. For a discussion of evangelical and humanitarian work abroad, see Tyrrell, *Reforming the World*, 4.

38. Webb, *"Not My Will,"* 90–92; Irving Hart to Camp Fire Girls, March 25, 1929, CFNH.

39. Roces, "Filipino Elite Women and Public Health."

40. Rafael, *White Love*, 81–83; "News from the Philippines."

41. Webb, *"Not My Will,"* 90–92, 107, 113; "International Friendship," *Montana Standard*, February 8, 1931, 31.

42. "Camp Fire Sparks," 19.

43. Mary O'Brien to Irving Hart, November 4, 1932, Manila, CFNH.

44. Anderson, "States of Hygiene," 94.

45. Rene R. Escalante, "American Public Health Policy on Leprosy, 1898–1941," in Diokno, *Hidden Lives, Concealed Narratives*, 94–96, 101–2; Gealogo and Galang, "From Collection to Release," 179–82.

46. Anderson, "States of Hygiene," 110.

47. Moran, *Colonizing Leprosy*, 5.

48. Anderson, "States of Hygiene," 97, 101–2.

49. Theodora Alebasa, Annual Report of Santa Barbara, Iloilo, Camp Fire Girls, January 14, 1935, CFNH.

50. "Leprosy News," 485–86, 489.

51. Irving Hart to Dr. E. D. Aguilar, August 27, 1934, Manila, CFNH.

52. Dr. C. Gavino to Irving Hart, December 3, 1928, Manila, CFNH.

53. Eugenio Hernando to Irving Hart, May 12, 1937, Manila, CFNH.

54. Gealogo and Galang, "From Collection to Release," 172–73. Culion prohibited marriage between 1928 and 1932.

55. Irving Hart to Mary R. O'Brien, August 29, 1932, Manila, CFNH.

56. For a discussion of pregnancy, see Rodriguez, "Island of Despair," 60.

57. Irving Hart to Dr. E. D. Aguilar, August 16, 1934, Manila, CFNH.

58. Irving Hart to Dr. E. D. Aguilar, August 27, 1934, Manila, CFNH.

59. Note by Irving Hart attached to José M. Raymound to Irving Hart, September 14, 1934, Culion, CFNH.

60. Camp Fire Girl quoted in Irving Hart to Mary R. O'Brien, May 31, 1939, Manila, CFNH.

61. Irving Hart to Mary R. O'Brien, July 19, 1935, Manila, CFNH; Irving Hart to Dr. José Tolentino, February 6, 1940, Manila, CFNH.

62. Irving Hart to Lola Duvall Williams, August 1, 1937, Manila, CFNH.

63. See, for example, Irving Hart to Mary R. O'Brien, February 15, 1939, Manila, CFNH.

64. Purificacion Vercres and Purita Zamora to Irving Hart, June 1, 1937, San Lazaro Hospital, CFNH; Irving Hart to Camp Fire Girls, San Lazaro Hospital, June 4, 1937, Manila, CFNH; and Irving Hart to Mary R. O'Brien, June 5, 1937, Manila, CFNH.

65. Camp Fire Girls, Department of Public Relations, "Camp Fire in the Philippines," n.d., CFNH.

66. On the Girl Scout preference in the Philippines, see Irving Hart to Martha F. Allen, August 6, 1946, Manila, CFNH.

67. For a discussion of how World War II shaped perceptions of people with disabilities, see Nielsen, *Disability History of the United States*, 148–49.

5. "Worship God"

1. Ossian, "Fragilities and Failures," 163. For a discussion of children on the American home front, see Tuttle, *Daddy's Gone to War*, x, 115; and Kirk, "Getting in the Scrap." For a broader discussion of the American home front, see Winkler, *Home Front U.S.A.*

2. See Enloe, *Maneuvers*, 1–34, for an extended definition and discussion of militarization.

3. *Highland (CA) Messenger*, March 20, 1948, newspaper clipping in Scrapbook, 1946–52, SAC-SB.

4. "Initial Week of Camp Vagabond Enjoyed by Quincy Girls Groups," July 9, 1945, newspaper clipping in Mabel H. Walter, Scrapbook of Camp Fire (Quincy MA), 1939–46, folio box 5, CFCEM. It might be noted that the Marines did not have a cute title or acronym. General Thomas Holcomb, though not a huge supporter of women in the military, was adamant that all who were accepted into the Marines were in fact Marines. National Park Service, "Free a Marine to Fight."

5. "Camp Vagabond Day Session Draws Record Attendance," July 25, 1945, newspaper clipping in Walter, Scrapbook, CFCEM.

6. K. M. Schultz, *Tri-Faith America*, 7.

7. Tuttle, *Daddy's Gone to War*, 115–16; De Schweinitz, *If We Could Change the World*, 182.

8. On the 4-H, see G. N. Rosenberg, *4-H Harvest*, 162; Alexander, *Guiding Modern Girls*, 163.

9. Mary Ritter Beard, "Plan of Action for Camp Fire Girls," address, National Council of Camp Fire Girls, New York, September 26–28, 1940, in Annual Meeting Minutes, 42–43, CFNH. On the right-wing orientation of Scouts and the Catholic youth organizations in France during the interwar years, see Kalman, *Extreme Right in Interwar France*, 146; Nizkor Project, "Trial of German Major War Criminals"; and Coutrot, "Youth Movements in France," 31.

10. Lester F. Scott for the Camp Fire Girls, press release, 1939, CFNH.

11. "Abiding Loyalties."

12. "Carry On."

13. Tuttle, *Daddy's Gone to War*, 121, 137; Dorn, *American Education*, 7–8; and Chafe, *Unfinished Journey*, 4–7.

14. "Service Review."

15. Martha F. Allen, Report to the National Council Meeting of the Camp Fire Girls, Annual Meeting Minutes, October 9, 1942, New York, 21, CFNH.

16. "Service Review," 1; and Sense, "Home Volunteers to the Front."

17. "Camp Fire Girls in Action."

18. Palladino, *Teenagers*, 66–71; and Reiman, *New Deal and American Youth*, 175–76.

19. "Home Service for Victory."

20. "Food Fights for Freedom."

21. "Colton Camp Fire Girls Sell Sugarless Recipes," *Colton (CA) Editor*, May 5, 1942, newspaper clipping in Scrapbook, May 18, 1937, to May 1, 1942, SAC-SB.

22. Mrs. W. F. Miller, "A Group with a Purpose."

23. "Food Fights for Freedom."

24. Camp Nawakwa brochure, Pomona Valley (CA) Council, 1942, SAC-SB.

25. "Service Review," 6.

26. Morris, *How the Camp Fire Girls Won World War II*, 17.

27. Griswold, *Fatherhood in America*, 162.

28. See, for example, "Camp Fire Girls Win Service Stripes."

29. "Listen! What's That?"

30. Scrapbook and Journal of Tankuloka Camp Fire, Roslindale MA, 1943–44, March 24, 1944, box 2, folder 62, CFCEM.

31. Morris, *How the Camp Fire Girls Won World War II*, 7–18.

32. "Women's Group Opens Two War Bond Booths," December 2, 1944, newspaper clipping in Walter, Scrapbook, CFCEM.

33. Scrapbook and Journal of Tankuloka Camp Fire, March 24, 1944, CFCEM.

34. "Democracy for Victory."

35. Pierce, "Why I Am Proud to Be an American."

36. "Service Review," 1.

37. Tuttle, *Daddy's Gone to War*, 167.

38. Camp Fire also collaborated with the Federal Public Housing Agency, which asked the organization to extend its recreation program to a few housing projects in emerging defense centers, especially Ypsilanti, Michigan; South Bend, Oregon; and Vancouver, Washington.

39. "Statement of Relationships, Camp Fire Girls, Inc., and War Relocation Authority," in Operating Agreements and Statements of Joint Policy, folder E2.09, JAERR, http://www.oac.cdlib.org/ark:/13030/k6h70p6f/?brand=oac4; and Matsumoto, *City Girls*, 156–57, 169.

40. In Tsuchida, *Reflections*, 135, 246.

41. "Statement of Relationships, Camp Fire Girls, Inc., and War Relocation Authority," in Operating Agreements and Statements of Joint Policy, folder E2.09, JAERR, http://www.oac.cdlib.org/ark:/13030/k6h70p6f/?brand=oac4.

42. Martha F. Allen, Report to the National Council Meeting of the Camp Fire Girls, Annual Meeting Minutes, October 9, 1942, New York, 23, CFNH.

43. Park, *Facilitating Injustice*, 363.

44. Allen, Report to the National Council Meeting, October 9, 1942, 23, CFNH.

45. Untitled announcement, *Herald and News* (Klamath Falls OR), August 3, 1942, 7.

46. In Tsuchida, *Reflections*, 348; and "Statement of Relationships, Camp Fire Girls, Inc., and War Relocation Authority," in Operating Agreements and Statements of Joint Policy, folder E2.09, JAERR, http://www.oac.cdlib.org/ark:/13030/k6h70p6f/?brand=oac4.

47. See "Around the Circuit," *Topaz (UT) Times*, June 17, 1944, 4; Mrs. Elmer (Mammie) Shirrell, diary, 1942–1945, September 7, 1942, 59, JAERR, https://digitalassets.lib.berkeley.edu/jarda/ucb/text/reduced/cubanc6714_b268r25_0010_2.pdf.

48. *Heart Mountain Sentinel* (Cody WY), April 14, 1945, 3, http://ddr.densho.org/media/ddr-densho-97/ddr-densho-97-228-mezzanine-80ae7054ff.htm. Unfortunately, no summary of the roundtable was given.

49. "Around the Circuit," *Topaz (UT) Times,* July 15, 1944, 10.

50. Harvey, *Amache,* 112.

51. On the similar internment camp schools' lessons on patriotic citizenship, see Tuttle, *Daddy's Gone to War,* 118.

52. Seton, *Woodcraft Manual for Boys,* 24.

53. Camp Fire Girls, *Book of the Camp Fire Girls* (1914), 42–43.

54. Minutes of the Board of Directors of the Camp Fire Girls, January 31, 1917, New York, CFNH.

55. Camp Fire Girls, *Book of the Camp Fire Girls with War Program,* 122.

56. Buckler, Fiedler, and Allen, *Wo-he-lo,* 84–85; Minutes of the Board of Directors of the Camp Fire Girls, September 24, 1919, New York, CFNH.

57. The Girls' Friendly Society and the Camp Fire Girls, *The Affiliation of the Girls' Friendly Society with Camp Fire Girls* (New York: Girls' Friendly Society and the Camp Fire Girls, ca. 1920s), pamphlet, 4, CFNH.

58. Minutes of the National Board of Directors and Executive Committee of the Camp Fire Girls, January 28, 1925, and February 18, 1925, New York, CFNH. The National Catholic Youth Organizations Federation finally included Camp Fire in 1973. On Catholic youth organizations, see National Federation for Catholic Youth Ministry, "NCCGSCF History."

59. Minutes of the National Council of the Camp Fire Girls, October 9, 1942, New York, 38, CFNH.

60. K. M. Schultz, *Tri-Faith America,* 44.

61. Mechling, *On My Honor,* 41–45, explains that the Boy Scout program also became more religious during the 1950s.

62. Herberg, *Protestant—Catholic—Jew,* 14, 40, 46–49.

63. Camp Fire Girls, Inc., *They Told Us What They Wanted: Report of the Camp Fire Girls Program Study,* 1946, CFNH.

64. For a discussion of how Jews and Catholics used the language of pluralism to carve out space for their religions as equals alongside Protestantism, see K. M. Schultz, *Tri-Faith America,* 9–10.

65. Minutes of the National Council of the Camp Fire Girls, October 10, 1941, Detroit MI, 23–32, CFNH.

66. Minutes of the National Council of the Camp Fire Girls, October 10, 1941, Detroit MI, 23–32, CFNH.

67. Minutes of the National Council of the Camp Fire Girls, October 10, 1941, Detroit MI, 23–32, CFNH.

68. Minutes of the National Board of Directors of the Camp Fire Girls, Semi-Annual Meeting, May 22, 1942, New York, CFNH.

69. Minutes of the National Council of the Camp Fire Girls, October 9, 1942, New York, 38, CFNH.

70. Runbeck, "Our Camp Fire Law."

71. Mrs. Edith Eskesen, "Observe 45th Anniversary," *Rialto (CA) Record*, March 11, 1955, newspaper clipping in Scrapbook, 1955, SAC-SB.

72. See, for example, "Aiding War on Homefront Theme for Camp Fire Girls Birthday Week," *Indianapolis (IN) Star*, March 14, 1943, 21; and "Candlelight Vesper Service," *Indianapolis Star*, March 14, 1943, 21.

73. "Winneconne Church to Hold Camp Fire Services Tomorrow," *Oshkosh (WI) Northwestern*, March 22, 1941, 7.

74. June 10, c. 1957, newspaper clipping in Scrapbook, 1954–1958, CFSD.

75. Minutes of the National Board of Directors and Executive Committee of the Camp Fire Girls, May 6, 1944, New York, CFNH.

76. Allen, "Religious Policies Committee."

77. Minutes of the National Board of Directors and Executive Committee of the Camp Fire Girls, January 16, 1948, New York, CFNH.

78. Report of the Religious Policies Committee, Minutes of the National Board of Directors of the Camp Fire Girls, Semi-Annual Meeting, May 20–21, 1948, New York, CFNH.

79. "Camp Fire and the Protestant Girl," "Camp Fire and the Catholic Girl," and "Camp Fire and the Jewish Girl" (New York: Camp Fire Girls, ca. 1950), pamphlets, CFNH.

80. "Camp Fire and the Protestant Girl," "Camp Fire and the Catholic Girl," and "Camp Fire and the Jewish Girl," pamphlets, CFNH.

81. "Camp Fire and the Protestant Girl," "Camp Fire and the Catholic Girl," and "Camp Fire and the Jewish Girl," pamphlets, CFNH.

82. Minutes of the National Board of Directors of the Camp Fire Girls, Semi-Annual Meeting, May 20–21, 1948, New York, CFNH.

83. "Camp Fire Girls Go to Church," *Evening Telegram* (San Bernardino CA), March 17, 1955, newspaper clipping in 1955 Scrapbook, SAC-SB.

84. Buckler, Fiedler, and Allen, *Wo-he-lo*, 84–85; and Minutes of the National Board of Directors of the Camp Fire Girls, Semi-Annual Meeting, May 20–21, 1948, New York, CFNH.

85. Rockwell, "Camp Fire and the Church."

86. "Camp Fire and the Protestant Girl," "Camp Fire and the Catholic Girl," and "Camp Fire and the Jewish Girl," pamphlets, CFNH. On the combination of civics and religion, see Allen, "Future of Camp Fire."

87. Camp Fire Girls, Committee on Intercultural Policies and Practices, *Opportunity for All* (New York: Camp Fire Girls, 1955), pamphlet, 3, CFNH.

88. "For Our Allies," 5.

89. Scully, "Brotherhood."

6. Being a "Homemaker—Plus"

1. "Camp Fire Girls Postwar Program," 1.

2. Allen, "We Study Our Objectives."

3. "Camp Fire Girls Postwar Program," 1.

4. May, *Homeward Bound*, xxiv–xxv.

5. Strub, "Clearly Obscene and the Queerly Obscene," 373.

6. Plant, *Mom*, 12, 21, 24, 38. See also McEnaney, *Civil Defense Begins at Home*, 77, for a discussion of how maternalism infused postwar civil defense work.

7. Meyerowitz, "Beyond the Feminine Mystique"; Evans, *Personal Politics*, 5–6; Rosen, *World Split Open*, 4–8, 19–27, 40–43; and Weiss, *To Have and to Hold*, 53–54, 205.

8. "Camp Fire Girls Postwar Program," 1.

9. Lynne Newman, email to author, February 13, 2004; and Sally Dunn, interview by author, Angels Camp CA, 2013.

10. Allen, "What Will She Be When She Grows Up?"; and Camp Fire Girls, *A Great Leader: Tribute to a Great Leader* (New York: Camp Fire Girls, 1966), pamphlet, 5–8, box 1, folder 7, CFCEM. On the Board of Directors of the Camp Fire Girls actively seeking a woman director, see Joseph E. Raycroft to Mrs. Elbert Williams, January 2, 1940, CFNH.

11. Allen, "What Will She Be When She Grows Up?"

12. Allen, "Camp Fire Girls in the Second Half Century."

13. Allen, "We Study Our Objectives."

14. Allen, "Camp Fire Girls in the Second Half Century."

15. Martha F. Allen to James P. Fitch, September 19, 1944, CFNH.

16. Allen, "We Study Our Objectives."

17. Allen, "Camp Fire Girls in the Second Half Century," 4.

18. "Together We Make Tomorrow: 1957."

19. Allen, "We Study Our Objectives."

20. Camp Fire Girls, *Constitution and By-Laws of the Camp Fire Girls*, New York [1912], 1, 2, CFNH. See discussion in Camp Fire Girls, Discussion Material on Objectives of Camp Fire Girls Including Report of Meeting on Objectives at National Council Meeting, April 1953, Omaha NE, 3–4, 11–13, CFNH.

21. Camp Fire Girls, "Camp Fire Girls Statement of Objectives."

22. Mrs. Warren C. Hunter, Report of the President, Minutes of the National Council of Camp Fire Girls, Annual Meeting Minutes, November 7–9, 1954, Kansas City MO, 2, CFNH.

23. Camp Fire Girls, Discussion Material on Objectives of Camp Fire Girls, April 1953, Omaha NE, 3, 11–12, CFNH; and Discussion of Objectives, Minutes of the National Council of Camp Fire Girls, Annual Meeting Minutes, November 7–9, 1954, Kansas City MO, 42–44, CFNH.

24. Camp Fire Girls, "Camp Fire Girls Statement of Objectives."

25. Allen, "Report on the Study of Our Objectives." Camp Fire did not formally

replace the 1914 Articles of Incorporation, finding it cumbersome to change them. Its new statement was used for publicity and programming decisions.

26. How, "We Pass Our Feelings On!"
27. Fiedler, "Why a Council Fire?"
28. Korman, "Being a Homemaker—Plus." It should be noted that Korman, too, resumed her career. By the early 1980s, she was dean at New York University's School of Social Work, where she was on the faculty for thirty-five years.
29. Lambert, "Jobs to Grow On."
30. Hammond, "The Fourth Rank."
31. Sally Dunn, interview by author, Angels Camp CA, 2013.
32. Camp Fire Girls, "Together We Make Tomorrow," 6.
33. "Around the Camp Fire."
34. Beard, "Mahawe's Memory Book."
35. Lowman, "Camping Adventure."
36. Lynne Newman, email to author, February 13, 2004; and Himmelberger, "Passing the Light," 9.
37. Finch, "Count Your Blessings."
38. Metro Chicago Camp Fire Council, "What Is Your Favorite Camp Fire Memory?," Alumni Reunion and 90th Birthday Celebration, 2000, CFNH.
39. "Camp Is So Much Fun."
40. Spear, "A Guide to Camping," 12, describes the 1946 Camp Fire program study, *They Told Us What They Wanted.*
41. Camp Fire Girls, Annual Report, 1954, CFNH.
42. Hazard, "More Fun Out of Doors."
43. Camp Fire Girls, Annual Report, 1961, CFNH.
44. Keyes, "So Much to Do in Summer."
45. Borchardt, "Growing Together."
46. Sally Dunn, interview by author, Angels Camp CA, 2013.
47. Scrapbook of Eastport ME, Camp Fire, ca. 1948–1952, October 1949, folio box 5, CFCEM. Rowe, "In the Camp Fire Tradition"; Rowe, "New Directions in Program"; and Schaumburg, "Camp Fire, 1961–1979," 263–65. The Junior Hi program was renamed the Discovery Program in 1971.
48. Burdett, "Report on Research Study"; Camp Fire Girls, Annual Report, 1928, 5, CFNH; Camp Fire Girls, Annual Report to the Board of Directors, 1964–65, CFNH; Camp Fire Girls, Annual Report, 1966–67, 3, CFNH. If the San Diego Council is representative, only about half of Camp Fire leaders had daughters in their group in 1936. Bennett, "Investigation of the Educational Practices," 56.
49. Mac Millan, "Beauty Found in Household Tasks."
50. Mann, "Blueprint for Beauty."
51. Mann, "Blueprint for Beauty."
52. Luther Gulick, "Symbolism and the Camp Fire Girls," ca. 1912, 9–10, CFNH.

53. Camp Fire Girls, *Book of the Camp Fire Girls* (1946), 64–65; and Frick, "What's Become of Health." On magazines for girls, see Schrum, "'Teena Means Business.'"

54. Veglia, "It's Work—But It's Fun!"

55. Teichmann, "Program Designs for Your Horizon Club."

56. Gladys Mae Jackson, "Lessons in Leadership," typed report of Torch Bearer Rank, 1943, Lincoln NE, CFNH. Gladys Mae Jackson (Gail Fullerton) would go on to be the first female president at San Jose State University (California). Perhaps her charm was the key!

57. Jackson, "Lessons in Leadership," typed report of Torch Bearer Rank, 1943, Lincoln NE, CFNH.

58. J. Lane, *Your Carriage, Madam!*, 9, 23.

59. Jackson, "Lessons in Leadership," typed report of Torch Bearer Rank, 1943, Lincoln NE, CFNH.

60. Brumberg, *Body Project*, 61.

61. Hunt, "Are You Good at Figures?"

62. Allen, "Fitness of American Youth."

63. Bricker, "Accentuate the Positive."

64. Brunst, "Sports for Older Girls."

65. Lippitt, "Boys and Girls Together."

66. Lippitt, "Boys and Girls Together"; and "Girls and Boys Together."

67. Horizon Club Scrapbook, 1939–1942, CFOKC.

68. *Camp Fire Girl* 33, no. 5 (January 1954): 1.

69. J. Brown, "A Is for Atom, B Is for Bomb"; Mickenberg, *Learning from the Left*, 186–90; and Scripps, "Science Fairs as National Security."

70. Kempthorne, "Doing It Differently."

71. Linda Lou Harris, Scrapbook, 1947–1949, CFOKC.

72. Camp Fire Girls, *Book of the Camp Fire Girls* (1946), 194.

73. Pitcher, "What Kind of Education for Girls?"

74. "More Fun with Science."

75. "The Camp Fire Scene," 16; and Lynne Newman, email to author, February 13, 2004.

76. Duvall, "The Girl Today," 5.

77. Scrapbook and Journal of Tankuloka Camp Fire, Roslindale MA, 1943–1947, February 1947, box 2, folder 62, CFCEM.

78. Freeman, *Sex Goes to School*, xi, 93.

79. Duvall, "Girl Today," 6.

80. Lippitt, "Boys and Girls Together."

81. "You've Told Us."

82. *Sun Telegram* (San Bernardino CA), May 6, 1962, newspaper clipping in Mary Jo Meade, Scrapbook of the Camp Fire Girls, 1962–64, SAC-SB.

83. Devlin, *Relative Intimacy*, 2.

84. "Preparing for the Future."

7. "Prejudices May Be Prevented"

1. Camp Fire Girls, Committee on Intercultural Policies and Practices, *Opportunity for All*, 20, CFNH.
2. Allen, "You Can Contribute Courage."
3. Haney, "Everybody's Job—Civil Defense."
4. Allen, "Future of Camp Fire," 1.
5. Allen, "Camp Fire Girls in the Second Half Century," 4.
6. Allen, "Future of Camp Fire," 2.
7. Dudziak, *Cold War Civil Rights*, 12, 113, 118.
8. For discussion of attitude changes regarding eugenics and disabilities, see Nielsen, *Disability History of the United States*, 148–49; Ladd-Taylor, "'Sociological Advantages' of Sterilization," 282, 289; Mitchell and Snyder, "Eugenic Atlantic"; and Gelb, "'Mental Deficients' Fighting Fascism," 310; Jennings, *Out of the Horrors of War*, 6–9. On the antiprejudice efforts of schools, see Tuttle, *Daddy's Gone to War*, 116–17; De Schweinitz, *If We Could Change the World*, 182; and Burkholder, *Color in the Classroom*.
9. K. M. Schultz, *Tri-Faith America*, 8.
10. "Camp Fire Girls Postwar Program," 2.
11. The 1946 YWCA charter is quoted in Izzo, *Liberal Christianity and Women's Global Activism*, 104. See also Robertson, *Christian Sisterhood, Race Relations, and the YWCA*; Bucy, *Women Helping Women*; Weisenfeld, *African American Women and Christian Activism*; and Simmons, *Crescent City Girls*. On the Girl Scouts, see Williams, *Bridge to the Future*, 10; and Perry, "Josephine Groves Holloway." On 4-H, see G. N. Rosenberg, *4-H Harvest*, 156, 160. On the Boy Scouts, see Jordan, *Modern Manhood and the Boy Scouts of America*, 200–201; Honeck, *Our Frontier Is the World*, 196; and "Scouts and NAACP Resolve Crisis." See also Helgren, *American Girls and Global Responsibility*, 44–46.
12. Allen, "Future of Camp Fire," 2.
13. "Picture of the Month."
14. "Tea Party."
15. Alpenfels, "Let's Pack Up Our Prejudices."
16. Alpenfels, "Let's Pack Up Our Prejudices."
17. Montgomery, "You Can Do Something about Prejudice."
18. Camp Fire Girls, Committee on Intercultural Policies and Practices, *Opportunity for All*, 4, CFNH.
19. Camp Fire Girls, Committee on Intercultural Policies and Practices, *Opportunity for All*, 5, CFNH; and Camp Fire Girls, Inc., *They Told Us What They Wanted: Report of the Camp Fire Girls Program Study*, 1946, CFNH.
20. "Inquiring Reporter," 1949, newspaper clipping in Scrapbook for Leader's Association, 1948–1951, CFSD.
21. Patricia Flammini, interview by author, February 19, 2004.

22. Hein, "Democracy—Blue Bird Size."

23. Camp Fire Girls, Committee on Intercultural Policies and Practices, *Opportunity for All*, 6, CFNH; and Committee on Intercultural Practices and Policies, *Opportunity for All*, draft, 1955, 9–12, CFNH.

24. Celia Anderson, interview by author, January 28, 2004.

25. Camp Fire Girls, Committee on Intercultural Practices and Policies, *Opportunity for All*, draft, 17.

26. "Colored Camp Fire Girls' Carnival," *Tyler (TX) Morning Telegraph*, January 31, 1952, 2.

27. Camp Fire Girls, Committee on Intercultural Practices and Policies, *Opportunity for All*, draft, 18, CFNH.

28. Scrapbook of Eastport, Maine, Camp Fire, ca. 1948–1952, October 1949, folio box 5, CFCEM. Photographs of Camp Fire Girls, CFISC, also show girls in blackface.

29. Camp Fire Girls, Committee on Intercultural Practices and Policies, *Opportunity for All*, draft, 6–8.

30. Regional Report, Minutes of the National Council of the Camp Fire Girls, November 11–12, 1957, Minneapolis MN, 56, CFNH.

31. Roll Call of the Regions, Minutes of the National Council of the Camp Fire Girls, November 10–11, 1958, Denver CO, 17, CFNH.

32. McRae, *Mothers of Massive Resistance*, 89, 140–42.

33. "B-PW Club Members Will Sponsor Negro Camp Fire Group," *Seminole (OK) Producer*, December 7, 1951, 1; "Ceramics Topic for Albany Club," *Abilene (TX) Reporter-News*, November 19, 1949, 13.

34. "Negro Camp Fire Girls to Attend Cleburne Camp," *Corsicana (TX) Daily Sun*, August 9, 1950, 3.

35. McRae, *Mothers of Massive Resistance*, 93, 94.

36. "Tyler to Don Yule Dress This Week," *Tyler (TX) Courier-Times*, November 28, 1954, 1.

37. Camp Fire Girls, Committee on Intercultural Policies and Practices, *Opportunity for All*, 6, CFNH.

38. "Negro Field Worker to Help Camp Fire Group," *Waco (TX) Tribune-Herald*, June 16, 1946, 25; and "1,126 on Camp Fire Rolls," *Waco (TX) Tribune-Herald*, March 21, 1954, 8.

39. Camp Fire Girls, Committee on Intercultural Practices and Policies, *Opportunity for All*, draft, 18, CFNH.

40. Camp Fire Girls, Minutes, November 7–9, 1954, National Council Meeting, Kansas City MO, CFNH.

41. Camp Fire Girls, Committee on Intercultural Practices and Policies, *Opportunity for All*, 10–12, CFNH.

42. On the Girl Scouts controversy, see Helgren, *American Girls and Global Responsibility*, 140–43.

43. McRae, *Mothers of Massive Resistance*, 183.

44. Martha F. Allen, Report of National Director, Minutes of the National Council of the Camp Fire Girls, November 5–9, 1955, Chicago, 15, CFNH.

45. Allen, "Forward Look."

46. Sonia Littrell, interview by author, February 18, 2004; and Lisa Reeder, email to author, January 29, 2004.

47. Littrell, interview.

48. Littrell, interview.

49. Camp Fire Girls, Committee on Intercultural Practices and Policies, *Opportunity for All*, draft, 15, CFNH.

50. Littrell, interview.

51. Buckler, Fiedler, and Allen, *Wo-he-lo*, 196.

52. Parker, Report of the Secretary, May 14, 1914, LHWP.

53. Schaumburg, "Camp Fire, 1961–1979," 299–300.

8. *"The War on Poverty"*

1. "National Camp Fire Girls Program Serves Many in All Walks of Life," *Arcadia (CA) Tribune*, December 29, 1966, 21.

2. Martha Allen, "Creative Adaptation to Change: Report of Seminars, Metropolitan Critical Areas Project" (New York: Camp Fire Girls, Inc., 1965), 1, CFNH. See also Allen, "Camp Fire Girls in the Second Half Century."

3. See Membership in Minority and Poverty Areas in "Working Papers: Background Information on Camp Fire Girls," Minutes of the National Council of the Camp Fire Girls, Annual Meeting Minutes, November 8–11, 1968, Scottsdale AZ, 2, CFNH; Camp Fire USA, "All About Us," 2004, http://www.campfireusa.org /all_about_us.

4. For a discussion of children's choices as political, see Berghel, Fieldston, and Renfro, introduction to *Growing Up America*, 2.

5. Camp Fire Girls, Annual Report, 1965, CFNH. Camp Fire, Inc., Agency Profile, 1986, 13, CFNH; and Ad Hoc Planning Committee of the National Board of Directors of the Camp Fire Girls, "It's a New Day," November 1974, 8, CFNH. The Agency Profile charts youth members and total members from 1949 to 1985. This report is among the most reliable, as it describes inconsistencies in data collection. From 1949 to 1976, children and adults were often counted together in membership numbers, and some children were double-counted in camp and club programs. Indeed, many of the annual reports list different numbers from the 1986 Agency Profile. A National Criminal Justice Service report on youth organizations' collaboration with the justice department indicates that Camp Fire grew slightly during the 1970s, but these numbers contradict the organization's internal records and are likely a result of Camp Fire's inconsistencies in counting members during these years. See Olson-Raymer, "National Nongovernmental Organizations Involved with the Juvenile Justice System." On the membership

struggles of Boy Scouts and Girl Scouts, see Arneil, "Gender, Diversity, and Organizational Change," 53–54, 57.

6. Annual Report for Mt. San Antonio Council of Camp Fire, 1972, CFISC.

7. Martha C. Burk, "Directions for the Future," address, National Council Meeting of the Camp Fire Girls, Houston TX, November 21–22, 1975, Annual Meeting Minutes, 3, CFNH.

8. For a discussion of the origins of the community chest, see Bookman, "Community Chest Movement."

9. Maynard J. Hammond, Developmental Study: Report to Camp Fire Girls (American City Bureau/Beaver Associates, 1964), 22–24, 34, CFNH; and Martha F. Allen, "The Group and I," address, Triennial Conference, Camp Fire Girls, San Francisco, November 15, 1963, in National Council Meeting Minutes, CFNH; and Martha F. Allen, "Challenge and Opportunity for Camp Fire Girls," address, Camp Fire Girls National Council, Dallas TX, November 9, 1964, in National Council Meeting Minutes, CFNH. For the gender divide in youth funding, see "Go West—Young Woman—Go West," ca. 1967, newspaper clipping in Dr. Hester Turner File at CFNH.

10. On urban migration, see Riessman, Culturally Deprived Child, 1. On urban life, see Farber and Bailey, Columbia Guide to America in the 1960s, 47, 84, 104–5, 264–69, 330; and Herman, Fighting in the Streets, 2, 75. On the Twenty-Sixth Amendment, see Cheng, "Uncovering the Twenty-Sixth Amendment," 57.

11. Cazenave, Impossible Democracy, 19; and Hinton, From the War on Poverty to the War on Crime, 23, 32–33.

12. Allen quoted in Eva Schindler-Rainman, "Looking Backward, Looking Forward," in Camp Fire Girls, "Innovation and Imagination for Youth: Report of Seminar IV Metropolitan Critical Areas Project," June 1967, 9, CFNH.

13. Camp Fire Girls, "Creative Adaptation to Change: Report of Seminars, Metropolitan Critical Areas Project" (New York: Camp Fire Girls, 1965), 4, CFNH.

14. Hinton, From the War on Poverty to the War on Crime, 42–44.

15. Eckelmann et al., Growing Up America, 7; and Elman, Chronic Youth, 20.

16. Organizations that Black girls might have joined included Jack and Jill, an invitation-only program for upper- and middle-class Black children, and the NACW affiliates, the National Association of Girls and the National Association of Colored Girls.

17. Camp Fire Girls, "Creative Adaptation to Change: Report of Seminars, Metropolitan Critical Areas Project" (New York: Camp Fire Girls, 1965), 17, CFNH. Edith Tufts disagreed with the term "culturally deprived." Tufts, a professor of social work at USC who directed Camp Fire's outreach program to elementary school girls in Los Angeles, believed "educationally disadvantaged" was a more accurate descriptor. Edith Miller Tufts, Group Work with Young School Girls, 1968, Los Angeles, xv, 3–4, 139, CFNH.

18. Eva Schindler-Rainman, interview by Charlotte S. Langley, January 10, 1992, Uni-

versity of Southern California Libraries, https://libraries.usc.edu/sites/default
/files/schindler-rainman_eva.pdf.

19. Camp Fire Girls, "Creative Adaptation to Change: Preview of the Learnings, Metropolitan Critical Areas Projects," presented at the Camp Fire Girls Quadrennial Conference, November 1967, 1, CFNH; Schaumburg, "Camp Fire, 1961–1979," 300–303; and Tufts, *Group Work with Young School Girls*, 5–7, CFNH.

20. Camp Fire Girls, *Final Report: Metropolitan Critical Areas Project, A Child Welfare Demonstration Project*, 1967, 11, CFNH.

21. Camp Fire Girls, *Final Report: Metropolitan Critical Areas Project*, 5, CFNH; Tufts, *Group Work with Young School Girls*, 9, 14, CFNH.

22. Camp Fire Girls, *Final Report: Metropolitan Critical Areas Project*, CFNH, 10–11.

23. Lola Beth Buckley, Janet Murray, and Jean Butman, *Camp Fire Girls Final Report: Detroit Area Council of Camp Fire Girls*, 1968, Detroit, 10, CFNH.

24. Buckley et al., *Camp Fire Girls Final Report: Detroit Area Council*, 7, CFNH.

25. Shirley D. McCune and Betty Jones, *Camp Fire Girls Final Report, Potomac Area Council*, 1967, Washington DC, 5, CFNH.

26. Camp Fire Girls, "Innovation and Imagination for Youth," 27, CFNH.

27. Camp Fire Girls, "Innovation and Imagination for Youth," 23, CFNH. For a discussion of white flight, see Boustan, *Competition in the Promised Land*, 7.

28. Buckley et al., *Camp Fire Girls Final Report: Detroit Area Council*, 30, CFNH. For a discussion of Detroit's racial politics, see Sugrue, *Origins of the Urban Crisis*, 213.

29. Davis and Weiner, *Set the Night on Fire*, 32–33; Stevenson, *Contested Murder of Latasha Harlins*, 18, 37.

30. Camp Fire Girls, "Innovation and Imagination for Youth," 28, CFNH.

31. Hinton, *From the War on Poverty to the War on Crime*, 48.

32. Camp Fire Girls, "Creative Adaptation to Change: Report of Seminars," 2–4, CFNH. On Camp Fire's covert advertisements, see Buckley et al., *Camp Fire Girls Final Report: Detroit Area Council*, 10, CFNH.

33. Eva Schindler-Rainman, interview by Charlotte S. Langley, January 10, 1992, University of Southern California Libraries, https://libraries.usc.edu/sites/default
/files/schindler-rainman_eva.pdf.

34. "Mozell Clarence Hill."

35. Camp Fire Girls, "Creative Adaptation to Change: Report of Seminars," 29, CFNH.

36. Camp Fire Girls, "Creative Adaptation to Change: Report of Seminars," 43, 45–46, CFNH.

37. Camp Fire Girls, "Creative Adaptation to Change: Report of Seminars," 88, CFNH.

38. For a discussion of Economic Research and Action Projects, see Evans, *Personal Politics*, 129–31.

39. Camp Fire Girls, "Creative Adaptation to Change: Report of Seminars," 82, 92, CFNH.

40. Vargus quoted in "National Camp Fire Girls Program Serves Many in All Walks of Life," *Arcadia (CA) Tribune*, December 29, 1966, 21; and Ione Vargus, interview by Daniel Koosed, 2005, Kountze Family Archival History Project, Brandeis University Library, https://www.brandeis.edu/repository/projects/westmedford /blog-static/index.html%3Fpage_id=35.html.

41. Advertisement in the *Daily Journal* (Vineland NJ), January 22, 1968, 4.

42. Shirley D. McCune and Betty Jones, *Camp Fire Girls Final Report, Potomac Area Council*, 1967, Washington DC, 62, 66, CFNH.

43. McCune and Jones, *Camp Fire Girls Final Report, Potomac Area Council*, 66, CFNH.

44. Tufts, *Group Work with Young School Girls*, 5–7, CFNH.

45. Camp Fire Girls, "Innovation and Imagination for Youth," 17, CFNH.

46. Buckley et al., *Camp Fire Girls Final Report: Detroit Area Council*, 24, CFNH.

47. Camp Fire Girls, *Final Report: Metropolitan Critical Areas Project*, 12, 14, CFNH; Tufts, *Group Work with Young School Girls*, 6, 40, CFNH.

48. Buckley et al., *Camp Fire Girls Final Report: Detroit Area Council*, 67–68, 77, CFNH.

49. Buckley et al., *Camp Fire Girls Final Report: Detroit Area Council*, 57, 60, CFNH.

50. Tufts, *Group Work with Young School Girls*, 67, 151, CFNH.

51. Camp Fire Girls, *Final Report: Metropolitan Critical Areas Project*, 13, CFNH.

52. Buckley et al., *Camp Fire Girls Final Report: Detroit Area Council*, 22, CFNH.

53. McCune and Jones, *Camp Fire Girls Final Report, Potomac Area Council*, 79, CFNH.

54. Buckley et al., *Camp Fire Girls Final Report: Detroit Area Council*, 21, 22, CFNH.

55. Camp Fire Girls, "Creative Adaptation to Change: Report of Seminars," 92, CFNH.

56. Buckley et al., *Camp Fire Girls Final Report: Detroit Area Council*, 33, CFNH; McCune and Jones, *Camp Fire Girls Final Report, Potomac Area Council*, 8, CFNH.

57. Buckley et al., *Camp Fire Girls Final Report: Detroit Area Council*, 21, CFNH; *Camp Fire Leadership*, Fall 1976, 8–9.

58. Camp Fire Girls, "Innovation and Imagination for Youth," 37, 42, CFNH.

59. Camp Fire Girls, *Final Report: Metropolitan Critical Areas Project*, 18, CFNH.

60. Tufts, *Group Work with Young School Girls*, 30–32, CFNH; McCune and Jones, *Camp Fire Girls Final Report, Potomac Area Council*, 40, CFNH.

61. Camp Fire Girls, *Final Report: Metropolitan Critical Areas Project*, 28, CFNH.

62. Tufts, *Group Work with Young School Girls*, 27, 50, CFNH.

63. Buckley et al., *Camp Fire Girls Final Report: Detroit Area Council*, 20, 27, 75, CFNH.

64. Camp Fire Girls, *Final Report: Metropolitan Critical Areas Project*, 28, CFNH; McCune and Jones, *Camp Fire Girls Final Report, Potomac Area Council*, 40, 55, CFNH.

65. Buckley et al., *Camp Fire Girls Final Report: Detroit Area Council*, 76, CFNH.

66. McCune and Jones, *Camp Fire Girls Final Report, Potomac Area Council*, 9, 55, 77, CFNH.

67. Tufts, *Group Work with Young School Girls*, 73–74, CFNH; Buckley et al., *Camp*

Fire Girls Final Report: Detroit Area Council, 76, CFNH; and McCune and Jones, *Camp Fire Girls Final Report, Potomac Area Council,* 60, CFNH.

68. Camp Fire Girls, *Final Report: Metropolitan Critical Areas Project,* 19, CFNH.

69. Buckley et al., *Camp Fire Girls Final Report: Detroit Area Council,* 18, 30, CFNH.

70. Buckley et al., *Camp Fire Girls Final Report: Detroit Area Council,* 38, CFNH.

71. "National Camp Fire Girls Program Serves Many in All Walks of Life," *Arcadia (CA) Tribune,* December 29, 1966, 21; and Camp Fire Girls, "Innovation and Imagination for Youth," 19–20, CFNH.

72. Camp Fire Girls, *Final Report: Metropolitan Critical Areas Project,* 19, CFNH; and McCune and Jones, *Camp Fire Girls Final Report, Potomac Area Council,* 10, CFNH.

73. Buckley et al., *Camp Fire Girls Final Report: Detroit Area Council,* 33, CFNH.

74. Camp Fire Girls, *Final Report: Metropolitan Critical Areas Project,* 20–21, CFNH; and Buckley et al., *Camp Fire Girls Final Report: Detroit Area Council,* 38, 41, 76, CFNH.

75. Camp Fire Girls, *Final Report: Metropolitan Critical Areas Project,* 20, CFNH.

76. Buckley et al., *Camp Fire Girls Final Report: Detroit Area Council,* 40, 45, CFNH.

77. Buckley et al., *Camp Fire Girls Final Report: Detroit Area Council,* 45, CFNH.

78. Camp Fire Girls, *Final Report: Metropolitan Critical Areas Project,* 27–28, CFNH.

79. Higginbotham, *Righteous Discontent,* 14–15, 187; and Cooper, *Beyond Respectability,* 19–22, 46.

80. McCune and Jones, *Camp Fire Girls Final Report, Potomac Area Council,* 43, CFNH; Tufts, *Group Work with Young School Girls,* 42, CFNH.

81. Buckley et al., *Camp Fire Girls Final Report: Detroit Area Council,* 93, CFNH.

82. Buckley et al., *Camp Fire Girls Final Report: Detroit Area Council,* 36, 37, 38, CFNH.

83. Buckley et al., *Camp Fire Girls Final Report: Detroit Area Council,* 100, CFNH.

84. Tufts, *Group Work with Young School Girls,* 72–73, CFNH.

85. Camp Fire Girls, "Innovation and Imagination for Youth," 18–19, CFNH.

86. Camp Fire Girls, *Final Report: Metropolitan Critical Areas Project,* 27–28, CFNH.

87. Buckley et al., *Camp Fire Girls Final Report: Detroit Area Council,* 101, CFNH.

88. "Camp Fire USA Stories," CFUSA webpage, 2001.

89. McCune and Jones, *Camp Fire Girls Final Report, Potomac Area Council,* 49, 51, CFNH. For the contemporary definition of Family Life Education, see World Confederation, *Teachers and Family Life Education.*

90. Camp Fire Girls, *Final Report: Metropolitan Critical Areas Project,* 21, CFNH; McCune and Jones, *Camp Fire Girls Final Report, Potomac Area Council,* 77, CFNH.

91. "Camp Fire Girls No Longer 'Indians,' Reflect Background," *World,* October 25, 1972, 10, clipping in Camp Fire Girls Organizational Materials, 1973–1975, Newspaper Clippings, folder 25, CFGSYC. See also "Many Cultures."

92. Buckley et al., *Camp Fire Girls Final Report: Detroit Area Council,* 21, 38, CFNH.

93. Camp Fire Girls, "Creative Adaptation to Change: Report of Seminars," 30, CFNH.

94. Camp Fire Girls, "Creative Adaptation to Change: Report of Seminars," 30, CFNH; Teal, "Moral Economy," 58–62; and Paris, *Children's Nature*, 270.

95. Eva Schindler-Raiman, Camp Fire Girls, San Gabriel Valley Council, Working with Special Girls in a Special Way, a Demonstration Project, report 3, 1967, 13, CFNH.

96. Camp Fire Girls, "Creative Adaptation to Change: Report of Seminars," 105, CFNH; Camp Fire Girls, *Final Report: Metropolitan Critical Areas Project*, 24, CFNH. From the Potomac region, thirteen girls camped during the three-year project.

97. Finney, *Black Faces, White Spaces*, 55–56, 59–60.

98. Camp Fire Girls, *Final Report: Metropolitan Critical Areas Project*, 23, CFNH; Buckley et al., *Camp Fire Girls Final Report: Detroit Area Council*, 51, CFNH; and Spensley, "Segregated Summer Camps."

99. McCune and Jones, *Camp Fire Girls Final Report, Potomac Area Council*, 78, CFNH.

100. See Girl Scout camp brochures, Vintage Girl Scout Online Museum, accessed November 7, 2020, https://www.vintagegirlscout.com/rockwood-national-camp; Buckley et al., *Camp Fire Girls Final Report: Detroit Area Council*, 17, CFNH.

101. Camp Fire Girls, *Final Report: Metropolitan Critical Areas Project*, 24, CFNH; Buckley et al., *Camp Fire Girls Final Report: Detroit Area Council*, 41, CFNH.

102. Chautauqua Area (NY) Girl Scout Council, Girl Scout Camping, brochure, 1964; Camp Minnetoska (NY) for Girl Scouts, brochure, 1954; Girl Scouts, Camp Tanasi (TN), brochure, 1965; Camp Weetamoe (NH), brochure, 1966, all in the collection of the author.

103. Buckley et al., *Camp Fire Girls Final Report: Detroit Area Council*, 41, 52, 56, CFNH.

104. Buckley et al., *Camp Fire Girls Final Report: Detroit Area Council*, 52, CFNH.

105. Camp Fire Girls, *Final Report: Metropolitan Critical Areas Project*, 24, CFNH.

106. Buckley et al., *Camp Fire Girls Final Report: Detroit Area Council*, 53, CFNH.

107. Buckley et al., *Camp Fire Girls Final Report: Detroit Area Council*, 55, CFNH; see also McCune and Jones, *Camp Fire Girls Final Report, Potomac Area Council*, 57, CFNH.

108. Buckley et al., *Camp Fire Girls Final Report: Detroit Area Council*, 52, CFNH.

109. Buckley et al., *Camp Fire Girls Final Report: Detroit Area Council*, 55, 58–59, CFNH.

110. Buckley et al., *Camp Fire Girls Final Report: Detroit Area Council*, 51–52, CFNH.

111. Buckley et al., *Camp Fire Girls Final Report: Detroit Area Council*, 53, 56, CFNH.

112. Camp Fire Girls, "Innovation and Imagination for Youth," 30, 80, 81, CFNH. In some councils, the community funds or grant stipulation declared that funded organizations could not collect dues from members.

113. Buckley et al., *Camp Fire Girls Final Report: Detroit Area Council*, 81, CFNH.

114. Buckley et al., *Camp Fire Girls Final Report: Detroit Area Council*, 68, CFNH.

115. Buckley et al., *Camp Fire Girls Final Report: Detroit Area Council*, 71, CFNH; and McCune and Jones, *Camp Fire Girls Final Report, Potomac Area Council*, 28, CFNH.

116. Buckley et al., *Camp Fire Girls Final Report: Detroit Area Council*, 18, 19, CFNH; McCune and Jones, *Camp Fire Girls Final Report, Potomac Area Council*, 59, CFNH.

117. Buckley et al., *Camp Fire Girls Final Report: Detroit Area Council*, 38–39, CFNH. Los Angeles MCAP provided girls with full uniforms and Blue Bird program materials to help them see themselves as part of the larger organization. Tufts, *Group Work with Young School Girls*, 64, CFNH.

118. Buckley et al., *Camp Fire Girls Final Report: Detroit Area Council*, 80, CFNH.

9. "It's a New Day"

1. Buckler, Fiedler, and Allen, *Wo-he-lo*, 14, 87; and "This Is a New Day."

2. Camp Fire Girls, Annual Report, 1976, 10, CFNH; and Camp Fire Girls, "New Day Implementation-Module II," 1976, CFNH.

3. Allen, "Camp Fire Girls in the Second Half Century," 4; Camp Fire Girls, "New Day Implementation-Module II," CFNH; and "Go West—Young Woman—Go West," newspaper clipping in Dr. Hester Turner File, CFNH.

4. Camp Fire Girls, "New Day Implementation-Module II," 1976, CFNH.

5. Hester Turner, interview by author, March 26, 2004; and Camp Fire, *Tradition and Transition*, annual report, 1977, CFNH.

6. Hinton, *From the War on Poverty to the War on Crime*, 82. See Olson-Raymer, "National Nongovernmental Organizations Involved with the Juvenile Justice System."

7. Camp Fire Girls, *Final Report: Metropolitan Critical Areas Project*, 37, CFNH.

8. Buckley et al., *Camp Fire Girls Final Report: Detroit Area Council*, 73, 75, 79, CFNH.

9. Tufts, *Group Work with Young School Girls*, 82, 88–90, 148, CFNH.

10. McCune and Jones, *Camp Fire Girls Final Report, Potomac Area Council*, 50, 66, 68, 73, 75–76, CFNH.

11. Maynard J. Hammond, Developmental Study: Report to Camp Fire Girls (American City Bureau/Beaver Associates, 1964), 37, CFNH; and Eva Schindler-Rainman, "Looking Backward, Looking Forward," in Camp Fire Girls, "Innovation and Imagination for Youth: Report of Seminar IV Metropolitan Critical Areas Project," June 1967, 13, CFNH.

12. Buckley et al., *Camp Fire Girls Final Report: Detroit Area Council*, 79, CFNH.

13. McCune and Jones, *Camp Fire Girls Final Report, Potomac Area Council*, 75, CFNH.

14. Camp Fire Girls, "New Day Implementation-Module II," CFNH.

15. *Camp Fire Leadership*, Fall 1976, 8–9; Camp Fire Girls, *Final Report: Metropolitan Critical Areas Project*, 22, CFNH. Although Camp Fire's New Day left local councils intact, providing programming through them, it established thirteen nationwide zones, each with its own board representatives. Individual girls and leaders were no longer members of the national organization but members of their councils, and the councils were members of the national. Each council's votes were proportional to its size in the new congress. Bylaws (revised November 22, 1975), in Camp Fire Girls, "New Day Implementation-Module II," CFNH.

16. Camp Fire Girls, "New Day Implementation-Module II," CFNH.

17. Camp Fire Girls, press release for *Christian Science Monitor*, March 22, 1976, CFNH.

18. Yukic, "TMR."

19. Camp Fire Girls, *Final Report: Metropolitan Critical Areas Project*, 6, CFNH. Camp Fire Girls, "Creative Adaptation to Change: Report of Seminars," 59, CFNH.

20. Buckley et al., *Camp Fire Girls Final Report: Detroit Area Council*, 104, CFNH.

21. Camp Fire Girls, "Creative Adaptation to Change: Report of Seminars," 60–62, CFNH. In 2007 the U.S. Commission on Civil Rights found ongoing misplacement of African American, Latino, and American Indian children in special education. The commission found teachers reported a disproportionate number of African American boys, though too few special needs diagnoses are also sometimes a problem, and many children of color do not receive needed assistance. U.S. Commission on Civil Rights, "Minorities in Special Education."

22. Camp Fire Girls, "Creative Adaptation to Change: Report of Seminars," 66, CFNH.

23. Camp Fire Girls, *Final Report: Metropolitan Critical Areas Project*, 21, CFNH; Buckley et al., *Camp Fire Girls Final Report: Detroit Area Council*, 46, CFNH. The report did not state the rationale for putting older girls with younger ones.

24. Buckley et al., *Camp Fire Girls Final Report: Detroit Area Council*, 46, CFNH.

25. Yukic, "TMR," 11.

26. Camp Fire Girls, "Innovation and Imagination for Youth," 22–23, CFNH.

27. Camp Fire Girls, "Creative Adaptation to Change: Report of Seminars," 63, CFNH.

28. *Camp Fire Program Summary*, 1981, Kansas City MO, 34, CFNH.

29. Harper, "Bread and Butter."

30. Camp Fire, "Agency Profile," January 1986, 1, 5, CFNH.

31. Minutes of the National Council of the Camp Fire Girls, November 2, 1971, Seattle WA, 3, CFNH. Camp Fire also had experimented, in the late 1960s, with coeducational programing through joint efforts with Boy Scouts and Girl Scouts. When Boy Scouts admitted girls to their Explorer program, Camp Fire left the collaboration and acted on its own in the 1970s to open Camp Fire to boys. See Schaumburg, "Camp Fire, 1961–1979," 337–39. Hester Turner, interview by author, March 26, 2004.

32. Proposal 2, Minutes of the National Council of the Camp Fire Girls, November 2–4, 1973, Detroit, 1–2, CFNH. Many groups with boys in them adopted the presumably more gender-neutral title Blue Jays instead of Blue Birds. See Schaumburg, "Camp Fire, 1961–1979," 397. On boys tagging along, see Turner, interview.

33. "Blue Jays Are Just for Boys," *Daily Democrat* (Woodland CA), January 24, 1977, Camp Fire Girls Organizational Materials, News Releases, 1970–1983, folder 20, CFGSYC.

34. "Camp Fire Girls Will Go Coed," *Sacramento Bee*, November 9, 1971, B1–2, news-

paper clipping in Camp Fire Scrapbook, Large Blue Scrapbook, 1946–1976, folder 41, CFGSYC.

35. *Issues* 1, no. 1 (Fall 1971): 3; "Camp Fire Opens Horizon Club Ranks to Boys."

36. In Camp Fire Girls, "New Day Implementation-Module II," CFNH.

37. "Questions."

38. "Blue Bird Leaders."

39. "Adventure."

40. "Camp Fire Girls Will Go Coed," *Sacramento Bee*, November 9, 1971, B1–2, newspaper clipping in Camp Fire Scrapbook, Large Blue Scrapbook, 1946–1976, folder 41, CFGSYC.

41. New Day Advisory Committee of Camp Fire Girls, Camp Fire Girls Councils' Implementation of the New Day Program (Princeton NJ: Opinion Research Corporation, 1977), 20-1, 9a-1, 9a-4, 64-1, 64-4, CFNH.

42. "Blue Jays Are Just for Boys," *Daily Democrat* (Woodland CA), January 24, 1977, Camp Fire Girls Organizational Materials, News Releases, 1970–1983, folder 20, CFGSYC.

43. Camp Fire Girls, Annual Report, 1979, CFNH. In the traditional club program, boys' highest proportions were in Camp Fire's youngest groups, followed by the high school–age groups. Their numbers were higher in day and resident camp programs. In 1986 boys were 30 and 25 percent of participants (Camp Fire, "Agency Profile," January 1986, 4, CFNH). In 2005 boys were 46 percent of Camp Fire members (Camp Fire USA, "All About Us," 2004, http://www.campfireusa .org/all_about_us).

44. "Camp Fire Looks Ahead to Challenging Programs," *Oregonian* (Portland OR), August 30, 1976, newspaper clipping at CFNH.

45. Schaumburg, "Camp Fire, 1961–1979," 398.

46. Burdett, "Report on Research Study."

47. Sally Dunn, interview by author, Angels Camp CA, 2013.

48. Girl Scouts Memo, October 26, 1975, box 7, Sheila Weidenfeld Files, Gerald R. Ford Presidential Library, https://www.fordlibrarymuseum.gov/library/document /0126/1489469.pdf.

49. *Washington Post*, October 28, 1975, newspaper clipping, box 7, Sheila Weidenfeld Files, Gerald R. Ford Presidential Library, https://www.fordlibrarymuseum.gov /library/document/0126/1489469.pdf. Title IX exempted voluntary youth service organizations such as Camp Fire, Girl Scouts, Boy Scouts, and YMCA youth programs.

50. Camp Fire, "Agency Profile," January 1986, 39, CFNH.

51. Barb Kubik, interview by author, August 11, 2011.

52. New Day Advisory Committee of Camp Fire Girls, Camp Fire Girls Councils' Implementation of the New Day Program (Princeton NJ: Opinion Research Corporation, 1977), 63-1, CFNH.

53. New Day Advisory Committee of Camp Fire Girls, 63-2, 63-4, CFNH.

54. "Pomona Camp Fire Girls' HQ Burned: Racist Arson Blamed," *San Bernardino County (CA) Sun,* January 8, 1971, 1; June Hyman, interview with author, March 11, 2006.

55. New Day Advisory Committee of Camp Fire Girls, 20-1, 9a-1, 9a-4, 64-1, 64-4, CFNH.

56. Hester Turner, interview by author, March 26, 2004.

57. Turner, interview.

58. Camp Fire, "Agency Profile," January 1986, 1, 11, CFNH.

59. Putnam, *Bowling Alone.* Putman identifies four exceptions to the decrease in civic participation: volunteerism, telecommunications, evangelical conservative grassroots movements, and an increase in self-help support groups.

60. Arneil, "Gender, Diversity, and Organizational Change," 55–58.

61. Camp Fire, "Agency Profile," January 1986, 10.

62. Camp Fire, "Agency Profile," January 1986, 5, 12, CFNH.

63. One poll showed that 66 percent of Americans had heard of Camp Fire, a number far below the 90 and 96 percent who were aware of the Girl Scouts and the Boy Scouts respectively. Camp Fire, "Agency Profile," January 1986, 35, CFNH.

Epilogue

1. Tisdale, "On My Mind."

2. Camp Fire Girls, *Handbook for Guardians of the Camp Fire Girls* (1924), 9.

3. "Boy Scouts"; World Organization of the Scout Movement, *Scouting 'Round the World.*

4. Proctor, *Scouting for Girls,* 158–159, 162; WAGGGS Membership Policy 2019, approved by the World Board, 02/20 (W.B. 4908d), 4, 5, https://duz92c7qaoni3 .cloudfront.net/documents/ENG-Membership-Policy-2020.pdf.

5. Camp Fire, "History," https://campfire.org/.

6. Camp Fire's Inclusion Statement, 2021, https://campfire.org/blog.article/inclusion -statements-why-specificity-matters/.

7. Camp Fire, "Why Are There Pronouns in Our Email Signatures?," https:// campfire.org/pronouns/.

8. Camp Fire, "Programs," https://campfire.org/programs/.

9. Greg Zweber, Ben Matthews, and Julia Fleenor, videoconference interview by author, September 23, 2020.

10. Girl Scouts USA, "Social Issues," 2021, https://www.girlscouts.org/en/footer /faq/social-isues-faq.html; and Boy Scouts of America, National Capital Area Council, "Info for Units Regarding Transgender Youth in Scouting," 2017, https:// www.ncacbsa.org/blog/2017/02/14/info-for-units-regarding-transgender-youth -in-scouting/.

11. Greg Zweber, letter, in Annual Report, 2019; and Annual Report, 2019, https:// campfire.org/wp-content/uploads/2019/11/AnnualReport2019October29-3 .pdf. Youth reached by the program are 59 percent white, 12 percent African

American, 2 percent American Indian, 3 percent Asian American, 14 percent Latinx, 1 percent Hawaiian and Pacific Islander, 6 percent multiracial, and 4 percent other. Thirty-seven percent are eligible for free/reduced lunches, a number that roughly accords with the nation's child poverty rates. Twelve percent are disabled.

12. See, for example, Camp Fire, El Dorado (AR), "About," https://campfireeldorado.org/index.php/about; and Camp Fire Central Puget Sound, Seattle WA, "Meeting Openings," https://campfireseattle.org/wp-content/uploads/2015/06/Meeting-Openings.pdf. See also Greg Zweber, Ben Matthews, and Julia Fleenor, videoconference interview by author, September 23, 2020.

13. Camp Fire, "WoHeLo," accessed September 27, 2020, https://campfire.org/wohelo-award-recipients/; "Foreign Service Youth Foundation's 2018 Youth Awards Ceremony"; Camp Fire Central Puget Sound News, "Profile of a Wohelo Award Recipient," May 2, 2013, https://campfireseattle.org/blog/profile-of-a-wohelo-award-recipient/.

14. Camp Fire, "Be A Spark Champion," 2019, https://campfire.org/blog/article/be-a-sparks-champion/.

15. Greg Zweber, Ben Matthews, and Julia Fleenor, videoconference interview by author, September 23, 2020.

16. Camp Fire, "Inclusive since 1910," June 4, 2018, https://campfire.org/blog/article/inclusive-since-1910/.

17. Greg Zweber, Ben Matthews, and Julia Fleenor, videoconference interview by author, September 23, 2020.

18. Greg Zweber, "Message from Our CEO: Expressing Solidarity with Our Black Youth and Families," Camp Fire, May 29, 2020, https://campfire.org/blog/article/solidarity/.

19. Cathy Tisdale, interview by author, July 18, 2018.

20. Camp Fire, "Fireside Chat"; and Greg Zweber, Ben Matthews, and Julia Fleenor, videoconference interview by author, September 23, 2020.

21. Greg Zweber, Ben Matthews, and Julia Fleenor, videoconference interview by author, September 23, 2020.

22. Stewart Smith, interview by author, January 14, 2004; Cathy Tisdale, interview by author, July 18, 2018; and Greg Zweber, Ben Matthews, and Julia Fleenor, videoconference interview by author, September 23, 2020.

23. A slightly larger percentage of girls in the population had been or were Camp Fire Girls since some quit each year.

24. Rene Riback, Messenger correspondence with author, May 2021; Ann Chenhall, interview by author, July 12, 2011.

Bibliography

Archives and Manuscript Materials

CFCEM. Camp Fire Council for Eastern Massachusetts Records. Schlesinger Library, Radcliffe Institute for Advanced Study, Harvard University, Cambridge MA.

CFGSTK. Register of the Camp Fire Girls (Stockton CA) Summer Camp Scrapbooks, 1919–1922. Holt-Atherton Special Collections, University of the Pacific, Stockton CA.

CFGSYC. Camp Fire Girls Sacramento-Yolo Council Records, 1910–2007. Center for Sacramento History, Sacramento CA.

CFISC. Historical Records of Camp Fire Inland Southern California, Upland CA.

CFNH. Historical Records of Camp Fire National Headquarters, Kansas City MO.

CFOKC. Historical Records of Camp Fire, Oklahoma City (OK) Council.

CFSD. Historical Records of Camp Fire, San Diego (CA) Council.

GFP. Gulick Family Papers, 65M-183. Special Collections, Houghton Library, Harvard University, Cambridge MA.

JAERR. Japanese American Evacuation and Resettlement Records. Bancroft Library, University of California, Berkeley.

LHWP. L. Hollingsworth Wood Papers. Special Collections, Haverford College, Haverford PA.

SAC-SB. Historical Record of Camp Fire, San Andreas Council, San Bernardino CA. (Closed Council.)

Published Works

"Abiding Loyalties." *The Guardian: A Bulletin of News and Suggestions for Leaders of Camp Fire Girls* 20, no. 1 (September 1940): 1:1.

Acosta, Teresa Palomo, María-Cristina García, and Cynthia E. Orozco. "Settlement Houses." *Handbook of Texas*. Texas State Historical Association, accessed June 19, 2020. http://www.tshaonline.org/handbook/online/articles/pwsgr.

Addams, Jane. *Twenty Years at Hull-House with Autobiographical Notes*. New York: MacMillan, 1911.

"Adventure." *Camp Fire Leadership* 54, no. 3 (Spring 1975): 7.

Alexander, Kristine. *Guiding Modern Girls: Girlhood, Empire, and Internationalism in the 1920s and 1930s*. Vancouver: University of British Columbia Press, 2017.

Allen, Martha F. "Camp Fire Girls in the Second Half Century." *Camp Fire Girl* 42, no. 3 (January–February 1963): 3–4.

———. "Fitness of American Youth." *Camp Fire Girl* 36, no. 2 (October 1956): 8–9.

———. "The Forward Look." *Camp Fire Girl* 41, no. 1 (September 1961): 4.

———. "The Future of Camp Fire." *Camp Fire Girl* 30, no. 7 (March 1951): 1–2.

———. "The Religious Policies Committee—Its Meaning for Us." *Camp Fire Girl* 28, no. 6 (February 1949): 3.

———. "A Report on the Study of Our Objectives." *Camp Fire Girl* 34, no. 8 (April 1955): 3.

———. "We Study Our Objectives." *Camp Fire Girl* 33, no. 10 (June 1954): 3–4.

———. "What Will She Be When She Grows Up?" *Camp Fire Girl* 36, no. 1 (September 1956): 6.

———. "You Can Contribute Courage." *Camp Fire Girl* 30, no. 4 (December 1950): 3.

"An All-Indian Camp Fire Girls' Group." *World Call* 12 (April 1930): 19.

Alpenfels, Ethel J. "Let's Pack Up Our Prejudices." *Camp Fire Girl* 28, no. 7 (March 1949): 4–5.

Altenbaugh, Richard J. "Where Are the Disabled in the History of Education? The Impact of Polio on Sites of Learning." *History of Education* 35, no. 6 (November 2006): 705–30.

Andersen, Nancy Keever. "Cooperation for Social Betterment: The Intellectual and Theological Rationale of Southern Methodists Associated with the Southern Sociological Congress, 1912–1914." *Methodist History* 34, no. 1 (October 1995): 30–37.

Anderson, Warwick. "States of Hygiene: Race 'Improvement' and Biomedical Citizenship in Australia and the Colonial Philippines." In *Haunted by Empire: Geographies of Intimacy in North American History*, edited by Laura Stoler, 94–115. Durham NC: Duke University Press, 2006.

Antle, Martina. "Surrealism and the Orient." *Yale French Studies* 109 (2006): 4–16.

Arboleda, Molly Quest. *Educating Young Children in WPA Nursery Schools: Federally-Funded Early Childhood Education from 1933–1943*. New York: Routledge, 2018.

Arneil, Barbara. "Gender, Diversity, and Organizational Change: The Boy Scouts vs. Girl Scouts of America." *Perspectives on Politics* 8, no. 1 (March 2010): 53–68.

"Around the Camp Fire." *Camp Fire Girl* 28, no. 6 (February 1949): 8.

Austin, Joe, and Michael Nevin Willard, eds. Introduction to *Generations of Youth: Youth Cultures and History in Twentieth-Century America*, 1–20. New York: New York University Press, 1998.

"An Autumn Council Fire." *Guardian* 10, no. 3 (November 1930): 2.

Bahba, Homi. *The Location of Culture*. New York: Routledge, 1994.

Beard, Mary Alice. "Mahawe's Memory Book." Accessed August 4, 2020. http://www.alicemariebeard.com/campfire/memories.htm.

Bederman, Gail. *Manliness and Civilization: A Cultural History of Gender and Race in the United States, 1880–1917*. Chicago: University of Chicago Press, 1995.

Begay, Marie D. "The Modern Indian Girl." *Native American* 30, no. 5 (March 8, 1930): 63–64.

———. "The Modern Indian Girl." *Native American* 30, no. 11 (June 7, 1930): 139, 142.

Bell, Ernest A. *Fighting the Traffic in Young Girls: Or, War on the White Slave Trade*. Chicago: G. S. Ball, 1910.

Bennett, Muriel. "An Investigation of the Educational Practices and Value of the Program of Activities for Camp Fire Girls in San Diego, California." MA thesis, Claremont Colleges, 1936.

Berghel, Susan Eckelmann. "'What My Generation Makes of America': American Youth Citizenship, Civil Rights Allies, and the 1960s Black Freedom Struggle." *Journal of the History of Childhood and Youth* 10, no. 3 (Fall 2017): 422–40.

Berghel, Susan Eckelmann, Sara Fieldston, and Paul Renfro, eds. Introduction to *Growing Up America: Youth and Politics Since 1945*, 1–16. Athens: University of Georgia Press, 2019.

Berrol, Selma. "Immigrant Children at School, 1880–1940." In *Small Worlds: Children and Adolescents in America, 1850–1950*, edited by Elliott West and Paula Petrik, 42–60. Lawrence: University Press of Kansas, 1992.

Berry, Sarah. *Screen Style: Fashion and Femininity in 1930s Hollywood*. Minneapolis: University of Minnesota Press, 2000.

Bird, S. Elizabeth, ed. Introduction to *Dressing in Feathers: The Construction of the Indian in American Popular Culture*, 1–12. Boulder CO: Westview, 1996.

Blanco F., José, et al. "Peasant Blouse." In *Artifacts from American Fashion*, edited by Heather Vaughan Lee, 27–33. Santa Barbara CA: ABC-CLIO, 2020.

Bloom, John. "'There Is Madness in the Air': The 1926 Haskell Homecoming and Popular Representations of Sports in Federal Indian Boarding Schools." In *Dressing in Feathers*, edited by S. Elizabeth Bird, 97–110. Boulder CO: Westview, 1996.

"Blue Bird Leaders." *Camp Fire Leadership* 54, no. 3 (Spring 1975): 6.

Bookman, C. M. "Community Chest Movement: An Interpretation." Presentation at the National Conference of Social Work, 1924. Virginia Commonwealth University Libraries Social Welfare History Project. https://socialwelfare.library.vcu.edu/organizations/state-institutions/community-chest-movement-an-interpretation/.

Borchardt, Ruth. "Growing Together." *Camp Fire Girl* 34, no. 7 (March 1955): 3.

Borish, Linda. "'An Interest in Physical Well-Being among the Feminine Membership': Sporting Activities for Women at Young Men's and Young Women's Hebrew Associations." *American Jewish History* 87, no. 1 (1999): 61–93.

Boustan, Leah Platt. *Competition in the Promised Land: Black Migrants in Northern Cities and Labor Markets*. Princeton NJ: Princeton University Press, 2017.

"Boy Scouts." *New World Encyclopedia*. Accessed September 26, 2020. https://www.newworldencyclopedia.org/entry/Boy_Scout.

"Boy Scouts and Camp Fire Girls." *American Journal of Care for Cripples* 2, no. 1 (1915): 51.

Bradt, Edith Virginia. "The New Patriotism." *American Monthly Magazine* 41 (July–November 1912): 179–82.

Bricker, A. June. "Accentuate the Positive." *Camp Fire Girl* 32, no. 6 (February 1953): 13.

Brown, JoAnne. "'A Is for Atom, B Is for Bomb': Civil Defense in American Public Education, 1948–1963." *Journal of American History* 75 (June 1988): 68–90.

Brown, Ruth A., and Florence Heintz. "Gypsying Both by Sea and Land." *Everygirl's* 13, no. 9 (May 1926): 7, 17.

Brown, Victoria Bissell. "Golden Girls: Female Socialization in Los Angeles, 1880–1910." In *Small Worlds: Children and Adolescents in America, 1850–1950*, edited by Elliott West and Paula Petrik, 232–54. Lawrence: University Press of Kansas, 1992.

Brumberg, Joan Jacobs. *The Body Project: An Intimate History of American Girls.* New York: Random House, 1997.

Brunst, Eunice. "Sports for Older Girls." *Camp Fire Girl* 36, no. 7 (March 1957): 7.

Buckler, Helen, Mary F. Fiedler, and Martha F. Allen, *Wo-he-lo: The Story of Camp Fire Girls, 1910–1960.* New York: Holt, Rinehart and Winston, 1961.

Bucy, Carole Stanford. *Women Helping Women: The YWCA of Nashville, 1898–1998.* Nashville TN: YWCA of Nashville, 1998.

Burchenal, Elizabeth. *Dances of the People: A Second Volume of Folk Dances and Singing Games.* New York: G. Schirmer, 1913.

———. *Folk-Dances and Singing Games.* New York: G. Schirmer, 1909.

———. *Folk-Dances from Old Homelands.* New York: G. Schirmer, 1922.

Burdett, Rita. "Report on Research Study." *Camp Fire Girl* 37, no. 7 (March 1958): 4–5.

Burkholder, Zoë. *Color in the Classroom: How American Schools Taught Race, 1900–1954.* New York: Oxford University Press, 2011.

Butler, Judith. *Gender Trouble: Feminism and the Subversion of Identity.* New York: Routledge, 1990.

Cahill, Cathleen D. *Recasting the Vote: How Women of Color Transformed the Suffrage Movement.* Chapel Hill: University of North Carolina Press, 2020.

Cahn, Susan. *Coming on Strong: Gender and Sexuality in Twentieth-Century Women's Sports.* Cambridge MA: Harvard University Press, 1998.

Camp Fire. "Fireside Chat: People & Impact!" Videoconference, August 28, 2020. https://campfire.org/firesidechat/.

"Camp Fire for All." *Guardian* 14, no. 8 (April 1935): 4.

"The Camp Fire Girl Afield." *Wohelo* 2, no. 5 (November 1914): 1.

Camp Fire Girls. *The Book of the Camp Fire Girls.* New York: Doubleday, Page, 1912.

———. *The Book of the Camp Fire Girls.* 3rd rev. ed. New York: George H. Doran, 1913.

———. *The Book of the Camp Fire Girls.* 4th rev. ed. New York: National Headquarters, 1914.

———. *The Book of the Camp Fire Girls with War Program.* 6th rev. ed. New York: National Headquarters, 1917.

————. *The Book of the Camp Fire Girls*. Rev. ed. New York: Camp Fire Girls, 1925.

————. *The Book of the Camp Fire Girls*. Rev. ed. New York: National Headquarters, 1933.

————. *The Book of the Camp Fire Girls*. New York: Camp Fire Girls, 1946.

————. *Handbook for Guardians of the Camp Fire Girls*. New York: Camp Fire Girls, 1924.

————. *Handbook for Guardians of the Camp Fire Girls*. Second printing. New York: Camp Fire Girls, 1925.

————. *Vacation Book of the Camp Fire Girls*. New York: National Headquarters, 1914.

"Camp Fire Girls in Action." *Camp Fire Girl* 24, no. 6 (November 1945): 2:2–3.

"Camp Fire Girls Postwar Program." *Camp Fire Girl* 24, no. 7 (March 1945): 1–2.

"Camp Fire Girls Statement of Objectives." *Camp Fire Girl* 35, no. 5 (January 1956): 3.

"Camp Fire Girls Win Service Stripes." *Guardian* 21, no. 6 (February 1942): 8.

"Camp Fire Is for Our Best Friends." *Wohelo: A Magazine for Girls* 3, no. 7 (January 1916): 9.

"Camp Fire Opens Horizon Club Ranks to Boys." *Camp Fire Girl* 51, no. 3 (January/February 1972): 30.

"The Camp Fire Scene." *Camp Fire Girl* 27, no. 3 (November 1947): 16.

"Camp Fire Sparks." *Everygirl's* 13, no. 4 (December 1925): 18–19.

"Camp Is So Much Fun." *Camp Fire Girl* 30, no. 9 (May 1951): 8.

"Candle Light and Ideals." *Wohelo* 2, no. 5 (November 1914): 7–8.

"Carry On." *Guardian* 20, no. 4 (December 1940): 1:1.

Cazenave, Noel A. *Impossible Democracy: The Unlikely Success of the War on Poverty Community Action Programs*. Albany: State University of New York Press, 2007.

Chafe, William. *The Unfinished Journey: America since World War II*. New York: Oxford University Press, 1991.

Chatelain, Marcia. *South Side Girls: Growing Up in the Great Migration*. Durham NC: Duke University Press, 2015.

Cheng, Jenny Diamond. "Uncovering the Twenty-Sixth Amendment." PhD diss., University of Michigan, 2008.

Choate, Anne Hyde, and Helen Ferris, eds. *Juliette Low and the Girl Scouts*. New York: Doubleday, Doran, 1928.

Cobb, Amanda J. *Listening to Our Grandmothers' Stories: The Bloomfield Academy for Chickasaw Females, 1852–1949*. Lincoln: University of Nebraska Press, 2000.

Cooper, Brittney C. *Beyond Respectability: The Intellectual Thought of Race Women*. Chicago: University of Illinois Press, 2017.

Cordery, Stacy A. *Juliette Gordon Low: The Remarkable Founder of the Girl Scouts*. New York: Viking, 2012.

"Cornwall-on-Hudson Camp Fire Girls." *Wohelo* 2, no. 3 (September 1914): 7.

Cott, Nancy F. *The Grounding of Modern Feminism*. New Haven CT: Yale University Press, 1987.

Coutrot, Aline. "Youth Movements in France in the 1930s." *Journal of Contemporary History* 5, no. 1 (1970): 23–35.

Cremin, Lawrence. *The Transformation of the School: Progressivism in American Education, 1876–1957*. New York: Vintage, 1961.

Cressy, David. *Gypsies: An English History*. Oxford: Oxford University Press, 2018.

Davis, Cynthia J. *Charlotte Perkins Gilman: A Biography*. Palo Alto CA: Stanford University Press, 2010.

Davis, Mike, and Jon Weiner. *Set the Night on Fire: L.A. in the Sixties*. Brooklyn NY: Verso Books, 2020.

Deloria, Philip J. *Playing Indian*. New Haven CT: Yale University Press, 1998.

DeLuzio, Crista. *Female Adolescence in American Thought, 1830–1930*. Baltimore MD: Johns Hopkins University Press, 2007.

D'Emilio, John, and Estelle B. Freedman. *Intimate Matters: A History of Sexuality in America*. Chicago: University of Chicago Press, 1997.

"Democracy for Victory." *Guardian* 21, no. 6 (February 1942): 9.

Demos, John, and Virginia Demos. "Adolescence in Historical Perspective." *Journal of Marriage and Family* 31, no. 4 (1969): 632–38.

De Schweinitz, Rebecca. *If We Could Change the World: Young People and America's Struggle for Racial Equality*. Chapel Hill: University of North Carolina Press, 2009.

Deutsch, Sarah. *Women and the City: Gender, Space, and Power in Boston, 1870–1940*. New York: Oxford University Press, 2000.

Devlin, Rachel. *Relative Intimacy: Fathers, Adolescent Daughters, and Postwar American Culture*. Chapel Hill: University of North Carolina Press, 2005.

Dewey, John. *The School and Society: Being Three Lectures*. Chicago: University of Chicago Press, 1899.

Diokno, Maria Serena I. *Hidden Lives, Concealed Narratives: A History of Leprosy in the Philippines*. Manila: National Historical Commission of the Philippines, 2016.

"Division News." *Locomotive Engineers Journal* 28, no. 1 (January 1894): 328–30.

Dorgan, Ethel Josephine. *Luther Halsey Gulick, 1865–1918*. New York: Bureau of Publications, Teachers College, 1934.

Dorn, Charles. *American Education, Democracy, and the Second World War*. New York: Palgrave Macmillan, 2007.

Dudziak, Mary L. *Cold War Civil Rights: Race and the Image of American Democracy*. Princeton NJ: Princeton University Press, 2000.

Dumenil, Lynn. *The Second Line of Defense: American Women and World War I*. Chapel Hill: University of North Carolina Press, 2017.

Duncan, Leanna. "'Every One of Them Are Worth It': Blanche Van Leuven Browne and the Education of the 'Crippled Child.'" *History of Education Quarterly* 60, no. 3 (August 2020): 324–50.

Duvall, Evelyn Mills. "The Girl Today." *Camp Fire Girl* 40, no. 6 (February 1961): 5–6.

Eastman, Charles A. *Indian Scout Talks: A Guide for Boy Scouts and Campfire Girls*. Boston: Little, Brown, 1914.

Ellis, Havelock. *Studies in the Psychology of Sex.* Vol. 6. Philadelphia: F. A. Davis, 1911.

Elman, Julie Passanante. *Chronic Youth: Disability, Sexuality, and U.S. Media Cultures of Rehabilitation.* New York: New York University Press, 2014.

Elshtain, Jean Bethke. *Women and War.* New York: Basic Books, 1987.

Enloe, Cynthia. *Maneuvers: The International Politics of Militarizing Women's Lives.* Berkeley: University of California Press, 2000.

Escalante, Rene R. "American Public Health Policy on Leprosy, 1898–1941." In *Hidden Lives, Concealed Narratives: A History of Leprosy in the Philippines,* edited by Maria Serena I. Diokno, 87–110. Manila: National Historical Commission of the Philippines, 2016.

Evans, Sara. *Personal Politics: The Roots of Women's Liberation in the Civil Rights Movement and the New Left.* New York: Vintage Books, 1979.

Farber, David, and Beth Bailey. *The Columbia Guide to America in the 1960s.* New York: Columbia University Press, 2003.

Fass, Paula. *The Damned and the Beautiful: American Youth in the 1920s.* New York: Oxford University Press, 1977.

————. *Outside In: Minorities and the Transformation of American Education.* New York: Oxford University Press, 1989.

Fiedler, Mary F. "Why a Council Fire?" *Camp Fire Girl* 28, no. 7 (March 1949): 3.

Finch, Catherine E. "Count Your Blessings." *Camp Fire Girl* 30, no. 7 (March 1951): 10.

Finney, Carolyn. *Black Faces, White Spaces: Reimagining the Relationship of African Americans to the Great Outdoors.* Chapel Hill: University of North Carolina Press, 2014.

Fluck, Winfried. "Was ist eigentlich so schlecht daran, reich zu sein? Zur Darstellung des Reichtums in der amerikanischen Kultur." In *Wie viel Ungleichheit verträgt die Demokratie? Armut und Reichtum in den USA,* edited by Winfried Fluck and Welf Werner, 267–303. Frankfurt: Campus Verlag, 2003.

Foley, Jessica L. "'Meeting the Needs of Today's Girl': Youth Organizations and the Making of a Modern Girlhood, 1945–1980." PhD diss., Brown University, 2010.

"Food Fights for Freedom." *Camp Fire Girl* 24, no. 3 (November 1944): 7.

"The Foreign Service Youth Foundation's 2018 Youth Awards Ceremony Honors Six AAFSW Merit Scholarship Recipients." Associates of the American Foreign Service Worldwide, accessed September 27, 2020. https://www.aafsw.org/the-foreign-service-youth-foundations-2018-youth-awards-ceremony-honors-six-aafsw-merit-scholarship-recipients/.

Forman-Brunell, Miriam. "Girls' Culture." In *Girlhood in America: An Encyclopedia,* edited by Miriam Forman-Brunell, 325–27. Santa Barbara CA: ABC-CLIO, 2001.

Forman-Brunell, Miriam, and Leslie Paris, eds. *The Girls' History and Culture Reader.* 2 vols. Chicago: University of Illinois Press, 2011.

"For Our Allies." *Camp Fire Girl* 24, no. 3 (November 1944): 4–5.

Freeberg, Ernest. *The Education of Laura Bridgman: First Deaf and Blind Person to Learn Language.* Cambridge MA: Harvard University Press, 2001.

Freeman, Susan K. *Sex Goes to School: Girls and Sex Education before the 1960s*. Urbana: University of Illinois Press, 2008.

Frick, Flora M. "What's Become of Health." *Camp Fire Girl* 25 no. 10 (June 1946): 12.

Gardner, Susan. "Subverting the Rhetoric of Assimilation: Ella Cara Deloria (Dakota) in the 1920s." *Hecate* 39, no. 1–2 (2013): 9–31.

Garland-Thomson, Rosemarie. *Extraordinary Bodies: Figuring Physical Disability in American Culture and Literature*. New York: Columbia University Press, 1997.

Gealogo, Francis A., and Antonio C. Galang Jr. "From Collection to Release: Segregated Lives in the Culion Colony, 1906–1935." In *Hidden Lives, Concealed Narratives: A History of Leprosy in the Philippines*, edited by Maria Serena I. Diokno, 163–89. Manila: National Historical Commission of the Philippines, 2016.

Gelb, Stephen A. "'Mental Deficients' Fighting Fascism: The Unplanned Normalization of World War II." In *Mental Retardation in America: A Historical Reader*, edited by Steven Noll and James W. Trent Jr., 308–21. New York: New York University Press, 2004.

Gerstle, Gary. *American Crucible: Race and Nation in the Twentieth Century*. Princeton NJ: Princeton University Press, 2017.

Gilmore, Glenda Elizabeth. *Gender and Jim Crow: Women and the Politics of White Supremacy in North Carolina, 1896–1920*. Chapel Hill: University of Northern Carolina Press, 1996.

"Girls and Boys Together." *Camp Fire Girl* 37, no. 8 (April 1958): 4–5.

Glassberg, David. *American Historical Pageantry: The Uses of Tradition in the Early Twentieth Century*. Chapel Hill: University of North Carolina Press, 1990.

Glenna, Leland L., Margaret A. Gollnick, and Stephen S. Jones. "Eugenic Opportunity Structures: Teaching Genetic Engineering at U.S. Land-Grant Universities since 1911." *Social Studies of Science* 37, no. 2 (2007): 281–96.

Gordon, Beverly. *The Saturated World: Aesthetic Meaning, Intimate Objects, Women's Lives, 1890–1940*. Knoxville: University of Tennessee Press, 2006.

Gordon, Linda. *Second Coming of the KKK: The Ku Klux Klan of the 1920s and the American Political Tradition*. New York: Liveright, 2017.

Griswold, Robert. *Fatherhood in America: A History*. New York: BasicBooks, 1993.

Gulick, Charlotte. "How Camp Fire Girls Are Being Educated in Babycraft." *Health News: Monthly Bulletin, New York State Department of Health* 9, no. 4 (April 1914): 124–26.

———. "A Message to Mothers from Hiiteni." *Wohelo* 3, no. 12 (June 1916): 4.

———. *The Shul U Tam Na of the Camp Fire Girls*. New York: Camp Fire Outfitting, 1915.

———. "What the Camp Fire Girls Stand For." *Ladies' Home Journal* 29 (July 1912): 51.

Gulick, Luther H. "Camp Fire Girl Movement and Education." *Journal of Education* 75, no. 25 (June 20, 1912): 700–701.

———. "Camp Fire Girls." *Association Monthly* 6 (March 1912): 43–48.

———. "The Ceremonial Gown." *Wohelo* 1, no. 2 (August 1913): 1.

———. "College Camp Fire Girls." *Wohelo* 3, no. 3 (August 1914): 1.

———. Editorial. *Wohelo* 3, no. 6 (December 1915): 7.

———. *The Efficient Life*. New York: Doubleday, Page, 1900.

———. *The Healthful Art of Dancing*. New York: Doubleday, Page, 1910.

———. "Will to Be Cheerful." *World's Work* 16, no. 3 (July 1908): 10496–98.

Gutiérrez, Ramón A. *When Jesus Came, the Corn Mothers Went Away: Marriage, Sexuality, and Power in New Mexico, 1500–1846*. Stanford CA: Stanford University Press, 1991.

Hahner, Leslie. "Practical Patriotism: Camp Fire Girls, Girl Scouts, and Americanization." *Communication and Critical/Cultural Studies* 5, no. 2 (June 2008): 113–34.

Hall, G. Stanley. *Adolescence: Its Psychology and Its Relations to Physiology, Anthropology, Sociology, Sex, Crime, Religion and Education*. Vol. 2. New York: Appleton, 1904.

———. "From Generation to Generation: With Some Plain Language about Race Suicide and the Instruction of Children during Adolescence." *American Magazine* 66 (1908): 248–54.

Hammond, June. "The Fourth Rank." *Camp Fire Girl* 40, no. 6 (February 1961): 14.

Hancock, Ian. "The Symbolic Function of the Gypsy Myth." In *Race and Ideology: Language, Symbolism, and Popular Culture*, edited by Arthur K. Spears, 105–13. Detroit: Wayne State University Press, 1999.

Haney, Nancy. "Everybody's Job—Civil Defense." *Camp Fire Girl* 31, no. 2 (October 1951): 12.

Hantover, Jeffrey. "Sex Role, Sexuality, and Social Status: The Early Years of the Boy Scouts of America." PhD diss., University of Chicago, 1976.

Harper, Gwendolyn. "Bread and Butter." *Camp Fire Leadership* 56, no. 1 (Fall 1976): 14–15.

Harvey, Robert. *Amache: The Story of Japanese Internment in Colorado during World War II*. Dallas: Taylor Trade Publishing, 2003.

Hazard, Margaret. "More Fun Out of Doors." *Camp Fire Girl* 40, no. 9 (May 1961): 12.

Heimlich, Evan. "Gypsy Americans." Countries and Their Cultures Forum, accessed October 8, 2020. https://www.everyculture.com/multi/Du-Ha/Gypsy-Americans.html.

Hein, Lucille. "Democracy—Blue Bird Size." *Camp Fire Girl* 28, no. 5 (January 1949): 6.

Helgren, Jennifer. *American Girls and Global Responsibility: A New Relation to the World during the Early Cold War*. New Brunswick NJ: Rutgers University Press, 2017.

———. "Native American and White Camp Fire Girls Enact Modern Girlhood, 1910–1939." *American Quarterly* 66, no. 2 (June 2014): 333–60.

Herberg, Will. *Protestant—Catholic—Jew: An Essay in American Religious Sociology*. Garden City NJ: Doubleday, 1955.

Herman, Max Arthur. *Fighting in the Streets: Ethnic Succession and Urban Unrest in Twentieth-Century America*. New York: Peter Lang Publishers, 2005.

Hetherington, Clark W. "Playgrounds: A Normal Course in Play for Professional

Directors." *Hygiene and Physical Education* 1, no. 1 (March 1909): 770–76, cont. 863–68, 957–60.

Higginbotham, Elizabeth. *Righteous Discontent: The Women's Movement in the Black Baptist Church, 1880–1920*. Cambridge MA: Harvard University Press, 1993.

Higham, John. *Strangers in the Land: Patterns of American Nativism, 1860–1925*. 2nd ed. New Brunswick NJ: Rutgers University Press, 1988.

Himmelberger, Barbara. "Passing the Light Undimmed to Others." *Camp Fire Girl* 37, no. 4 (December 1957): 9.

Hinderaker, Eric. "Translation and Cultural Brokerage." In *A Companion to American History*, edited by Philip J. Deloria and Neal Salisbury, 357–75. Malden MA: Blackwell, 2004.

Hinton, Elizabeth. *From the War on Poverty to the War on Crime: The Making of Mass Incarceration in America*. Cambridge MA: Harvard University Press, 2016.

Hoganson, Kristin L. *Consumers' Imperium: The Global Production of American Domesticity, 1865–1920*. Chapel Hill: University of North Carolina Press, 2007.

"Home Service for Victory." *Guardian* 21, no. 6 (February 1942): 4.

Honeck, Mischa, *Our Frontier Is the World: The Boy Scouts in the Age of American Ascendancy*. Ithaca NY: Cornell University Press, 2018.

Horowitz, Helen Lefkowitz. *The Power and Passion of M. Carey Thomas*. Urbana: University of Illinois Press, 1999.

How, Beatrice. "We Pass Our Feelings On!" *Camp Fire Girl* 30, no. 9 (May 1951): 10–11.

"Howard Chandler Christy Paints One of Us." *Everygirl's* 12, no. 8 (April 1925): 2.

"How to Do It without Money." *Guardian* 14, no. 8 (April 1935): 4.

Hoxie, W. J. *How Girls Can Help Their Country: Handbook for Girl Scouts*. Reprint. New York: Cosimo Classics, 2010.

Hull, Carrie R., and Linda T. Wynn. "Blue Triangle YWCA, 1919–1974." Annual Local Conference on Afro-American Culture and History. Tennessee State University Library and Media Centers, accessed October 9, 2020. http://ww2.tnstate.edu /library/digital/Blue.htm.

Hunt, Terry. "Are You Good at Figures?" *Camp Fire Girl* 27, no. 9 (May 1948): 5.

Hunter, Jane. *How Young Ladies Became Girls: The Victorian Origins of American Girlhood*. New Haven CT: Yale University Press, 2002.

Imada, Adria L. "A Decolonial Disability Studies?" *Disability Studies Quarterly* 37, no. 3 (2017). https://dsq-sds.org/article/view/5984/4694.

"Incidents of Indian Life at Hampton." *Southern Workman* 10 (January 1881): 7.

Inness, Sherrie. "Girl Scouts, Camp Fire Girls, and Woodcraft Girls: The Ideology of Girls' Scouting Novels, 1910–1935." In *Continuities in Popular Culture: The Present in the Past and the Past in the Present*, edited by Ray B. Browne and Ronald Ambrosetti, 229–40. Bowling Green OH: Bowling Green State University Popular Press, 1993.

———, ed. Introduction to *Nancy Drew and Company: Culture, Gender, and Girls' Series*, 1–14. Bowling Green OH: Bowling Green State University Popular Press, 1997.

Izzo, Amanda L. *Liberal Christianity and Women's Global Activism: The YWCA of the USA and the Maryknoll Sisters*. New Brunswick NJ: Rutgers University Press, 2018.

Jacobson, Lisa. *Raising Consumers: Children and the American Mass Market in the Early Twentieth Century*. New York: Columbia University Press, 2004.

James, Anthony. "Political Parties: College Social Fraternities, Manhood, and the Defense of Southern Traditionalism, 1945–1960." In *White Masculinity in the Recent South*, edited by Trent Watts, 63–85. Baton Rouge: Louisiana State University Press, 2008.

Jennings, Audra. *Out of the Horrors of War: Disability Politics in World War II America*. Philadelphia: University of Pennsylvania Press, 2016.

Jordan, Benjamin René. *Modern Manhood and the Boy Scouts of America: Citizenship, Race, and the Environment, 1910–1930*. Chapel Hill: University of North Carolina Press, 2016.

Kalman, Samuel. *The Extreme Right in Interwar France*. New York: Routledge, 2016.

Kearns, Carrie Wallace. "The Problem." In *National Education Association, Addresses and Proceedings of the 54th Annual Meeting*, 828–29. New York, July 1–8, 1916.

Keller, Helen. "Nature Has the Power to Renew and Refresh Our Minds, Our Bodies, and Our Spirits." *Guardian* 14, no. 8 (April 1935): 1.

——. *The Story of My Life and Selected Letters*. New York: Chartwell Books, 2006.

Kempthorne, Edith. "Doing It Differently." *Camp Fire Girl* 26, no. 1 (September 1946): 4.

Kennedy, David M. *Freedom from Fear: The American People in Depression and War, 1929–1945*. New York: Oxford University Press, 1999.

——. *Over Here: The First World War and American Society*. New York: Oxford University Press, 1982.

Kessler-Harris, Alice. *In Pursuit of Equity: Women, Men, and the Pursuit of Economic Citizenship in Twentieth-Century America*. New York: Oxford University Press, 2001.

Kett, Joseph. *Rites of Passage: Adolescence in America 1790 to the Present*. New York: Basic Books, 1977.

Keyes, Cynthia H. "So Much to Do in Summer." *Camp Fire Girl* 30, no. 10 (June 1951): 3.

Kirk, Robert William. "Getting in the Scrap: The Mobilization of American Children in World War II." *Journal of Popular Culture* 29, no. 1 (Summer 1995): 223–33.

Kirk, Ruth, and Carmela Alexander. *Exploring Washington's Past: A Road Guide to History*. Seattle: University of Washington Press, 1995.

Kloppenberg, James T. *Uncertain Victory: Social Democracy and Progressivism in European and American Thought, 1870–1920*. New York: Oxford University Press, 1986.

Kopper, R. S. *Virginia Woolf: Fashion and Literary Modernity*. Edinburgh: Edinburgh University Press, 2009.

Korman, Eleanore Z. "Being a Homemaker—Plus." *Camp Fire Girl* 36, no. 5 (January 1957): 11.

Koven, Seth, and Sonya Michel. "Womanly Duties: Maternalist Politics and the Origins of Welfare States in France, Germany, Great Britain, and the United States, 1880–1920." *American Historical Review* 95, no. 4 (October 1990): 1076–108.

Ladd-Taylor, Molly. *Mother-Work: Women, Child Welfare, and the State, 1890–1930*. Urbana: University of Illinois Press, 1994.

———. "The 'Sociological Advantages' of Sterilization: Fiscal Policies and Feeble-Minded Women in Interwar Minnesota." In *Mental Retardation in America: A Historical Reader*, edited by Steven Noll and James W. Trent Jr., 281–99. New York: New York University Press, 2004.

Lambert, Clara. "Jobs to Grow On." *Camp Fire Girl* 29, no. 9 (May 1950): 6.

Lane, Janet. *Your Carriage, Madam! A Guide to Good Posture*. New York: John Wiley and Jones, 1934.

Lane, Winthrop. "The Camp Fire Girls: A Readjustment of Women." *Survey* 18 (May 1912): 320–22.

Langdon, William Chauncy. *Book of Words: The Pageant of Thetford, in Celebration of the One Hundred and Fiftieth Anniversary of the Granting of the Charter*. White River Junction VT: Vermonter Press, 1911.

Leake, Albert H. *The Vocational Education of Girls and Women*. New York: Macmillan, 1920.

Lears, T. J. Jackson. *No Place of Grace: Antimodernism and the Transformation of American Culture, 1880–1920*. New York: Pantheon Books, 1981.

Leon, Janice M. "Bethlehem House, Nashville." *Tennessee Encyclopedia*. Tennessee Historical Society, 2017. https://tennesseeencyclopedia.net/entries/bethlehem -house/.

"Leprosy News." *International Journal of Leprosy* 2, no. 4 (1934): 485–90.

Lieffers, Caroline. "Empires of Play and Publicity in G. P. Putnam's 'Boys' Books by Boys.'" *Diplomatic History* 43, no. 1 (January 2019): 31–56.

Lighthouse International. "A Look Back at Two Forward Thinkers: The Holt Sisters, Founders of the Lighthouse." 2001. http://www.lighthouse.org/lighthouse_news /winter2001/lighthouse_news_winter2001_founders.htm.

Lippitt, Rosemary. "Boys and Girls Together." *Camp Fire Girl* 26, no. 2 (November 1946): 11.

"Listen! What's That?" *Camp Fire Girl* 24, no. 6 (February 1945): 2:10.

Lomawaima, K. Tsianina. *They Called It Prairie Light: The Story of Chilocco Indian School*. Lincoln: University of Nebraska Press, 1995.

Lomawaima, K. Tsianina, and Teresa L. McCarty. *To Remain an Indian: Lessons in Democracy from a Century of Native American Education*. New York: Teachers College Press, 2006.

Lombardo, Paul A. *Three Generations, No Imbeciles: Eugenics, the Supreme Court, and Buck v. Bell*. Baltimore MD: Johns Hopkins University Press, 2008.

Lott, Eric. "Love and Theft: The Racial Unconscious of Blackface Minstrelsy." *Representations* 39 (Summer 1992): 23–50.

Lowman, Noel. "Camping Adventure." *Camp Fire Girl* 30, no. 8 (April 1951): 4.

Lyons, Scott Richard. *X-Marks: Native Signatures of Assent*. Minneapolis: University of Minnesota Press, 2010.

Macleod, David. *The Age of the Child: Children in America, 1890–1920*. New York: Twayne, 1998.

———. *Building Character in the American Boy: The Boys Scouts, YMCA, and Their Forerunners, 1870–1920*. Madison: University of Wisconsin Press, 1983.

Mac Millan, Violet. "Beauty Found in Household Tasks." *Everygirl's* 17, no. 8 (April 1930): 26.

Malaquias, Catia. "'Usefulness' Is Not a Measure of Human Worth: It's a Dangerous Ideology." Starting with Julius, 2016. http://www.startingwithjulius.org.au /usefulness-is-a-dangerous-measure-of-human-worth/.

Mann, Eleanor. "Blueprint for Beauty." *Camp Fire Girl* 25, no. 8 (April 1946): 12.

"Many Cultures." *Camp Fire Girl* 51, no. 3 (January/February 1972): 20–22.

Martin, Frances. *Elizabeth Gilbert and Her Work for the Blind*. London: Macmillan, 1887.

Matsumoto, Valerie J. *City Girls: The Nisei Social World in Los Angeles, 1920–1950*. New York: Oxford University Press, 2014.

Matthews, Jodie. "Back Where They Belong: Gypsies, Kidnapping and Assimilation in Victorian Children's Literature." *Romani Studies* 20, no. 2 (December 2, 2010): 137–59.

———. *The Gypsy Woman: Representations in Literature and Visual Culture*. London: I. B. Tauris, 2018.

May, Elaine Tyler. *Homeward Bound: American Families in the Cold War Era*. New York: Basic Books, 1999.

McAllister, Lester G., and William Edward Tucker. *Journey in Faith: A History of the Christian Church (Disciples of Christ)*. St. Louis MO: Chalice, 1975.

McCallum, Mary Jane. "'The Fundamental Things': Camp Fire Girls and Authenticity, 1910–20." *Canadian Journal of History* 40 (2005): 45–66.

McCulloch, James Edward, ed. *The Call of the New South: Addresses Delivered at the Southern Sociological Congress, Nashville, Tennessee, May 7 to 10, 1912*. Nashville TN: Southern Sociological Congress, 1912.

McEnaney, Laura. *Civil Defense Begins at Home: Militarization Meets Everyday Life in the Fifties*. Princeton NJ: Princeton University Press, 2001.

McRae, Elizabeth Gillespie. *Mothers of Massive Resistance: White Women and the Politics of White Supremacy*. New York: Oxford University Press, 2018.

McRobbie, Angela, and Jenny Garber. "Girls and Subcultures." In *Feminism and Youth Culture: From "Jackie" to "Just Seventeen,"* edited by Angela McRobbie, 12–25. Boston: Unwin Hyman, 1991.

Mechling, Jay. "Male Gender Display at a Boy Scout Camp." In *Children and Their Organizations: Investigations in American Culture*, edited by R. Timothy Sieber and Andrew J. Gordon, 136–60. Boston: G. K. Hall, 1981.

———. *On My Honor: Boy Scouts and the Making of American Youth*. Chicago: University of Chicago Press, 2001.

Methodist Episcopal Church. *Fourth Annual Report of the Woman's Missionary Council*. Nashville TN: Methodist Episcopal Church, South, 1914.

—————. *Ninth Annual Report of the Woman's Missionary Council of the Methodist Episcopal Church, South, for 1918–1919*. Nashville TN: Publishing House of the Methodist Episcopal Church.

Meyerowitz, Joanne. "Beyond the Feminine Mystique: A Reassessment of Postwar Mass Culture 1946–1958." In *Not June Cleaver: Women and Gender in Postwar America*, edited by Joanne Meyerowitz, 229–62. Philadelphia PA: Temple University Press, 1994.

Meyers, Susanna. "Following Indian Trails." *Guardian* 16, no. 8 (April 1937): 1:2–3.

Mickenberg, Julia L. *Learning from the Left: Children's Literature, the Cold War, and Radical Politics in the United States*. New York: Oxford University Press, 2006.

Miller, Mrs. William F. "A Group with a Purpose." *Camp Fire Girl* 24, no. 6 (February 1945): 2:8.

Miller, Susan A. "Assent as Agency in the Early Years of the Children of the American Revolution." *Journal of the History of Childhood and Youth* 9, no. 1 (Winter 2016): 48–65.

—————. *Growing Girls: The Natural Origins of Girls' Organizations in America*. New Brunswick NJ: Rutgers University Press, 2007.

Mintz, Steven. *Huck's Raft: A History of American Childhood*. Cambridge MA: Harvard University Press, 2004.

Mintz, Steven, and Susan Kellogg. *Domestic Revolutions: A Social History of American Family Life*. New York: Free Press, 1988.

Mitchell, Claudia, and Jacqueline Reid-Walsh, eds. *Girl Culture: An Encyclopedia*. Westport CT: Greenwood Press, 2007.

Mitchell, David, and Sharon Snyder. "The Eugenic Atlantic: Race, Disability, and the Making of an International Eugenic Science, 1800–1945." *Disability & Society* 18, no. 7 (December 2003): 843–64.

Mitchell, Reavis L., Jr. "George Edmund Haynes." *Tennessee Encyclopedia*. Tennessee Historical Society, 2017. https://tennesseeencyclopedia.net/entries/george-edmund-haynes/.

Montgomery, Gail. "You Can Do Something about Prejudice." *Camp Fire Girl* 31, no. 4 (December 1951): 14.

Moran, Michelle T. *Colonizing Leprosy: Imperialism and the Politics of Public Health in the United States*. Chapel Hill: University of North Carolina Press, 2007.

"More Fun with Science." *Camp Fire Girl* 33, no. 1 (September 1953): 12.

Morris, Rebecca G. *How the Camp Fire Girls Won World War II*. Self-published, 2017.

"Mozell Clarence Hill." In *Biographical Dictionary of Modern American Educators*, edited by Frederick Ohles, Shirley M. Ohles, and John G. Ramsey, 160. Westport CT: Greenwood, 1997.

Nadkarni, Asha. *Eugenic Feminism: Reproductive Nationalism in the United States and India*. Minneapolis: University of Minnesota Press, 2014.

Nash, Roderick Frazier. *Wilderness and the American Mind*. 3rd ed. New Haven CT: Yale University Press, 1982.

National Federation for Catholic Youth Ministry. "NCCGSCF [National Catholic Committee for Girl Scouts and Camp Fire] History." Accessed July 29, 2020. https://nfcym.org/programs/nccgscf/nccgscf-history/.

National Park Service. "Free a Marine to Fight." November 9, 2017. https://www.nps .gov/articles/womenmarinesworldwarii.htm.

Newman, Louise Michelle. *White Women's Rights: The Racial Origins of Feminism in the United States*. New York: Oxford University Press, 1999.

"News from the Philippines." *Everygirl's* 12, no. 1 (September 1924): 6–7.

"Newsyviews of Camp Fire Girls." *Guardian* 21, no. 2 (October 1941): 2:5.

"New York Association for the Blind." In *New York Charities Directory*. New York: Charity Organization Society, 1920.

Nielsen, Kim E. *A Disability History of the United States*. Boston: Beacon Press, 2012.

———. "Helen Keller and the Politics of Civic Fitness." In *The New Disability History: American Perspectives*, edited by Paul K. Longmore and Lauri Umansky, 268–90. New York: New York University Press, 2001.

The Nizkor Project. "The Trial of German Major War Criminals: Transcript of Trial of Baldur von Schirach." Nuremberg, Germany, May 14–24, 1946. Nizkor Project, vol. 14, accessed March 11, 2005. http://www.nizkor.org/hweb/imt/tgmwc/tgmwc -14/tgmwc-14-137-05.shtml.

Noble, David W. *The Progressive Mind, 1890–1917*. Minneapolis MN: Burgess, 1981.

Norwood, Vera. *Made from This Earth: American Women and Nature*. Chapel Hill: University of North Carolina Press, 1993.

O'Leary, Margaret R., and Dennis S. O'Leary. *Adventures at Wohelo Camp: Summer of 1928*. Bloomington IN: iUniverse, 2011.

Olson-Raymer, Gayle. "National Nongovernmental Organizations Involved with the Juvenile Justice System: Focus on the Serious and Violent Juvenile Offender." National Criminal Justice Service, 1983. https:// www .ojp .gov /pdffiles1 /Digitization/93867NCJRS.pdf.

Ortner, Sherry. "Is Female to Male as Nature Is to Culture?" In *Woman, Culture, and Society*, edited by M. Z. Rosaldo and L. Lamphere, 68–87. Stanford CA: Stanford University Press, 1974.

Ossian, Lisa L. "Fragilities and Failures, Promises and Patriotism: Elements of Second World War English and American Girlhood, 1939–1945." In *Girlhood: A Global History*, edited by Jennifer Helgren and Colleen A. Vasconcellos, 162–78. New Brunswick NJ: Rutgers University Press, 2010.

"Our Foreign Camp Fires." *Wohelo* 5, no. 3 (September 1917): 37.

"Our Heritage from the American Indians." *Guardian* 9, no. 5 (January 1930): 8.

Page, James Franklin. *Socializing for the New Order of Educational Values of the Juvenile Organization*. Rock Island IL: Augusta College, 1919.

Palladino, Grace. *Teenagers: An American History*. New York: Basic Books, 1997.

Paris, Leslie. "The Adventures of Peanut and Bo: Summer Camps and Early-Twentieth-Century American Girlhood." *Journal of Women's History* 12, no. 4 (2001): 47–76.

————. *Children's Nature: The Rise of the American Summer Camp.* New York: New York University Press, 2008.

Park, Yoosun. *Facilitating Injustice: The Complicity of Social Workers in the Forced Removal and Incarceration of Japanese Americans, 1941–1946.* New York: Oxford University Press, 2020.

Parker, Dorothy. *Phoenix Indian School: The Second Half-Century.* Tempe: University of Arizona Press, 1996.

Parris, Guichard, and Lester Brooks. *Blacks in the City: A History of the National Urban League.* Boston: Little, Brown, 1971.

Paterek, Josephine. *Encyclopedia of American Indian Costume.* New York: Norton, 1996.

Peiss, Kathy. *Cheap Amusements: Working Women and Leisure in Turn-of-the-Century New York.* Philadelphia PA: Temple University Press.

————. *Hope in a Jar: The Making of America's Beauty Culture.* Philadelphia: University of Pennsylvania Press, 1998.

Pendry, Elizabeth R., and Hugh Hartshorne. *Organizations for Youth: Leisure Time and Character Building Procedures.* New York: McGraw Book, 1935.

Perry, Elisabeth Israels. "Josephine Groves Holloway." *Tennessee Encyclopedia of History and Culture,* December 25, 2009, updated January 1, 2010. http://tennesseeencyclopedia.net/entry.php?rec=641.

"Picture of the Month." *Camp Fire Girl* 25, no. 9 (May 1946): 2.

Pierce, Mildred. "Why I Am Proud to Be an American." *Camp Fire Girl* 24, no. 3 (November 1944): 2:4.

Pitcher, Evelyn Goodenough. "What Kind of Education for Girls?" *Camp Fire Girl* 43, no. 4 (March–April 1964): 3–4.

Plaine, Ann Marie. *Colonial Intimacies: Indian Marriage in Early New England.* Ithaca NY: Cornell University Press, 2000.

Plant, Rebecca Jo. *Mom: The Transformation of Motherhood in Modern America.* Chicago: University of Chicago Press, 2010.

"Post Scripts." *Saturday Evening Post* 207, no. 10 (September 8, 1934): 24, 68.

"Preparing for the Future." *Camp Fire Girl* 33, no. 4 (December 1953): 14.

"The Presidency: Happy Birthday." *Time* 79, no. 22 (June 1962): 13.

Proctor, Tammy M. *Scouting for Girls: A Century of Girl Guides and Girl Scouts.* Santa Barbara CA: Praeger, 2009.

Putnam, Robert D. *Bowling Alone: The Collapse and Revival of American Community.* New York: Simon and Schuster, 2000.

Putney, Clifford. *Muscular Christianity: Manhood and Sports in Protestant America, 1880–1920.* Cambridge MA: Harvard University Press, 2001.

"The Question of Dues." *Wohelo* 8, no. 2 (February 1916): 16.

"Questions." *Camp Fire Leadership* 54, no. 3 (Spring 1975): 4.

Rafael, Vicente L. *White Love and Other Events in Filipino History.* Durham NC: Duke University Press, 2000.

Rankin, Louise W. Goodwin. "Gypsying." *Everygirl's* 10, no. 9 (May 1923): 280–81.

"Recreation for Crippled Children." *Playground: World at Play* 11, no. 1 (April 1917): 204–5.

Reiman, Richard A. *The New Deal and American Youth: Ideas and Ideals in a Depression Decade.* Athens: University of Georgia Press, 2010.

Reinhardt, Claudia, and Bill Ganzel. "Farming in the 1930s: Gypsies." Wessels Living History Farm, York NE, accessed October 8, 2020. https://livinghistoryfarm.org /farminginthe30s/life_33.html.

"Relocation." *Camp Fire Leadership* 56, no. 1 (Fall 1976): 1.

Remus, Emily. *A Shopper's Paradise: How the Ladies of Chicago Claimed Power and Pleasure in the New Downtown.* Cambridge MA: Harvard University Press, 2019.

Riessman, Frank. *The Culturally Deprived Child.* New York: Harper and Row, 1962.

Robertson, Nancy Marie. *Christian Sisterhood, Race Relations, and the YWCA, 1906–46.* Urbana: University of Illinois Press, 2007.

Roces, Mina. "Filipino Elite Women and Public Health in the American Colonial Era, 1906–1940." *Women's History Review* 26, no. 3 (June 2017): 477–502.

Rockwell, Margaret R. "Camp Fire and the Church." *Camp Fire Girl* 24, no. 7 (March 1945): 4.

Rodgers, Daniel T. "Socializing Middle-Class Children: Institutions, Fables, and Work Values in Nineteenth-Century America." In *Growing Up in America, Children in Historical Perspective,* edited by N. Ray Hiner and Joseph Hawes, 119–32. Chicago: University of Illinois Press, 1985.

Rodriguez, Ma. Christina V. "Island of Despair." In *Culion Island: A Leper Colony's 100-Year Journey toward Healing,* edited by Ma. Cristina Verzola Rodriguez, 50–72. Makati City, Philippines: Culion Foundation, 2003.

Roediger, David. *Working toward Whiteness: How America's Immigrants Became White.* New York: Basic Books, 2005.

Rogers, D. Fiske. "New York Association for the Blind." *New Outlook for the Blind* 7 (1914): 33–34.

Roosevelt, Theodore. *The Works of Theodore Roosevelt.* Vol. 12. Project Gutenberg, Ebook, 2019.

Rosen, Ruth. *The World Split Open: How the Modern Women's Movement Changed America.* New York: Penguin Books, 2000.

Rosenberg, Gabriel N. *The 4-H Harvest: Sexuality and the State in Rural America.* Philadelphia: University of Pennsylvania Press, 2015.

Rosenberg, Rosalind. *Beyond Separate Spheres: Intellectual Roots of Modern Feminism.* New Haven CT: Yale University Press, 1982.

Rosenzweig, Linda W. *The Anchor of My Life: Middle-Class American Mothers and Daughters, 1880–1920.* New York: New York University Press, 1993.

———. "'Another Self'? Middle-Class American Women and Their Friends, 1900–1960." In *An Emotional History of the United States,* edited by Peter N. Stearns and Jan Lewis, 357–73. New York: New York University Press, 1998.

Rothschild, Mary Aickin. "To Scout or to Guide? The Girl Scout–Boy Scout Controversy, 1912–1941." *Frontiers: A Journal of Women's Studies* 6, no. 3 (1981): 115–21.

Rotundo, E. Anthony. *American Manhood: Transformations in Masculinity from the Revolution to the Modern Era.* New York: Basic Books, 1993.

Rowe, Helen. "In the Camp Fire Tradition." *Camp Fire Girl* 40, no. 9 (May 1961): 3–4.

———. "New Directions in Program." *Camp Fire Girl* 41, no. 7 (May–June 1962): 3–4.

Runbeck, Margaret Lee. "Our Camp Fire Law." *Camp Fire Girl* 29, no. 5 (January 1950): 1–2.

Rury, John L. "Vocationalism for Home and Work: Women's Education in the United States, 1880–1930." *History of Education Quarterly* 24, no. 1 (Spring 1984): 21–44.

Schalk, Sami. "Ablenationalism in American Girlhood." *Girlhood Studies: An Interdisciplinary Journal* 9, no. 1 (March 2016): 36–52.

Schaumburg, Ron. "Camp Fire, 1961–1979." In *Wo-he-lo: The Camp Fire History*, by Helen Buckler, Mary F. Fiedler, Martha F. Allen, and Ron Schaumburg, 249–413. 2nd ed. Kansas City MO: Camp Fire, 1980.

Schmitt, Peter J. *Back to Nature: The Arcadian Myth in Urban America.* Baltimore MD: Johns Hopkins University Press, 1990.

Schrepfer, Susan R. *The Fight to Save the Redwoods: A History of Environmental Reform, 1917–1978.* Madison: University of Wisconsin Press, 1983.

———. *Nature's Altars: Mountains, Gender, and American Environmentalism.* Lawrence: University Press of Kansas, 2005.

Schrum, Kelly. *Some Wore Bobby Sox: The Emergence of Teenage Girls' Culture, 1920–1945.* New York: Palgrave Macmillan, 2004.

———. "'Teena Means Business': Teenage Girls' Culture and *Seventeen* Magazine, 1944–1950." In *Delinquents and Debutantes: Twentieth-Century American Girls' Cultures*, edited by Sherrie Inness, 134–63. New York: New York University Press, 1998.

Schultz, Joy. "Crossing the *Pali*: White Missionary Children, Bicultural Identity, and the Racial Divide in Hawai'i, 1820–1898." *Journal of the History of Childhood and Youth* 6, no. 2 (Spring 2013): 209–35.

Schultz, Kevin M. *Tri-Faith America: How Catholics and Jews Held Postwar America to Its Protestant Promise.* New York: Oxford University Press, 2011.

"Scouts and NAACP Resolve Crisis." *Crisis* (March 1975): 100.

Scripps, Sarah. "Science Fairs as National Security: Adolescent Culture in Postwar America, 1950–1965." In *Growing Up America: Youth and Politics since 1945*, edited by Susan Eckelmann Berghel, Sara Fieldston, and Paul M. Renfro, 54–74. Athens: University of Georgia Press, 2019.

Scully, Dorothy. "Brotherhood." *Camp Fire Girl* 24, no. 6 (February 1945): 1:1.

Seitler, Dana. "Unnatural Selection: Mothers, Eugenic Feminism, and Charlotte Perkins Gilman's Regeneration Narratives." *American Quarterly* 55, no. 1 (March 2003): 61–88.

Selig, Diana. *Americans All: The Cultural Gifts Movement.* Cambridge MA: Harvard University Press, 2008.

Sense, Eleanor. "Home Volunteers to the Front." *Guardian* 21, no. 6 (February 1942): 12.

"Service Review." *Camp Fire Girl* 24, no. 3 (November 1944): 1–2.

Seton, Ernest Thompson. *The Birch-Bark Roll of the Woodcraft Indians*. New York: Doubleday, Page, 1907.

——. *Two Little Savages*. New York: Doubleday, Page, 1903.

——. *The Woodcraft Manual for Boys*. 15th ed. Garden City NY: Doubleday, Page, 1917.

Simmons, LaKisha Michelle. *Crescent City Girls: The Lives of Young Black Women in Segregated New Orleans*. Chapel Hill: University of North Carolina Press, 2015.

Sims, Anastatia Hodgens. "Juliette Gordon Low: Late-Blooming Daisy." In *Georgia Women: Their Lives and Times*, edited by Ann Short Chirhart and Betty Wood, 370–90. Athens: University of Georgia Press, 2007.

"The Slacker's Dream." *Wohelo* 6, no. 5 (November 1918): 135.

Smith-Rosenberg, Carroll. "The Female World of Love and Ritual." In *Disorderly Conduct: Visions of Gender in Victorian America*, 53–76. New York: Oxford University Press, 1985.

Solomon, Barbara Miller. *In the Company of Educated Women*. New Haven CT: Yale University Press, 1985.

"Sparks from the Camp Fires." *Wohelo* 6, no. 2 (August 1918): 65.

Spear, Elizabeth. "A Guide to Camping." *Camp Fire Girl* 29, no. 10 (June 1950): 12.

Spensley, Allie. "Segregated Summer Camps." *US History Scene*, February 16, 2020. ushistoryscene.com/article/segregated-summer-camps/.

Stage, Sarah. Introduction to *Rethinking Home Economics: Women and the History of a Profession*, edited by Sarah Stage and Virginia B. Vincenti, 1–13. Ithaca NY: Cornell University Press, 1997.

Stedman, Raymond William. *Shadows of the Indian*. Norman: University of Oklahoma Press, 1982.

Steinson, Barbara. *American Women's Activism in World War I*. New York: Garland, 1982.

Stephens, Katherine Bernice. "American Gypsies: Immigration, Migration, Settlement." MA thesis, California State University, San Bernardino, 2003.

Stevenson, Brenda E. *The Contested Murder of Latasha Harlins: Justice, Gender, and the Origins of the L.A. Riots*. New York: Oxford University Press, 2013.

Stewart, Jane L. *A Campfire Girl in Summer Camp*. Akron OH: Saalfield, 1914.

——. *A Campfire Girl's Chum*. Akron OH: Saalfield, 1914.

Strong, Pauline Turner. *American Indians and the American Imaginary: Cultural Representation across the Centuries*. New York: Routledge, 2013.

Strub, Whitney. "The Clearly Obscene and the Queerly Obscene: Heteronormativity and Obscenity in Cold War Los Angeles." *American Quarterly* 60, no. 2 (June 2008): 373–98.

Sugrue, Thomas J. *The Origins of the Urban Crisis: Race and Inequality in Postwar Detroit*. Princeton NJ: Princeton University Press, 2014.

Summers, Mark Wahlgren. *The Gilded Age, or, The Hazard of New Functions*. Upper Saddle River NJ: Prentice Hall, 1997.

Sway, Marlene. *Familiar Strangers: Gypsy Life in America*. Urbana: University of Illinois Press, 1988.

Teal, Orion A. "The Moral Economy of Postwar Radical Interracial Summer Camping." In *The Economic Civil Rights Movement: African Americans and the Struggle for Economic Power*, edited by Michael Ezra, 58–74. New York: Routledge, 2013.

"Tea Party." *Camp Fire Girl* 27, no. 4 (December 1947): 12.

Tedesco, Laureen. "Making a Girl into a Scout: Americanizing Scouting for Girls." In *Delinquents and Debutantes: Twentieth-Century American Girls' Cultures*, edited by Sherrie A. Inness, 19–39. New York: New York University Press, 1998.

Teichmann, Ruth. "Program Designs for Your Horizon Club." *Camp Fire Girl* 26, no. 1 (September 1946): 12.

"This Is a New Day." *Wohelo* 1, no. 7 (January 1914): 1.

Thompson, Barbara. *West by Northwest*. Spencer Creek Press, 2000.

Thurston, Ida Tredwell. *The Torch Bearer*. New York: Fleming H. Revell, 1913.

Tisdale, Cathy. "On My Mind: Radical Notions of Inclusion." Camp Fire, June 14, 2016. https://campfire.org/blog/article/on-my-mind-radical-notions-of-inclusion/.

"Together We Make Tomorrow: 1957 Birthday Project." *Camp Fire Girl* 36, no. 1 (September 1956): 4–5.

"Together We Make Tomorrow: 1958 Birthday Project." *Camp Fire Girl* 37, no. 1 (September 1957): 6.

Trawick, A. M. "The Play Life of Negro Boys and Girls." In *Southern Sociological Congress*, edited by James Edward McCulloch, 354–62. Washington DC: Southern Sociological Congress, 1918.

"Treasure Trails of Indian Lore." *Guardian* 21, no. 10 (June 1942): 1:7.

Tsuchida, John Nobuya, ed. *Reflections: Memoirs of Japanese American Women in Minnesota*. Covina CA: Pacific Asia Press, 1994.

Tuttle, William M., Jr. *Daddy's Gone to War: The Second World War in the Lives of America's Children*. New York: Oxford University Press, 1993.

Tyack, David. *The One Best System: A History of American Urban Education*. Cambridge: Harvard University Press, 1974.

———. *Seeking Common Ground: Public Schools in a Diverse Society*. Cambridge MA: Harvard University Press, 2003.

Tyrrell, Ian. *Reforming the World: The Creation of America's Moral Empire*. Princeton NJ: Princeton University Press, 2010.

Untitled editorial. *American Indian Magazine* 4, no. 1 (March 1916): 60–64.

U.S. Commission on Civil Rights. "Minorities in Special Education: A Briefing before the United States Commission on Civil Rights." Briefing Report, December 3, 2007. https://www.usccr.gov/pubs/docs/MinoritiesinSpecialEducation.pdf.

"The Vagrant." *Living Age* 322 (1924): 334.

Vandercook, Margaret. *The Camp Fire Girls at Sunrise Hill*. Philadelphia PA: John C. Watson, 1913.

Van Slyck, Abigail A. *A Manufactured Wilderness: Summer Camps and the Shaping of American Youth, 1890–1960*. Minneapolis: University of Minnesota Press, 2006.

Veglia, Romana. "It's Work—But It's Fun!" *Camp Fire Girl* 26, no. 1 (September 1946): 1.

Wallach, Stephanie. "Luther Halsey Gulick and the Salvation of the American Adolescent." PhD diss., Columbia University, 1989.

Washington, Mary H. Introduction to *A Voice from the South*, by Anna Julia Cooper. Oxford: Oxford University Press, 1988.

Watson, Thomas E. "The Wonderful Career of a Cripple, and the Beautiful Mission Work He's Engaged In." *Watson's Magazine* 23, no. 2 (June 1916): 61–75.

Webb, Mary. *"Not My Will": A Christian Martyr in the Philippines*. Pasig City, Philippines: Anvil, 1997.

Weinbaum, Alys Eve, et al. *The Modern Girl around the World: Consumption, Modernity, and Globalization*. Durham NC: Duke University Press, 2008.

Weisenfeld, Judith. *African American Women and Christian Activism: New York's Black YWCA, 1905–1945*. Cambridge MA: Harvard University Press, 1998.

Weiss, Jessica. *To Have and to Hold: Marriage, the Baby Boom, and Social Change*. Chicago: University of Chicago Press, 2000.

Wells, Amos Russel. *Social Evenings: A Collection of Pleasant Entertainments for Christian Endeavor Societies and the Home Circle*. Boston: United Society of Christian Endeavor, 1894.

Wells, Zillam E. "White Mountain Gypsying." *Everygirl's* 13, no. 2 (October 1925): 10.

West, Elliott. *Growing Up with the Country: Childhood on the Far Western Frontier*. Albuquerque: University of New Mexico Press, 1989.

"What Camp Fire Girls Are Doing." *Wohelo* 6, no. 1 (July 1918): 25.

"What Camp Fire Girls Are Doing." *Wohelo* 6, no. 6 (December 1918): 25, 184–85.

Williams, Lillian S. *A Bridge to the Future: The History of Diversity in Girl Scouting*. New York: Girl Scouts USA, 1996.

Winkler, Allan M. *Home Front U.S.A.: America during World War I*. Wheeling IL: Harlan Davidson, 2000.

Winter, Thomas. *Making Men, Making Class: The YMCA and Workingmen, 1877–1920*. Chicago: University of Chicago Press, 2002.

World Confederation of Organizations of the Teaching Profession. *Teachers and Family Life Education: Report of WCOTP/IPPF/GNAT Seminar*. Bolgatanga, Ghana, November 1976.

World Organization of the Scout Movement. *Scouting 'Round the World: Facts and Figures on the World Scout Movement*. Geneva, Switzerland: World Organization of the Scout Movement, 1990.

Wright, Audrey. "Grand Rapids Gypsies." *Everygirl's* 14, no. 2 (October 1926): 14.

Wright, Rowe. "The Makers of America." *Wohelo* 6, no. 7 (February 1919): 211–12.

———. "On the Trail of the Gypsy." Part 1. *Wohelo* (May 1919): 309.

———. "On the Trail of the Gypsy." Part 2. *Wohelo* (June 1919): 355.

"You've Told Us." *Camp Fire Girl* 28, no. 8 (April 1949): 8–9.

Yukic, Eleanor. "TMR." *Camp Fire Leadership* 56, no. 1 (Fall 1976): 8–11.

Zelizer, Viviana A. *Pricing the Priceless Child: The Changing Social Value of Children.* Princeton NJ: Princeton University Press, 1994.

Ziegler, Mary. "Eugenic Feminism: Mental Hygiene, the Women's Movement, and the Campaign for Eugenic Legal Reform, 1900–1935." *Harvard Journal of Law & Gender* 31 (2008): 211–35.

Index

American Indians (*cont.*)
56, 57, 64–69; special needs diagnoses of, 308n21; and stereotypes
about women, 70, 72
Americanization honors, 102–6, 108
American Legion, 205
American Legion Women's Auxiliary,
101, 150
American Monthly Magazine, 25
American Red Cross, 51, 52, 53, 149, 151,
168
Anderson, Celia, 47, 95, 201, 206
Anderson, Warwick, 133
anniversary projects, Camp Fire, 53,
92, 146
anticommunism, 143, 166, 194
antifascism, 142, 143, 144–45
anti-immigration laws, 4, 89, 103, 119
antipoverty programs, 2, 211, 216, 258
antiprejudice ideals, 16, 95, 144, 150, 164,
193–99, 208, 263. *See also* inclusion
anti–Vietnam War protests, 213
Apaches, 74
Argentina, 10
arts and crafts movement, 29
Ashton, Haroldean, 221, 222
Asian American Camp Fire Girls, 90,
218, 283n3, 284n4. *See also* Filipina
Camp Fire Girls; Japanese American Camp Fire Girls
Asibal, Petra, 135
assimilation, 263; in boarding schools,
57–58, 72, 77; as Camp Fire ideal,
4–5, 63, 74–75, 96, 102, 105, 116, 143;
of girls with disabilities, 118; in the
Philippines, 129–31. *See also* Americanization honors
athletics, 184; in boarding schools,
58; for boys, 4, 32, 37–38, 106; folk
dance as alternative to, 106–7; for
girls and women, 2, 14, 19, 25, 32–

33, 37, 38, 42–43, 65, 185, 262; in the
New Day program, 245
Atlanta Council of Camp Fire Girls, 202
atomic age, 165–66, 186–87, 194
Austin, Mary, 58

baby boom, 17, 213
baby care lessons, 1, 46, 168, 176, 189
babysitting, 146, 176, 224, 227, 228, 229
Baden-Powell, Agnes, 9
Baden-Powell, Robert, 9, 20
Baltimore, 216, 218, 226. *See also* Poto-
mac Area Council of Camp Fire
Girls
Barnett, Ida B. Wells, 115
Beard, Daniel Carter, 9, 25, 274n12
Beard, Lina, 21
Beard, Mary Alice, 176
Beard, Mary Ritter, 144
beauty ideals: and appearance, 72, 179–
85, 190; as attitude, 22, 26, 30, 45–48,
53, 57, 61, 64, 76, 262; and girls of
color, 75, 76, 225. *See also* charm
lessons
Becker, Beatrice, 83
Beegle, Mary, 23
Bee Hive Girls (Church of Jesus Christ
of Latter-day Saints), 154, 163
Belgium, 53
Berry, D. Wellington, 114, 288n88
Bethlehem Settlement House (Nash-
ville), 104, 110, 112, 113, 114–15, 287n67
Bicol Treatment Station (Legaspi,
Albay), 127
Bird, S. Elizabeth, 57, 58
Bitner, Carol, 245
Black American(s), 109, 217, 218, 230;
activists, 31, 230; childhood, 16, 215–
16; girls, 5, 109; perceived as threat-
ening, 89; special needs diagnoses
of, 247, 308n2; women, 109, 230–31

children with disabilities (*cont.*)
meeting across lines of ability, 124–26; as objects of service, 126; as primitive, 123; and racial segregation, 122; schools and institutions for, 118, 120–22; as standard setters, 126. *See also* disabilities; *and specific institutions*
Chile, 10
Chilocco Indian School (OK), 72
China, 10, 38, 106
Christy, Howard Chandler, 93, 94
Church of Jesus Christ of Latter-day Saints, 154, 163
Church Welfare Bureau (Los Angeles), 221
citizenship: Black American claims to full, 109, 142; models of, for girls, 2, 4–5, 15, 17, 19, 22, 26, 50–51, 117, 139, 166, 193–94, 231, 241, 262–63; models of, for youth, 241, 242; racialized, 2, 4, 10, 15; women's claims to full, 51
citizenship honors, 150, *159*, 163, 180. *See also* patriotism honors
civic nationalism, 4, 17
civic participation: decline of, in America, 257, 310n59; of girls and women, 3, 109, 139, 141, 166–67; religion as, 154, 156, 159
Civil Rights Act (1964), 235, 249
civil rights movement, 16, 194–95, 204–5, 211, 213, 214, 261
class hierarchies and divisions, 54, 95–102, 201. *See also* middle-class girls; working-class women and girls
Cobb-Greetham, Amanda, 72
coeducation, 3, 31, 250, *251*, 253–54, 263–64, 308n31
Cold War, 16, 151, 166, 173; anticommunism during, 143, 205, 235; civil rights and, 193–94

Collier, John, 58
Collins, Viola, 47
colorblindness, 93, 214
Commission on Civil Rights (U.S.), 308n21
Committee on Religious Education of Youth for the International Council of Religious Education, 159–60
community chests, 213–14, 239
consumerism, 2, 14, 82, 135; and Camp Fire products, 98–99; girls' critiques of, 66, 82; and training girls for wise choices, 45, 97; and women's roles, 190
Cooper, Anna Julia, 111
Costa Rica, 10
council fires, 47, 55, 60–61, 71, 92, 94–95, 111, 134, 160
counterculture, 17, 213
Creel, George, 52
Cuba, 10
Cub Scouts, 250, 264
Culion Sanitarium (Philippines), 119, 127, 129–31, 133–34, 135–37, 138, 155, 291n54
cultural appropriation, 4, 15, 55, 64, 78, 263, 267–69. *See also* American Indian imagery; Gypsy imagery
cultural gifts movement, 15, 90, 103, 106, 108, 115

Daily People, 96
Dakota Sioux, 59, 63
dating, 185–86, 189, 190, 232, 253
Deloria, Ella, 58, 59–60
Deloria, Philip, 56, 58
democracy, U.S.: Camp Fire's commitment to, 93, 96, 145, 150, 172, 193, 194, 195, 269; as consistent with segregation, 116; girls as symbols of, 52; in Japanese American incarceration camps, 152; meaning of, 91, 143, 165,

48, 63, 66, 70, 75, 77; labor of, 109, 141, 147–48; as modern, 7, 45, 48, 63, 64, 65, 70, 71, 73, 75–77, 80, 104, 130–31; relationships of, with their mothers, 30, 275n33; reproductive contributions expected of, 20, 171, 241–42; responses of, to the Camp Fire program, 42–43, 46–48, 50, 61, 63–73, 74, 75, 76–77, 87, 134, 137, 174, 176–78, 181–83, 186, 226–28, 229–30, 232–33, 238; and same-sex attraction and intimacy, 35–36, 65; spending money of, 46, 99, 227; writings of, 12, 42, 47–48, 50, 63–65, 66–70, 75–76, 83. *See also* children; girlhood; youth

Girls' Branch of the Public School Athletic League (New York City), 274n12

Girl Scouts (Clara Lisetor-Lane's organization), 21, 23, 274n18

Girl Scouts of the USA, 9, 11, 21, 201; adopted by the Philippines national government, 139; and Catholics, 70, 92, 155, 157; coeducation rejected by, 254; communist infiltration alleged against, 204–5; compared to Camp Fire, 10, 11–12, 21–22, 28, 77, 168, 170, 196–96, 213, 253, 257, 259, 264–66, 275n21; in Hansen's disease treatment centers (Philippines), 136; and integration and inclusion, 195–96, 257; in Japanese American incarceration camps, 151, 153; and LGBTQ+ youth, 265; membership challenges of, in the 1960s and 1970s, 213, 254, 257; merger rejected by, 24; oath of, 157; public familiarity with, 310n63; as single-sex organization, 264; and Title IX exemption, 309n49; and transgender youth, 265

girls' culture, 5, 6, 7, 10, 15, 54, 71, 75–77, 87, 95, 125

girls' fiction, 7, 85–86, 96–97, 100

Girls' Friendly Society, 154

girls of color in the Camp Fire Girls, 15, 108, 212–13, 215, 233, 246. *See also specific social groups*

Girls of the Forward Quest, 109, 112–13, 114, 115, 287n67

girls' organizations, 21; attempt to merge, 23–24, 274n18; funding gap of, compared to boys' organizations, 214. *See also* youth organizations; *and specific organizations*

Goitin, Juan, 136

Gold Wings Camp Fire Girls (Decatur IL), 111

Great Depression, 100–101, 284n11, 285n32, 286n34

Greater Boston Council of Camp Fire Girls (later Camp Fire Council for Eastern Massachusetts), 150, 158, 163, 189, 216, 217, 220, 223

Greeley area Camp Fire Girls, 11

Guardian (magazine), 123, 152, 284n11

guardians. *See* leaders ("guardians") of Camp Fire clubs

Guardians Associations, 158, 246

Gulick, Charlotte Vetter, 21, 30, 53, 63, 66, 67, 241; and American Indian imagery, 2, 56, 57, 60, 61, 63; on bicycle riding, 37; and camp movement, 8, 24, 41; on changing conditions for girls, 1–2; education of, 21; and expansion of girls' opportunities, 262; on glorifying work, 29–30, 46; on motherhood, 41–42, 44; on outdoor activity for girls, 41–42, 61; pregnancy of, 37; on racial inheritance, 20, 61; role of, in Camp Fire origins, 1, 8, 21, 24; on sex education, 34–35; and suffrage, 49

World Organization of the Scout Movement, 264

World War I, 115, 142, 151; and Black youth, 111; Camp Fire during, 50–53, 100, 111, 262

World War II, 16, 140, 164, 167, 195; and American childhood, 141, 148–49; Camp Fire during, 92, 141, 142–43, 145–50, 147, 164, 262; and Camp Fire in the Philippines, 138; and children's contributions, 145–46; Double Victory campaign and, 195; and girls' contributions, 141; Japanese American Camp Fire Girls during, 143, 151–53, 153

"The Wraggle-Taggle Gypsies" (folk song), 83

Wright, Rowe, 103, 105–6

Wylie, Philip, 166

Yakamas, 72–73, 73, 281n53

Yakima Indian Christian Mission, 57, 72, 73, 102

Young Ladies' Mutual Improvement Association (Church of Jesus Christ of Latter-day Saints), 154, 163

Young Men's Christian Association (YMCA), 8, 38, 53, 309n49; Black branches of, 100; and Camp Fire work, 266; and integrated summer camps, 235; and Japanese American incarceration, 151

Young Men's Hebrew Association (Louisville), 92

Young Women's Christian Association (YWCA), 21, 24, 58, 111, 114, 223; in Black communities, 111, 115; and Camp Fire affiliation, 113, 115, 154;

and integration, 195; and Japanese American incarceration, 151; in Nashville, 113–14, 115. See also Blue Triangle League; Girl Reserves (YWCA)

Your Carriage, Madam! (Lane), 183

youth, 62; citizenship models for, 241, 242; improving social conditions for, 193, 241; plasticity of, 215; as untainted, 193. See also boys; children; girls

Youth Committee on Civilian Defense, 149

youth culture, 71, 261, 269

youth organizations: and American Indian imagery, 70; antiprejudice efforts of, 195; as assimilative agencies, 129; belief of, in plasticity of youth, 215; Black children's access to, 114–15, 195–96; and democratic training, 193; difficulties recruiting leaders for, in the 1960s and 1970s, 213; early history of, 8–10; gender distinctiveness in, 22–23, 64; for health and morale, 127; membership decline in, 16–17, 213, 257; and sexual orientation policies, 264; in Sweden, 264; and threat of fascism, 142, 144–45; and Title IX exemption, 309n49; as transnational, 10; in twenty-first century, 263–64; in the United Kingdom, 264. See also specific organizations

youth work, 9, 21, 114. See also youth organizations

Zweber, Greg, 267

In the Expanding Frontiers series

To order or obtain more information on these or other University of Nebraska Press titles, visit nebraskapress.unl.edu.

CPSIA information can be obtained
at www.ICGtesting.com
Printed in the USA
LVHW110957181022
730956LV00002B/110

9 781496 233080